DR. DAVID RALPH MATTHEWS
1 Brady Lane
Guelph, Ontario   N1L 1A2

Common Property Resources

Common Property Resources

Ecology and community-based sustainable development

edited by
Fikret Berkes

BELHAVEN PRESS
A division of Pinter Publishers
London

© The editor and contributors, 1989

First published in Great Britain in 1989 by
Belhaven Press (a division of Pinter Publishers),
25 Floral Street, London WC2E 9DS

ISBN 1 85293 080 2

Published in Association with The International Union for
the Conservation of Nature and Natural Resources

Library of Congress Cataloging-in-Publication Data

Common property resources : ecology and community-based sustainable
    development / edited by Fikret Berkes.
        p.   cm.
    Includes papers presented at the Conference on Conservation and
Development: Implementing the World Conservation Strategy, held June
1986, Ottawa, and the Fourth International Congress of Ecology, held
Aug. 1986, Syracuse, N.Y.
    "Published in association with the International Union for the
Conservation of Nature and Natural Resources" — T.p. verso.
    Includes index.
    ISBN 1−85293−080−2 : £29.50
    1. Economic development—Environmental aspects—Congresses.
2. Conservation of natural resources—Congresses.   I. Berkes,
Fikret.   II. Conference on Conservation Development: Implementing
the World Conservation Strategy (1986 : Ottawa, Ont.)   III. World
Congress of Ecology (4th : 1986 : Syracuse, N.Y.)   IV. International
Union for Conservation of Nature and Natural Resources.
HD75.6.C647 1989
333.7′2—dc20   89−7091
                                                                                          CIP

Filmset by Mayhew Typesetting, Bristol, England
Printed and bound by Biddles Ltd,
Guildford and King's Lyn

Contents

vi Contents

Foreword

Sustainable development has been defined by the World Commission on Environment and Development as 'development that meets the needs and aspirations of the present without compromising the ability of future generations to meet their own needs'. Yet these very needs have been heavily mortgaged by past development activities and practices many of which have been conceived, financed and controlled by development agencies, multilateral development banks, and consultants only marginally affected by their strategies and decisions, however well meaning. Needs and aspirations must now be built upon a heritage of the devastating loss of forest land, the loss of soil through erosion, nutrient depletion, salination, and the extensive desertification of other lands. Our waterways, shorelines, and oceans have been spoiled through the dumping of domestic and industrial wastes, many of which are highly toxic. We still seek ways of dealing with radioactive wastes whose environmental impacts will last well into the next millenium.

Present needs and aspirations are built upon the base of living resources of the biosphere. These resources are renewable if managed properly with care and with concern, but they are not limitless. They will have to be shared by a global population that will double in the early part of the next millenium.

Of the living resources of the planet, an enormous reservoir are used and managed as 'common property', property that is shared by a wide array of social groups. Sustainable management strategies associated with the use of common property are as diverse as the social, cultural, and ecological contexts in which they are practiced. Those practices emphasize respect, responsibility, and stewardship and are highly participatory. The planning for and the management of resources held as common property is carried out by those most directly affected by their decisions, decisions that are designed to contribute to the continuing sustained use of the living resources. These practices emphasize local control, self management, and to the extent possible, self sufficiency.

They are based on co-operation rather than competition, the collective sharing of a resource rather than the individual attempting to maximize yield without reference to the community. Common property resource management practices incorporate a rich and varied library of traditional knowledge, knowledge that has been developed over extensive periods of time, knowledge that has sustained the living resource base upon which social communities depend.

The global commons of the atmosphere and the oceans has received a great deal of attention in the world press. The impact of CFC's on the ozone layer of the stratosphere, the increasing impacts of acid rain on the health of our forests and lakes, and the cumulative effect of carbon dioxide emissions that contribute to the 'greenhouse effect' have become common subjects of discussions. This volume emphasizes the local and regional commons: pasturelands, forest stands, and fishing grounds that are used communally and sustained collectively. The practices inherent to common property resource management at the local and regional scale frequently incorporate sustainable technologies, and are based invariably, on institutional structures and organizations that are socially appropriate and highly adaptive. Much can be learned through a careful analysis of these traditional and varied management practices that have contributed to sustainable development for so long and in so many different contexts.

The concept of sustainable development is not new. In 1980, the International Union for Conservation of Nature and Natural Resources (IUCN) produced the World Conservation Strategy (WCS), which highlighted the need to protect essential ecological processes, to preserve biological and genetic diversity, and to reconcile conservation with development through the sustainable use of biological resources. The World Commission on Environmental Development developed many of the themes introduced in the WCS in the report for 'Our Common Future'. The WCS has been extremely successful in promoting greater conservation awareness, but much more needs to be done. Six years after its launch, a major international conference was held in Ottawa to review progress in implementing the principles of the WCS and to address the human aspects of conservation in the future. The conference endorsed the concept of sustainable development as the basis for human self-betterment, and concluded that a series of books aimed at a broad readership should be launched to promote the theme. This series addresses the social, ecological, economic and political dimensions of sustainable development with the intent of influencing policy and programmes locally, nationally and globally.

Series Editor: Peter Jacobs
Chairman, IUCN Commission on Sustainable
Development.

Preface and Acknowledgements

This volume has its origins in two conferences. The first was the Conference on Conservation and Development: Implementing the World Conservation Strategy, which met in June 1986 in Ottawa and included a workshop on common property resources. The second was the Fourth International Congress of Ecology (IV INTECOL), which met in August 1986 in Syracuse, New York, and included a workshop/symposium on the ecological management of common property resources.

Initially, a publication was planned with the seven papers presented at INTECOL (those by Regier, Cox, Miller, Freeman, Gadgil, Goodland and Berkes), supplemented by papers from two authors (Ruddle and Watson) who were unable to attend. Subsequently, Taghi Farvar, then Senior Advisor to the IUCN on sustainable development, proposed that the volume include some of the Ottawa papers. Thus, we added the chapters by Gibbs and Bromley and Cruz. To supplement these, there were four later additions: Acheson, Baines, Grima and Berkes and Moorehead.

From the start, we were aiming to compile a book which would give due attention to ecology and resource-management science. We felt ecological aspects of common-property management had been largely neglected in the dozen or so meetings on common-property resources between 1983 and 1986. This was no fault of the organizers; ecologists themselves seemed reluctant to get involved in common-property issues. But here was a chance to put humans back into the ecosystem, so to speak – a common-property focus around which natural sciences and social sciences could be integrated for sustainable resource use.

To make a long story short, the volume before you represents a remarkable interdisciplinary assembly in which natural science and social science perspectives are in balance. Applied ecologists, human ecologists and policy-oriented ecologists together make up the single largest group of authors. Resource economists and geographers constitute an almost equally large group. There are other social scientists as well (anthropologists, sociologists, political scientists), all addressing their tasks in an interdisciplinary spirit.

In preparing the volume, we aimed for the highest possible scholarly standards by carrying out a thorough peer review of the chapters. Each author undertook to review two other chapters; some did three. As well, Taghi Farvar arranged for a set of IUCN reviewers. As a result, each chapter has been reviewed by an average of three referees; virtually all chapters were rewritten, some twice.

This kind of thorough and intimate reviewing created another problem:

how to incorporate all these good comments into the text. There were suggestions, true to the spirit of communal management, that perhaps all chapters
could be prepared collaboratively, relegating the original author's name to a
footnote. But, alas, the individualist–scholarly tradition can not allow this.
Besides, there were reasonable differences in opinion among the authors
which would have made it difficult to claim that we had produced a
consensus. Nevertheless, in the end we did integrate reviewers' comments
into the text more than is usual in book or journal articles. As a result, many
of the chapters incorporate good-sized chunks of other contributors' writings.

Thanks are due to the following additional people for their assistance with
the review process. In alphabetical order:

Patrick Dugan
David Feeny
Jeffrey A. Gritzner
J. Honculada-Primavera
Barbara Lausche
Bonnie J. McCay
Jeffrey McNeely
David Pitt
James L. Wescoat, Jr.
John C. Wilkinson

Our IUCN advisor, Peter Jacobs made many helpful suggestions, including
those on the organization of the book. Stephanie Flanders and Liz Hopkins
were in charge of the file at the IUCN and, together with Robin Pellew,
Director of the Conservation Monitoring Centre at Cambridge, contributed to
the creation of the book. Brock University provided logistic support. Marilyn
Koop and Gina Armstrong provided able secretarial assistance. Loris
Gasparotto prepared many of the figures. I gratefully acknowledge the
support of the Social Sciences and Humanities Research Council of Canada
(SSHRC) for my work.

Fikret Berkes
St. Catherines, Ontario
December 1988

1 Introduction and overview
Fikret Berkes and M. Taghi Farvar

This volume is organized in four parts, preceded by this Introduction. The Introduction sets out the *problematique*, definitions, various concepts of common property and resource-management regimes, and provides an overview of the significance of common-property systems. The four chapters that make up Part 1 deal with perspectives on resource management. Part 2 consists of four chapters exploring a range of issues in the background of resource management: the appropriate role and limitations of science; the shortcomings and misuse of neoclassical economics; the science and ideology of conventional exploitive development of resources; and alternative approaches and management frameworks. The last two parts provide case studies. Those in Part 3 deal with single-resource case studies, and those in Part 4 with multiple-resource cases.

The 16 original essays collected here are the work of an interdisciplinary group of scholars with backgrounds in applied ecology and various fields of the social sciences. Three of the chapters deal primarily with fisheries (Ruddle, Acheson, Miller); three with lands and wildlife (Watson, Freeman, Berkes); one with water (Cruz); and four with a mix of resource types (Gadgil and Iyer, Baines, Moorehead, Goodland et al.). The rest are not resource-specific (although two use illustrations from fisheries) and are concerned with broader, cross-cutting issues.

It is the aim of the volume as a whole to identify and deal with certain concepts of the natural and social sciences which are central for the management of common-property resources as a class. It is hoped this will help social scientists appreciate the relevant ecological concepts, and in turn, help ecologists appreciate some key considerations in the social sciences and human ecology. For example, the chapter by Goodland et al. explains the significance of the economic concept of discount rates with regard to long-term conservation. In general, the book attempts to show how natural sciences and social sciences fit together towards the management of common-property resources for sustainable development.

Concepts developed in the volume are relevant to a diversity of renewable natural-resource types from forestry to pasture and range management, wildlife, fisheries and water. Each of these subjects has its own technical literature, but the commons dilemma cuts across the various aspects of specialization. The volume is designed to help specialists see similarities in such management dilemmas across these disciplines. This perspective is particularly important for integrated resource-management planning and for integrated economic programs (for example, chapters by Gadgil and Iyer, Baines, Goodland et al.).

The case-study material in the volume comes from a variety of geographic settings and a variety of cultures, many of which may be unfamiliar to readers of conventional resource-management literature. Much of resource-management thinking – for example the 'tragedy of the commons' model (Hardin, 1968) – is Western ethnocentric, emphasizing competition rather than cooperation and assuming the supremacy of individualism rather than communitarianism. Many of the chapters, for example those by Ruddle, Gadgil and Iyer, and Berkes, show these assumptions to be inappropriate. There are often cultural and institutional constraints on self-interested behaviour which may damage the collective interest.

The major area of emphasis here is on communal resource-management systems. The 'tragedy of the commons' model overemphasizes the solutions of privatization and central administrative controls at the expense of local-level controls and self-management. This book attempts to redress the balance, inviting resource managers and development planners to integrate local-level management ('planning with the people') into the existing common-property resource-management framework. Chapter 6, by Freeman, exemplifies this approach in the context of a specific example on the essential inadequacy of scientific data in population models. Chapter 12, by Acheson does the same, in the context of integration of local- and state level management systems or co-management. Taken as a whole, the selections in this volume show that different kinds of solutions to the commons dilemma may be complementary.

Books on common-property resources are rare. However, two recent volumes – those by McCay and Acheson (1987) and the National Research Council (1986) – summarize a growing and rich body of evidence relevant to common-property resources. Both volumes highlight social-science approaches. By contrast, the present volume emphasizes environment and resource systems and the ecological dimensions of the commons dilemma. It focuses on resources, applied ecology and human ecology. Both *The World Conservation Strategy* (1980) and the report of the World Commission on Environment and Development (1987) deal mainly with international, global commons. By contrast, this book is concerned with the local and regional commons.

The problematique

One of the major messages of the *World Conservation Strategy* (1980) was that the economic well-being of most countries is ultimately related to conservation of living resources. Environmental systems have to be used sustainably – that is, without compromising the interests of future generations (World Commission on Environment and Development, 1987; Chapter 9). With increasing human needs, population growth and economic growth, there is an increasingly greater need for new resource-management systems. Resources such as forests, pastures, water, wildlife and fish have to be utilized on a sustainable basis if they are to provide annual benefits in perpetuity. To do otherwise is to risk the destruction of the resource base and the ability of future generations to meet their own needs.

Increasingly, in many circles, there is general agreement that resources should be used sustainably, and detailed analyses are beginning to appear (Turner, 1988). A major issue now is the means to achieve this objective. Should the appropriate resource management systems come from the 'top down' or the 'bottom up'? Should they be based on resource management techniques of the industrialized countries? Or should they be developed by rehabilitating and adapting 'indigenous' resource-management systems and upgrading traditional local-level institutions? How can the two systems (scientific and traditional) be integrated? These are the central questions addressed by this volume.

Until recent years, scientists and policy-makers knew little about traditional management systems and accorded them little credibility. One of the authors' main objectives is to seek a new balance in the use of both 'scientific' and 'traditional management' systems. Specifically, the book explores the appropriate role of local, community-level institutions in the management of common-property resources. What we are working towards is a recognition of the importance of indigenous knowledge, a more eclectic choice set of institutional arrangements, and the use of whatever formal scientific knowledge is appropriate for the purposes of managing specific resources.

Resource management systems

Renewed interest in traditional management systems stems partly from the past failures of development projects, and the search for viable and sustainable alternatives to current models of resources use (Chapter 9, by Goodland et al.; 7, Regier et al.). Renewed interest is partly due to a new-found pride in traditional values and institutions, both in the Third World and in the West. Most cultures – certainly most of those in Third World countries – emphasise *responsibility* to the community, rather than the unbridled

Table 1.1 A sampling of traditional resource-management systems

System	Country/region	Resource type or function	Reference
boneh	Iran	irrigation water systems	Farvar (1987)
huerta	Spain	irrigation water systems	Maass and Anderson (1978)
zanjera	Philippines	irrigation water systems	Cruz (this volume)
subak	Bali, Indonesia	irrigation, rice	Geertz (1972)
jessour	Tunisia	water runoff management	Novikoff and Skouri (1981)
hema	Arab Middle East	pasture reserves	Gilles et al. (1986)
agdal	Morocco	range/pasture	Gilles et al. (1986)
common of pasture	England	range/pasture	Cox (1985); Dahlman (1980)
dina	Mali	grazing, fishing, farming	Moorehead (this volume)
iriaichi	Japan	village forests and meadows	McKean (1986)
iriai	Japan	coastal fishing	Ruddle (this volume)
valli	Adriatic, Italy	lagoon fishing	Lasserre and Ruddle (1983)
tambak	Java, Indonesia	brackish water fish ponds	Lasserre and Ruddle (1983)
acadja	West Africa	lagoon fishing	Lasserre and Ruddle (1983)
nituhuschii	eastern subarctic Canada	wildlife hunting territories	Berkes (this volume)
jhum	NE India	swidden (shifting cultivation)	Atal (1984); Watson (this volume)
ladang	Indonesia; Malaysia		
kaingin	Philippines		

individualism glorified in some Western industrial cultures. Communalism is an important mode of thinking and of managing resources throughout the world, from the nomads of the Arabian peninsula to native Amerindian people. It is no accident that traditional resource-management systems are often community-based. Table 1.1 provides a sampling of some of these systems, from different continents and for a number of different resource types.

These traditional management systems have been of interest to a number of international organisations in recent years. For example, in 1983 UNESCO started a series of regional studies on traditional knowledge and management of coastal systems (Lasserre and Ruddle, 1983; Ruddle and Johannes, 1985). Among other United Nations bodies, the FAO has interests in small-scale and community-based fisheries (for example, Christy, 1982), has a programme on forestry for Local Community Development.

The International Union for the Conservation of Nature and Natural Resources (IUCN) has produced several volumes including *Culture and Conservation* (McNeely and Pitt, 1985) and *Conservation with Equity* (Jacobs and Munro, 1987) relevant to the issue, and maintains a Working Group on Traditional Ecological Knowledge. Established under the Commission on Ecology, the working group publishes a newsletter, *Tradition, Conservation and Development*, edited by G. Baines. The IUCN Commission on Environmental Planning (which changed its name in 1987 to Commission on Sustainable Development), has maintained major interest in traditional management systems.

Following several conferences and workshops (McCay and Acheson, 1987), a major international initiative was the Conference on Common Property Resource Management organized by the US National Research Council (1986). One of the outcomes of this initiative, *The Common Property Resource Digest*, started publication in 1986 (available from: 332 E Classroom Office Building, 1994 Buford Avenue, University of Minnesota, St. Paul, MN 55108 U.S.A.). As of 1988, it has an international distribution of 1500 individuals and 1600 institutions.

Since traditional management systems invariably involve social institutions as an integral part, much of the writing on these topics has been done by social scientists, especially geographers (Klee, 1980) and anthropologists (Ruddle and Akimichi, 1984; McCay and Acheson, 1987). But the subject of traditional management and common property is not in the exclusive realm of any one discipline. Much recent work has been done by researchers who can deal with social as well as environmental systems. The subject is inter-disciplinary, cutting across several fields.

The economist studying communal resource-management systems might concentrate on how joint control saves scarce resources, as compared to state management or individual control. The sociologist might suggest that communal organization has to do with group cohesion. The anthropologist might relate resource-management practice to the maintenance of culture and values in that society. The political scientist may emphasize the importance of institutions in the success or failure of resource management. The planner may be interested in the ability of local communities to participate effectively in development decisions. The ecologist would look for the long-term survival value of traditional management and how local knowledge of the resource translates into management strategies that make ecological sense.

All of the above are important perspectives; complementary rather than alternative views. As Bromley (1986) pointed out, 'the common thread, obviously, is that the group as a whole has some abiding interest in survival, in cohesion, in the benefits and costs attendant to a particular use regime, and on economizing on perceived scarcities.' The truth is that traditional systems, such as those in Table 1.1, have been the main means by which societies have managed their natural resources over millennia on a sustainable basis. It is only as a result of this that we have any resources today to speak about.

For example, we find that *qanat*-based societies in Iran continue to survive if they have maintained their *boneh*s and perish if they have not. (*Qanat*s are underground networks of galleries tapping subsurface water.) We see that those communities in the nomadic societies of the Middle East and Africa that have kept their traditional range-management systems do better than those which have had to abandon them through external pressures. We note that those West African fishing communities which are able to maintain the *acadja* system have fish to eat, and those unable to manage these lagoon fisheries see the yields diminish. The notion advanced in the *State of the World* – that the general economic decline of Africa is largely attributable to the non-sustainable use of forest, grazing land, water and soil resources (Brown and Wolf, 1986) – is now widely accepted. It is of critical importance, therefore, that pathways to sustainable use of such common-property resources be developed.

The recent explosion of interest in traditional communal systems has provided us with much material on the ecological, economic and social values of these systems. UNESCO, for example, points out that traditional management often makes good scientific sense (Johannes, 1981; Lasserre and Ruddle, 1983). But in the contemporary world, sound technical information is also necessary for the management of common-property resources, especially those that are exploited by more than one user-group or resource community.

There is often potential for useful interplay between traditional and technical/scientific knowledge. A suitable analogy may be found in some of the early work with the highly successful experimental farms devoted to replicating and explaining in more scientific terms the best practice of experienced farmers (D. Feeny). It is the commonalties, rather than differences, between traditional and scientific systems of 'knowing' and using resources that make the study of commons interesting.

Different concepts of common property

All common-property resources share two important characteristics. First, exclusion (or control of access) of users to these resources is problematic. Secondly, each user is capable of subtracting from the welfare of other users. Hence, in this book, common-property resources are defined as 'a class of resources for which exclusion is difficult and joint use involves subtractability.' This definition follows the one developed by Feeny and colleagues, reported by Berkes et al. (1989), and is similar to the ones in Ostrom (1986) and Fortmann and Bruce (1988, p.2).

The present authors are concerned mainly with water, wildlife, fish, forests and pastures. All of these resources are renewable; all but one (water) living. However, there are other resources which show characteristics of common property. Oakerson (1986) included public parks, highways and oil pools among commons. Ostrom (1986) included radio wavelengths. S. Torres, at the Conference on Conservation and Development (Jacobs and Munro, 1987) included genetic resources. An interesting case of common-property resource is the geosynchronous orbit, a band of space above the equator in which most communication satellites are placed. Signal interference effectively limits the number of satellites to about 180, and so the geosynchronous orbit has become a scarce and limited global commons. The deep seabed and Antarctica are other examples of global commons.

Use of the term 'common property' has been controversial. This is partly because of differences at the philosophical basis of traditional views as opposed to Western scientific resource management. The contemporary Western view is that property is either private or it belongs to the state. In this view, resources which are not amenable to private appropriation are called 'common property'. But contrary to traditional view, 'common property' in this sense does not mean that the resource is owned collectively by a group; it means it is not owned by anyone. It is a free good. For example, marine resources, including fisheries, are defined in law in most Western nations including the United States as being 'owned by no one and belonging to everyone' (NOAA, 1985, p.2). According to this definition of common property, such resources are basically open-access and freely available to any user.

According to a second view, common property should be restricted to communally owned resources – that is, those resources for which there exist communal arrangements for the exclusion of non-owners and for allocation among co-owners.

> Economists are not free to use the concept of 'common property resources' or 'commons' under conditions where no institutional arrangements exist. Common property is not 'everybody's property'. The concept implies that potential resource users who are not members of a group of co-equal owners are excluded. The concept of 'property' has no meaning without this feature (Ciriacy-Wantrup and Bishop, 1975).

The concept of common property in this second sense is well established in formal institutions such as the Anglo-Saxon common law and the Roman Law (Ciriacy-Wantrup and Bishop, 1975). It is also well established in informal institutional arrangements based on custom and tradition. There is a particularly rich documentation of this from Oceania and Asia (Ruddle and Johannes, 1985; Ruddle and Akimichi, 1984).

The distinction between the two concepts is crucially important with regard to the 'tragedy of the commons' model of Hardin (1968) which guides the thinking of many resource managers in the Western world. Hardin's model makes the critical assumption that common-property resources are really open-access, which we know not to be true in the example of the medieval English grazing commons that Hardin used (Cox, 1985; Dasgupta, 1983, p.13; Dahlman, 1980). According to Hardin's model, such resources held in common are doomed to overexploitation since each resource-user places immediate self-interest above community interest. This way, the model makes a second critical assumption that resource-users are individualistic and unable to cooperate towards the greater community interest. Thus they eventually become both villain and victim of resource depletion. The Hardin model leads to the conclusion that resources should be either privatized or controlled by central government authority to ensure sustainable use. Hardin depicted the solution as 'mutual coercion, mutually agreed upon', and referred to government control; he made no mention of the possibility of communal management.

Many case studies indicate that resource-users can, and in fact do, cooperate. Valuable natural resources are almost never open-access but are managed under traditional rules governing use. To be sure, 'traditional' is difficult to define and many resource-use practices disappear over time; ecological wisdom is lost. However, at the same time, new knowledge and institutions can appear. It is a dynamic process. For example, new common-property institutions have developed within 15 years in the case of some Turkish coastal fisheries (Berkes 1986).

Cooperation for communal interest is not restricted to marginal societies in exotic, far-away places. It frequently occurs in Western societies as well; for example, in contemporary commercial fisheries in the United States, Great Britain and Canada – countries in which the supremacy of the individual interest is held without question (Berkes, 1985). Nevertheless, the tragedy of the commons model and the economic theory which preceded it (Gordon,

1954; Scott, 1955) are entrenched in resource-management textbooks, university curricula, and in the conventional wisdom of many contemporary managers of common-property resources. This thinking is also dominant in models of development exported to Third World countries.

Differences over the use of the term 'common property' are likely to persist, given the legal definition of resources such as fisheries as common property in the first, 'free goods' sense. Although we much prefer the second, 'communal ownership', sense of common property, we will acknowledge that 'common property' is used by many as a 'catch-all concept for a variety of essentially different circumstances' (Dorfman from chapter by Cox), and as a term that denotes a number of different types of resource status to different people.

Property-Rights Regimes

One solution to the impasse over the use of the term 'common property' is to distinguish between the *resource* and the *regime*. This distinction between the resource itself and the property-rights regime under which it is held is critically important (Ostrom, 1986; Bromley, 1989). This is because a particular resource may be held under more than one regime. For example, as Cox points out in this volume (Chapter 8), a resource such as salmon may quite plausibly fall under any of several management regimes depending on where it is located and harvested. In general, common-property resources may be held within:

1 open-access;
2 communal property;
3 state property; or
4 private property (Table 1.2).

In reality, few resources are purely open-access, communal or state property. Most are mixtures of these idealized types. For example, the lobster resource in the Acheson chapter is both communal property and state property; fishermen use it as communal resource but the state maintains management jurisdiction. In many traditional societies, communal property resources are nationalized and turned into state property. This complicates the ownership status of the resource, and often leads to resource depletion, as pointed out by Gibbs and Bromley in Chapter 2.

To bring out the distinction between communal property and state property, Repetto's illustration is useful (1986 p.30–1). 'Villagers who ruthlessly cut trees for firewood and fodder in government forests will zealously nurture and protect groves that belong to them or – if their community organization is sufficiently strong – to their village.' Repetto's observation has universal

Table 1.2 Idealized types of property-rights regimes relevant to common-property
resources.[1] The fourth property-rights regime is 'private property'

1. Open-access (*res nullius*)[2]	Free-for-all; resource-use rights are neither exclusive nor transferable;[3] these rights are owned in common but are open-access to everyone (and therefore property to no one).[4]
2. State property (*res publica*)	Ownership and management control is held by the nation state or crown; public resources to which use-rights and access rights have not been specified.
3. Communal property (*res communes*)	Use-rights for the resource are controlled by an identifiable group and are not privately owned or managed by governments; there exist rules concerning who may use the resource, who is excluded from using the resource, and how the resource should be used;[5] community-based resource management systems; common property.[6]

Notes
1. Ostrom (1986) advocates the use of the term 'common pool resource' for the resource itself, reserving the use of 'common property' to refer specifically to communal property-management systems.
2. Latin terminology follows Hugo Grotius (see Cox, Chapter 8).
3. After Grima and Berkes, Chapter 3, and Regier et al, Chapter 7.
4. After Gibbs and Bromley, Chapter 2, and Grima and Berkes, Chapter 3.
5. After Jacobs and Munro (1987), Workshop 14, p. 442; National Research Council (1986); Bromley (1985).
6. In the sense of Cirriacy-Wantrup and Bishop (1975); Bromley (1985); Ostrom (1986); Bromley (1989).

application and brings to mind the Turkish saying, 'Devletin mali deniz, yemeyen domuz.' (Liberally translated: 'One would have to be a despicable fool not to help oneself to state property.')

Of the four property-rights regimes in Table 1.2 (which are discussed further in Chapter 2 by Gibbs and Bromley), the one that comes close to being a null set is open-access resources. Notwithstanding Hardin's model, there are extremely few examples of resources which are truly open and freely available to everyone. Several centuries ago, ocean resources may have been open-access; under the 1982 United Nations Law of the Sea they have either become state property or have come under joint international jurisdiction. Whenever a society has needed a natural resource – whether medieval common-grazing lands in England or wild beaver in subarctic Canada – rules for its orderly use have been worked out.

Multiple functions of common-property systems

For purposes of this discussion, common-property (or communal-property) systems will include all community-based resource-management systems. To avoid some of the anthropological complications, 'community' is defined as 'resource community' – the group of people that uses a certain resource. 'Traditional' is defined here to denote practices which have had historical continuity among a group of people. Resources involved in common-property systems may be communal property or those which, although not legally owned by the community, are managed in accordance with community-based norms and rules. Common-property systems have certain critical roles in local communities. These roles may be summarized under five headings.

1 Livelihood security

Community-based management is traditionally one of the principal means of ensuring livelihood security (Korten 1986). With guaranteed access rights to a vital resource, everyone in the community is assured of the opportunity of meeting their basic needs. To guarantee that no one in the group starves, many societies have elaborate rules for sharing food (and other vital resources such as water in the case of arid environments).

Sharing rules are widely found in hunting–gathering societies, such as Amerindian groups, but also among agricultural societies. Reciprocal obligations for sharing and mutual help appear to be important for group survival, especially in cases where food supplies fluctuate in space and time. All common-property systems are characterized by the presence of arrangements for allocation of the resource among co-owners (Bromley, 1985; Ostrom, 1986).

2 Access equity and conflict resolution

Common-property systems normally provide mechanisms for the equitable use of resources with a minimum of internal strife or conflict. Rules mutually agreed upon by all members of the group provide an efficient means of conflict resolution and reduce 'transaction costs' in the enforcement of these rules. Often, users themselves point out that their local rules serve primarily to reduce conflict in resource use, over and above other possible functions (Berkes, 1986).

In cases where collective labour is needed for the operation of the production process (as in irrigation), common-property systems include rules to even out the work by allowing for equal participation based on producers' relative rights to the resource. In some cases, the means of production (for example, the water pump) is held communally as well as the resource itself (the water).

3 Mode of production

Community-based resource-management systems often form the basis for the system of production. Typically, these management systems tend to be set up at the sub-village or sub-tribal levels, and consist of work teams that include a number of households. Within the community, work teams may be fluid and flexible, with different individuals and households teaming up on different occasions. Community members share a common culture, knowledge of the resource and knowledge of resource-use rules, facilitated by the simple rule, 'you must live in this community to use this resource' (Ostrom, 1985).

Common-property systems serve as interface, not only between society and resource, but also between the individual and the society at large. Social roles and obligations are often defined in terms of one's participation in work teams. Common-property systems are an integral part of the local culture. Hunting, fishing and fruit gathering are a way of life rather than merely a means of earning a living.

This is fundamentally different from industrial societies with their hired workers, hierarchical organizations and single-minded quest for profits or production quotas. Nevertheless, there are examples of industrial systems incorporating some of the characteristics of the communal-property mode of production. Industrial organization in Japan – with its emphasis on cooperation, maximum employee participation, consensus decision-making, extended 'corporate families', shared values, common goals and cradle-to-grave social security – is a notably successful case in point (Ouchi, 1981).

4 Resource conservation

Common-property systems are basically conservative in the way resources are utilized; many aim at local self-sufficiency. The emphasis is on taking what is needed; there are social sanctions against excessive individual gain from a communal resource and against the accumulation of surplus. This has created tension between community-level resource-use rules and state-level rules, and between communal-level interests and 'economic development' interests (see chapter 16 by Baines). Some Western-oriented development planners have even regarded common-property systems as an impediment to economic progress, whereas others increasingly see the value of incorporating them in the development process as a primary means of mobilizing people and resources for community-based sustainable development.

5 Ecological sustainability

It can be argued that common property systems deserve credit for many of those resources which have remained productive through the generations. The traditional use of resources often incorporates rituals to help synchronize harvesting with natural cycles (Johannes 1981). These serve to reinforce social controls in maintaining a productive resource from generation to generation.

The implementation of foreign economies (Farvar and Milton, 1972) and technologies (Commoner, 1971) have often upset age-old and time-tested resource-use rules developed over generations in each successful common-property system. Note, however, that in traditional societies that have remained reasonably stable and admitted technological and economic development at a pace that could be accommodated, traditional systems have remained remarkably successful. For example, McKean's (1986) detailed historical study of Japanese common lands (*iriaichi*) did not turn up a single example of a 'commons that suffered ecological destruction while it was still a commons'. (See Chapter 10 by Ruddle.)

Common property institutions and development

Because of the crucial role played by common-property systems in sustainable resource use, their most significant application in the contemporary world context is their relevance to development. Since common-property systems provide, in effect, long-term and 'grass-roots' institutions, these systems are the most important candidates for popular participation in development decision-making.

Common property resource management systems such as those in Table 1.2 have a political and socioeconomic context. The effective functioning of these systems depends on the existence of appropriate institutions. With many common property resources, these institutions are local and informal, community-based rather than government-sponsored (Korten, 1986). Ignored by much development planning in the past, there is now abundant evidence from detailed case studies that these institutions play a crucial role in economic development (Ostrom et al. 1988).

Institutions seen as necessary for development planning cannot be created anew. In areas earmarked for development projects, the local people cannot be divorced from the social structures of which they are a part. The logical approach for development planners is to deal intelligently with existing community structures, including those for handling production and resource-management issues. However, care has to be taken to put common-property systems in their proper perspective when considering transferability from one area or resource type to another. Having developed within specific historical, cultural and ecological contexts, their strength is in their suitability for specific areas and resource types.

Whereas the Japanese common-property fishery system, *iriai*, may not be transferable in its exact form to, say, coastal fisheries in Thailand, some of its basic characteristics may be. The Japanese system is instructive in showing how modern natural-resource-management legislation can be designed to support and strengthen traditional common-property systems successfully. Likewise, whereas the *zanjera* system of water management in the Philippines may not be directly applicable to a Latin American situation, it does demonstrate how irrigated agriculture can benefit from communally managed allocation systems.

To be sure, not all traditional practice is ecologically adaptive, and some practices and beliefs deserve to be abandoned. But the rejection of all traditional practice, including those of common-property systems that make ecological sense is a case of 'throwing out the baby with the bathwater' – something Third World decision-makers can ill afford to do. Just as traditional knowledge of medicinal plants is no longer taken lightly by medical scientists, traditional practices in common-property resource management are taken very seriously indeed by many resource conservationists and managers. To learn from traditional users, however, it is necessary for scientists, economists and development planners to overcome the narrow technical perspectives of their disciplines, and become sensitive to other world views.

Many resource users in traditional common-property systems still act as if the earth's resources were given to them for use with care, not to do as they please under the forces of market economies or state production quotas. The ecological wisdom of many common-property systems emphasizes respect, responsibility and stewardship; some provide real-life examples of 'deep ecology' (Naess, 1973). In implementing an 'ecosystem view' in which humans are considered part of the ecosystem, there is much to learn from traditional societies such as those in the Pacific Islands, the Sahara and the Canadian subarctic. An ecosystem view of people–nature relations is a richer, more informative and ultimately more sustainable approach than a disembodied study of the resources or social institutions by themselves.

Are common-property systems of continuing and future relevance? They are under a great deal of pressure. They are not museum pieces but living, adapting, sometimes disappearing and reappearing systems. Many exist despite official government policies to privatize and nationalize resources. Perhaps the most important practical reason for governments to encourage common-property systems is economic. It makes administrative and economic sense to involve user-groups in management, especially in cases where these groups have proven their ability for self-management. As several chapters in this volume point out, shared governance (co-management), or state regulation jointly with self-management is often a viable option.

Depending on the resource type, combinations of private and communal-property regimes may also be viable. The long-term coexistence of communal-property systems and private property in Swiss alpine grazing meadows today (Netting, 1981), strongly hints that communal property is not merely lack of private property but rather a system with ecological survival value in its own right. The Swiss-meadows case and all the management systems indicated in Table 1.2 provide evidence that communal-property systems are not evolutionary relics about to be replaced by 'newer and better' management regimes. They exist in the Swiss Alps and elsewhere because they provide certain advantages over other property-rights regimes.

It is the task of careful empirical and theoretical studies, such as those in this book, to investigate these advantages. A new theory of common-property resources has to be able to account for sustainable resource management under communal-property regimes. Alternative models based on more complete theory, rather than the misleading 'tragedy of the commons' model, could provide the basis for the sustainable use of common-property resources for the future.

Acknowledgements

We thank David Feeny for thoughtful and detailed comments and Peter Jacobs for suggesting new approaches and organization.

References

Atal, Y., 1984: 'Swidden cultivation in Asia: The need for a new approach', *Nature and Resources*, 20(3), pp. 19–26.

Berkes, F. 1985: 'Fishermen and "the tragedy of the commons"', *Environmental Conservation*, 12, pp. 199–206.

Berkes, F. 1986: 'Local-level management and the commons problem: A comparative study of Turkish coastal fisheries', *Marine Policy*, 10, pp. 215–29.

Berkes, F., Feeny, D., McCay, B.J. and Acheson, J.M., 1989: 'Reassessing the "tragedy of the commons"', *Nature* (in press).

Bromley, D.W., 1985: 'Common property issues in international development', *Developments*, 5(1), pp. 12–15.

Bromley, D.W., 1986: 'The common property challenge', in *Proceedings of the Conference on Common Property Resource Management*, National Academy Press, Washington DC, pp. 1–5.

Bromley, D.W., 1989: *Economic Interests and Institutions*, Blackwell, London.

Brown, L.R. and Wolf, E.C., 1986: 'Reversing Africa's decline', in *State of the World 1986*, Worldwatch Institute/Norton, New York.

Christy, F.T. Jr., 1982: 'Territorial use rights in marine fisheries: Definitions and conditions', *FAO Fisheries Technical Paper No. 227*.

Ciriacy-Wantrup, S.V. and Bishop, R.C., 1975: '"Common property" as a concept in natural resources policy', *Natural Resources Journal*, 15, pp. 713–27.

Commoner, B., 1971: *The Closing Circle*, Knopf, New York.

Conklin, H.C., 1961: 'Study of shifting cultivation', *Current Anthropology*, 2, pp. 27–61.

Cox, S.J.B., 1985: 'No tragedy on the commons', *Environmental Ethics*, 7, pp. 49–61.

Dahlman, C., 1980: *The Open Field System and Beyond*, Cambridge University Press, Cambridge, UK.

Dasgupta, D.S., 1983: *The Control of Resources*, Harvard University Press, Cambridge, MA, USA.

Farvar, M.T., 1987: 'Local strategies for sustainable development', in *Conservation with Equity: Strategies for Sustainable Development*, Jacobs, P. and Munro, D.A., eds, IUCN, Cambridge, UK, pp. 233–43.

Farvar, M.T. and Milton, J.P., eds, 1972: *Careless Technology: Ecology and International Development*, Natural History Press, Garden City, New York.

Feeny, D., Berkes, F., McCay, B.J. and Acheson, J.M. *The tragedy of the commons: Twenty years later* (in preparation).

Fortmann, L. and Bruce, J.W., eds, 1988: *Whose Trees? Proprietary Dimensions of Forestry*, Westview Press, Boulder and London.

Geertz, C., 1972: 'The wet and the dry: Traditional irrigation in Bali and Morocco', *Human Ecology*, 1, pp. 23–39.

Gilles, J.L., Hammoudi, A. and Mahdi, M., 1986: 'Oukaimedene, Morocco: A high mountain *agdal*', *Proceedings of the Conference on Common Property Resource Management*, National Academy Press, Washington, DC, pp. 281–304.

Gordon, H.S., 1954: 'The economic theory of a common property resource: the fishery', *Journal of Political Economy*, 62, pp. 124–42.

Hardin, G., 1968: 'The tragedy of the commons', *Science*, 162, pp. 1243–8.

Jacobs, P. and Munro, D., eds, 1987: *Conservation with Equity: Strategies for Sustainable Development*, IUCN, Cambridge, UK.

Johannes, R.E., 1981: *Words of the Lagoon: Fishing and Marine Lore in the Palau District of Micronesia*, University of Berkeley Press, Berkeley and Los Angeles.

Klee, G.A., ed., 1980: *World Systems of Traditional Resource Management*, Winston, New York.

Korten, D.C., ed., 1986: *Community Management. Asian Experience and Perspectives*, Kumarian Press, West Hartford, CT, USA.

Lasserre, P. and Ruddle, K., 1983: 'Traditional Knowledge and Management of Marine Coastal Systems', in *Report of the ad hoc Steering Group*, UNESCO, Paris. (Also published as: Biology Internations Special issue 4.)

Maass, A. and Anderson, R.L., 1978: *And the Desert Shall Rejoice. Conflict, Growth and Justice in Arid Environments*, MIT Press, Cambridge, MA, USA.

McCay, B.J. and Acheson, J.M., eds, 1987: *The Question of the Commons*, University of Arizona Press, Tucson.

McKean, M.A., 1986: 'Management of traditional common lands (*iriaichi*) in Japan', in *Proceedings of the Conference on Common Property Resource Management*, National Academy Press, Washington, DC.

McNeely, J.A. and Pitt, D., eds, 1985: *Culture and Conservation*, Croom Helm, London.

Naess, A., 1973: 'The shallow and the deep, long-range ecology movement. A summary', *Inquiry*, 16, pp. 95–100.

National Research Council, 1986: *Proceedings of the Conference on Common Property Resource Management*, National Academy Press, Washington, DC.

Netting, R.M., 1981: *Balancing on an Alp: Ecological Change and Continuity in a Swiss Mountain Community*, Cambridge University Press, Cambridge, UK.

NOAA, 1985: *Fishery Management – Lessons From Other Resource Management Areas*, National Oceanic and Atmospheric Administration, Washington, DC.

Novikoff, G. and Skouri, M., 1981: 'Balancing development and conservation in pre-Saharan Tunisia', *Ambio*, 10, pp. 135–41.

Oakerson, R.J., 1986: 'A model for the analysis of common property problems', in *Proceedings of the Conference on Common Property Resource Management*, National Academy Press, Washington, DC, pp. 13–30.

Ostrom, E., 1985: 'The rudiments of revised theory of the origins, survival, and performance of institutions for collective action', *Working Paper 32*, Workshop in Political Theory and Policy Analysis, Indiana University, Bloomington.

Ostrom, E., 1986: 'Issues of definition and theory: some conclusions and hypotheses', in *Proceedings of the Conference on Common Property Resource Management*, National Academy Press, Washington, DC, pp. 597–615.

Ostrom, V., Feeny, D. and Picht, H., eds, 1988: *Rethinking Institutional Analysis and Development*, International Centre for Economic Growth, San Francisco.

Ouchi, W.G., 1981: *Theory Z. How American Business Can Meet the Japanese Challenge*, Addison-Wesley, Reading.

Repetto, R., 1986: *World Enough and Time*, World Resources Institute/Yale University Press, New Haven and London.

Ruddle, K. and Akimichi, T., eds, 1984: *Maritime Institutions in the Western Pacific*, Senri Ethnological Studies No. 17., National Museum of Ethnology, Osaka.

Ruddle, K. and Johannes, R.E., eds, 1985: *The Traditional Knowledge and Management of Coastal Systems in Asia and the Pacific*, UNESCO, Jakarta.

Scott, A.D., 1955: 'The fishery: The objectives of sole ownership', *Journal of Political Economy*, 63, pp. 116–24.

Turner, R.K., ed., 1988: *Sustainable Environmental Management. Principles and Practice*, Belhaven, London and Westview, Boulder.

World Commission on Environment and Development, 1987: *Our Common Future*, Oxford University Press, Oxford.

World Conservation Strategy, 1980: *Living Resource Conservation for Sustainable Development*, IUCN/UNEP/WWF, Gland.

Part 1 Perspectives on the Commons Debate

> One of the troubles of our age is that habits of thought cannot change as quickly as techniques, with the result that as skill increases, wisdom fades.

Thus noted the philosopher, Bertrand Russell. One of these habits of thought is the consideration of natural resources as mere commodities to be exploited. Western industrial nations learned early on how to generate material wealth from resources with the application of capital and human labour. Techniques were developed to exploit resources singlemindedly, efficiently and quickly – but not sustainably and equitably. Environmental and social repercussions of the triumph of Western science and technology are becoming increasingly apparent.

In recent years, a new idea has been gaining currency: the ecologically sustainable use of resources to provide long rather than short-term economic returns (world conservation strategy, see also Chapter 1). This is a revolutionary change in thinking; notable also for its irony.

For decades, many developing countries have been ignoring the time-tested resource-use practices of their own people, trying instead to emulate the developed countries, with their imprudence and excess in resource use. Meanwhile, scholars and resource managers in industrialized countries have been seeking new paradigms of resource use and developing a keen interest in traditional resource-use wisdom and ecological knowledge as found in some developing areas of the world. Thus, there is renewed interest, for example, in *acadjas* of Western Africa, *hemas* of the Middle East, and *zanjeras* of the Philippines.

The four chapters in this section of the book deal with a selection of perspectives relevant to the common-property debate: different views, background concepts and definitions. This section comes to grips with a variety of views on management regimes; institutions and social systems; ecology and economics; development planning; and evolution of resource-management systems.

Chapter 2 by Gibbs and Bromley starts out with some of the basic concepts: resources, property and property rights, and common-property regimes, defined as the set of accepted social norms and rules governing resource use. Focusing on communal ownership of resources, the chapter briefly reviews common-property regimes in practice, pointing out the universality of communal-management systems. The authors promote these common-property regimes as a foundation for institutional innovation towards sustainable development – a challenging task for world-wide implementation.

Chapter 3 by Grima and Berkes deals with the ecosystem view of resource management and attempts to infuse ecological thinking into resource economics. The chapter argues that the narrow definition of resources as commodities ignores the interdependency of various ecosystem components and understates the ecological value of resources. The chapter explains why the disembodied analysis of resources does not work, using examples, such as the 'maximum-sustainable-yield' approach which deals with one resource at a time, independently of the ecosystem. It explains how a more comprehensive, longer-term view of resources can be developed.

Chapter 4 by Watson takes a development-planning perspective. Using the example of shifting cultivation in Sarawak, Malaysia, the chapter explores what happens when traditional resource-management systems do not keep pace with changing economic and demographic conditions. While traditional 'passive management' systems may have provided a man–nature balance in the past, they have been overtaken by population growth. Watson foresees the evolution of more intensive resource-management systems, integrating new ecological knowledge with greater individual control over the resource. The chapter raises the question of whether privatization may be the more appropriate solution in some cases, while communal ownership is better for others.

Berkes (Chapter 5) takes an evolutionary ecological view in dealing with cooperation among users of a resource – cooperation which is essential to common-property systems. How does cooperation evolve and persist? What conditions lead to cooperation or lack of it? Using the case study of Cree Amerindian hunting territories in subarctic Canada, the chapter traces the emergence of family-based territories out of a community-based system by intensification of resource use; its collapse with the creation of open-access conditions by intrusion from outsiders; and its subsequent recovery by the restoration of closed-access conditions. The chapter shows that the recovery of common-property systems and the resource itself is possible, and that users can cooperate to their mutual advantage once the critical problem of open-access is resolved.

The chapters in Part 2 obviously do not cover all possible perspectives on common property resources. But they do represent a diverse sampling: an institutional–economic approach, an ecological–economic approach, a development-planning view and an evolutionary–ecological view. These perspectives are different but complementary. Part 2 thus progresses from institutional issues to a consideration of economics tempered with ecological concerns.

There are differences among authors regarding such issues as population growth. Watson raises fundamental questions about the viability of traditional 'management' systems in the face of population pressure, and searches for planning solutions. Berkes, on the other hand, deals with population merely as one factor among many and focuses instead on cooperation as the driving force in maintaining viable communal-property systems. The debate on the relative importance of the population issue brings to mind another quote, this one attributed to Mahatma Gandhi: 'Earth has resources for everyone's need, but not for everyone's greed.'

2 Institutional Arrangements for Management of Rural Resources: Common-Property Regimes

Christopher J.N. Gibbs and *Daniel W. Bromley*

Summary

Institutional arrangements are defined as the rules and conventions which establish peoples' relationships to resources, translating interests into claims, and claims into property rights. Common-property rights are a special class of property rights which assure individuals access to resources over which they have collective claims. Common-property regimes are forms of management grounded in a set of accepted social norms and rules for the sustainable and interdependent use of collective goods such as forests, grazing grounds, fisheries and water resources. This chapter defines terms and concepts necessary to analyse common-property regimes, and briefly illustrates their application to a number of renewable resources. The chapter concludes that common-property regimes can be efficient and equitable mechanisms for sustainable resource management, and may provide an appropriate foundation for the design or adaptation of institutional arrangements in the future.

Introduction

Resources may be defined as those components of an ecosystem which provide goods and services useful to man. The majority of the world's people, being rural and impoverished, directly employ the earth's resources of land, water, forests and fisheries for their livelihoods. Such resources should be recognized as potentially renewable, capable of sustaining people and of being sustained indefinitely. However, whether or not this potential will be realized depends on numerous factors, including the institutional arrangements that people choose to adopt concerning resource utilization.

Institutional arrangements, which here refer to the conventions that societies establish to define their members' relationships to resources, translate interests in resources into claims, and claims into property rights. These relationships in turn strongly affect resource-use patterns worldwide. This chapter will identify the role and significance of one particular set of institutional arrangements: those defining common-property resource management.

Common-property rules and conventions are found in rural areas of the world from Switzerland to the Sahara (Netting, 1978; Thompson, 1979). These arrangements are of special interest to conservationists because they have provided access to resources equitably, sustainably and at reasonable cost. This has been achieved through the persistent acceptance of rules which regulate individual behaviour in the continuing interest of the group as a whole. Continued acceptance of the rules has meant both survival of the community and maintenance of the resource base.

This volume argues that our understanding of, and respect for, customary rules and conventions for management of resources as common property must be increased. Furthermore, the design of new arrangements for the sustainable management of renewable resources in particular could benefit from such lessons. Initially, therefore, this chapter defines resources and property, continues with a discussion of the characteristics, functions and performance of common-property regimes, and concludes by relating institutional arrangements to the depletion of renewable rural resources. The overall argument relates to institutional innovation for the future.

Resources

Components of nature such as soil, water, forests, fish and wildlife are considered to be resources when they provide means of sustenance to mankind. However, there are good ecological reasons to broaden the concept of resources to something beyond the provision of short-term utility. Wood has been a resource for thousands of years; solar powered electricity has been a resource for only decades. As natural resources, they exist within a particular technical and institutional environment. The technical environment provides the tools and knowledge which define how a resource is used as a factor of production. The institutional environment defines who can control the resource and how the technique is applied.

Irrigation based on groundwater, for example, is a combination of both a technique – involving pumps, water, soil, seed, labour and tools – and of supporting institutions which define rights to water, land tenure and labour relations. Techniques and supporting institutions must complement each other if irrigation technology is to function efficiently and sustainably. In the absence of effective institutions, groundwater flows are wasted and the pool becomes overdrawn.

Natural resources exist as *stocks*, such as coal or mineral deposits, or *flows* such as water, sunlight, forests or fisheries. For stock resources the physical quantity available for use is more or less fixed: what is used now will not be available later. Stock resources are therefore exhaustible and non-renewable and it is possible to identify an optimum rate of depletion based on extraction costs and demand. Determining the optimum rate of extraction is the puzzle faced by owners of coal, oil and mineral deposits.

Unlike stock resources, flow resources are renewable and can be managed to yield goods and services sustainably. Where property rights in flow resources are privately owned – such as for livestock on a farm or trees in a private plantation – the management problem is similar to that of the mine owner looking for a private optimum based on prices and costs. However, where property rights in flow resources are not exclusively owned, the management problem is more complex.

For flow resources, the physical quantity available changes over time: what is used now may not necessarily affect what is available later. For example, in the case of solar energy, winds or tides, present use does not diminish future use. However, some flow resources have a critical zone below which a decrease in flow cannot be reversed. A fish or wildlife population, for example, can be driven to extinction once the population is reduced below a certain critical minimum size (Ciriacy-Wantrup, 1952).

Forests, grasslands and soils are further examples of flow resources with critical zones. These are also the resources on which the majority of the rural people in the developing world depend directly for their welfare. Whether these potentially renewable resources are managed sustainably depends largely on how property rights or use rights are assigned and the pattern of incentives they create for conservation or depletion.

Property and property rights

Property is the result of a secure claim to a resource or the services that resources provide. Property rights in resources exist in a variety of forms but most commonly as:

1 State property, where the secure claim rests with the government – as in a public forest or a national park;
2 private property, where the claim rests with the individual or the corporation; and
3 common property or communal property, where individuals have claims on collective goods as members of recognized groups.

In addition, resources may exist where there are no secure claims, and therefore cannot be considered as property: access to everyone means property to no one. Complications with the Western notion of 'property' are dealt with in Chapter 3.

There is nothing inherent in a resource itself to determine absolutely the nature of property rights. Fisheries, wildlife, water and forests are all capable of being nationalized, privatized or managed collectively. All are also equally capable of being unspecified and unmanaged. The nature of property and the specification of rights to resources are determined by members of a society and the rules and conventions they choose to establish – not by the resource itself.

Common-property rights are a special class of property rights which assure individuals access to resources over which they have collective claims. Villager's interest in forests, grazing lands, irrigation water, fisheries and wildlife all provide examples of resources which may be managed as common property. Common property is created when members of an interdependent group agree to limit their individual claims on a resource in the expectation that the other members of the group will do likewise. Rules of conduct in the use of a given resource are maintained to which all members of the interdependent group subscribe.

For a resource to be managed as common property, each individual confidently relies on every other group member's contribution to management. If individuals contribute to the management of a collective good when they do not expect others to contribute, they are behaving altruistically. If individuals fail to contribute to the management of a collective good when they expect that others will, they are behaving as 'free riders'. Free riders respond to incentives to shirk responsibility to the group to which they belong (Runge, 1983).

The importance of these distinctions rests upon the realization that altruism cannot be depended upon to sustain renewable resources, and free riding is the basis for the so-called 'tragedy of the commons'. Finally, when all members of a group fail to subscribe to the rules governing use of a collective good, anarchy prevails and the commons inevitably disappear.

Common-property regimes

Resources are managed as common property by rules for user-group behaviour when their continuing use is conditional upon the interdependent behaviour of group members. Since common property is grounded in a set of accepted social norms and rules, the term 'common-property regimes' will be used to refer to this type of property management. Common-property regimes provide assurance that the resources on which all persons collectively depend will be available sustainably. The same assurances could not be provided by the adoption of private or state-property rights since the consequences for productivity, sustainability and equity would be different. For people in the developing world who are directly dependent on the availability of renewable resources, common-property regimes can provide equitable and sustainable access to the resource with minimal cost.

Case studies demonstrate that rules or norms for the interdependent use of collective goods develop in the face of uncertain or limited resource-availability. These rules originate within the group, are mutually accepted by the group, and contain their own means for resolving conflicts. The rules, moreover, prescribe individual functions within the group and thus eliminate the need for members to negotiate every new transaction with each other. Negotiating each transaction individually would be costly, and would lead to outcomes dependent on individual bargaining power which could have injurious consequences distributionally (Runge, 1983).

For resources such as forests, grasslands and fisheries on which whole communities may depend and where the potential for free riding exists, questions of efficiency, equity and sustainability are inextricably bound together. In situations of uncertain resource-availability, common-property-regime members prefer to trade off some of the individual benefit generated by a system of private-use rights, for the collective assurance that the resource will be used equitably and, as a consequence, sustainably.

A well-functioning common-property regime will probably be distinguished by:

1 a minimum (or absence) of disputes and limited effort necessary to maintain compliance: the regime will be efficient;
2 a capacity to cope with progressive changes through adaptation, such as the arrival of new production techniques: the regime will be stable;
3 a capacity to accommodate surprise or sudden shocks: the regime will be resilient; and
4 a shared perception of fairness among the members with respect to inputs and outcomes: the regime will be equitable.

Using these four criteria – efficiency, stability, resiliency and equitability – the institutional performance of such regimes can be appraised and their value as foundations for institutional innovation can be assessed.

In order to meet these criteria and to guide the use of collective resources, numerous variables must be defined by the group implementing common-property resource management:

1 what constitutes membership of the group having a right to the resource and who is not a member with the duty to respect the rights of members;
2 what constitutes agreement – unanimity, consensus or majority;
3 on what basis the right will apply over time, i.e., annually or seasonally;
4 how rights are transmitted between generations;
5 where control resides, i.e., vested in a community board, in village or district elders, or in the households;
6 how compliance with agreed rules and conventions is to be maintained;

7 how departures from the rules are to be corrected and sanctions imposed;
8 and how disputes are to be settled.

Common-property regimes in practice

Examples of common-property regimes can be found in the management of water resources, pasture or rangelands, forests, wildlife, fisheries, and agriculture. The most highly developed examples of common-property regimes are probably found in irrigations, where effective water management is dependent on the interrelated actions of a unified set of water users (Chapter 13).

For irrigation, the physical scope of the system and the pattern of water rights largely help to define the organization which must manage the system. Government agencies by themselves cannot provide sufficient resources to manipulate water flows down to the level of farmers' fields, maintain every canal, or settle every conflict. The farmers must participate through organization based on an acceptable set of rules for collective water management.

Successful irrigation organizations require legal status, although this may be founded either in customary or contemporary law. The law defines who owns the water and water facilities, and who has the responsibility for operating and maintaining the system. In general, irrigator's organizations perform three sets of related activities (Bob Yoder, International Irrigation Management Institute, personal communication). The first set includes system-development activities (design, construction, operation and maintenance); the second includes water-management activities (water acquisition, allocation, distribution and drainage); and the third includes organizational activities (decision-making, mobilizing resources, communication and conflict resolution). Irrigator organizations perform well collectively when all three sets of activities intersect. For example, users must be able to make decisions about system design as it relates to water acquisition, or to mobilize resources for the operation of water distribution. Managing the common-water resource may break down if one or more aspect is neglected.

There are considerable variations in method around the world. However, the activities must be performed if water is not to be used inefficiently or the system itself to cease to function. Associations of irrigators therefore exist under the law to innovate and adapt collective means for water management which are not only relatively efficient but also equitable. By maintaining equity in claims on the water resource and by distributing operating costs and benefits fairly, members of well-functioning irrigation associations have an incentive to contribute to their maintenance.

Livestock farmers using common pastures or rangelands innovate rules for pasture use in much the same way as irrigators collectively manage water.

Common pasture and rangelands are shared by individual members of groups and by competing groups. Unless rules are followed for opening and closing the pasture and for limiting stock rates, the productivity of the pasture may be depressed through the depletion of desirable forage species. If desirable species are extinguished, the capacity of the pasture to renew itself is impaired.

Common-property regimes developed by livestock-owning communities may enforce periodic closure of rangelands in rotation to allow them to regenerate (Dani et al., 1987). Tribal taxation systems and social expenditure may also be imposed to reduce the size of herds as they approach critical limits. Types of livestock may also be regulated – such as a preference for goats over sheep – to limit pressure on range grasses and to maintain the range ecosystem. In functioning the rangeland common-property regimes, these rules are backed by sanctions imposed if rules are violated. The sanctions incur costs to violators which exceed the benefit gained from breaking the code.

The immediacy of cohesive collective management associated with a well-functioning irrigation system is not so apparent for a common pasture. However, the underlying need for operational common-property rules still applies. Where traditional management regimes for rangelands are still strong, it has been shown that range deterioration is minimized. It has also been shown that common-property regimes can be economically more efficient than private property rights (Dahlman, 1980). However, both commercialization of the livestock industry and contemporary legislation and administration have tended to undermine or replace the institutional base upon which traditional common-property regimes were founded.

A third kind of common-property regime concerns the community management of forests. Throughout much of the world, forests have been managed collectively for generations through traditional management regimes. Communities have established rules for cutting firewood and forage, and for the harvest of fruits, timber, fibres and other products (see Chapters 14 and 16). Special rules have been innovated for certain products, such as gum arabic and other resins. Other rules have evolved defining who has rights in forests. These rules may specify both individual and group rights which might coexist with respect to the same piece of land, and may distinguish land tenure from tree tenure. As in the cases of irrigation water and rangelands, these forest codes have been developed within communities to specify who has use rights and what form the rights take. Collective rights to forests may specify the right to plant, use and dispose of trees, use forest products, use the ground under or between trees, or to take livestock into the forest (Fortmann and Riddell, 1985).

Common-property regimes for the use and sharing of wildlife resources were perhaps the earliest developed in the history of humankind, considering that hunter-gatherer societies appeared earlier than did pastoralist and agricultural societies. Surviving hunting societies have been of particular interest because of their special relationships to land and animals; even when Christianized, some hunting societies retain their animist or pantheist roots (Tanner, 1979).

For hunter-gatherers, cooperation has strong survival value because coordinated action is often necessary for the successful hunting of large animals. Hunting areas tend to be under the control of tribes, family or kin groups. Such communal hunting territories are still in existence in parts of Africa and northern North America (Chapters 5 and 6). In Amazonia, parts of Indo-Pacific and northern Asia, hunting supplements small-scale agriculture or animal husbandry, which are themselves communal activities. In the relatively crowded Indian subcontinent, there still exist special hunting rights by caste (Chapter 14), an example of the resilience and persistence of common-property regimes in wildlife.

Such wildlife common-property regimes, however, have declined greatly with increasing pressure on the land resources from the expansion of agriculture, commercial forestry and mineral-exploitation activities. A hunting-gathering mode of life requires large areas in which the community of hunters must control access to the wildlife resource. Thus, hunting societies are often displaced and marginalized by other users of land resources who tend to be more numerous and politically more powerful.

A fifth example of common-property regimes concerns fisheries in marine coastal areas, lakes and rivers. The legal definition of the sea as an open-access resource by many Western industrialized nations is responsible for the neglect of common-property regimes in fisheries. Many non-Western societies, including those in Oceania and the Arctic, do not share this Western bias against marine environments, and view sea tenure in a manner similar to that of land tenure. Common-property regimes in fisheries are particularly well developed in the Pacific area, especially in Japan (Chapter 10), the Pacific (Chapter 16) and, historically, the North American Pacific coast, but they do occur throughout the world.

The basic and probably universal factor of common-property regimes in fisheries is the limitation of access to the resource (Scudder and Conelly, 1985). Without some kind of access limitation, a productive fishery sooner or later attracts enough fishermen to render it unproductive (Chapter 3). To solve this commons dilemma, many different societies have independently developed management regimes whereby the right to fish in a particular area is controlled by a family, clan, community or group of communities. As Johannes (1978) puts it, 'it was in the best interests of those who controlled a given area to harvest in moderation. By doing so they could maintain high sustainable yields, all the benefits of which would accrue directly to them.' In some societies, there are fishing leaders to oversee harvesting activities, and to enforce often elaborate rules and prohibitions.

Resource conservation and institutions in transition

Throughout the world, processes of resource depletion are at work. In the developing world, Bromley (1985) identifies three main classes of resource degradation. The first is the deliberate conversion of natural resources to other forms of capital. Minerals, forests and fisheries are being mined or harvested for export sales to raise foreign exchange. The demand for foreign exchange creates competition for resources among governments, concessionaires, and rural communities as well as pressure to redefine property rights and acquire rents.

Redefinition of property rights is the second major source of resource depletion. In post-colonial societies throughout the world, new legislation has been enacted which redefines the rights of the state and the duties of individuals. In particular, land and water resources have been nationalized in the interest of the state. Villagers have seen customary rights replaced, local organizations superseded and their incentives to conserve resources removed. Governments have acted as if they had the capacity to manage resources down to the local level. However, this has created conflicts between local and national interests which individuals rationally exploit in the absence of common-property regimes.

The final class of resource depletion is indirect, and results from the unintended side-effects of policies which appear to be unrelated. Most notable are policies to develop commercial agriculture for food self-sufficiency or for commercial export in the irrigated lowlands. When agriculture cannot absorb an increased population, because of mechanization and capital intensification, individuals become marginalized and migrate either to cities or uplands. However, it is in the uplands especially that the institutional arrangements are least able to cope with sudden waves of immigration or inappropriate techniques. Upland resource use has, until very recently, been guided frequently by custom, local institutional arrangements and individual membership in groups. Traditional upland production techniques have also evolved locally to promote sustainability in diverse and fragile environments. However, under pressure from population expansion, commercialization of resource use and technical change, these local arrangements may adapt or disappear depending upon their usefulness in changed circumstances, their capacity for change and their resilience.

Conclusions

Institutional arrangements, as rules and conventions, are clearly important elements in resource conservation, translating claims on resource into property rights for some and duties for others. In Western society, while vestiges of the commons still exist, property rights have become centred on the state and the individual. A belief has also arisen that common property is inherently unstable, subject to inevitable pressure from free riders, and bound to be degraded in the 'tragedy of the commons'. A more careful analysis of the foundation of common property, combined with closer investigation of management of collective goods in the developing world, suggests that common-property regimes not only can be viable, but in some circumstances, such as irrigation at the local level, are essential.

Common-property regimes have the capacity to manage rural resources in ways that meet multiple criteria of importance to rural people. Efficiency, equity and sustainability appear to be optimized by resource-poor rural communities dependent on collectively managed renewable resources. A significant measure of resource conservation for forests, ranges, water resources and fisheries is inherent in these management systems which have evolved to meet the direct needs of people in uncertain environments. For this reason alone, common-property regimes are worthy of more careful analysis. The designers of new institutional arrangements for conservation and development need to be aware of the strengths and weaknesses of such regimes to guide their work. State and private property are not the property-right norms for many societies and they may not be the most appropriate foundations for future institutional arrangements.

Promoting exploration of common-property regimes as acceptable foundations for institutional innovation will not be easy. Acknowledging institutional arrangements which are responsive to local conditions and which are locally managed implies a willingness to accept that ecosystem and social-system variation should be reflected in policy and administration. This in turn may imply an acceptance of participatory approaches to resource management and more decentralized administration. However, this involves a major shift in the role of resource-management agencies and bureaucracies unaccustomed to sharing power (see Chapter 6). Nevertheless, reversals of this kind may be necessary if the potential of rural people as resource conservationists is to be realized.

References

Bromley, Daniel W., 1985: 'Resources and economic development: An institutionalist perspective', *Journal of Economic Issues*, 3, September, pp. 779–96.
Campbell, B. and Godoy, R.A., 1986: 'Commonfield agriculture: The Andes and medieval England compared', in *Proceedings of the Conference on Common Property Resource Management*, National Academy Press, Washington, DC, pp. 323–58.
Ciriacy-Wantrup, S.V., 1952: *Resource Conservation: Economics and Policies*, University of California Press, Berkeley, California.

Dahlman, Carl J., 1980: *The Open Field System and Beyond: A Property Rights Analysis of an Economic Institution*, Cambridge University Press, Cambridge, UK.

Dani, Anis A., Gibbs, Christopher J.N. and Bromley, Daniel W., 1987: 'Institutional development for local management of rural resources', *Workshop Report No. 2*, East-West Environment and Policy Institute, Honolulu, Hawaii.

Fortmann, Louise and Riddell, James, 1985: *Trees and Tenure: An Annotated Bibliography for Agroforesters and Others*, Land Tenure Center, University of Wisconsin, Madison, Wisconsin, and International Council for Research in Agroforestry, Nairobi, Kenya.

Johannes, R.E., 1978: 'Traditional marine conservation methods in Oceania and their demise', *Annual Review of Ecology and Systematics* 9, pp. 349–64.

Netting, R.M., 1978: 'Of men and meadows: Strategies of Alpine land use', *Anthropological Quarterly*, 45, pp. 132–44.

Runge, Carlisle F., 1983: 'Common property and collective action in economic development', a paper prepared for the Board on Science and Technology for International Development (BOSTID), Office of International Affairs, National Research Council, Washington, DC.

Scudder, T. and Conelly, T., 1985: 'Management systems for riverine fisheries', *FAO Fisheries Technical Paper No. 263*.

Tanner, A., 1979: *Bringing Home Animals. Religious Ideology and Mode of Production of the Mistassini Cree Hunters*, Hurst, London.

Thompson, James, 1979: 'Public choice analysis of institutional constraints on firewood production strategies in the West African Sahel', in Russell, Clifford S. and Nicholson, Norman K., eds, *Public Choice and Rural Development*, Research Paper Number 2, Resources for the Future, Washington, DC, pp. 119–52.

3 Natural Resources: Access, Rights-to-Use and Management

A.P. *Lino Grima* and *Fikret Berkes*

Summary

This chapter addresses several interrelated themes and issues, starting with a discussion of the shortsighted and narrow definition of resources, as opposed to the ecosystem view; and complications with the notion of 'property' as it applies to resources. Resource-use rights can be characterized in terms of property and access relations and their allocation can be characterized in terms of the exclusivity and transferability of these rights. In Western industrialized nations, especially in North America, common-property ideals still survive. But in the absence of workable common-property regimes, these ideals are more appropriately labelled 'open-access ideals' (or 'frontier ethics'), leading to resource-use patterns which are not sustainable in the long run.

Resource scarcity, including problems with sustainability, has led to the development of 'resource management', basically a field of applied ecology and economics. Community-based resource management is offered as an alternative to resource management by central government agencies, with or without the use of market mechanisms. However, the choice is not always clear cut and the two alternatives not always distinct.

Definitions of resource

Resources are assets for the creation of human satisfaction or utility, including income. However, this misleadingly narrow definition of resources ignores the interdependency of the various components of ecosystems and understates the ecological value of resources. The broader view of human-nature systems, or the ecosystem approach, as the basis for sustainable development broadens the definition of resources. In particular it makes their values consistent with the notion of sustainability in the long term.

According to the view of resources as mere factors of production, they are not desirable in themselves, but rather means to an end. They are valuable only to the extent that they can be used to create goods and services – water for hydro-electric power, for example, or fishery resources for food and recreational opportunities. This view of resources if found in most textbook and dictionary definitions. The *Concise Oxford Dictionary*, for example, defines resources as 'means of supplying a want or stock that can be drawn upon'; this concept may be conveniently summarized by Zimmerman's (1951) dictum: 'resources are not, they become.' Resources are culturally defined; to the North American Indians of 1800, oil and gas were not resources; for the contemporary North American society they are. Such definitions embody the ideas of 'usefulness', now or later, and the 'resource supply', available to be used by humans.

Traditionally, economists have identified three broad categories of factors of production: natural resources, human resources, and capital. Natural resources were considered 'free gifts of nature'. In reality, however, natural resources are almost never altogether free. This is so for both renewable and non-renewable resources. In the case of the former, they are free only if they can be wholly replenished without cost. If the amount taken exceeds the natural capacity of the resource to replenish itself, then the resource will eventually disappear unless it is restored at some cost. The overfishing of a lake or the overharvesting of a forest are examples of this. Even where the level of exploitation of the resource does not exceed the self-renewal capacity, one group of users may be restricting another use of the resource or displacing another group of users dependent on that use.

In the case of non-renewable resources, the very depletion of the resource may be considered a cost to society. Even where there is still a large supply of the resource left elsewhere, these remaining supplies are likely to be more costly to develop than the supplies just exhausted. Furthermore, the use of a resource as a factor of production may impose costs on the use of other resources in that ecosystem. For example, the burning of high-sulphur coal may affect fisheries by the acidification of lakes, or forests by making trees more susceptible to disease. These are part of the social costs of production or 'externalities' in the environmental economist's jargon – the cost which is not accounted for in the market. An externality is really a failure of the market system. As Kneese and Bower (1968) point out, this market failure is pervasive in the economy rather than rare.

In this sense, then, natural resources are not free. The depletion of fish by one group of fishermen creates externalities for another group. The pollution of a river's waters by an industrial plant creates externalities for the recreational users of that river. It may be true that the first group of fishermen and the industrial plant in the above examples treated their resources as free goods. Sooner or later, some other groups – or society as a whole – end up paying the cost of treating resources as free goods.

Implications of the market-centred definition of resources

In the ecosystem perspective, resources cannot be treated as mere factors of production. Take the example of wetlands, which have a relatively low market value (except as potential agricultural land when drained). However, they serve extremely important ecological functions such as water-flow regulation, flood control, the absorption of oxygen-demanding wastes, critical habitat for waterfowl and fur animals, area of high biological productivity, and spawning and nursery areas for some types of fish. These valuable ecological functions are normally not captured by the market process. Therefore the market value of wetlands, as an economic resource to individual owners, grossly underestimates the long-term ecological value of this resource, and its potential national or regional value. If left to market forces, wetlands would disappear (and have been disappearing very rapidly in most countries of the world). Some wetland areas have been protected as parks; this effectively serves to take these areas out of private ownership. It makes them what the economist calls a public good. However, it would be impossibly costly to turn all wetlands into national parks and other protected areas.

There is another reason why market decisions based on returns to individual owners tend to be shortsighted. The investor in a resource-based enterprise would want to get an annual rate of return comparable to other opportunities for investment. Consider a renewable resource in which the value of a renewable harvest is lower than the return on investment at a usual interest rate, say 10 per cent. What would be the economically rational decision for the private resource user: to use the resource within its margin of renewability, or to mine it?

Clark (1973) has dealt with just such a resource issue. Using the example of the blue whale, which has a relatively slow rate of replenishment (about 5 per cent), Clark has shown that 'an annual discount rate of between 10 and 20 per cent would be sufficient for extinction to result from maximization of present value of harvests.' The same logic is applicable to other renewable resources such as forests (Regier and Baskerville, 1986).

The discounting of the future economic value of a resource (or rate of time preference) has another important consequence: ecological resources which we may want to sustain, say 30 years from now, have almost no present monetary value to the rational decision-makers at a high discount rate. A resource that would be worth, say $800,000 30 years from now, would have a present value of $100,000, assuming an interest rate of 7 per cent. At higher rates, the present value would be even smaller. In fact, as pointed out by Ophuls (1977), 'for all practical purposes, costs and benefits more than 20 years into the future are discounted to zero – it is a rare economic decision-maker whose time horizon extends more than ten years into the future.' These considerations create problems also in development planning (see Chapter 9).

Helliwell (1975) pointed out that discounting future values at prevailing interest rates is appropriate for commodities such as cars, buildings and machines. However, when this is done with resources, 'our grandchildren may have to do without such basic necessities as timber, fertile soils, clean oceans, and pleasant countryside. All these will have been deemed *uneconomic*.' As a solution, one may try to avoid the use of discount rates, or use a variable rate according to the risks involved. The risk of the invest-ment becoming redundant in, say, 70 years' time is very small with resources that have long-term ecological value. With such resources, which are capable of providing 'a perpetual stream of annual benefits', Helliwell considers that for the purposes of governmental cost–benefit studies, a discount rate of 1 per cent may be more realistic than one based on the prevailing interest rate.

In brief, the market mechanism is not capable of, or is not designed to, accurately reflect the long-term value of resources. An alternative approach is to value the existence of a resource in the present very highly, thus obtain-ing a 'non-trivial' future value after discounting at prevailing interest rates. The two approaches are not equivalent: the choice of a low discount rate effectively takes the valuation out of the market. By contrast, ascribing a high value to the resource is a clearer expression of valuing resources.

While resources may be defined in terms of human wants, they cannot be treated as mere tradeable assets because much of the ecological value of resources is not reflected in the short-term market value. Thus the ecosystem or holistic view that takes into account all ecosystem components and their interactions (including those involving human societies), is a realistic approach in the long term. The ecosystem view of resources makes more sense than the more narrowly market-oriented definition of resources.

Problems with the concept of property

Who owns common-property resources? The wisdom of many cultures ancient and contemporary is that humans as mere mortals cannot own natural resources. Nature has a temporal existence of a different magnitude than human life span, and humans are merely given (by whatever higher powers) rights to use natural resources, with the injunction that people act as good 'stewards'. This basic idea is very pervasive; it cuts across many cultures from Amerindians to Africans to Pacific islanders (see Chapters 5, 15 and 16). It also appears in the conservation traditions of Western cultures (White, 1967) but tends to be overlooked in many industrial societies, as pointed out by some of the most respected early conservationists (Marsh, 1864).

The notion of property implies exclusion of non-owners. Some scholars have therefore argued that the term 'common property' should be restricted to those resources for which there exist communal arrangements for exclusion of non-owners and for allocation among the co-owners. Ciriacy-Wantrup and Bishop (1975) are among the proponents of this more restricted definition of common property. The confusion of definition is likely to persist since resources such as fisheries are defined in law as 'common property' in many countries, but only in the sense that the resource belongs to the public (*res publica*). It is not automatically available to all; users are subject to government licensing and regulations.

> The mischief to arise from the term 'common property' is that many . . . do not understand the critical distinction between 'open-access resources' (*res nullius*) and 'common property' (*res communes*). Open-access is a free-for-all, while common property represents a well defined set of institutional arrangements concerning who may make use of a resource, who may not make use of a resource, and the rules governing how the accepted users shall conduct themselves   (Bromley, 1985).

To carry this argument further, property arrangements over natural resources are often thought to be at two extremes: there is either private property or there is a free-for-all. Since a free-for-all will almost certainly result in the degradation of the resource, it is concluded that the solution is to create private property over scarce and valuable resources. Bromley (1985) notes that economics as practised in the market-oriented societies of Western industrial nations, is itself a product of the Industrial Revolution. It is, therefore, 'small wonder that our paradigm starts with the assumption that all valuable resources are individually owned, fully mobile, and exchangeable in small increments in well functioning markets. We will then conclude that these conditions will assure an efficiently operating system' (Bromley, 1985).

The challenge is that cultural relativity operates not only with the definition of resources, but also with the definition of what constitutes a workable arrangement for the sustainable management of resources. In many Western societies, the individual self-interest is seen as supreme. In many other societies, however, as well as within certain groups in Western cultures, the individual is not the dominant locus of choice; the community is the relevant decision-making unit. This is true among North American native peoples who never had – and under the present reservation system still do not have – individual ownership of land or resources (see Chapter 5). Is the Western practice of individual ownership somehow superior to communal ownership? Is there a general trend for the evolution of property systems from the communal to the individual? Or are these systems alternative viable arrangements for the management of resources?

Western Europeans developed their own particular view of land and resources, defined in legal and economic terms, over a period of centuries.

This view assured that resources were used to their fullest extent, and it served capitalism very well. At the time the Europeans started the fur trade in the seventeenth century, for example, European countries such as England had already been depleted of beaver. The colonial-era Western man thought himself to be a superior being, the master of his natural environment. His new view of land and resources helped reinforce the belief that he was 'civilized'. It helped justify the colonization of America, Asia, Africa and Oceania where the 'natives' had not reached this stage of development.

Property and access

Instead of emphasizing the ownership status of a resource, it may be more useful to examine the diversity of relationships involving property and access conditions under which a resource is held. To carry out such an analysis, a two-dimensional classification of resources may be proposed, as to whether they are used under limited-access or open-access regimes; and whether they are privatized or commonly-owned. This gives four possible combinations.

1 Open-access, commonly owned resources are typically subject to Hardin's (1968) 'tragedy of the commons'. These are resources for which management institutions are non-existent or have broken down; the 'tragedy' occurs when the supply of the resource is smaller than the amount that the users are taking. As long as the resource holds up at a given rate of uncontrolled exploitation, the short-term situation may be quite favourable. But such open-access exploitation is not sustainable if scarcity develops.
2 In contrast to the first case, sustainable use is possible with limited-access, commonly owned resources. This case may include two property-rights regimes covered earlier in Chapters 1 and 2. Resources may be managed mainly under some kind of local-level arrangement or institution (communal property) or solely by the government (state property). The two are not always distinct; joint jurisdiction (*co-management*) is also possible.
3 Resources may also be successfully managed if they are privatized and held under limited-access conditions. In this case, there are clear rights to exclusive use and transferability.
4 On the other hand, a resource which is privatized but held under open-access conditions could not be expected to remain viable for long. Such a situation could occur if the owner of the resource is unable to defend it – if the rules of enforcing exclusion have broken down. The resource will decline by trespassing and poaching by unauthorized users.

Property and access relations, treated in more detail in Chapter 7, can be made more complicated by explicitly indicating a continuum of conditions on both axes. The point is that, even with a simple, two-dimensional classification of resources, it is possible to identify more than one set of conditions that could lead to resource degradation. More to the point, privatization – which seems to be the obvious solution under the market-economy paradigm – is not the only solution. If access is open only to the community, and if the resource is controlled under enforceable rules, a sustainable system is possible. As Farvar points out (in a personal communication), the truth is that these community-based systems have been the main way in which societies have run their management systems for natural resources over millennia – otherwise we would have had no resources left today to speak about.

However, once a market economy has developed, communal ownership and control are extremely difficult to maintain. Even Amerindian peoples cheat each other because there is a world outside the reservation where the fruits of cheating is called success. As Hardin (1968) pointed out, there is need for *mutual coercion* whether it be the force of law that respects the right of property or the community's peer pressure that enforces responsible use.

Institutional instruments for resource allocation

Since wants are ever-expanding with human aspirations and expectations, resources tend to be scarce – that is, we cannot increase supply without incurring costs. We therefore need to allocate resources either through the market process, communal agreement, kingly fiat or coercive decision. Allocation not only provides an interesting entry into the problem of making resource use consistent with an ecosystem approach, it is the institutional instrument for achieving a well-functioning ecosystem – or failing to achieve it.

The most common dictionary synonyms of allocation are 'allotment', 'apportionment' and 'assignment'. Allocation confers rights to access and use of a resource, rather than the right to the resource. For example, ownership of land is constrained by official land-use plans or other regulations. Such rights to the use of a resource need to be based on a common interest or sense of commonality if they are to be successfully implemented through policy. Above all, the allocation of rights-to-use needs to be perceived as being fair within the institutional–cultural context. Lack of explicit allocative decisions or allocations perceived to be unfair – or unenforceable – lead to resource degradation and the related injustice among resource users (Regier and Grima, 1985).

The first step in the allocative process is to assign rights of access. As noted above, open access is a free-for-all and implies either that the allocative process is underspecified, or that the rules of its operation have broken down.

	Exclusive right	Nonexclusive right
Nontransferable	Rights to use administered by government with a centralized bureaucracy, regulatory boards, courts — Rights to use privatized in part and administered by a community of users	Rights to free access to common property, in a tradition of untrammelled exploitive use — Rights to free access to community resources in tradition of individual stewardship
Transferable	Rights to legitimate use exchanged for money in a free market institution — Rights to legitimate use exchanged by informal bartering openly in public	Rights to use conferred through a patronage establishment, publicly condoned — Rights to uses purportedly exchanged, but fraudulently, by criminal swindlers

Figure 3.1 A perspective on the variety of ways in which rights to fish and similar resources are managed. In the four inside characterizations the exclusivity and transferability of user rights are satisfied in a partial manner. User rights in these four inside types are less sharply defined than those in the four corners. The schema may be viewed to have a soft core with a more sharply defined hard shell or edge. (After Regier and Grima 1985.)

If access is limited, the allocative instruments need to specify the rights to use (or property rights) in terms of their transferability and exclusivity.

Figure 3.1 is a perspective on societal devices for allocation expanded by Regier and Grima (1985) from a schema by Dales (1975). In the four corners, the types of right-to-use are more sharply defined than the four inside characterizations. In the top two of the four inside characterizations, the exclusivity and transferability of user rights are not as clearly defined because some of these rights are held in common (they have features of communal property). For example, access to forest products such as nuts and fibre are granted to individual gatherers by the community which controls the resource. In the bottom two of the four inside characterizations, it is the mode of exchanging rights which makes the rights-to-use less defined. Patronage confers real rights – and real wealth – but the right may prove to be less than permanent. Similarly, the rules of exchange in a barter system are less flexible than in a monetary system partly because of indivisibilities and partly because the needs of buyers are likely to fluctuate from one 'market day' or 'market place' to another.

The four outside corners in Figure 3.1 form a more sharply defined edge or shell in the sense that they are all easily categorised in terms of rights-to-use (or property rights). However, these four characterizations coexist in the real world and in a sense complement each other: it would be hard to regulate or to privatize every right-to-use; the reality is a kind of pragmatic mix-and-match where institutions step in to correct abuses and to create checks and balances in a mixed economy (a market system with government regulation and intervention). In societies in which communal-property systems predominate, government regulation and intervention may again be necessary, if only to provide legitimation for traditional authority structures (see Chapters 10 and 16).

It should be noted that allocative disorder – as in the tragedy of the commons – or poaching, or illegal land transfers, may arise in three ways:

1 open access conditions and a demand greater than annual sustainable level of harvest;
2 poorly defined 'rights-to-use'; and
3 breakdown in the system of enforcement of either limits to access or the rights-to-use (ie, exclusivity and transferability).

Whether the resources are owned in common or privately, the two keys to workable allocative processes are control of access and legal enforcement of the rights-to-use. However, as Dales (1975) noted, there is no intrinsically superior allocative instrument: the market mechanism works better in some circumstances, regulation works better in others and so on. In rare cases, even open access makes most sense, for example information that should be freely accessible in the public interest.

The specific institutional or policy instruments that emerge from the taxonomy in Figure 3.1 include prohibition and regulation, as practised in both industrial and traditional societies. In the former, there are also grants and tax incentives, direct government intervention (buy-back programs of fisheries, pest control programs etc), compulsory insurance to cover third-party damages, demand management through peak-responsibility pricing and transferable quotas, etc. In the latter, the repertoire of institutional instruments relies relatively more heavily on social and cultural conventions, and may be strongly based on ethical/cultural considerations.

The evaluation or assessment of institutional instruments is outside the scope of this chapter, but those for water and fishery resources have been addressed elsewhere for North America (see Regier and Grima, 1985; Grima and Allison, 1983; Grima 1981). However, it is important to note that such assessments and evaluations need to take into account the cultural, economic, political and social context. The superiority of one type of institutional instrument or mode of ownership over another is difficult to determine. The costs of monitoring, enforcement and other transaction costs are important in evaluating the suitability of an institutional instrument; unfortunately these costs are often unknown. It should be noted that the preference of the analyst often reflects his/her ideological stance rather than the flow of pure reason. One observer notes that 'arguments (about tenure systems) belong to the realm of belief systems since so few marshall any evidence in support of their claims . . . where both methodology and data are open to independent scrutiny' (Noronha, 1986). In sum, the choice of allocative instruments is not value-free (see also Chapter 7).

It is important to emphasize that some combination of instruments are likely to be required under both private and communal ownership. For example, the government needs to regulate the activities of private-resource users; the community needs to enforce regulations on members. Regulation, monitoring, policing and enforcement – all these are the instruments of 'mutual coercion'. The rhetoric of the ecological romantics and of the hard-nosed economists differ; the instruments for allocating rights-to-use are quite similar.

Indirect allocation and sensitive uses

In the political decisions to allocate rights to access and use, it is possible – and convenient – to mask the detailed allocation and its consequences by making indirect allocations. By indirect allocations, we mean allocations of a resource (like grazing land) through the decisions about another resource (construction of a dam for power production and irrigation which floods part of that land). Indirect uses such as waste disposal in a river foreclose other uses, such as the provision of drinking water from that river.

Allocative decisions should be carefully examined so that the consequences are clear to all users, and the societal trade-offs can be openly discussed. Indirect allocations mask such trade-offs to the detriment of losers, and often divert attention from the critical allocative decisions. For example three groups of fishermen on the Canadian Great Lakes are busy battling one another while the resource base on which all three depend is being lost to pollution (Whillans and Berkes, 1986).

Consider the mix of uses of an aquatic ecosystem. Some of the uses, such as fishing, crabbing, the collection of water reeds for mats (see Chapter 14) and recreation are dependent on the health of the ecosystem. These are sensitive uses: they are affected by degradative uses but they do not in turn affect degradative uses. Relations among uses are not symmetrical. Permits for degradative uses of ecosystems (or anti-pollution legislation) in effect involve major allocations of natural resources, often in indirect ways.

The activities of some groups of users are detrimental to others. For example, one of the most pervasive kinds of fishery conflicts in the world concerns that of small-scale inshore fisheries against large-scale operations such as trawlers. The appearance of powerful outside interests often combine with the degradation of the resource base to result in the dispossession of local users and the disappearance of community-based management systems. There are many other examples of this, including the Sahel herders of Africa (Sinclair and Fryxell, 1985) and users of wild animal and plant resources in parts of India (see Chapter 14).

In this general sense, ecosystems (wildlife, fish, water) constitute a 'common-pool resource': consumption or other use by one user can adversely affect all other potential and actual users (Ostrom and Ostrom, 1971). Allocative decisions should take this feature of ecosystems into account, preferably by arranging either for a cascading pattern of resources (from most sensitive to least sensitive) wherever possible; by protecting the most sensitive users; or by making compensation a condition of resource use by insensitive users.

Commons dilemma: coping with scarcity and conflict

The commons dilemma develops when there are too many users to a limited resource. As noted above, allocative disorder arises when the limits to access and/or the right-to-use are underspecified or not enforced and there are demands on the ecosystem that conflict with sustainability or other users, leading to the possibility of conflict and the degradation of the resource. Figure 3.1 indicates that the rights for the use of the resource may be established in at least seven different ways, or a combination of these. How have these various mechanisms for the establishment of the rights-to-use emerged in recent historical times?

Ostrom and Ostrom (1971), Loftus et al. (1982) and Grima and Allison (1983) have elaborated five ideals that reflect the pervasive traditions in North America on the use of natural resources such as fish, wildlife and water. Historically, these ideals applied to forestry and grazing lands as well but these latter two resource types were either privatized or brought under state management. It should be noted that the ideals in question emphasize rights of society at large to the exclusion of community-based rights such as those of the salmon-fishing Amerindian tribes of the Pacific coast of North America, which has already been discounted because of their incompatibility with the rights of society at large (Rogers, 1979). The following list of North American open-access ideals was formulated specifically with the fishery resource in mind.

1 Natural resources should be held or owned in common by all citizens.
2 Access is to be open to all citizens (or 'residents').
3 Access to and use are to be free of royalty or rent.
4 Any limitation of one or more of the above ideals is to be permitted only

when all current users of a resource willingly consent to the specific limitations.

5 Property rights of some kind and degree accrue to the users as a consequence of access and use – whether it be opportunistic, permitted or licensed – and these rights are not to be swept aside arbitrarily.

As Regier and Grima (1985) point out, these ideals, in pure form, may be internally inconsistent (particularly the first three with the last two) and also incompatible with some of the following major societal goals.

1 The productivity of the resource should be sustainable in perpetuity.
2 The regime of resource use and management should not lead to undue burdens on the users (for example loss of the source of livelihood).
3 The administration of the resource and user system should not be costly or unduly oppressive.
4 The owners of the resource (the public) should share with the users the 'resource rent' (the returns from exploiting the resource after all costs have been met).

In Canada, the enunciation and adherence to that set of five ideals was not a universal or a powerful force (Tuomi, 1982; Comeau 1983). In the USA, as a reaction to the inequities in European countries – where landowners and aristocrats owned the land and fish and wildlife – apparently predisposed that society toward open-access ideals (Stroud et al., 1982). But there may be another reason. As David Feeny noted (in a personal communication), these ideals were formed under conditions of incredible resource abundance and obvious lack of need to restrict access at that time. Until some shortage or conflict develops with the use of a resource, it is effectively valueless in trade and in no danger of direct overuse; it would be pointless to specify and police a system of rights with respect to allocation. This frontier mentality persisted in the USA until a few decades ago.

In addition to an excessive commitment to open-access ideals, there are other conditions which would lead to intensification of the commons dilemma. One is inertia with respect to the introduction of an effective reform because an abusive-user regime that would be defended by current users (including private owners). Another is the deliberate sacrifice of an ecosystem in the name of conventional economic development (see Chapters 7 and 9).

In traditional societies, the commons dilemma is often solved by the emergence of communal-property institutions to define the rights and duties of the co-owners of the resource, or of the right to use the resource. If the users are individualistic and competitive and have no interest or capacity to protect the sustainability of the resource on which their livelihood depends, then communal-property management (mutual coercion in the form of peer pressure) does not work. In such cases the rights to use the resource must be administered by centralized regulatory authorities and/or by free market mechanisms. The next section discusses the principles and limitations of a market-based solution.

Rise of resource-management science

Gordon (1954) translated the commons dilemma into the concepts of market economics more than three decades ago, and since then resource economists of this tradition have been urging a larger role for the market (for example, Pearse 1979; Anderson, 1977). Gordon's basic argument is that in an open-access fishery (or other type of resource), resource rents will dissipate over a period of time. Resource rents, defined as a surplus value over and above the opportunity costs for all factors of production, arise from ownership of or access to a valuable resource in limited supply. Maximum resource rents are obtained at a certain level of effort, E_1, in Figure 3.2. This point is called the maximum economic yield or MEY point (where marginal revenue equals marginal cost). It is in the best interests of the resource owner that resource rents be maximized because these rents are the return to the ownership of the resource. In an open-access fishery, however, resource rents are non-appropriated income that attract new entrants into the fishery until effort

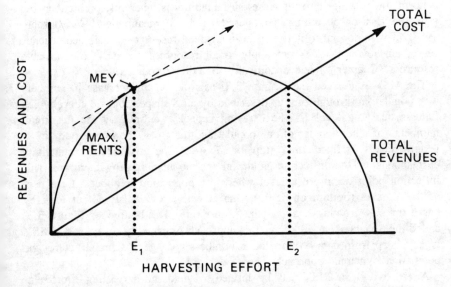

Figure 3.2 Resource rents in an open-access fishery and the formulation of the maximum economic yield (MEY).

expands to E_2. This is the point at which costs have risen to equal revenues and all resource rents have been competed away.

The fishery economists' solution to the commons dilemma is to limit the numbers of users of the resource and to allocate among the users the total allowable yearly harvest in such a way that the race to catch fish before others catch them is prevented. Instead, the fishermen concentrate on reducing costs per unit effort. The more efficient resource users, the argument goes, should be able to expand at the expense of the less efficient and inept; in the market economy, order is produced out of chaos in a manner analogous to natural selection. (The similarity between Adam Smith's *laissez-faire* economics and Charles Darwin's 'struggle for existence' is not accidental, as discussed in Chapter 5.)

The remaining issue, the argument goes, is to determine the allowable harvest or the amount that could safely be taken from year to year without depleting the resource, a biological problem. Resource management has developed the tools to try to solve this problem. The basic concept of sustained yield (SY) first appears in forestry. The mathematical approach to maximise this SY is best developed in fisheries, but it is widely applied to wildlife and forestry resource management as well. This is the concept of maximum sustainable yield (MSY), the maximum yield or harvest that can be obtained from year to year without depleting the natural resource stock.

The MSY is discussed here in some detail because the idea of 'sustainability' in sustainable development descends partially from this ecological concept. In its wider current sense, sustainability is inherently ambiguous and runs the risk of becoming 'so abused as to be meaningless' (O'Riordan, 1988). It is important to note that in its original resource-management-science sense, sustainability does not apply to all resources but only to renewable resources (Chapter 2) and specifically to living resources.

The MSY is derived (see Figure 3.3) as follows: the increase in numbers of a population through time is described by an S-shaped logistic curve which flattens out at a level K, the carrying capacity, defined as the maximum numbers of individuals of a population that can be supported in a geographically defined area (top of figure). The maximum productivity corresponds to the inflection point on the population growth curve. This inflection point occurs at a level where the population is about 50 per cent of the K level (bottom of figure); this is where a population, cut back by harvesting, is growing again at the fastest rate. The bottom of Figure 3.3, called the Schaefer curve, shows this approach graphically. In practice, MSY is calculated from data on population numbers and age and sex structure: the population dynamics approach.

Alternatively, the MSY may be defined by yield and harvesting effort relationships. Any point to the right of the MSY indicates overharvesting (Fig. 3.4). Catch per unit of harvesting effort (CPUE) is useful for management

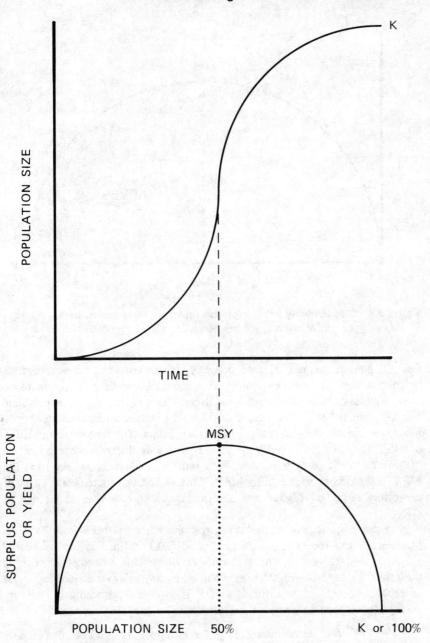

Figure 3.3 The logistic curve (top) and the Schaefer curve (bottom), showing the formulation of MSY from basic ecological considerations.

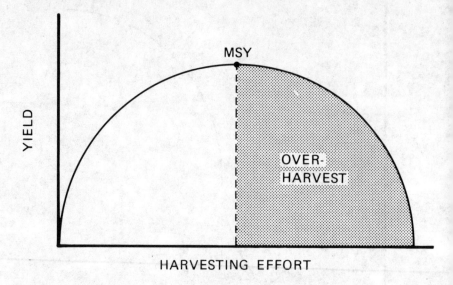

Figure 3.4 Formulation of MSY in practical resource management, based on catch per unit of effort (yield per harvesting effort) considerations.

(see Chapter 6) because, if used properly, it can provide feedback controls on each successive year's harvesting. It is also closer to the resource management logic and practice of traditional users – that is, it may be 'appropriate science', but it has the drawback that it is difficult to operationalize due to inconsistencies in quantifying the harvesting effort. This second formulation of MSY is analogous to MEY (Fig. 3.2), the only difference being that, in the MEY, the yield is multiplied by a unit price. Note, however, that the MEY point occurs sooner than MSY. This is because incremental costs of harvesting effort are higher than the incremental revenues in that range of effort.

In resource management, the trend over the years has been from MSY to MEY and, most recently, to optimum yield (OY), defined as the amount of effort deemed to provide the greatest overall benefits to society, which is prescribed on the basis of MSY as modified by any relevant economic, social or ecological factors. As difficult as OY is to define operationally, it is an attempt to respond to some of the criticisms of the MSY concept:

1 The MSY focuses on biological yields as a goal and ignores other important goals such as providing high economic returns to labour, capital and risk-taking.

2 The MSY does not take into account year-to-year variations in the harvestable surplus which are, in turn, due to year-to-year variations in

the natural environment (for example, weather).

3 The MSY focuses on single species or stocks (population units for management purposes) and ignores a myriad of ecological interactions within the ecosystem, such as predation, competition, and time lags. It deals with populations as if they could be managed in isolation of their living and non-living environments.

Resource management science has developed an impressive body of tools and approaches in pursuit of the cherished goal of industrialized societies: how to squeeze the maximum amount of benefit from a resource. The ecological critique of this tool has been strong and to the point: the theoretical MSYs often do not work in the real world and stocks keep on collapsing (Larkin, 1977; Regier and McCracken, 1975).

Thus, the resource manager's solution to the commons dilemma – limiting the number of users (by licence limitation) and allocating among them the allowable harvest (by assigning individual harvest quotas) – has encountered some difficult conceptual and operational problems. There are very few fully fledged, scientifically designed limited-entry systems (Young, 1983) – and there are inevitably 'people problems' in quota-management systems run by government administrators with the help of market controls (Berkes and Pocock, 1987). In contrast, community-based management systems have the potential of solving the commons dilemma by internalizing the high information and transaction costs. The community has a built-in incentive to stay well within the biological limits of the resource which have been learnt by experience. The community also has at its disposal the requisite social coercive mechanisms to force compliance with expected harvests.

From sequential exploitation to sustainable use

Many resources throughout the world were traditionally used as the common property of communities of users. This is true with respect to fisheries and wildlife, forests, rangelands, agricultural lands in some areas, and water resources, especially in irrigation (McCay and Acheson, 1987; NRC 1986; chapters in the last two parts of this volume). Such resources were rarely, if ever, managed as open-access. However, for many of these resources, open-access conditions were imposed by outside pressures during a relatively short historical period which often coincided with the period of rapid economic development. Some of the pressures that led to this included colonialism, the rise of capitalism, commercialization of subsistence resources into export staples, population growth, and the development of technology for increasingly more efficient exploitation (Berkes, 1985). Some of these factors are of course interrelated.

As the traditional governance of common property with limited access was replaced by open access and intensive competition, the demand exceeded the sustainable harvest. The phenomenon is not unique to any one area or resource type. In many fisheries, for example, including the salmon fisheries of the Pacific northwest (Rogers, 1979), the general trend was that development-oriented fisheries (as opposed to subsistence fisheries and steady-state commercial fisheries) followed a predictable sequence of geographical expansion from more accessible to less accessible areas, and from the more valuable to the less valuable species. Area after area and stock after stock was depleted in a systematic fashion in the course of resource development.

This pattern has been noted, among other places, in the Great Lakes area of North America, both in forestry and in fisheries (Regier and Baskerville, 1986; Whillans and Berkes, 1986). The historical development of Canada's major resource exports – fur, fish and lumber – as described by Innis (1930 and other works), all follow the pattern of a succession of resource exports from successive geographical frontiers. Comparable detailed historical information on living resource use in other geographical areas of the world is not readily available. But a general pattern of *sequential exploitation* – from the more accessible to increasingly less accessible areas and from the most valuable to the less and less valuable species – appears to be a common feature of living resources development in general; it is not unique to North America or to fisheries.

Sequential exploitation can be viewed as a failure of the market system under open-access resource use. Traditional communal-property systems are brushed aside or otherwise rendered unworkable to make room for development and for the creation of economic surplus. But communal-property systems are not usually replaced with any other kind of institution initially. Exceptions to this may include the privatization of grazing lands once controlled communally by societies of migratory herders in the Sahel region of Africa (Sinclair and Fryxell, 1985). More generally, open-access conditions persist until the resource is so badly depleted that there is no longer any profit to be made.

Consider the following historical sequence.

1 Before outside influences disrupt them, there exist communal-property systems for a given resource in a given area. Communal-property institutions, where they exist, generally provide for both the sustainable use of the resource in question and for its allocation. It is a general feature of communal-property systems that resource-use rules and resource-sharing rules are inextricably tied together. This is the case, for example, with Pacific Island societies in both marine and terrestrial resource use (see Chapter 16), and with Cree Amerindian society in the use of wildlife resources (see Chapter 5).

2 As communal-property systems disappear with the creation of free access to the resource, the traditional allocation system also collapses. Open-access conditions lead eventually to the collapse of the ecological resource base as well. The loss of resource rents forces a search for the solution of the commons dilemma thus created. The solution may take one of three forms.

3(a) Market solutions cannot work if the open-access condition persists. To make the market solutions work, resource-use rights have to be made exclusive and transferable (Fig. 3.1). This is difficult to do with fish, wildlife and water resources, but relatively less difficult with land resources (agricultural, grazing or forest land). Chapter 4, for example, argues that the market solution (privatization) meets the requirements of the new economic context better than does the revamping of the traditional shifting cultivation system in Sarawak, Malaysia.

3(b) More commonly, where market solutions are difficult to institute, central governments have stepped in to regulate the rights to use. This is the case, for example, with fisheries resources throughout most of the industrialized countries. In Third World countries, there is a variation on this theme. In some cases, central governments have declared a particular resource to be state property or have nationalized a communal-property resource. This has happened with elephants or the ivory resource in Zaire (Kisangani, 1986) and with hill forests in Nepal (Arnold and Campbell, 1986).

3(c) The alternative solution to the commons dilemma is the redevelopment of communal-property systems. Much of the present volume is about this alternative. Successful examples include Japanese fisheries in which open-access conditions never lasted for long and in which communal-property institutions go back several centuries (see Chapter 10); Amerindian wildlife-management systems in Canada in which open-access conditions were created at least twice – both cases followed by the recovery of local-level systems (Chapter 5); and Pacific Island marine and terrestrial resource-use systems which have recovered, in some cases, after more than a century of neglect (Chapter 16).

The sequential exploitation idea helps to emphasize the time dimension of resource-use systems. All resources have a history, as do all communities of users. In some cases, the systems are obviously very ancient, but they can also develop quite rapidly, in less than 20 years in the case of three Turkish coastal fisheries (Berkes, 1986). It is possible, however, that these local-level fishery-management systems were borrowing from a rich Near Eastern tradition of communal property with water and grazing systems.

Community-based management systems may exist with government support or enabling legislation, may exist *despite* government regulation, or may be actually created by government legislation (Chapters 16, 12 and 13 respectively). The creation of communal-property rights consistent with traditional and neotraditional practices, where they exist, has a better chance of success than 'top down' solutions in addressing commons problems. The legal specification of user rights at the community level lowers management costs and helps solve implementation problems. However, there has been little progress in integrating community-level with government-level management measures. It may be argued that such integration may become even more difficult to achieve in the future because government-level and market-oriented solutions – such as individual harvest quotas – create property rights for individual users, whereas local-level management generally results in the creation of communal rights.

Access limitation and the allocation of exclusive rights in the commons is a zero-sum game in terms of rights-to-use. The creation of exclusive rights for one groups necessarily means the exclusion of some other group. As some anthropologists have pointed out, there are not only 'tragedies of the commons' but also 'tragedies of the commoners', when inequities and losses occur with privatization of resources (McCay, 1984). This occurs when powerful interest groups usurp the commons rights enjoyed by less intensive or politically less powerful users of a resource. In our preoccupation to safeguard ecosystems, we should not forget that the creation of selective closed access is necessarily accompanied by injustices to the people who are excluded.

Communal-property systems do exist and are very widespread. The real issue is no longer the feasibility of communal systems but rather if and how they can be viable in the contemporary world. To the extent that no community lives any more in splendid isolation and self-sufficiency, none of the alternative solutions to the commons dilemma should be rejected out of hand. Access, rights-to-use and management approaches need to be imaginatively brought together in workable combinations that enhance ecological sustainability and, at the same time, ensure fairness to users.

Acknowledgements

We thank David Feeny and Taghi Farvar for their searching and insightful critique of this chapter. The work was supported, in part, by grants from the Max Bell Foundation and the Social Sciences and Humanities Research Council of Canada.

References

Anderson, L.G., 1977: *The Economics of Fisheries Management*, Johns Hopkins Press, Baltimore, MD.

Arnold, J.E.M. and Campbell, J.G., 1986: 'Collective management of hill forests in Nepal: The community forestry development project', in *Proceedings of the Conference on Common Property Resource Management*, National Academy Press, Washington, DC, pp. 425–54.

Berkes, F., 1985: 'Fishermen and the "tragedy of the commons"', *Environmental Conservation*, 12 pp. 199–206.

Berkes, F., 1986: 'Local-level management and the commons problem: A comparative study of Turkish coastal fisheries', *Marine Policy*, 10, pp. 215–29.

Berkes, F. and Pocock, D., 1987: 'Quota management and "people problems": A case history of Canadian Lake Erie fisheries', *Transactions of the American Fisheries Society*, 116, pp. 494–502.

Bromley, D.W., 1985: 'Common property issues in international development', *Developments*, 5(1), pp. 12–15.

Ciriacy-Wantrup, S.V. and Bishop, R.C., 1975: '"Common property" as a concept in natural resource policy', *Natural Resources Journal*, 15, pp. 713–27.

Clark, C.W., 1973: 'The economics of over-exploitation', *Science*, 181, pp. 630–4.

Comeau, P.A., 1983: 'Allocation process in Canada', in Reintjes, J.W., ed., *Improving Multiple Use of Coastal and Marine Resources*, American Fisheries Society, Bethesda, MD, pp. 92–6.

Dale, J.H., 1975: 'Beyond the market place', *Canadian Journal of Economics*, 8, pp. 483–503.

Gordon, H.S., 1954: 'The economic theory of a common property resource', *Journal of Political Economy*, 62, pp. 124–42.

Grima, A.P., 1981: 'Institutional instruments for water pollution control', *GeoJournal*, 5, pp. 503–11.

Grima, A.P. and Allison, W.R., 1983: *Allocation of fishery resources with special reference to the Great Lakes*, report to the Great Lakes Fishery Commission, Ann Arbor, MI.

Hardin, G., 1968: 'The tragedy of the commons', *Science*, 162, pp. 1243–8.

Helliwell, D.R., 1975: 'Discount rates and environmental conservation', *Environmental Conservation*, 2, pp. 199–201.

Innis, H.A., 1930: *The Fur Trade in Canada: An Introduction to Canadian Economic History*, 2nd edn, University of Toronto Press, Toronto.

Kisangani, E., 1986: 'A social dilemma in a less developed country: The massacre of the African elephant in Zaire', in *Proceedings of the Conference on Common Property Resource Management*, National Academy Press, Washington, DC, pp. 137–60.

Kneese, A.V. and Bower, B.T., 1968: *Managing Water Quality: Ecosystems, Technology, Institutions*, Johns Hopkins Press, Baltimore, MD.

Larkin, P.A., 1977: 'An epitaph for the concept of maximum sustained yield', *Transactions of the American Fisheries Society*, 106, pp. 1–11.

Loftus, K.H., Holder, A.S. and Regier, H.A., 1982: 'A necessary new strategy for allocating Ontario's fishery resources', in Grover, J.H., ed., *Allocation of Fishery*

Resources, Food and Agricultural Organization, Rome, pp. 255–64.

Marsh, G.P., 1864: *Man and Nature or Physical Geography as Modified by Human Action*, Scribners, New York.

McCay, B.J., 1984: 'Capturing the commons: A foray into the field', *Annual Meeting of the Society for Applied Anthropology*, Toronto.

McCay, B.J. and Acheson, J.M., eds, 1987: *The Question of the Commons*, University of Arizona Press, Tucson.

Noronha, R., 1986: As quoted in *Common Property Resource Digest*, no. 1 (December).

NRC, 1986: *Proceedings of the Conference on Common Property Resource Management*, National Academy Press, Washington, DC.

Ophuls, W., 1977: *Ecology and the Politics of Scarcity*, Freeman, San Francisco.

O'Riordan, T., 1988: 'The politics of sustainability', in Turner, R.K., ed., *Sustainable Environmental Management*, Belhaven, London and Westview, Boulder, pp. 29–50.

Ostrom, V. and Ostrom, E., 1971: 'A political theory for institutional analysis', in Butrico, F.A., Touhil, C.J., and Whitteman, I.L., eds, *Resource Management in the Great Lakes Basin*, Heath Lexington Books, Lexington, MA.

Pearse, P.H., eds, 1979: 'Symposium on politics for economic rationalization of commercial fisheries', *Journal of the Fisheries Research Board of Canada*, 36, pp. 711–866.

Regier, H.A. and McCracken, F.D., 1975: 'Science for Canada's shelf-seas fisheries', *Journal of the Fisheries Research Board of Canada*, 32, pp. 1887–1932.

Regier, H.A. and Grima, A.P., 1985: 'Fishery resource allocation: An exploratory essay', *Canadian Journal of Fisheries and Aquatic Sciences*, 42, pp. 845–59.

Regier, H.A. and Baskerville, G.L., 1986: 'Sustainable redevelopment of regional ecosystems degraded by exploitive development', in Clark, W.C. and Munn, R.E., eds, *Sustainable Development of the Biosphere*, IIASA/Cambridge University Press, Cambridge, pp. 75–103.

Rogers, G.W., 1979: 'Alaska's limited entry program: Another view', *Journal of the Fisheries Research Board of Canada*, 36, pp. 738–88.

Sinclair, A.R.E. and Fryxell, J.M., 1985: 'The Sahel of Africa: Ecology of a disaster', *Canadian Journal of Zoology*, 63, pp. 987–94.

Stroud, R.H., Radonski, G.C. and Martin, R.G., 1982: 'Evolving efforts at best-use allocations of fishery resources', in Grover, J.H., ed., *Allocation of Fishery Resources*, Food and Agriculture Organization, Rome, pp. 418–31.

Tuomi, A.L.W., 1982: 'The role and place of sportfishing in water-based recreation', *Canadian Water Resources Journal*, 7(3), pp. 53–68.

White, L., 1967: 'The historical roots of our ecologic crisis', *Science*, 155, pp. 1203–7.

Whillans, T.H. and Berkes, F., 1986: 'Use and abuse, conflict and harmony: The Great Lakes fishery in transition', *Alternatives*, 12(3), pp. 10–18.

Young, O.R., 1983: 'Fishing by permit: Restricted common property in practice', *Ocean Development and International Law Journal*, 13, pp. 121–69.

Zimmerman, E.W., 1951: *World Resources and Industries*, Harper, New York (first published 1933).

4 The Evolution of Appropriate Resource-Management Systems

Dwight J. Watson

Summary

Environmental and social problems may be created if the development of resource-management systems does not keep pace with changing social, economic and environmental conditions in less developed countries. Shifting cultivation in Sarawak, Malaysia is an example of a passive resource-management system which was appropriate under conditions of low population density. Increasing demand for the limited resources of agricultural land has forced shifting cultivators to shorten fallow periods, farm marginal land and invade state forest reserves and wildlife preserves. Subsequent deforestation is causing flooding, erosion and soil impoverishment, and endangering wildlife through habitat destruction or fragmentation. At the same time, declining yields have contributed to chronic malnutrition. Development of active management systems which enhance natural productivity in order to meet increased demands for limited renewable resources is recommended. These systems should integrate the creation and assimilation of new scientific knowledge with greater individual control over the resource.

Introduction

The term 'management' in the context of resource use requires careful definition at the outset. For the purposes of this chapter, seasonal migrations of human populations synchronized with the natural seasonal cycle of renewable-resource availability (such as grassland pasture) are considered to be *passive* management systems. This is because migrations synchronized to natural cycles of resource productivity are also characteristic of many animals. *Active* resource-management systems, however, should involve the balancing of labour and material inputs to the natural system in order to enhance its carrying capacity and achieve a profitable and sustainable level of production. Both passive and active management can be characteristic of the use of specific kinds of resources in many traditional as well as modern societies.

Passive systems include extraction or exploitation management whether in a traditional or modern context. Although often based upon sophisticated research and technology, management for commercial capture fisheries and whaling are examples of passive systems which have been maintained by many modern societies. These systems are intended to control harvests of natural production from a resource – rather than enhance that production – by determining priority access to resources through stratification of factors such as social status, season, location, expertise, and technology. This allocation of the quantity and quality of specific resources among members of a society, or among human populations, might be considered analogous to that associated with reef and riverine fish assemblages which partition essential resources to minimize energy loss through active competition (Watson and Balon, 1984).

It may eventually be shown that, as in fish ecology, a high degree of specialization among human populations expressed by progressively finer partitioning along specific resources axes also reduces their resilience to unpredictable 'environmental' perturbations. Climatic, economic or social perturbations within a previously predictable socioeconomic environment may directly or indirectly affect the availability of some resources – and may eliminate some specialized life styles. Therefore, many arcane societal specializations in less developed countries (LDCs), such as those on the Indian subcontinent described by Gadgil and Iyer (Chapter 14), may now represent uncompetitive life styles within the changing national socioeconomic environment.

Active resource-management systems reduce dependency on natural cycles of resource productivity, and may be instituted only when production through passive management cannot keep pace with growth in demand. In the case of land resources designated for food production, mixed farming on intensified plots (systematic application of organic and inorganic fertilizers to selected cultivars on a fixed area) probably represents the most productive land-management system so far developed. Passive systems such as some forms of shifting cultivation, on the other hand, can represent the least productive systems in terms of annual sustainable yield per unit area, but require minimal technical expertise. Active systems of land management are often associated with greater individual control over the resource (if not total privatization), more intensive management, and the systematic application of scientific knowledge. However, the indigenous ecology is usually replaced by one which is fundamentally different and artifically maintained.

Many LDCs have traditional societies in transition from subsistence to commercial economies, and most LDCs have ambitious plans for accelerating this process. In this Chapter I use a case study of shifting cultivation in Sarawak, Malaysia, to examine the social, economic and environmental consequences for traditional societies which continue to rely upon passive systems for management of their essential resources when undergoing socioeconomic transformations, and provide a framework for guiding such transformations.

Shifting cultivation and land resource management in Sarawak

Shifting cultivation or *swidden* agriculture is still a worldwide practice in tropical and subtropical regions although it is basically only a step removed from hunting and gathering. Whilst being a very simple form of agriculture, it can also be quite productive if the human society functions as an integral part of the indigenous natural ecology.

Historically, shifting cultivators have lived in relative balance with their environment, and the natural productivity of the forest ecosystem was preserved by observing a sufficiently long fallow period between cropping. Since subsistence farmers were preoccupied with the need to produce enough food to last until the next harvest, it is unlikely that traditional societies observed fallow periods out of concern for the ecology or their environment. Most probably, experience had indicated that yield reductions from cropping the same plot in successive years resulted in harvests that were not in accordance with the effort expended. Since higher yields could be obtained by farming new plots, the fallow period became incorporated in order to maximise a yield-effort ratio.

In the case of Sarawak, Malaysia, the indigenous tribes were pacified during the reign of James Brook and his descendants, the 'White Rajas', from the last half of the nineteenth century up to 1940, and later governed by the British colonial and Malaysian national governments following the Japanese occupation. During this period of strong central rule, tribal boundaries were established, trade was encouraged, modern government services such as health-care systems were introduced, and the transition from a subsistence to commercial economy began. Improved health care and the stable political environment contributed to a steady increase in the human population. Population growth rate is estimated at an average 2.5 per cent per year but may be as high as 4.4 per cent in rural areas (Hatch and Lim, 1978).

During 1978, there were an estimated 40,000 households involved in some form of shifting cultivation. This represented some 250,000 people, or about 20 per cent of the Sarawak population. The most important crop grown under shifting cultivation was hill paddy (dryland rice), usually intercropped with cassava, cucumber, squash and other vegetable crops. In the 1975/76 planting season, approximately 65,980 hectares (or 0.5 per cent of total Sarawak land area), was slashed and burned for hill paddy cultivation. However, air photographs indicated that some 2,854,000 hectares were either actively within the shifting cultivation cycle or had been slashed and burned at least once. This figure accounted for an impressive 23 per cent of the total land area.

Because of its low population density (about 18 persons per square kilometre) Sarawak land resources had not previously been considered subject to population pressures. However, data derived from a recent land capability classification indicates that Sarawak lands are generally hilly, steeply dissected, and covered with shallow and infertile soils (Maas and Tie, 1978). Therefore, almost 80 per cent of Sarawak's total land area is now considered unsuitable for commercial or settled agriculture. Although the economic potential of forestry on these lands is relatively more promising than agriculture, government priorities for economic land use have often conflicted with the immediate needs, agricultural capability and traditions of the native farmers.

In areas where primary jungle is burned each year, the yield from hill paddy can exceed 1100kg per hectare. This is approximately equivalent to yields from wet paddy cultivation. However, in heavily populated, shifting cultivation regions of western Sarawak, yields are frequently as low as 330 to 450Kg per hectare (Hatch and Lim, 1978). Since sustainable crop yields from shifting cultivation are low when compared to modern intensive agriculture, the traditional shifting-cultivation system functionally breaks down under population pressure. Increasing population pressure on the limited resources of good agricultural land eventually forces shifting cultivators to shorten the fallow period. It may take several generations, but gradually shortening fallow periods manifest themselves in lower yields through soil impoverishment and erosion.

Recent studies indicate that some Sarawak shifting cultivators are already experiencing chronic malnutrition as a result of continuous food insufficiency rather than periodic scarcity or famine (Anderson, 1977). Shifting cultivation works reasonably well when population densities are low, and can yield high returns to labour (Dove, 1986) as long as there is an abundance of fertile land. However, as the land resource becomes limiting, declining yields and malnutrition are inevitable unless more productive systems are introduced.

Since shifting cultivation is a subsistence form of agriculture, it is not normally geared for surplus production. Therefore, socioeconomic development places an additional burden on the family. It is no longer sufficient to produce enough food to feed a family – a cash income is also required to purchase modern necessities such as soap, clothing, motor fuels and school supplies. In order to offset declining yields and an increasing financial burden, shifting cultivators compensate by slashing larger areas each season, farming marginal land and invading state forest reserves. Such a breakdown of the traditional shifting cultivation system leads to a deteriorating cycle of events which is both environmentally disruptive and difficult for the farmer to break free of in his struggle to survive.

Environmental impact of shifting cultivation

Ultimately, soil is the most valuable natural resource an agricultural country can possess. Soil must be conserved if either agriculture or silviculture is to thrive. Traditional shifting cultivation has seldom resulted in significant soil erosion as long as the fallow period was sufficiently lengthy, and relatively small areas were involved each season. Limited shifting cultivation could arguably be considered beneficial to the ecosystem by promoting habitat diversity.

Appropriate fallow periods are determined by the slope and nature of soil on individual parcels of land. Some steep and rocky slopes may be effectively cultivated only once in a lifetime, while flat alluvial valleys may be cultivated every few years and still produce acceptable yields. Among upland farmers in Sarawak, 25 years is considered sufficient for land to yield a hill paddy crop almost equivalent to that from virgin forest.

Where no fallow management is practised, the percentage recovery to original yield is expected to equal the recovery to original soil fertility (Figure 4.1). Assuming that the original successional pattern will recur, the time required to achieve 100 per cent recovery would be dependent on both degree of erosion/impoverishment of the original topsoil prior to the beginning of the fallow period and length of the fallow period. Therefore, as fallow period is shortened, fertility (and expected yield) will be reduced. The recovery pattern is assumed to be sigmoidal because of factors associated with biological recolonization and succession. The curve becomes increasingly attenuated as the degree of soil erosion/impoverishment increases.

The recovery of original species diversity should also follow a similar pattern. Therefore, a reduction in average fallow period should produce a reduction in original species diversity. Species possessing a rapid rate of reproduction and strong invasion capacity (niche generalists) would be able to recolonize successfully, while those species occurring late in the recovery period would be eliminated.

It has become apparent that in some areas of Sarawak the average fallow period (Table 4.1) has fallen to a point where soil impoverishment and erosion can become a serious problem. In West Sarawak, gully erosion and landslide have occurred on steep slopes and where the fallow periods have been greatly reduced or essentially abandoned. Habitat fragmentation has also disrupted the migratory pattern of orangutans, and in combination with a change in habitat structure and diversity over wide areas, has threatened the survival of many birds and mammals.

Loss of forest cover within a catchment basin can result in flash flooding when the terrestrial ecosystem loses its ability to buffer the runoff from intense tropical rainstorms. Under natural conditions a dense forest cover, the protective layer of plant debris and open soil structure ensure maximum

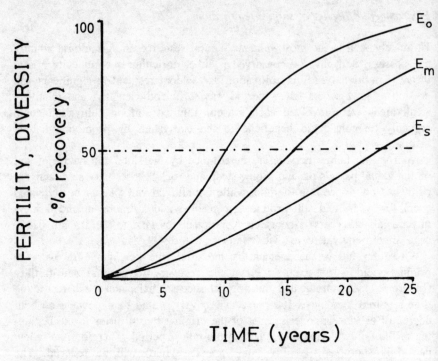

Figure 4.1 Expected recovery pattern to original fertility (yield) and biological diversity of a shifting cultivation plot in fallow, assuming no erosion (Eo), moderate erosion (Em) and severe erosion (Es).

infiltration of water and slows release of runoff to streams. Runoff from primary forest is about 40 per cent. Where forest cover is removed in partially urbanized watersheds the runoff to infiltration ratio of rainwater increases sharply to about 65 per cent (Whitton, 1975). The problem of flash flooding has become acute in several river systems including the Sadong, Kayan, Lemanak and Tinjar as a result of extensive shifting cultivation (Hatch and Lim, 1978).

Deforestation results in an increase in the flood peak discharge and a decrease in the low water flow as well as an increase in the total amount of water flowing from the watershed. The extreme fluctuations in river level alternately churn and expose the gravel terraces used by fishes, including many *Puntius* and some rare *Tor* species, as spawning grounds (Watson, 1982). Siltation of gravel terraces reduces the number and size of spawning areas and suffocates eggs incubating within the gravel interstices.

The fragility of some tropical aquatic ecosystems (Watson and Balon 1983, Watson and Balon, 1984; Goulding, 1981) and the importance of tropical forest cover in maintaining ecological stability in general has only recently

Table 4.1 Fallow periods in shifting cultivation regions of Sarawak (adopted from Lim, 1978)

Shifting cultivation regions	Land under shifting cultivation (ha)	Forested land (ha)	1978 Native population	Estimated fallow period (years)
West Sarawak	169,971	136,786	46,370	6
Simganggang	74,464	25,900	11,307	11
Ai-Lemanak	152,165	56,657	13,929	18
Layar	64,751	0	7,518	14
Skrang	44,921	22,258	4,539	17
Krian	97,936	0	16,368	10
Julau	210,846	82,152	29,211	12
Katibas	79,725	249,292	5,826	23
Ngemah	66,370	62,728	7,893	14
Mid-Rajang	176,851	112,100	18,700	16
Upper Rajang	30,757	206,394	3,672	14
Baleh	143,262	1,080,939	14,488	17
Balui	65,560	1,177,256	9,326	12
Linau-Plieran	2,833	286,524	661	7
Belaga	12,546	255,767	610	34
Mukah	165,115	191,016	13,582	20
Kakus	70,012	368,677	7,180	16
Kemena	129,502	492,918	13,576	16
Niah	37,637	228,652	6,259	10
Bakong-Tinjar	57,062	144,071	6,172	15
Upper Tinjar	28,329	189,397	1,972	24
Mid-Baram	99,555	468,636	11,483	14
Upper Baram	69,607	749,899	6,239	19
Upper Limbang	27,519	315,662	4,172	11
Trusan-Lawas	29,947	200,728	2,191	23
Semado-Bareo	40,874	164,306	2,746	25

been fully realized. Widespread destruction of the forest cover in some areas of Sarawak has led to soil erosion, siltation of waterways and fish spawning grounds, and flooding. Although the social and ecological ramifications of shifting cultivation are widely recognized, intensified agricultural systems are not readily implemented because of the growing number of shifting cultivators, their limited expertise, and the modest resources available to the department of agriculture.

Economic impact of shifting cultivation

Sarawak has a total land area of some 123,260 square kilometres, of which over 70 per cent is covered with tropical hardwood forests. Log timber accounted for nearly 19 per cent (US$ 150 million; exchange rate of approximately M$ 2.80 per US$ in 1977) of Sarawak's 1977 export earnings, and 66 per cent of non-oil exports. However, it is estimated that for every log that was exported, another was burned by shifting cultivators (Hatch and Lim, 1978).

The Sarawak Forest Department has estimated that, on average, 60,220 hectares of mature forest are destroyed each year for paddy cultivation. This figure includes illegal encroachment on state forest reserves as well as customary lands not previously used for paddy cultivation. A typical six-person family practising shifting cultivation will obtain a total annual income of US$ 217 per hectare of mature forest destroyed. This compares with US$ 2455 per hectare from commercial timber and employment opportunities if the same land were managed as production forest. Silviculture on private lands may be managed directly by the family, via a village cooperative, or contracted to a private company. When individual resource ownership is established the owner can profit directly from commercial timber cropping while the state will benefit via higher employment and tax revenues. Currently, the net revenue loss per year to the state economy from shifting cultivation is estimated at about US$ 130 million including US$ 5.1 million in timber royalties to the state and federal governments (Lau and Chung, 1978).

Land tenure and ownership

Problems associated with shifting cultivation and land use in general are inextricably linked to rationalization of traditional systems of land tenure. As of 1978, the lands and survey department of Sarawak had been able to determine private land ownership status for less than 5 per cent of the state's total land area.

Under the tribal system of land management, the village farmers would gather with the chief, or *tua kampong*, prior to the start of each planting season. The farmers would discuss the areas where they intended to plant that year, and new farmers would be allocated lands from the communal reserve. Land allocations would be determined according to the individual's social status and ability to cultivate. Disputes concerning historical cultivation rights were settled by the knowledgeable village elders since, once lands were given, the farmer and his descendants normally maintained the right-to-use, or *hak pakai*, for those lands.

Recognition of inherited territorial use rights represents a relatively 'advanced' form of shifting cultivation. In societies which are transforming from hunter-gatherer to settled-subsistence – such as those found in Timor, Indonesia – villages have genealogical rather than territorial integrity, all land is communal property, and no inherited land-use rights are recognized. This system is similar to that used by the Penans, the only remaining hunter-gatherer tribe of Sarawak, as well as the Karen tribesmen of Thailand described by Hinton (1985).

In Sarawak, hereditary land rights have become infinitely complex over the generations because of complicated social structures, customs, and changing fortunes of the descendants. For example, it was not uncommon for slaves, taken in raids on neighbouring tribes, to be eventually allocated lands for cultivation by their masters. Descendants of the slaves, once integrated into the community, by marriage, may claim customary right to use of those lands, especially if they have become relatively wealthy and influential. Also, governmental erosion of traditional leadership – hence maintenance of requisite knowledge by village elders of individual resource rights – has contributed to complications in the modern legal determination of land ownership.

Discussion

The government of Malaysia has established a legal slope limit of 20 degrees for agricultural use of hilly land. Land steeper than this is declared unsuitable for agriculture and must remain under forest cover. In Sarawak, lands ranging from 25 to 40 degrees are still commonly used for shifting cultivation. Since exploitation rights to the best agricultural land have already been allocated, the less agriculturally productive lands are being progressively brought into the shifting cultivation cycle.

When it is assumed that shifting cultivation requires approximately 0.6 hectares to support one person, given yields at less than 450kg per hectare presently obtained in many upland regions, acute land shortages may develop before the year 2000. When considering the progressively declining agricultural suitability of, and expected yields from, new lands available to be incorporated into the shifting cultivation cycle, the demand for new land is expected to increase at 10 per cent per year although the natural population increase is estimated at 2.5 per cent per year (Lim, 1978).

The risk of total crop failure combined with the effort required to farm on increasingly marginal land has created a class of landless farmers who invade wildlife preserves and forest reserves just to survive. The higher population density associated with socioeconomic transformation to a modern commercial state has meant a net reduction in the standard of living for subsistence farmers. Unlike western societies, no family support subsides are paid. Subsides have become an essential component of Western government efforts to regulate destructive resource exploitation ventures. This occurs for example with Canada's commercial capture fishery which is still critical to the social and economic well-being of many coastal provinces but perennially unprofitable from a national perspective (see Mitchell, 1980).

Subsides tend to foster both social and political procrastination in dealing with the roots of the problem. However, without alternative support mechanisms, the immediate needs of shifting cultivators will continue to conflict with government attempts at rational land-used planning to improve the quality of life for all Sarawak citizens. Allowing shifting cultivation to continue may itself be interpreted as a form of social welfare executed at the expense of the environment rather than directly on the state treasury.

In most developing countries human death rates have decreased faster than birth rates, trapping these countries in the second stage of demographic transition, unable to achieve the economic and social progress necessary to reduce birth rates (Brown, 1987). A critical problem for developing societies is, then, how to sustain a growing population at a desirable standard of living on a limited resource base. If the objective is higher than fulfilling the basic needs for survival, the solution probably does not lie with preserving extractive or exploitative resource-management systems.

Modernization in the LDCs needs to be accompanied by new systems which use natural resources more efficiently and effectively. In many instances, scientific research can accelerate the evolution of indigenous systems and the knowledge associated with them to produce new systems which are acceptable to both the unique ecological and cultural character of a region. Evolution of indigenous systems is preferable to imposing foreign ones which may eventually be found to have had only limited regional validity (Watson and Balon, 1983). However, in the rush toward modernization, LDCs seldom have adequate finances to support basic research in any form. Consequently, renewable resources are frequently sacrificed for short-term economic gain, or inadvertently as a result of preserving or adopting inappropriate management systems.

A recommendation to prosecute shifting cultivators (Lau and Chung, 1978) who invade state forest reserves does not address the roots of the problem. A long-term solution to both environmental and social problems should involve accelerated development of more productive land-management systems. However, the knowledge required to execute a management system is context-specific and often not wholly appropriate to new conditions. New and existing knowledge must be synthesized in order to understand and execute a new system.

The acquisition and synthesis of knowledge which lays the foundation for successful social transformation has been historically a long process, although the transformation itself may be relatively rapid. Despite its importance, the creation of new knowledge and its subsequent communication between people and government agents are key components which often receive inadequate attention in Western countries (Pringle, 1985) as well as in LDCs' plans for accelerated socioeconomic development. Consequently, individuals who function within the context of an old society often find themselves at the periphery of LDC development, and ill-equipped to cope with impinging realities created by changing social conditions or imposed by government.

Once public education, retraining or extension efforts have achieved some critical mass of knowledge, individuals are in a position to adapt to the new conditions. For example, it has been found that some innovative farmers combine shifting cultivation on smaller plots with inputs of fertilizer and intensive weeding to achieve increased yields per hectare of hill paddy (Cramb, 1978). The labour saved in cultivating a smaller plot is devoted to estate crops such as pepper and rubber to increase cash incomes. The effect has been a net reduction in the land area actively within their shifting cultivation cycle and an increase in the length of the fallow period. Such innovations represent effective interim measures in the transition from shifting cultivation to modern commercial agriculture.

LDC research into the functioning of indigenous ecosystems – of which traditional human societies have heretofore formed an integral part – is essential to understand how changes in socioeconomic patterns may affect the environment, and to plan for change based on knowledge of the limitations and potentials of their natural resources.

In the case of Sarawak, general complacency about shifting cultivation practices, fostered by assumptions based on low population density, has given way to a sense of looming social and environmental crisis. As a result of coordinated research in the areas of health and nutrition, economics, ecology, and natural resources, the government is in a position to develop corrective policies and programmes. However, since this research occurred rather late in the evolution of the problem, it may not be possible to implement remedial measures in time to prevent extensive environmental damage to forest reserves, parks and wildlife preserves as well as on other land.

In order to manage the socioeconomic transformation of modernizing societies, it is necessary to develop an action plan which focuses and directs the activities of government, researchers, and the private sector. In the case of Sarawak's shifting cultivators, an action plan could build upon the following framework:

1 A multidisciplinary task force should be formed to advise on government policy, to establish geographic priorities, to plan and coordinate sectoral programs, to initiate and evaluate research (especially in the areas of ecology and agro-forestry), and to identify support requirements

(financial, physical, and human resources) for government departments.

2 An immediate assessment of the type, quality, and quantity of renewable resources, including their economic and ecological significance, within priority regions is essential for land-use planning purposes. This should be accompanied by a study of traditional patterns of resource use in order to identify potentially useful/harmful practices that could be adapted/prohibited within a new resource-management system.

3 The new management structure should build upon the strengths of the extant structure rather than attempt immediate wholesale replacement. Therefore, the sociocultural structure, traditions, and attitudes of the individual tribal populations should be studied in order to gain insights into their historical management and enforcement structures, identify potential technical or legal problems (such as land tenure), and address local concerns or special interests (resistance factors). The results of 2 and 3 should be combined to produce a regional profile.

4 Based on research results and the regional profile, a regional master plan should be developed as closely as possible from all key aspects (geographical, demographic, economic, ecological, etc). A master plan should remain flexible, and therefore receptive to new findings, but provide a uniform standard by which government departments can establish programme priorities and budgets, coordinate activities, and monitor progress.

5 Technical education and extension programmes must be developed which are appropriate to the human socioeconomic stage of development, and the economic potential of resources in each region (forest industries, estate crops, food crops, tourism, etc). Direct consultation with the target population will facilitate feedback to planners as well as the transfer of research and technical knowledge required by the people at each stage in their transformation. Therefore, effective two-way communication links between government and the people should be established early in the planning process. Traditional leaders should participate in all aspects of decision-making in order to promote understanding and encourage cooperation. This aspect is especially important when government plans call for land reform, or the establishment of wildlife preserves, protected forests and national parks.

6 Public-sector commitments to fund research and implement programmes in a coordinated manner must be maintained at a scale which is sufficient to reverse the trend of environmental damage in the near term, and eventually eliminate the negative social and environmental consequences of shifting cultivation as a resource-management system.

The coordinated efforts of ecologists and other researchers should provide technical options that can be applied at each stage in the shifting cultivation cycle. In the case of land clearing, research on the optimal size, shape and spacing of individual plots could minimize erosion and contiguous ecological disruption in order to promote biological recolonization. Research on inter-cropping of improved dryland rice cultivars with leguminous crops could increased crop yields and overall production. Fallow management through the planting of leguminous cover crops, or reforestation with timber and other commercial tree crops, could speed the recovery cycle. In each instance the farmers must share in the increasing body of technical knowledge and provide a greater measure of input into the maintenance of their renewable resources.

Conclusion

Socioeconomic change requires human adjustment within all segments of society in order to adapt to new conditions. Since in most cases it is almost impossible accurately to predict what adjustments will be necessary, even over the short term, development planning should be introspective, incremental and sectorally balanced. For instance, better health care should be accompanied by alternative methods of social welfare and demands for family planning.

Prior to an induced social change, cultural attitudes and habits should be studied in order to predict and account for the probable outcomes of particular innovations. But perhaps most critically, a capacity for basic scientific research must be developed early in the process to produce the new knowledge required for informed decision-making in government as well as at all socioeconomic strata within the changing societies. This implies the active participation of ecologists and other scientists in both research and interpretation of their research for the public benefit.

Researchers, however, often lack sufficient perspective to provide practical syntheses of their work. Researchers on traditional resource management may have focused excessively on descriptions of those systems without sufficient appreciation of the social, economic and environmental conditions which nurtured them, and which may be rapidly changing. A Neroistic tendency among academics – perhaps combined with a reluctance to acknowledge that the actual functioning of traditional systems may not be as egalitarian or idyllic as is often portrayed – may contribute to the current fashion of promoting a return to traditional community-based management. Because most traditional societies are feudal in structure, sharing of communal resources is often elitist and subject to dishonesty (see Chapter 16). This is contrary to the basic objectives of modern community development theory.

Elitism and the potential for dishonesty in sharing of communal resources among traditional societies, as well as the much publicized low production from collective farms when compared to private plots in modern communist nations, indicate that basic human nature is a major factor influencing the overall performance of any management system. Since population growth in LDCs implies that a progressively smaller share of essential resources will be available to any individual, passive management must give way to active and intensive management systems if production is to meet the growing demand. Individual energy and innovation are essential to increasing the carrying capacity of a community's resources, and should be encouraged by ensuring that individual effort will be suitably rewarded.

Therefore, the unravelling and fixing of resource rights or ownership will remain an important aspect of managing socioeconomic transformations and solving the environmental and social problems that may be created. Although intensified agriculture and agro-forestry techniques offer opportunities for increased and sustainable production per unit area in Sarawak, no farmer is likely to invest in land improvement unless there is some appropriate legal guarantee that he will benefit from those improvements.

Acknowledgements

This Chapter is based on data presented at a workshop on shifting cultivation in Kuching, Sarawak, Malaysia from 7th to 8th December, 1978. However, I have adapted and interpreted the data and in consequence they not necessarily reflect the opinion of the workshop participants or the Malaysian government. I am grateful to F. Berkes who encouraged and stimulated my thoughts on the issue of common-property resource management.

References

Anderson, A.J.U., 1977: *Malnutrition Among Sarawak Shifting Cultivators and Remedies*, Sarawak Medical Service, Kuching, Malaysia.
Brown, L.R., 1987: 'Analysing the demographic trap', in *State of the World 1987*, Worldwatch Institute, Norton, New York.
Cramb, R., 1978: *The Transition from Shifting Cultivation to Commercial Agriculture – a Case Study from the Layar River*, Sarawak Department of Agriculture, Kuching, Malaysia.
Dove, M., 1986: 'The ideology of agricultural development in Indonesia', in MacAndrews, C., ed., *Central Government and Local Development in Indonesia*, East Asian Social Science Monographs, Oxford University Press, Singapore, pp. 221–40.
Goulding, M., 1981: *Man and Fisheries on an Amazon Frontier*, Dr. W. Junk Publishers, The Hague.
Hatch, T., and Lim, C.P., 1978: *Shifting Cultivation in Sarawak: A Report Based*

upon the Workshop on Shifting Cultivation held in Kuching on 7-8th December, 1978, Sarawak Department of Agriculture, Kuching, Malaysia.

Hinton, P., 1985: 'An approach to the study of traditional systems of coastal resources management in Thailand', in Ruddle, K. and Johannes, R.E., eds, *The Traditional Knowledge and Management of Coastal Systems in Asia and the Pacific*, UNESCO, Jakarta, pp. 279–93.

Lau, B.T. and Chung, K.S., 1978: *Forest Protection Against Shifting Cultivation*, Sarawak Department of Agriculture, Kuching, Malaysia.

Lim, C.P., 1978: *Areas Under Shifting Cultivation in Upland Sarawak and their Agricultural Potential*, Sarawak Department of Agriculture, Kuching, Malaysia.

Maas, E.F. and Tie, Y.L., 1978: *Land Capability Classification and Evaluation for Agricultural Crops*, Department of Agriculture, Kuching, Malaysia.

Mitchell, C.L., 1980: *Canada's Fishing Industry: A Sectoral Analysis*, Department of Fisheries and Oceans, Ottawa.

Pringle, J.D., 1985: 'The human factor in fishery resource management', *Canadian Journal of Fisheries and Aquatic Sciences* 42(2), pp. 389–92.

Watson, D.J., 1982: 'Subsistence fish exploitation and implications for management in the Baram River System, Sarawak, Malaysia', *Fisheries Research*, 1, pp. 299–310.

Watson, D.J. and Balon, E.K., 1983: 'Structure and production of fish communities in tropical rain forest streams of northern Borneo', *Canadian Journal of Zoology*, 62, pp. 927–40.

Watson, D.J. and Balon, E.K., 1984: 'Ecomorphological analysis of fish taxocenes in rainforest streams of northern Borneo', *Journal of Fish Biology*, 25, pp. 371–84.

Whitton, B.A., 1975: *River Ecology*, Blackwell Scientific Publications, London.

5 Cooperation from the Perspective of Human Ecology

Fikret Berkes

Summary

Many ecologists have overemphasized competition and underestimated cooperation in ecological relationships. There is reason to believe that the root cause of this bias goes back to Charles Darwin and Adam Smith. The 'tragedy of the commons' notion is merely an extension of this bias into the area of resource management. But there is a tradition in animal ecology which focuses on prudent predation and offers the beginnings of a theory of cooperation – cooperation that confers selective advantage to a population at the ultimate (or evolutionary) level of causation. But how does cooperation evolve?

Three possible mechanisms – kin selection, group selection and reciprocity – can act in concert when human populations live in territorial, extended-kin groups. Such groups offer the most promising case material on which to base a theory of cooperation in human ecology. The chapter considers historical data on the hunting-territory system of Cree Amerindian people from James Bay, eastern subarctic Canada, to illustrate how community-based resource systems can and do work. A simple historical model is offered to explain how the hunting-territory system has adapted to changes, and how it has collapsed and recovered at least twice since the 1700s – an indication of the persistence and resilience of such cooperative resource-use systems.

Introduction

Human cultural behaviour is noted for its flexibility. It responds appropriately to prevailing conditions in the social and physical environment. Just as humans can be peaceable or warlike depending on the situation, use of resources by a group may or may not be sustainable depending on the situation (analogy suggested by M. Gadgil, personal communication). Users of a common-property resource will not necessarily behave in ways leading either to overexploitation or to sustainable use. Depending on the situation, neither the 'tragedy of the commons' (Hardin, 1968), nor sound management is inevitable.

Where societies are fluid, with large numbers of individuals only in casual contact, all having access to the commons, the tragedy is relatively likely. Hence, to many whose worldviews are shaped by the urban–industrial society in which they live, with little intimate contact with neighbours and other members of society, the 'tragedy' may appear inevitable. By contrast, use of commons for long-term sustainable yields is relatively more likely in the case of people living in small groups with tight communal control over the resource base and over social behaviour. Not being familiar with such societies, many Western-trained, urban-based resource managers and scientists overlook possibilities for sustainable management of commons in such situations (M. Gadgil, personal communication).

The first part of this chapter examines some of the background to the idea that communally owned resources are destined to be overexploited, a notion which necessarily emphasizes competitive aspects of resource utilization. Yet there is a tradition in the ecological literature which focuses on prudence and cooperation in joint resource use, and on the evolution of such positive interactions. The second part deals with a case study in which resource users live in small groups with tight communal control over the resource base. This is the hunting and trapping territory system of Cree Amerindian people of James Bay, eastern subarctic Canada. The case study is used to investigate how common-property systems can develop, persist or collapse, and how they can be re-established, more than once, following classical 'tragedies of the commons'.

The 'tragedy' as a cultural bias

The tragedy does no doubt occur with many resources owned collectively by society. Perhaps more remarkable, many common-property resources are used without an accompanying tragedy. Users cooperate with one another rather than compete. A great many examples of this are found in this volume and others (National Research Council, 1986; Ruddle and Johannes 1985; McCay and Acheson 1987; McNeely and Pitt 1985). Even the common grazing lands in Hardin's (1968) own paradigm were well looked after for many centuries, before they declined for reasons unrelated to any inherent flaw in the commons system (Cox, 1985). Judging by the literature summarized in Chapter 1, common-property resource tragedies in the Hardin sense seem not to be the rule but the exception. The tragedy tends to be related to the breakdown of existing commons systems due to disruptions that have originated externally to the community. As with the English commons example (Cox, 1985), such tragedies are not due to any built-in shortcoming of common-property institutions themselves. From an historical point of view, they tend to be episodic, with recovery sometimes following disruption (Berkes, 1985a).

Given that the tragedy is not all-pervasive, and that there are many successes as well as failures of the commons, there is an apparent paradox: Why has there been so much attention on the tragedy?

Suppose that Hardin (1968) had written an essay entitled 'Cooperation in the commons'. Is it likely that this hypothetical essay would have been cited in the technical literature as frequently as the one on 'the tragedy of the commons'? It is well known that people have a morbid fascination with disasters and tragedies. But there is a second major reason: Western culture tends to overemphasize competition as opposed to cooperation, and this may be affecting scientists' worldviews as well. Ecologists such as Odum (1983) and den Boer (1986) have pointed out that Western ecologists have been overly indulgent with the concepts of competition, predation and parasitism, as opposed to positive ecological interactions such as cooperation, commensalism and mutualism.

> The widespread acceptance of Darwin's idea of 'survival of the fittest' as an important means of bringing about natural selection has directed attention to the competitive aspects of nature. As a result, the importance of cooperation between species in nature has been underestimated. Until recently, positive interactions have not been subjected to as much quantitative study as have negative interactions. One might reasonably assume that negative and positive relations between populations eventually tend to balance one another, and that both are equally important in evolution of species and in stabilization of the ecosystem (Odum 1983, p. 393).

This lack of systematic balance may be related to the general emphasis on negative interrelationships in the very culture that nurtures Western ecologists (and economists, political scientists etc: see Axelrod 1984, p. 40). The issue has so far been little analysed by philosophers of science (Pepper, 1984). The point here is that cooperation has received relatively little attention in the population ecology literature, and this is perhaps the key to understanding why there has not been much interest in the past on the cooperative use of common-property resources.

Prudent predators and the evolution of cooperation

The literature of ecology contains the beginnings of a theory of cooperation in which the observed cooperation at the proximate (or explanatory) level is related to the survivorship of the species at the ultimate (or evolutionary) level. Slobodkin (1964) noted that evolution is like a game, a non-zero-sum game in which the only payoff is to stay in the game. In a later paper, he observed that 'predators generally acted as if they were behaving prudently' and sought a general theory that would help distinguish between the behaviour of a 'wise' hunter and that of a 'foolish' one. He pointed out that the human hunter/resource user was not unique among species with respect to the benefits of a policy of prudent predation (Slobodkin, 1968).

A major theoretical problem has been the question of how prudent predation could evolve. It is known from the work of Rosenzwieg and MacArthur (1963) and others that there generally is selective pressure on predators to improve their exploitation efficiency. If so, one would expect the destabilization of the supposed ecological steady-state between the predator and prey. The dilemma is that overly efficient predators would cause the extinction of their prey, thus endangering their own existence.

Yet there must be ways in which prudent predation can develop. It is well known from the literature of coevolution, for example, that predator–prey and parasite–host interactions generally tend to become less negative through time. Three classes of processes have been proposed to account for the evolution of such adaptations and cooperation, or 'helping behaviour' in general (Peck and Feldman, 1986). Such behaviour is promoted by

1 *kin selection* in animals living in populations in which genetically related individuals are often found together;
2 *reciprocity*, where specific individuals have repeated contact (likely in many human societies – and a few animal examples have been suggested); and
3 *group selection*, which is likely in animals only under special scenarios of prey–predator and host–parasite interactions. Boyd and Richerson (1985) argued that cultural group selection is very plausible for human populations.

As pointed out by Gadgil (personal communication), all three can act in concert when human populations live in territorial, extended kin groups – the situation with many hunter-gatherers and shifting cultivators, as also with Indian rural society (see Chapter 14), Pacific island societies (Chapter 16) and others. None of these may be operative in a highly fluid, mobile, urban-industrial society.

Gilpin (1975) argued that group selection provides an insight as to how coevolution can occur. Using a catastrophe theory model, he showed that if two parasite strains were present in the same host, the more efficient and faster multiplying strain would be favoured by natural selection. But in cases where the efficiency of parasitism kills the host, the slower multiplying strain would be favoured by group selection between hosts (Gilpin, 1975). The model shows that group selection begins to act after the evolution of even higher exploitation efficiency has precipitated the destabilization of the ecological steady-state.

Reciprocity is of particular interest in human ecology because it is a good match for cultural evolution. As Bronowski (1978, p. 22) put it, 'natural selection in human societies has been largely dominated by human cultures themselves for at least the last million years'. A promising application of the reciprocity concept at the level of the individual is the use of the game-theoretic approach known as Prisoner's Dilemma.

In the Prisoner's Dilemma game, the evolution of cooperation requires that the individuals have a sufficiently large chance to meet again so that they have a stake in their future interactions. If this requirement is fulfilled, then even in a world full of selfish, non-cooperating meanies, cooperation can evolve from small clusters of individuals who base their cooperation on reciprocity. It has been demonstrated both mathematically and empirically (with a computer tournament) that a strategy based on reciprocity can thrive in a world where many different strategies are possible, and it can protect itself from invasion by less cooperative strategies (Axelrod, 1984, p. 20). In its application to biological evolution, it can be made compatible with kin selection theory by assuming that genes favouring reciprocity and cooperation may be first established by kin selection. Cooperation can then spread among individuals who are less and less genetically related (Axelrod and Hamilton, 1981).

Cultural evolution and common-property institutions

Currently, no theory of cultural evolution has achieved the status of conventional wisdom. While Axelrod's (1984) game-theoretic framework is appealing, it does not purport to be *the* model of cultural evolution. Some theories of cultural evolution are based on analytical models from evolutionary biology including group selection (for example, Boyd and Richerson, 1985) and others on cultural selection processes.

Boehm (1982) speculated that cultural selection mechanisms probably include both blind variation and selective retention, as well as rational variants of the same process. As Durham (1981) put it, the mechanism may be the 'trial-and-error perseverance of individuals or . . . some process of intuition and rational ''pre-selection'' or . . . a group level mechanism . . . We simply do not know enough about the levels of mechanisms of cultural evolution.' Bonner (1980) pointed out that cultural evolution is not limited to human societies, but that a surprising array of simple forms of cultural transmission (by learning) occur among animals. While social scientists emphasize the uniqueness of humankind, biologists see in mankind quantitative extensions of qualities present in other species (Bonner, 1980).

Many social scientists believe that cultural differences among human societies are not necessarily related to differences in their biophysical environment, as once held by proponents of 'environmental determinism', a dominant school of geographical thought in the past. Environmental determinism was popular among geographers who rationalized colonialism – another case of simplistic science underpinning bad politics (see Pepper, 1984). Currently, there are basically three views. The first view is that differences among societies may be arbitrary, a result of 'cultural drift', akin to genetic drift. A second view, closer to 'environmental determinism', is that different cultures are adaptations to different environmental conditions. A third and perhaps more realistic view is that different human cultures and practices may represent alternate stable systemic adaptations.

There is considerable empirical support for this third view. Flowers et al. (1982) found that each of four central Brazilian Indian groups grew numerous crop species together (polyculture), but the mixes of crops were different and highly patterned. In Hawaii, Kirch (1982) noted three distinct adaptive strategies of marine exploitation from archeological evidence. 'The population which colonized Hawaii carried as part of its cultural baggage a set of marine exploitation strategies which over time were modified in response to the local environment.' Over historical time, agriculture intensification resulted in the division of fields into smaller units. Shifting cultivation developed into a highly productive but labour-intensive crop-rotation system. With the intensification of inshore marine exploitation, fish weirs (stone traps) evolved into fish ponds (Kirch, 1980).

The literature on common-property resources also supports the view that different cultures represent alternative stable adaptations. Examples in this volume and elsewhere document the existence of a variety of common-property institutions in many different areas and groups as a solution to the 'tragedy of the commons'. What is striking is the diversity of these institutions, from the reef and lagoon tenure system of Pacific islands, to resource specialization by castes in India, to lobster fishing territories in Mexico and Maine. A great many variations of the same basic theme (communal resource-management institutions with access control) seem to have evolved repeatedly in different areas and in different groups elsewhere on earth – obviously an optimal (or a minimax) solution, but very diverse. This cultural diversity, in turn, may be closely related to and essential for the conservation of biological diversity (Gadgil, 1987), inextricably linking social concerns in resource use with ecological concerns.

The literature on human ecology is rich in documentation of diversity of resource-use patterns and their change over time. Human ecologists, however, have a major methodological problem: they cannot control all the variables as can a laboratory-based ecologist. But some human ecologists have an advantage over their laboratory-bound colleagues: they can use historical data to add a time dimension to the study of interactions of human groups with their resources. Such historical data are crucially important for the study of change of resource-use patterns over time, and for the study of special mechanisms of resource use such as territoriality. A case study of Amerindian hunting territories serves to illustrate the point.

Hunting territories in James Bay

The study area is eastern James Bay in the Canadian subarctic (Fig. 5.1). The Cree Amerindian village of Chisasibi (formerly Fort George, pop. 2000), located some 1000km north of Montreal, is one of eight Cree communities in the area. Relatively isolated until the construction of a large hydroelectric project on the La Grand River, Chisasibi has had a road connection since the mid-1970s to the south.

As shown in Fig. 5.1, Chisasibi has a community hunting, fishing and trapping area with a reasonably well defined boundary. Under the James Bay Agreement of 1975, Chisasibi hunters and fishermen have exclusive rights to most of the western-quarter of this area, and for trapping purposes they have exclusive use-rights for the entire area. The community hunting area is divided into some 40 'traplines' or hunting territories (in Cree, *nituhuschii*, 'my hunting land'). Henceforth, we shall refer to the *nituhuschii* system or simply 'the system'. How does the system work?

Each territory is seasonally occupied by a hunting group, traditionally consisting of two or three nuclear families, usually ten to 20 people, spending most of the year together in bush camps. Much has been written about Cree hunting territories, the extended-kin groups which occupy them, and the age-old rules for resource use. The system operates by consensus, cooperation and reciprocity. The traplines were formalized by the government in the 1950s as a beaver management system, but the basic land-tenure system has existed for a long time (Bishop and Morantz, 1986).

The leader of the hunting group, (*amiskuchimaaw*, 'beaver boss'), effectively controls more than just the beaver resource. Under the traditional management system in Chisasibi, all persons wishing to hunt, fish or trap are expected to obtain permission from the boss of that area. Such requests would rarely be turned down, but nevertheless this arrangement ensures that the boss controls access to his area and knows about all harvesting activities taking place in it. A good beaver boss has a mental map of all the beaver colonies over an area of several hundred square kilometres, and a pretty good idea of the age and sex composition of the beaver in each (Feit, 1986). He also knows which other animals can be harvested productively – and where – in 'his' area. The hunting boss is the repository of specialized knowledge needed to travel to an area and to hunt successfully after getting there (Berkes, 1977).

In addition to beaver, the Canada goose is also hunted on a territorial basis

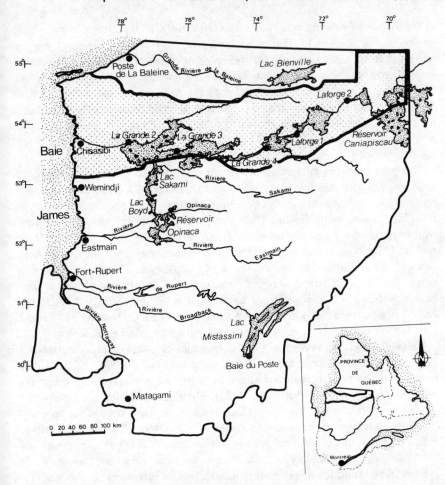

Figure 5.1   The James Bay area and the hunting, fishing, trapping territory of the
Cree Indian community of Chisasibi.

in Chisasibi (Berkes, 1982). This is a more specialized subsystem of the
overall hunting-territory system. Goose territories exist only during April-
May and September when the geese are present; they are found only along
the James Bay coast (elsewhere geese are not abundant); and they are
controlled by the *paaschichaauchimaaw* ('goose-shooting boss'). The goose
territory system is not formalized or mapped. It is more fluid than the
government-sanctioned beaver trapline system but just as real within the
traditional management sphere. The two kinds of bosses are not necessarily
the same people, and the boundaries of the two kinds of territories do not
usually coincide.

Both types of hunting bosses in Chisasibi often talk about their 'ownership' of the land and animals. However, the word used – *nitipaaihtaan* – means 'ownership to take care of' or 'to control', and differs from the term *nitipiwaawsiiun*, which is used to refer to the ownership of personal belongings, things that can be bought and sold (J. Mailhot, personal communication). Chisasibi hunters say that the land and animals belong to God; the boss does not really own the animals but has the responsibility for the distribution of the wealth of the land. (Interestingly, Pacific islanders have a similar concept of stewardship; see Chapter 16.)

The boss manages harvesting activity for the benefit of the community as a whole: he leads the hunt, supervises the sharing of food to make sure that no one goes hungry, and enforces customary laws with respect to conservation and appropriate hunting behaviour. The boss inherits the hunting territory, usually from his father or other relative, but he cannot sell it or buy it. If he does not manage it for the community benefit, he can be held accountable and forced by social pressure to step down. This does not happen often. In Chisasibi, there was only one case of this in recent years. The beaver boss in question neglected to pull out his traps (usually done at the end of March) – a fairly serious violation of trappers' customary law – and was subsequently forced to relinquish his authority (Berkes, 1986).

Chisasibi land-use system is a good example of common-property institutions (term used in the sense of Ciriacy-Wantrup and Bishop, 1975). Here, common property is a regime distinct from private property, state property, or open-access regimes (Bromley, 1986). Hunting territories are clearly not private property in the Euro-American sense. They are communal property in which hunting bosses exercise leadership ('stewardship' as Feit, 1986, calls it) by mutual consent, mostly tacit consent, of the community of hunters. The present day territorial arrangement is a common-property system with traditional or neotraditional institutions partially backed by government legislation. Local-level management plays a more important role than government management. Land and the animals are *res communes*, not *res nullius*. Everyone's property is *not* no one's property.

The land-use system in Chisasibi is not particularly unique among northern native peoples of North America. In contrast to the dominant tradition among the Europeans who colonized the land, Amerindians never considered land or wildlife as a commodity (Usher, 1987). According to Sutton (1975), probably all native peoples in North America had systems of land tenure which involved allocation within the group, control of access to resources, and the prerogative to convey certain resource-use rights but not outright alienation. In this regard, the Amerindian communal-property systems were similar to those described in this volume from many different continents and for different kinds of resources.

Unlike some of the other communal-property systems in North America and elsewhere, the system of the Chisasibi Cree has survived colonialism. This is remarkable in itself and worthy of investigation. But furthermore, the land-tenure system of the James Bay area has been of considerable interest to anthropologists investigating the cultural impact of the European fur trade, and to economists theorizing on the origins of private property as an institution.

The debate in anthropology concerns the role of the commercialization of fur animals, principally beaver, in the appearance of family hunting territories. The main point of debate has been the claim that territories were not aboriginal (or traditional) but a response to the fur trade, and that the origin of territoriality must be sought in the shift from a subsistence economy to a commercial one (Feit, 1978; Bishop and Morantz, 1986). Some economists have interpreted the presumed evolution of family hunting territories as indicating private hunting rights. On scant evidence of individual ownership they have based a theory of evolution of private-property-rights systems (Demsetz, 1967). Both the anthropological debate and the economic proposition require re-examination. This will be done by constructing a model of common-property use with hunting territories (Berkes, 1986).

A model of James Bay hunting territories

The model proposed in Fig. 5.2 is an extension of that in Berkes (1986) and is based on the following considerations.

1 Use of common-property resources may change over time. These changes would not necessarily be unidirectional; there may be cycles in the structure and dynamics of resource-use systems. Thus, a model of hunting territories has to be dynamic and able to accommodate cycles of use patterns and resource abundance. There is, in fact, evidence of several cycles in the abundance of beaver since the beginning of the fur trade in the James Bay area (for instance, see Feit, 1978).

2 Resources which are abundant relative to needs do not require any special arrangements such as territories. However, when the resource becomes scarce relative to needs, then special care has to be taken. Privatization may be one rather extreme response. Alternatively, common-property institutions may evolve in ways to enable sufficient control of the resource in question. A relatively loose communal-property system may be strengthened by having community-appointed stewards to exercise resource-management leadership on behalf of the community. The evidence behind this proposition comes directly from interviews with Cree hunters. Also, comparative studies of Amerindian

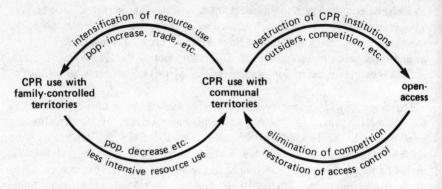

Figure 5.2 Relationship between common-property-resource (CPR) use and the development of common-property institutions and conservation practices: a systems view.

coastal resource-tenure systems provide additional support: there is a documented relationship between increasing relative scarcity of resources and increasing emphasis and concentration of control of access to the resource (Richardson, 1982).

3 Creation of open-access conditions due to external disruptions and the destruction of existing common-property institutions often lead to the depletion of the resource. This is particularly well documented in the case of fisheries (Berkes, 1985b), and no doubt applies as well to many other types of communally owned resources. As Regier (personal communication) noted, 'disruption has always served imperialism – *divide et impera* as a special case. In this regard, creation of private property may be a means of dividing a community internally to make it subservient to an external market.'

4 Once a resource is badly depleted, it is no longer profitable to exploiters from the outside. This may enable the local resource community to reassert its control over the resource. State-level management, such as government regulations on resource use, may be of further assistance, permitting the resource to recover. This appears to have happened, for example, in North American Great Lakes fisheries; there have been not one but several cycles of overcapitalization–overfishing–resource depletion–resource recovery in Lake Erie (Berkes, 1985a).

The most likely land-tenure system in James Bay at the time of contact with Europeans is shown at the centre of Fig. 5.2. The land was held communally at the level of the band or sub-band. There were groups of families who traditionally occupied specific areas, with hunters exploiting the land most familiar to them. (This expression is reversed in the Cree language; hunters are more likely to have hunting success when 'the land is familiar with them'.) There is little doubt that there was fluidity in the use of hunting areas and in reciprocal exchanges of use-rights; hunting lands within the community territory were not clearly demarcated. Note that the model is not dependent on the specification of the above; it would be applicable if there had been family hunting territories at the time of contact.

It is more likely, however, that family hunting territories appeared with the intensification of resource use. It is the fur trade that triggered increasing levels of exploitation of beaver, marten, lynx, fox and Canada goose resources. But the point is that the fur trade is not the control (or key) variable – intensification is. Increased exploitation of resources could in theory have been caused by change in technology and population growth, even in the absence of the fur trade. With the fur trade, however, the demand to create surplus probably resulted in the tightening of the system. More care had to be taken with the harvest. Hunting bosses – senior hunters who knew their areas particularly well – became more important in society and started to control more closely those resources which were intrinsically controllable. As a relatively stationary and predictable resource, beaver met this requirement very well. Over a period of time, this new arrangement may have reverted back to the more loosely managed system if there had been reduced market demand for fur, or depopulation of the area as a result of epidemics caused by the contact with the Europeans.

The other direction in which the system may go is the creation of open-access conditions by external pressures and the destruction of the local common-property institutions. Destructive competition between two rival fur companies vying for market control, itinerant fur trappers who have no regard for the local rules, and the coercion of the local trappers themselves, all appear to be part of the recipe for depletion of the resource. The key aspect of the failure of the territory system, according to this model, is the creation of open-access conditions; the trapper is no longer able to reap the benefits of his own restraint. Once local control has failed, if the trapper does not harvest the resource first, someone else will – the tragedy of the commons.

Nevertheless, the system has the capacity to recover. Diminishing returns to the trapper make it unlikely that beaver over such a large area would be completely depleted. However, with economic overhunting, the sustained yield will be much lowered. The collapse of the supply may in turn result in the collapse of the fur companies, making mergers or consolidation likely. For the business to recover, fur companies are likely to become generally more cautious and conservation-oriented. The government may also decide to protect the fur producer from the competition of outsiders, and may initiate conservation measures such as closed seasons and beaver preserves. Since the resource in question is renewable, given adequate protection it should eventually recover. However, the key aspect of the recovery, according to the model, is not the action of fur companies or governments, but the restoration of limited-access conditions. Just as living resources usually have the capacity to recover from past abuses, it appears that common-property institutions also have the ability to bounce back when the local community is once more able to control access to the land and resources.

Testing the model

There is suitable ethnohistorical information from the James Bay area to examine whether the proposed model approximates reality. Historically one of the most important industries of the colony now known as Canada, fur trade started in the James Bay–Hudson Bay area with the granting of exclusive trade rights by the King of England to the Hudson's Bay Company (HBC) in 1670 (Francis and Morantz, 1983). The meticulous data kept by the HBC in the form of fur return statistics and daily journals make it possible to document that beaver were scarce in the James Bay area around 1740 and again in 1769, during the period of intense competition between the HBC and French traders (Francis and Morantz, 1983, p. 55). Nevertheless, there is insufficient information to document the kind of land-tenure system that was present in that period and whether the effect of competition on communal-property systems could be held responsible for the decline in beaver numbers.

Somewhat better documentation to test the model comes from the nineteenth century. In the early 1800s, the main competition in the fur trade was between the HBC and The North West Company. The demand for fur was high; and increasingly larger numbers of beaver were being taken by native trappers, seduced by trade items like rum. But this was not a sustainable resource use pattern; returns gradually declined until, in 1821, the HBC absorbed its rival. Following this, beaver returns recovered from a low in 1825–29 to reach a high in 1830–34, according to Rupert's River District (James Bay) records (Francis and Morantz, 1983, p. 130). But the HBC was not able to maintain its status as the sole buyer. Private traders, some of them Abenaki Indians from the south (whose land had already been depleted of beaver) started to make incursions into parts of the Cree area through the 1830s and 1840s (Francis and Morantz, 1983, p. 132). Beaver returns declined to a new low in 1845–49 before recovering again after about 1860, as the intruders were gradually expelled from Cree communal hunting areas (Francis and Morantz, 1983, p. 130).

The next major beaver-depletion cycle, which occurred in the early twentieth century, provides a good test for the model. In this case, not only are statistical data available but the events occurred in living memory and have been analysed extensively by Feit (1978) and others.

In the late 1920s and early 1930s beaver populations were depleted in the James Bay area, especially in the southern portion of it, which had by then become accessible by railway. Non-native trappers from the outside began to enter the James Bay area during the period of high fur prices in the late 1920s, depleting one hunting territory after another. With the control of access to the beaver resource gone, and unable to stop the intruders, the Cree hunters themselves contributed (by their own admission) to the overhunting of beaver rather than letting outsiders take them all (Feit, 1978, 1986).

The land-tenure system of the James Bay Cree at the time was relatively well known. In the early 1900s, anthropologists described family hunting territories and even mapped them in parts of the James Bay area. Whatever more loosely organized communal-property system had existed earlier, by the turn of the century it was clear that a more tightly controlled family-level system with hunting bosses had emerged.

When the beaver reached an all-time low in the 1930s and the outsiders who had already made their 'killing' left, the Cree people of James Bay were able to re-establish their system, backed by government regulations. Under conservation laws introduced after 1930, beaver killing by outsiders was banned and Cree communal territories legally recognized. Within the communal area, family hunting territories were mapped and beaver bosses were put officially in charge of their own territories. Beaver populations recovered in ten to 20 years, depending on the region (in Chisasibi, by the mid-1950s), resulting in productive harvests once more.

Discussion and conclusions

As Gadgil (1987) has observed:

> The colonization of the world by the dominant technological culture pouring out of Europe is now nearing completion, and with this, traditions of sustainable use of biological resources and conservation of diversity are reappearing. They have reemerged most readily in regions where the technological revolution was first completed.
>
> Thus the Japanese have successfully established highly sustainable use of their inshore fisheries, basing it on earlier communal controls by artisanal fishermen . . . The control over local resources is reverting to local people as resources are reduced to levels too low for profitable exploitation by those employing more sophisticated and hence more expensive technologies. . .

Traditions of resource conservation can re-emerge, not in their original form but by borrowing from the wisdom of ancient practices, in ways that are well adapted to the contemporary world, as in the case of Japanese inshore fisheries (Chapter 10). Slobodkin (1964) commented that evolution may be considered an existential game that Sartre or Kafka might have created. If extinction represents a kind of losing, then the only point in the evolution game is persistence. Analogous to Gilpin's (1975) example of host–parasite systems, societies which deplete their resources for short-term economic gains are losers in the long run; those which use them sustainably are likely to be the ultimate winners by minimizing the chance of extinction.

Cooperation among the users of a resource towards sustainable management is possible and confers selective advantage to the population in question. This is true for populations of humans as well as for those of other species. Contrary to Hardin's (1968) 'tragedy-of the-commons' model which unidirectionally predicts resource depletion, sustainable and adaptive strategies of common-property resource use are both theoretically possible and empirically observed. However, institutions for the use of such resources do change over time and sometimes break down due to factors that impinge on the system.

The 'ecosystem view' (Chapters 3 and 7) is a powerful tool in investigating the components of a resource-use system and their interrelationships: it emphasizes the interdependence of humans with their environment. The 'man-in-nature' view, as opposed to the 'man-against-nature' view, necessarily accents a cooperative approach.

The case study of Cree Amerindian hunting territories illustrates the use of a systems approach to explain the evolution, demise and subsequent recovery (more than once) of communal resource-management systems. A fundamental assumption behind this case study, and several others in this volume, is that the traditional lifestyle of the populations involved is an ecologically viable option.

Territoriality may be considered a behavioural self-regulatory mechanism. Territorial use of resources is found among many hunting peoples – and among other predatory mammalian species. It serves at the ultimate level of causation to limit population with respect to resources. In human societies, these mechanisms tend to be more complex than those found in non-human groups. Many animal populations have territories; many human societies have common-property institutions which are often systems of access rules, together with rules about resource sharing, conservation and appropriate harvesting behaviour.

Selective pressures towards cooperation and the prudent use of resources are present in human as well as non-human populations. Among human groups, however, cultural evolution is likely to be relatively more important than biological evolution. Hence, the reciprocity/game-theory approach of Axelrod (1984) appears to be a suitable tool to explain the evolution of cooperation among human groups. Actual cases of cooperation from fishing communities have been investigated using Prisoner's Dilemma formulation, and realistic results have been obtained (Berkes and Kence, in press). In general, lessons from human-ecology case studies appear to indicate that evolutionary mechanisms of reciprocity, kin selection and group selection converge rather than diverge, consistent with Wilson (1983 and in progress).

As Gadgil (personal communication) noted, in highly fluid urban-industrial societies, however, none of these three mechanisms promoting cooperation may be operative. In smaller communities and among extended kin groups of the kind found in rural areas of the world, cultural and biological selective pressures toward cooperation are likely to be strong. But even in such societies, resource users, including individuals in leadership positions, cheat on occasion. In societies with tight communal control over resources, persistent cheaters are likely to be caught and free-ridership penalized. Small communities are not pleasant places for those who violate local rules and norms of cooperative behaviour.

Some ecologists have indeed overemphasized the competitive aspects of nature at the expense of cooperation. Hardin's (1968) 'tragedy of the commons' is merely an extension of this bias into the realm of resource management. (Then again, he did note that the solution may be found in 'mutual coercion, mutually agreed upon'.) Scientists are creatures of the culture which nurtures them, and ecologists are not alone in this regard. Some of their biases are shared with scholars in other disciplines as well. How else can one explain the economist Demsetz's (1967) enthusiasm to interpret family-controlled communal hunting territories as merely a step in the evolution of private-property regimes?

Systematic biases in Western ecology and resource management are partially related to the fact that economics and biology have been borrowing ideas from one another. The case in point is Darwin's notion of 'survival of the fittest' which was borrowed from the *laissez-faire* economics of Adam Smith (Gould, 1980, p. 66). Likewise, many contemporary ecologists and resource managers accept without question the 1950s economic paradigm that resources will decline unless privatized or else regulated by central governments, thanks to Hardin's (1968) rediscovery of these ideas. Paradigms die hard, but they do die − as more and more evidence accumulates that cannot be explained by the body of theory based on them (Kuhn, 1970).

In resource management, we may be nearing that point: a new theory of common-property resources has to be able to move beyond the 'tragedy of the commons'. It must explain resource-use successes as well as failures, and persistent cooperation among users under certain conditions and lack of it under other circumstances. Many western-trained ecologists and resource managers have been writing off the possibility of sustainable management of communal-property systems despite empirical evidence for their effectiveness. The search for alternative theories of (and management approaches for) the commons will have to take into account this paradox.

Acknowledgements

For the development of the ideas in this paper and for their critique, I am thankful to many colleagues including Taghi Farvar, John Middleton, Mina Kislalioglu Berkes, José Mailhot, David Pitt and David Sloan Wilson. Some of the material in the text incorporates extensive comments by Madhav Gadgil and Henry Regier to whom I am especially grateful. The work was supported by the Social Sciences and Humanities Research Council of Canada.

References

Axelrod, R., 1984: *The Evolution of Cooperation*, Basic Books, New York.

Axelrod, R. and Hamilton, W.D., 1981: 'The evolution of cooperation', *Science*, 211, pp. 1390–6.

Berkes, F., 1977: 'Fishery resource use in a subarctic Indian community', *Human Ecology*, 5, pp. 289–307.

Berkes, F., 1982: 'Waterfowl management and northern native peoples with reference to Cree hunters of James Bay', *Musk-ox*, 30, pp. 23–35.

Berkes, F., 1985a: 'The common property resource problem and the creation of limited property rights', *Human Ecology*, 13, pp. 187–208.

Berkes, F., 1985b: 'Fishermen and the "tragedy of the commons"'. *Environmental Conservation*, 12, pp. 199–206.

Berkes, F., 1986: 'Common property resources and hunting territories', *Anthropologica*, 28, pp. 145–62.

Berkes, F. and Kence, A., in press, 'Fisheries and the Prisoner's Dilemma game: Conditions for the evolution of cooperation among users of common property resources', *Middle Eastern Technical University Journal of Pure and Applied Sciences*, Ankara.

Bishop, C.A. and Morantz, T., eds, 1986: 'Who owns the beaver? Northern Algonquian land tenure reconsidered', *Anthropologica*, 28, nos. 1–2.

Boehm, C., 1982: 'A fresh outlook on cultural selection', *American Anthropologist*, 84, pp. 105–25.

Bonner, J.T., 1980: *The Evolution of Culture in Animals*, Princeton University Press, Princeton, NJ.

Boyd, R. and Richerson, P.J., 1985: *Culture and Evolutionary Process*, University of Chicago Press, Chicago.

Bromley, D.W., 1986: 'Closing comments', *Proceedings of the Conference on Common Property Resource Management*, National Academy Press, Washington, DC, pp. 593–8.

Bronowski, J., 1978: *The Origins of Knowledge and Imagination*, Yale University Press, New Haven and London.

Ciriacy-Wantrup, S.V. and Bishop, R.C., 1975: '"Common property" as a concept in natural resources policy', *Natural Resources Journal*, 15, pp. 713–27.

Cox, S.J.B., 1985: 'No tragedy on the commons', *Environmental Ethics*, 7, pp. 49–61.

Demsetz, H., 1967: 'Toward a theory of property rights', *American Economic Review, Papers and Proceedings 57*, pp. 347–59.

den Boer, P.J., 1986: 'The present status of the competitive exclusion principle', *Trends in Ecology and Evolution*, 1, pp. 25–8.

Durham, W.H., 1981: Comment in: Winterhalder, B. and Smith, E.A., eds, *Hunter/Gatherer Foraging Strategies*, University of Chicago Press, Chicago.

Feit, H.A., 1978: *Waswanipi Realities and Adaptations: Resource Management and Cognitive Structure*, PhD thesis, McGill University, Montreal.

Feit, H.A., 1986: 'James Bay Cree Indian management and moral considerations of fur-bearers', in *Native People and Resource Management*, Alberta Society of Professional Zoologists, Edmonton, pp. 49–65.

Flowers, N.M., Gross, D.R., Ritter, M.L. and Werner, D.W., 1982: 'Variations in swidden practices in four central Brazilian Indian societies', *Human Ecology*, 10, pp. 203–17.

Francis, D. and Morantz, T., 1983: *Partners in Furs. A History of the Fur Trade in Eastern James Bay 1600–1870*, McGill-Queen's University Press, Montreal.

Gadgil, M., 1987: 'Diversity: Cultural and biological', *Trends in Ecology Evolution*, 2(12), pp. 369–73.

Gilpin, M.E., 1975: *Group Selection in Predator–Prey Communities*, Princeton University Press, Princeton, NJ.

Gould, S.J., 1980: *The Panda's Thumb. More Reflections in Natural History*, Norton, New York.

Hardin, G., 1968: 'The tragedy of the commons', *Science*, 162, pp. 1243–8.

Kirch, P., 1980. 'Polynesian prehistory: Cultural adaptation in island ecosystems', *American Scientist*, 68, pp. 39–46.

Kirch, P.V., 1982: 'The ecology of marine exploitation in prehistoric Hawaii', *Human Ecology*, 10, pp. 455–76.

Kuhn, T.S., 1970: *The Structure of Scientific Revolutions*, Second Edition, University of Chicago Press, Chicago.

McCay, B.J. and Acheson, J.M., eds, 1987: *Capturing the Commons*, University of Arizona Press, Tucson.

McNeeley, J.A. and Pitt, D., eds, 1985: *Culture and Conservation*, Croom Helm, London.

National Research Council, 1986: *Proceedings of the Conference on Common Property Resource Management*, National Academy Press, Washington, DC.

Odum, E.P., 1983: *Basic Ecology*, Saunders, Philadelphia.

Peck, J.R. and Feldman, M.W., 1986: 'The evolution of helping behavior in large randomly mixed populations', *American Naturalist*, 127, pp. 209–221.

Pepper, D.M., 1984: *The Roots of Modern Environmentalism*, Croom Helm, London.

Richardson, A., 1982: 'The control of productive resources on the northwest coast of North America', in Williams, N.M. and Hunn, E.S., eds, *Resource Managers: North American and Australian Hunter/Gatherers*, AAAS Selected Symposium 67, Washington, DC, pp. 93–112.

Rozenzweig, M.L. and MacArthur, R.H., 1963: 'Graphical representations and stability conditions of predator–prey interactions', *American Naturalist*, 97, pp. 209–23.

Ruddle, K. and Johannes, R.E., eds, 1985: *The Traditional Knowledge and Management of Coastal Systems in Asia and the Pacific*, UNESCO, Jakarta.

Slobodkin, L.B., 1964: 'The strategy of evolution', *American Scientist*, 52, pp. 342–57.

Slobodkin, L.B., 1968: 'How to be a predator, *American Zoologist*, 8, pp. 43–51.

Sutton, I., 1975: *Indian Land Tenure*, Clearwater, New York.

Usher, P.J., 1987: 'Indigenous management systems and the conservation of wildlife in the Canadian North', *Alternatives*, 14(1), pp. 3–9.

Wilson, D.S., 1983: 'The group selection controversy: History and current status', *Annual Review of Ecology and Systematics*, 14, pp. 159–87.

Part 2 Critique of Conventional Resource Management Science

Henry Regier, one of the authors in Part 2, observed in *A Balanced Science of Renewable Resources* (1978), that the yin–yang model of East Asia may be useful in summarizing the ecologist's dilemma. Yang can be identified very approximately with Western science, and yin with an alternative approach emphasizing more intuitive, non-hierarchic networks and holistic, non-linear systemic and qualitative concepts.

Considering the essential inadequacy of Western reductionistic science in dealing with environmental and resource problems, Regier suggested that we develop a flexible, balanced approach by conserving what is useful in Western science and nurturing some of its more radical components. Ecology qualifies as one of these components because, as a science concerned with the whole (rather than with its parts), it stands at the fringes of the reductionistic tradition of Western science. (There are divisions of ecology in mainstream science, too, but we are not concerned with those.)

Seen this way, ecological thinking is sympathetic to yin and to systems of logic characteristic to East Asian, African and Amerindian cultures. As Regier put it, certain approaches to systems studies, including ecology, may be considered as part of the yin element within the predominant yang of Western science.

One of the major issues in common-property resources is how to integrate scientific management with traditional knowledge and management. To use the yin–yang analogy further, how do we put these two complementary halves together?

The four chapters in Part 2 take a critical look at yang. Chapters 6 and 7 take different paths in examining shortcomings of current resource-management science and exploring promising alternatives; Chapter 8 and 9 deal with the political and economic dimensions, respectively, of resource management.

The lead chapter in Part 2, by Freeman, offers a 'cautionary tale' for resource managers, based on recent controversies in the conservation of caribou in northern Canada. The uncertainty inherent in scientific findings, and the public misperception of 'the power of science to deliver the truth', presents scientist-managers with a particularly difficult problem. But the solution is not merely the acquisition of more data, which is the 'instinctive' reaction of many scientists. Freeman argues that more science does not necessarily mean better management. Instead, he suggests that conventional science be cut to size and made more consistent with traditional management approaches, with more effort directed to re-establishing conditions under which local-level management systems can be made to work.

Chapter 7 by Regier, Mason and Berkes deals with related issues in the search for alternative management approaches. Focusing on resource-use rights and allocation mechanisms, the chapter extends the critique of Western resource management science and its practitioners, and examines the phenomenon of short-term exploitive development as a manifestation of Western science and technology. Noting the variety of alternative approaches proposed in the West to deal with the ecological and social shortcomings of conventional exploitive development, the authors explore types of user rights and allocative mechanisms that are more likely to be compatible with the sustainable use of resources. Development, the authors point out, may be a misnomer: many resources are not unused or underused but rather misused and degraded. Thus, the aim of resource management must be sustainable 'redevelopment', rather than merely development.

Chapter 8 by Cox, deals with the problem of resources under different and often conflicting jurisdictions. Throughout the world, many resources are used by a diversity of users and often came under the authority of several different political authorities. In formulating management approaches, the resource manager/administrator faces the problem of developing a conceptual framework: which characteristics of the resource should be counted as contributing to critical similarities and differences? Cox develops such a typology applicable to common-property resources as a class, based on the nature of the resource, property rights, and the scale of the user pool. The typology is then applied to Chesapeake Bay fisheries of the eastern United States. The chapter alerts Third World resource managers to the implications of the resource-management bureaucracy that threatens to come from the West, strangling the community with laws. Cox shows how impossibly complicated government institutions and regulations could become when the state insists on managing resources without sharing responsibility with communities of users.

The final chapter in Part 2 by Goodland, Ledec and Webb, deals with the economics–ecology interface in the context of development projects in Third World countries. Extending the critique of economic practice introduced in Chapter 3, the authors provide a rich set of examples, showing how environmental degradation may result from the breakdown of traditional common-property systems; economically unjustified development projects; and interestingly, even from economically justified projects. An eye-opener on the yang of conventional neoclassical economics, the chapter explains how economic analysis can be modified and supplemented by ecological criteria, and suggests policy changes by which such an objective can be achieved.

Collectively, the four chapters in Part 2 provide a soul-searching, critical review of issues and a questioning of the commonly held assumptions behind resource-management theory and practice. Having dealt with yang and evaluated what is worth conserving in Western management science, Part 2 sets the stage for the consideration of case studies to deal with some of the yin.

6 Graphs and Gaffs: A Cautionary Tale in the Common-Property Resources Debate

Milton M.R. Freeman

An opening proposition

In relation to the issue of improving common-property-resources management I wish to examine a paradox from a sociology-of-science perspective. With so much empirical evidence now suggesting that traditionally-based local-level management can often be effective, and with an equally large literature suggesting that many non-local state-management systems are both costly and often ineffective, why is more effort not directed to re-establishing the conditions whereby local-level management systems can be made to work?

The caribou crisis reconsidered

To address the question of why there is not more development of renewable-resources management to local-level users I will refer to a long-standing phenomenon of common-property-resource management in arctic and subarctic North America: namely, the recurring appearance of the 'caribou crisis'. This event has surfaced periodically and perhaps most dramatically in Canada (due to media attention) in the 1950s. A more recent episode was announced around 1980, and featured the same two herds that were in crisis 30 years earlier. The 'crisis' is noted by state managers of the resource, whose population surveys periodically indicate progressive decline in the numbers of one or other of the migratory barren-ground caribou herds. The traditional users, having a longer association with caribou, frequently view caribou demography quite differently – often in far less alarmist terms. In the latest 'caribou-crisis', the state management agencies predicted the virtual extinction of two formerly very large caribou herds occupying an extensive range immediately to the west of Hudson Bay. This 'extinction' was to occur within a very few years unless remedial actions were taken immediately by way of harvest restriction and wolf removals (Calef, 1979; Graves, 1980; Munro, 1981; Thomas, 1981). As in earlier 'caribou crises', the state management biologists claimed to have diagnosed the problem, predicted the inexorable outcome and devised a solution, all with quantitatively precise intelligence.

But there are several worrisome features to this particular state-management model, some of which are addressed by other authors in this volume. Though I will not deal with the issues comprehensively here I do wish briefly to address three particular concerns. First, one main aspect of the theoretical basis of northern wildlife management practice; second, caribou census data and the manner of its manipulation; and third, the nature and limitation of natural science as a basis for wildlife management.

Theoretical basis of state wildlife management

The orthodox and widely accepted position taken by manager-biologists is that man (in the arctic and subarctic) and the renewable resources upon which he depends exist in a modified prey–predator relationship. This essentially biological model proposes that in historic times the human predator was kept in balance with food supply in such Malthusian checks as starvation, disease and density-dependent suppression of natural fertility. The primitive technology available in pre-modern times precluded the possibility of overharvesting. From this mostly traditional situation, subsequent contact with modern society caused serious ecological imbalances to occur. For example, new imported technology made killing animals much easier; medical and welfare services resulted in a human population explosion; and population density increased dramatically as people exchanged their nomadic and traditional ways for sedentary living in permanent settlements.

This transformation, the argument goes, occurring over the past one or two generations in Northern Canada, has resulted in the complete loss of natural checks on overharvesting and the consequent need for externally imposed regulations to protect wildlife and fish stocks from the uncontrolled and excessive harvesting that will be the inevitable result (Calef, 1981, p. 166–8; Macpherson, 1981; Mitchell and Reeves, 1980, p. 693; Theberge, 1981). This particular scientific orthodoxy necessarily denies the existence of any traditional resource-management systems, citing as evidence the notion of 'Pleistocene overkill' which is alleged to have occurred when early hunters first came into contact with large mammal species following the ice ages (discussed in Freeman, 1985). If such views reflected reality, we would expect wildlife to be scarce over much of the Canadian north where the native population has about doubled in the past 20 years; where few state-imposed harvest quotas are in place or strictly enforced; and where the wildlife harvesting technology has undergone profound improvement.

The actual situation in the north, however, bears little resemblance to the outcome predicted by this particular model. If we consider caribou, one of the most sought-after food species, we find that not only are the populations exceedingly numerous and increasing all over the north at this time, (Bergerud, 1985, p. 155; Sibbeston, 1986, p. 154, 157), but they occur in close proximity to many of the hunting communities. The evidence also suggests that, with a few localized exceptions, marine animals are probably as plentiful as ever. Some of the populations seriously depleted by non-native commercial exploitation in the past (such as bowhead whale, harp seal and walrus) are now evidencing, through increasing numbers, the resilience that characterizes arctic species in general, even in the face of continued hunting activity.

The nature of the database – and of natural science

The nature of western science is generally not well understood by its practitioners, though it has been well studied by the historians, philosophers and sociologists of science. However, the writings of these scholars remain unread by many practical men and women of science, who obtain their understanding of scientific culture, usually informally, from their practitioner-mentors. In this way, the ideals and myths of science are passed on to succeeding generations of scientists. For example, science is generally held to be objective, critical, directed toward rigorous searching for and uncovering of the 'truth'. It is quantitative, hence precise, and it tests its findings by means of objective experimentation and replication. As an institution, it relies upon a critical and impartial peer-review system to ensure high standards of work, and this internal review system is quite capable of uncovering any professional improprieties.

It follows from the above that cases of fraud (say by falsifying data or results, by selectively withholding information or by plagiarism) would easily be detected, exceedingly rare and perhaps, over time, might even be eradicated. One troubling feature, however, is that in practice fraud is very hard to detect, harder to prove, and yet is by no means uncommon according to a number of writers (references in Broad and Wade, 1982; Kilbourne and Kilbourne, 1983). Fraud in science is not something associated with 'losers'; the list includes many of the great names: Ptolemy, Galileo, Newton, Dalton, Darwin, Mendel, as well as a host of lesser players (though including at least two Nobel laureates). These lesser players' exploits are noteworthy nevertheless, because they were perpetrated at leading research institutes like Harvard, Yale, the Sloan Kettering Research Institute, the US National Institutes of Health, the US National Cancer Institute and the Rockerfeller Institute to name some of the better known (Broad and Wade, 1982).

In considering problems associated with resource management, however, it is especially important that agency scientists ascertain with honesty the true status of the resource stocks whose management is their responsibility.

Indeed, scientists in government employment are often the only people with the financial and technical resources to obtain this information. There is certainly a widely held public perception that government science-based management agencies are quite neutral in respect to management problems and therefore can be expected to provide objective information on the resource stock. On the other hand, it is a widely held belief among state management personnel, that resource users' objectivity is necessarily compromised by the evident self-interest that users have in the resources upon which, to varying degrees, they depend.

However, with respect to scientists' detachment from the issues they study, investigations indicate that scientists are not guided by objectivity and logic alone, but also by a host of decidedly personal (subjective) dispositions. In this sense scientists are no different from other people (see Chapter 7). 'In donning the white coat at the laboratory door, [scientists] do not step aside from the passions, ambitions and failings that animate those in other walks of life. *Modern science is a career.* Its stepping stones are published articles in the scientific literature' (Broad and Wade, 1982, p. 19; emphasis added).

Keeping science honest

Various writers have discussed aspects of the problem of keeping scientists honest and ethical in regard to publishing the results of their work. These problems include, for example, failure to comply with requests for raw data (Wolins, 1962; Craig and Reese, 1973), of publishing trivia (May, 1968; Mulkay and Williams, 1971), or publishing repetitively and obscurely (Wade, 1983). But as one commentator observed: 'Scientists know the games of science. They are all aware of trivial publications, fudged data, edifice complexes and outright theft. There is nothing new to the insider here. But scientists do not admit these sorts of things to the laity' (Higgins, 1983. p. 13).

Why should resource-management biologists fudge data – if indeed they do? Why should they make extravagant claims about the predictive power of their theories? Some of the problems associated with 'keeping science honest' in general (Freeman, 1977) and among wildlife biologists in particular (Campbell, 1982) are discussed elsewhere, but in connection with the present discussion I would offer three answers.

The first has already been alluded to: scientists are like most other people in having strong personal feelings about issues close to them, including ensuring advancement in their careers. Second, scientists have been trained to believe that their approach to understanding nature, and their resulting expertise, represent the best available approximation to 'the truth' and should therefore form the basis of rational decision-making in management matters.

And third, we need to remember that many issues involving science and society take place in a public, as well as a scientific, arena. In public situations lower standards of proof are asked for and offered. The result is often utterances by scientists of mere supposition, offered as scientifically proven fact – a class of evidence that has been labelled 'trans-science' (Weinberg, 1976, p. 341).

In these public debates (as well as in some scientific discussions) it is not uncommon to find scientists willing to assume an advocacy position on one side or another of a controversial issue. Such positions often require resorting to trans-science opinions due to limitations of available data, or the inherent limitations of science to produce definitive answers to complex problems.

The limitation of science

The uncertainty inherent in scientific findings presents a real problem to scientists having to deal with the widespread misperception of the power of science to deliver the truth. The stark reality is that, over time, nearly all current scientific knowledge will be replaced by new knowledge; the later knowledge being found, in turn, to be imperfect. Not only are current scientific facts not the truth (merely some approximation), science is unable to say what form the truth, if discovered, will take. 'The clearest induction from the history of science is that science is always mistaken . . . [so] then we have no reasonable alternative but to suppose that much or all of what we ourselves vaunt as scientific knowledge is itself presumably wrong' (Rescher, 1984, p. 86).

From the perspective of the epistemology of science, wildlife and fishery biologists face a particularly vexing and insoluble problem: in science there is always a trade-off between the precision of a finding and the extent of its general applicability (see for example, Levins, 1966). In the sense that scientists often aim to discover universal theories, precision is necessarily sacrificed. Science, within a particular paradigm, advances by successively refining these imprecise estimations of reality. However, increased certainty of the estimate can only be purchased at the cost of its detailed content (Rescher, 1984, p. 78–80; Levins, 1966, p. 422). This suggests that scientific rigour (in the quantitative sense of laboratory-based research) in renewable-resources management will remain problematic.

Yet another reason for this biological approach to be flawed is the limitation of orthodox reductionist, linear thinking to solving problems of an ecological nature. The orthodox, reductionist, analytic approach used by most biologists is a hold-over from much earlier times when a limited mechanistic view of the universe was applied to living systems. Rational thinking in those days required linear thinking, whereas 'ecosystems' are sustained in dynamic balance involving cycles and fluctuations anything but linear (see also Chapters 3 and 7).

For true ecological understanding to be gained, it may well be that we need to

combine our rational knowledge with an intuition for the non-linear nature of our environment. Such intuitive wisdom is characteristic of traditional, non-literate cultures, in which life was organized around a highly refined awareness of the environment. In the mainstream of our culture, on the other hand, the cultivation of intuitive wisdom has been neglected   (Capra 1982:25).

These remarks, by a theoretical physicist, call for the recognition of the importance and reintegration of intuition, of human consciousness, into the biological sciences that has already occurred in modern physics. Later in this chapter, the views of mathematician S. Tanaka will be introduced in order to illustrate how such an intuition-based system can be used to rationalize renewable resource management.

The caribou case study

Gaff: To fix for the purpose of cheating; hoax, fraud; trick, abuse.
                    (Webster's Seventh New Collegiate Dictionary)

Caribou occupy a special place in the mind of the Canadian public, for in important ways they symbolize the northern wilderness that is so quintessentially Canadian. Insofar as the Canadian public reacts to adverse accounts of the status of northern caribou, the species has considerable political significance. The federal government, for example, has for many years funded and maintained a fairly impressive caribou research programme.

Given the foregoing considerations, it is not surprising that a federal government report, entitled *Environmental Issues in Canada: A Status Report* selected caribou to illustrate the importance of wildlife-conservation programmes in Canada. In this report, graphical representation of the population status of nine northern caribou herds was presented (Canada, 1985, p. 17). Figure 6.1 suggests that in the 1970–80 decade overall caribou numbers were declining in the arctic, and furthermore that only three of the nine herds were increasing in size.

However, there are serious reasons to question this particular representation of overall and specific herd decline. Though the published material was assembled in 1984, by that date government reports were readily available indicating that four of the caribou herds shown in the 1985 report as decreasing were, in fact, increasing.

Figure 6.1 is misleading, for with respect to each herd, the top line is given a negative slope thereby creating the impression that each of the nine

Estimated Caribou Herd Populations 1970-1980

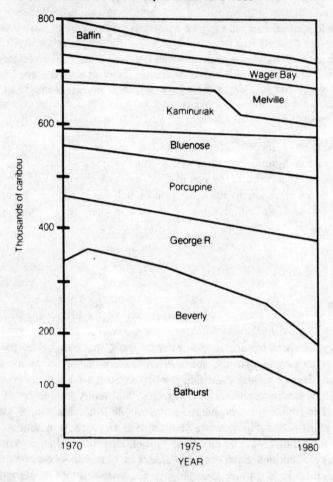

Figure 6.1 Graph of barren-ground-caribou population trends published by the
Department of the Environment (Canada 1985).

herds is declining in size. More careful examination, however, indicates that
only the Bathurst, Beverly, Kaminuriak and Baffin herds are represented as
declining in size. Furthermore, in Figure 6.1 the George River herd is
represented as doubling in size over the 1970–80 decade; however, in Figure
6.2, utilizing readily available official reports, this herd is seen to be
quadrupling over the same span of time.

The misrepresentation of information in Figure 6.1 occurs for all herds in
relation to official data available in 1984. For present purposes of illustration
here, however, only two herds are chosen, one of which was subject to the

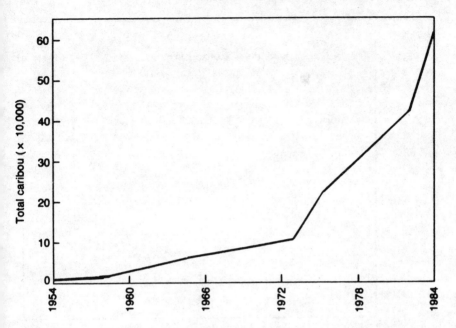

Figure 6.2 Graph of the George River caribou population trend (Jackson 1986).

most recent 'caribou crisis' episode (the Kaminuriak herd) and another (the Melville herd) which reflects a general problem in caribou management – namely the relative paucity of population data.

In Figure 6.3, available data indicate that the estimated population of the Kaminuriak herd was believed to be around 30,000 animals, with little evidence of either a population decline or increase during the 1970-80 decade. However, by 1982, government studies indicated that the herd had suddenly increased about five-fold, and over the next one or two years a nine-fold increase was registered. Whatever the explanation for this unexpected increase, it should at the very least suggest that the census results from the immediately preceding years require critical re-evaluation (see, for example, Anon, 1982: 4,12).

In similar fashion, though with less research to support the conclusions, the 'explosive' population increase in the Melville herd (illustrated in Figure 6.4) clearly does not support the representation in Figure 6.1. Since caribou rarely have more than one young per year, a rate of increase greater than 25 per cent per year is biologically unlikely. It follows, therefore, that the changes shown in Figures 6.3 and 6.4 are not biologically 'real', and are very probably due to problems associated with censusing the caribou herds. Once the methods were improved, resulting in larger population estimates, the earlier data clearly became suspect, yet appear to have been deliberately used

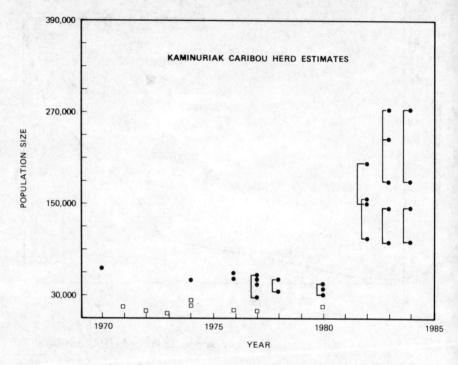

Figure 6.3 Plot of all existing population estimates for the Kaminuriak caribou herd, published and unpublished sources, 1970–1985. Open symbols denote calving ground surveys only.
Note: The author is able to provide on request bibliographic references for the 23 sources used to construct Figures 6.3 and 6.4.

by the state managers to support the notion of another 'caribou crisis'. In this sense, the gaff that has occurred results less from the dubious representation of negative population trends in Figure 6.1, and more from use of data that at the time should have been acknowledged as problematic and unreliable.

This recent incident suggests that state-management agencies are not always critical, nor rigorous, nor objective, and that the 'science' used in support of management objectives may well be more 'trans-science' than real science. (Chapter 12 has some parallels.)

In regard to the case study being considered here, what reasons would state managers have for misrepresenting caribou population trends by engaging in trans-science? First, the possibility may exist that the publication in question was the result of poor work: that is was not checked against the most recent information. However, this appears unlikely to be the case (Macpherson, 1985). A more likely explanation depends upon considering the increasingly intense competition for budgetary resources, and especially for research funds

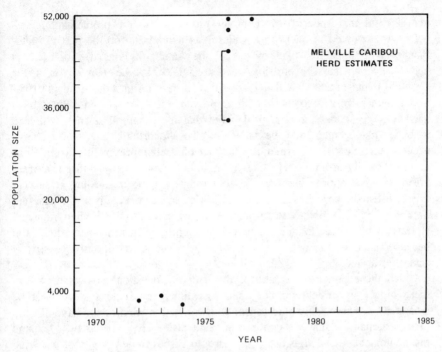

Figure 6.4   Plot of all existing population estimates for the Melville caribou population, published and unpublished sources, 1970–1985.

(Anon, 1985, p. 2) at a time when the state-manager's role in wildlife management is being challenged as never before by progressive advances in native self-government. Under such agency-threatening circumstances, an announcement that the great northern caribou herds are faced with the danger of extinction might reasonably be expected to generate public support (for mitigative action) that any government department would be pleased to receive at the best of times. However, the caribou report was not released at the best of times: Environment Canada was facing a loss of 400 positions, including 84 in the Canadian Wildlife Service (a staff reduction of 23 per cent) whose budget was reduced by 17 per cent; hardest hit were research programmes (Anon, 1985, p. 10).

The search for new management approaches

> The science that claims a monopoly on the road to knowledge, forfeits its claim that it is a good road or that the destination will be constructive for humankind
> (Forthman 1983:224).

Where does this discussion leave state management vis-a-vis local management in respect to the common-property-resource problematique?

I have attempted to question a widespread assumption on the part of state-management agencies that more of the same (biological) research is necessarily the most promising road to follow in the search for better resource management. I will not deny that more relevant ecological information is generally a precondition for improved state management. But I have tried to suggest that the uncritical belief that more natural science will lead to better management may be fallacious. To support this conclusion I have argued that scientific information does not of itself represent the 'truth', nor is it necessarily progressively 'better' in an operational sense. Indeed, current information or approaches may be so wrong as to be misleading. I suspect this is often the case in fishery and wildlife management, given the inherent limitation both of field-based scientific research itself, the limited financial resources allocated to the complex problem(s) under investigation, and because much of the debate takes place in a public, as opposed to strictly scientific arena.

Given these possible limitations, the daunting question remains: how can these highly dynamic, complex, and essentially stochastic systems best be managed? In answer, I would repeat with conviction what others have already proposed, namely that we continue to look elsewhere – not only to expand the ecological knowledge base, but also to discover new ways of knowing how best to mediate our environmental interdependencies.

Looking elsewhere is currently being done by individual scientists (and various science-based international agencies) who recognize the relevance of traditional resource-users' knowledge in the search for improved management practices. An extensive literature now exists with respect to this issue, involving various resource stocks and geographical areas (for example, Lasserre and Ruddle, 1983; Morauta et al. 1982; Ruddle and Johannes, 1985; Williams and Hunn, 1982; see also Berkes, 1985).

With respect to North American caribou management more especially, some recognition now exists as to the shortcomings of the scientific research upon which state management is based (Bergerud, 1979, p. 556). Moreover, in northern Canada, innovative changes in management institutions have occurred in order to improve the situation by having scientist-managers and traditional users jointly constituting the management authority (Monaghan, 1984; Drolet et al, 1987). This has also resulted in new approaches being taken to setting the governmental research agenda for caribou.

The efficacy of traditional resource-management systems in various northern Canada societies has been reported upon. For example, Cree Indian management of beaver (Feit, 1973), fish (Berkes, 1977), geese (Berkes, 1982) and moose (Feit, 1987) in historic and contemporary subarctic subsistence harvesting arrangements. Elsewhere I have supposed that a similar case can be made in respect of the legitimacy and relevance of Inuit environmental knowledge to contemporary resource management activities (Freeman, 1975; 1979; 1985; in press).

In seeking new approaches to managing exploited living-resource stocks, it is important to institute feedback-control systems so that the management system itself will signal the need to reduce harvest levels when the stock falls below some appropriate size. In this regard, it can be noted that a common feature of many of the traditional management systems referred to earlier is that the harvesters have access to a lengthy time-series of data by species, season and locality, in addition to extensive information that tends to emphasize relationships between species and various environmental parameters. Moreover, it should be recognized that determination of the 'appropriate' size of harvest is not a question for science alone to decide, as indeed the continuing disputes over wildlife and fishery management means and goals indicate. As discussed in Chapter 3, technical solutions, such as offered by MSY, are open to criticism on both ecological and social grounds.

For the purpose of the present discussion about alternative common-property resource-management systems, instituting a traditional user-based approach seems especially appropriate. First, such an empirically-based approach represents a movement away from the highly abstract modelling techniques currently in vogue among managers – techniques that depend upon large inputs of unknown, and often unknowable, data. Second, this tradition-based approach is especially significant as it relies upon data and techniques of analysis that local resource users can control and utilize in real time, so as to take locally sanctioned corrective actions with a minimum of delay. And third, it moves the focus of responsibility for management to those with the greatest direct stake in the sustainable utilization of the resource stock.

The traditional user/steward approach to management, based, *inter alia*, upon changes in catch per unit of harvesting effort (CPUE), is unlikely to require any modification in values or beliefs among local resource users. However, acceptance of this approach by scientist-managers requires their recognition that alternative ways of comprehending the complexities of resource-stock dynamics are possible and may indeed lead to improved management programmes even if based upon apparently 'non-scientific' systems of knowledge. Whereas some biological modellers remain doubtful of the utility of this particular approach (for example, de la Mare 1986a; 1986b), other scientists are calling for just such an integration of intuitive approaches which appears to be an especially promising way out of the stagnation that current paradigms force upon the natural sciences (Capra, 1975) and upon biological research more especially (Capra, 1982). One proposal to adopt such a new renewable-resource-management scheme is that of Tanaka (1986) which will be briefly and generally described below.

Feedback and learning in management systems

Tanaka introduces his new management proposal by reference to two contrasting ways of cracking an egg. The first means is the usual household method of taking the egg in one or two hands and applying an appropriate amount of force to the shell. A second method could be by constructing a robot which simulates the motions of human fingers, hands and arms. It is clear that in the latter case a small error in measuring the strength of each individual eggshell (a key component in the mathematical model required to programme the robot) would result in failure. The person cracking an egg can also experience failure, especially on the first few occasions of attempting the task. However, for most people, the complex and coordinated actions required are successfully learned after minimal trial and error. Despite the high degree of success an experienced egg-cracker can quickly attain, the actions are varied, delicate and highly integrated: to pick up the egg without cracking the shell, grip the egg in the fingers with sufficient firmness to control it without damage, apply the exact amount of force to the shell to ensure controlled breakage without damaging the yolk within the egg, or shattering the shell so that it mixes with the content of the egg.

According to Tanaka, management of whale stocks (he could as easily have referred to caribou or other wildlife or fishery stocks) has been elaborated on procedures analogous to those required to build an egg-cracking machine, even though ascertaining values of MSY – MSY level and population size for example – are far more difficult than ascertaining the strength of individual egg shells. Therefore, he suggests that due to the inherent variability and consequent uncertainties of determining biological stock-population parameters, the basis of managing these stocks should be reoriented away from approaches that appear to be based upon the concept of building a machine, and toward the concept based upon a human hand. Tanaka suggests that basic to the new, 'intuitive', approach are two essential requirements: feedback of information and learning. He urges that both simplicity and an empirical basis be adopted in developing models/approaches which are necessarily based upon insufficient data and insufficient understanding of reality; he cautions that any other approach to problem-solving can lead to dangerously wrong results.

Tanaka proposes a management approach that does not require knowing various stock parameters nor undertaking complex modelling exercises, but rather, is based upon easily and empirically derived indirect measures of stock circumstance, in this case CPUE. Rather than attempt to ascertain catch limits by complex modelling exercises and computer-based calculation of MSY or RY (replacement yield), it is more easily determined that if CPUE declines, then the catch exceeds RY. The management response will be to reduce the harvest level so as to allow the stock to recover to the level where CPUE values regain their normative/acceptable level.

In the case of depleted stocks, the decision as to what proportion of RY would be allocated to the increase in stock, as opposed to harvest quota, is another management decision based on empirically weighing many of the local considerations (socioeconomic as well as environmental) that have appropriate bearing upon management decisions yet cannot ordinarily be factored into complex mathematical models. Following this approach, catch limits for any year can be determined by increasing or reducing the catch limits set the preceding year. It is not necessary to know various population values; however, the experience of the past (which reflects the integrated value of all these unknown variables) is used in an intuitive feedback system to determine a new harvest level by modification of an earlier empirically derived value. The important feature of this approach is that CPUE is used as a relative index of population, obviating the need for accurately determining the absolute population figure.

Tanaka refers to simulation studies undertaken to test the resilience of this approach in the face of possible misapplication. Some of his findings show, for example, that the system becomes unstable under certain conditions, namely where significantly elevating catch limits because CPUE values are higher than should be the case. In such instances, he found that a 1 per cent decrease in CPUE should be followed by a 5 per cent decrease in harvest level. However, he observed that if such precautions are followed, very stable catches are possible from a stable population (of unknown size).

It is known that even empirically derived values of CPUE can contain errors. Tanaka's simulation studies indicated that ten-year averages overcame the adverse effects of inadvertent error, and that applying appropriate modification to harvest levels reduced the mathematical possibility of stock extinction to zero.

An important feature of this approach is that being locally and empirically based, any environmental change that requires modification of the assigned harvest level is applied automatically. Over time, knowledge that accumulates from operating this type of management system becomes intuitively incorporated into the system to improve its sensitivity.

This is precisely the manner in which tradition-based systems worldwide have successfully operated for long periods of time.

Conclusion

This chapter opened with a question: Why is so little effort directed to re-establishing the conditions whereby local-level management systems can be made to work? The evidence presented here, as a case study, suggests that self-interest on the part of state managers constitutes one very real impediment to progressive change that might allow the introduction of more effective management institutions.

The practice of science necessarily involves uncertainty. In scientific wildlife management these uncertainties can be readily mobilized in the service of non-science goals if the spectre of biological extinction is introduced as a potential consequence of imprudent resource exploitation. Extinction implies irreversible finality, as well as invoking such emotive and accusatory notions as tragedy, ignorance, greed and human weakness. Clearly, no decision-making officials or their advisors wish to stand accused of permitting such failures to overtake common-property resources whose conservation is their direct responsibility.

Science-based management, however, appears to offer managers a way of restricting the uncertainty inherent in natural-resource management; it is, after all, 'scientific', thus promising a degree of rationality and precision that non-scientific approaches are believed to lack. It is therefore to be expected that decision-makers, grounded in the belief that science offers a powerful means of exerting 'control', and largely ignorant of alternative non-western cultural traditions, will necessarily remain partial to the advice originating from science-based state-management institutions. For their part, scientists are generally held to be purveyors of certified knowledge, and are unlikely to seek to diminish their professional stature by admitting to non-scientists the tenuousness of their findings (see Mulkay, 1979, p. 117).

In conclusion therefore, it is suggested that until public awareness of the efficacy of traditional systems of management becomes widespread, public policy will continue to favour a conservative approach toward resource management, ensuring continuation of orthodox science-based approaches. However, at the same time as various environmental agencies are slowly acknowledging the value of tradition-based alternative systems of management, philosophers are independently beginning to recognize the serious limitations associated with the mechanistic approaches to investigating natural processes, an awareness sparked by recent advances in physics and new approaches to health and healing. The practical, if limited, success of various cooperative management arrangements in northern North America demonstrate that in certain circumstances (often, it seems, precipitated by crisis) resources users and state-management officials can work together effectively to improve resource management. Insofar as these cooperative institutions work in the best interest of both local users and state managers by ensuring socially aware sustainable utilization of resources, there are grounds for optimism with respect to the further introduction of progressive change and fewer gaffs in future graphs.

Acknowledgements

The author acknowledges the research assistance provided by Leonard Smith and the helpful criticism of an earlier draft of this paper by Fikret Berkes and three anonymous reviewers. Support from the Social Sciences and Humanities Research Council of Canada is also acknowledged.

References

Anon, 1982: 'Population increases cast doubt on previous counts', *Caribou News* 2(3), p. 4,12.

Anon, 1985a: 'Endangered species at the CWS', *Caribou News* 4(5), p. 2.

Anon,1985b: 'Environment Canada budget cuts strike hard at much Canadian Wildlife Service Research', *Caribou News* 4(5), p. 10.

Bergerud, A.T., 1979: 'A review of the population dynamics of caribou and wild reindeer in North America', in Reimer, E., Gaare, E. and Skienneberg, S., eds, *Proceedings of the Second Reindeer/Caribou Symposium*, Trondheim.

Bergerud, A.T., 1985: Letter to the editor, *Arctic*, 38(2), p. 155–6.

Berkes, Fikret, 1977: 'Fishery resource use in a subarctic Indian community', *Human Ecology*, 5, pp. 289–307.

Berkes, Fikret, 1982: 'Waterfowl management and northern native peoples with reference to Cree hunters of James Bay', *The Musk-ox*, 30, pp. 23–35.

Berkes, F., 1985: 'Fishermen and the tragedy of the commons', *Environmental Conservation*, 12(3), pp. 199–206.

Broad, William and Wade, Nicholas, 1982: *Betrayers of the Truth*, Simon and Schuster, New York.

Calef, G.W. 1979: 'The population status of caribou in the Northwest Territories', *Progress Report 1*, NWT Wildlife Service, Yellowknife.

Calef, George, 1981: *Caribou and the barren-lands*, Canadian Arctic Resources Committee, Ottawa and Firefly Books, Toronto.

Campbell, Brian, 1982: *Disputes among experts: a sociological case study of the debate over biology in the Mackenzie Valley Pipeline Inquiry*, PhD dissertation, McMaster University, Hamilton, Ontario.

Canada, 1985: *Environmental Issues in Canada: A Status Report*, Environment Canada, Ottawa.

Capra, Fritjof, 1975: *The Tao of physics*, Shambhala, Berkeley.

Capra, Fritjof, 1982: *The Turning Point: Science, Society and the Rising Culture*, Simon and Schuster, New York.

Craig, J.R. and Reese, S.C., 1973: 'Retention of raw data: a problem revisited', *American Psychologist*, 28, p. 723.

de la Mare, W., 1986a: 'Further consideration of the statistical properties of catch and effort data models to indices of relative abundance', in *Report of the International Whaling Commission*, 36, pp. 419–23.

de la Mare, W., 1986b: 'Fitting population models to time series of abundance data', in *Report of the International Whaling Commission*, 36, pp. 399–418.

Drolet, C.A., Reed, A., Breton, M. and Berkes, F., 1987: 'Sharing wildlife management responsibilities with Native groups: case histories in Northern Quebec', in *Transactions of the 52nd North American Wildlife and Natural Resources Conference*, pp. 389–98.

Feit, H.A., 1973: 'The ethno-ecology of the Waswanipi Cree: or how hunters can manage their resources', in Cox, B., ed., *Cultural Ecology: Reading on Canadian Indians and Eskimos*, McClelland and Stewart, Toronto.

Feit, H.A., 1987: 'North American native hunting and management of moose populations', *Swedish Wildlife Research*, 1987 Suppl. 1, pp. 25–42.

Forthman, Robert C., 1983: 'Summary: three perspectives on deviance in science', in Kilbourne, B.K. and Kilbourne, M.T., eds, *The Dark Side of Science*, American Association for the Advancement of Science, San Francisco.

Freeman, Milton M.R., 1975: 'Assessing movement in an arctic caribou population', *Journal of Environmental Management*, 3(3), pp. 251–7.

Freeman, Milton M.R., 1977: 'Anthropologists and policy-relevant research: the case for accountability', in Applied Anthropology in Canada, Proceedings no. 4, Canadian Ethnology Society, Hamilton, Ontario.

Freeman, Milton M.R., 1979: 'Traditional land users as a legitimate source of environmental expertise', in Nelson, J.G., Needham, R.D., Nelson, S.H. and Scace, R.C., eds, *Canadian National Parks: Today and Tomorrow, Conference II*, volume 1, Studies in Land Use History and Landscape Change, no. 7. Waterloo.

Freeman, Milton M.R., 1985: 'Appeal to tradition: different perspectives on arctic wildlife management', in Brøsted, J., Dahl, J. et al, eds, *Native Power: The Quest for Autonomy and Nationhood of Indigenous Peoples*, Universitetsforlaget, Oslo.

Freeman, Milton M.R., in press: 'The Alaska Eskimo whaling commission: successful co-management under extreme conditions', in Pinkerton, E., ed., *Co-operative management of local fisheries*, University of British Columbia Press, Vancouver.

Graves, Jonquil, 1980: *Barren-ground caribou of the Northwest Territories*, Arctic Wildlife Series, NWT Wildlife Service, Yellowknife.

Higgins, A.C., 1983: 'The games of science: science watching', in Kilbourne, B.K. and Kilbourne, M.T., eds, *The Dark Side of Science*, American Association for the Advancement of Science, San Francisco.

Jackson, Lawrence, 1986: 'World's largest caribou herd mired in Quebec-Labrador boundary dispute', *Canadian Geographic*, 105(3), pp. 25–33.

Kilbourne, Brock K. and Kilbourne, Maria T., eds, 1983: *The Dark Side of Science*, Proceedings of the 63rd Annual Meeting, American Association for the Advancement of Science, San Francisco.

Lasserre, Pierre and Ruddle, Kenneth, 1983: 'Traditional knowledge and management of marine coastal systems', *Biology International*, Special Issue 4.

Levins, R., 1966: 'The strategy of model building in population biology', *American Scientist*, 54, pp. 421–31.

Macpherson, A.H., 1981: 'Commentary: wildlife conservation and Canada's north', *Arctic*, 34(2), pp. 103–7.

Macpherson, A.H., 1985: 'Environmental issues in Canada: a status report', *Environmental Awareness*, 8(4), p. i.

May, K.O., 1968: 'Growth and quality of the mathematical literature', *Isis*, 59, pp. 363–71.

Mitchell, E.D. and Reeves, R.R., 1980: 'The Alaska bowhead problem: a commentary', *Arctic*, 33(4), pp. 686–723.

Monaghan, Hugh J., 1984: 'The Caribou Management Board and its early growth', in *National and Regional Interests in the North: Third National Workshop on People, Resources and the Environment North of 60*, Canadian Arctic Resources Committee, Ottawa.

Morauta, Louise, Pernetta, John and Heaney, William, eds, 1982: *Traditional conservation in Papua New Guinea: implications for today*, Institute of Applied Social and Economic Research, Monograph 16, Boroko, Papua New Guinea.

Mulkay, M.J., 1979: *Science and the Sociology of Knowledge*, George Allen and Unwin, London.

Mulkay, M.J. and Williams, A.T., 1971: 'A sociological study of a physics department', *British Journal of Sociology*, 22, pp. 68–82.

Munro, John C., 1981: 'Letter from Minister of Indian and Northern Affairs', *Caribou News*, 1(1), p. 2.

Rescher, Nicholas, 1984: *The Limits of Science*, University of California Press, Berkeley.

Ruddle, Kenneth and Johannes, R.E., eds, 1985: *The Traditional Knowledge and Management of Coastal Systems in Asia and the Pacific*, UNESCO, Jakarta.

Sibbeston, N., 1986: 'Economic development and renewable resources in the Northwest Territories', in *Native People and Renewable Resource Management*, Alberta Society of Professional Biologists, 1986 Symposium, Edmonton.

Tanaka, S., 1986: 'On a practical method for stock assessment', International Whaling Commission, *Document SC/A86/CA5*, Cambridge.

Theberge, John B., 1981: 'Commentary: Conservation in the north: an ecological perspective', *Arctic*, 34(4), pp. 281–5.

Thomas, D.C., 1981: *At the crossroads of caribou management in Northern Canada*, Canadian Nature Federation, Ottawa.

Wade, Nicholas, 1983: 'Frauds from 1960 to the present: bad apples or a bad barrel?', in Kilbourne, B.K. and Kilbourne, M.T., eds, *The Dark Side of Science*, American Association for the Advancement of Science, San Francisco.

Weinberg, Alvin M., 1976: 'Science in the public forum: keeping it honest', *Science*, 191, p. 341.

Williams, N.M. and Hunn, E.S., eds, 1982: *Resource Managers: North American and Australian Hunter-gatherers*, American Association for the Advancement of Science, Selected Symposium 67, Westview Press, Colorado.

Wolins, Leroy, 1962: 'Responsibility for raw data', *American Psychologist*, 17, pp. 657–8.

7 Reforming the Use of Natural Resources

Henry A. Regier, Richard V. Mason and Fikret Berkes

Summary

The conventional approach to the development of natural resources is in need of reform. Our experience with the most 'successful' conventional exploitive development is that it is not ecologically sustainable and often leads to the marginalization of local populations dependent on these resources. In the contemporary world, there are precious few healthy and productive ecosystems that are waiting for sustainable development to occur. Most ecosystems of the world are already degraded and have to be nursed back to a productive state before appropriate redevelopment may take place. We use the term 'reform-sustainable redevelopment' to refer to this task of transforming degraded ecosystems into ones in which uses are sustained ecologically and allocated equitably.

The chapter explores ways and means of reforming resource use, and concludes that mere fine tuning of current practice, addressing symptoms rather than root causes, is unlikely to lead to productive man–nature ecosystems. Governance regimes dependent upon hard-core administrative and market controls are not as likely to succeed as those emphasizing stewardship and community-based self-help. Our own experience with the rehabilitation of the Great Lakes of North America is that appropriate Western science for resource use cannot be the conventional, reductionistic science often used by resource-management agencies but rather *ecosystem science* explicitly dealing with human societies as part of natural systems. Such people-oriented ecosystem approaches are consistent with various stewardship traditions in the West, as well as with many Third World communal-property systems incorporating an apparent understanding of the interconnectedness of resources and people.

Introduction

The concept of common-property resource, CPR, is anything but simple and transparent – as other chapters of this volume demonstrate. Each of the three words in the concept has complex connotations, some of which have become strongly coloured by ideological content. Paint them red, blue, green – whatever! Is it possible to transcend much of these conventional polarizations and deal with some of the CPR issues in an unconventional way?

In this chapter we sketch some rather general trends of recent history as they relate to CPR. We propose reform-sustainable redevelopment as an alternative to conventional exploitive development for large regions of the world that have become degraded due to the latter process. We examine trends in governance regimes as societies try to cope with the systematic interconnectedness that now permeates all aspects of our locales, regions and global community. We re-examine the old heartland–hinterland motif. We end with an examination of recent progress with an ecosystem approach in the Great Lakes Basin and its implication for other areas. Throughout, our dominant theme is CPR as the concept relates to human uses of natural resources. (We use the term 'resource' in the broader sense, as in Chapter 3, of natural phenomena). We also highlight the role of science and scholarship because their currently dominant paradigms generally support the currently dominant ideologies with respect to resource use.

Conventional exploitive development and reform-sustainable redevelopment

Natural resources the world over are being degraded because of direct overuse as with excessive exploitation and because of indirect abuse through pollution, habitat destruction and so on. This has been apparent to informed observers for over a century. Degradation has become more intense and widespread because of increasingly more powerful techniques with massive impact on and deep penetration of ecosystem processes; concentration of the demand for resources and of power to deliver them in distant 'technically advanced' centres; and saturation of use and abuse of ecosystems to the extent that vast ecosystemic slums result. A large proportion of the world's population suffers the consequences of such degradation. Some partial or local corrective measures have been undertaken successfully but at the levels of regions, continents and the globe, degradation has been intensifying on average and in total.

Issues of common-property resources are usually addressed in Western countries with respect to what may be called conventional exploitive development, CED. CED is our characterisation of the dominant nature of the 'development' process wherever it occurs in the world today – East or West, North or South, Occident or Orient (Figure 7.1). In its early stages, CED served its European creators well, in their international imperial and

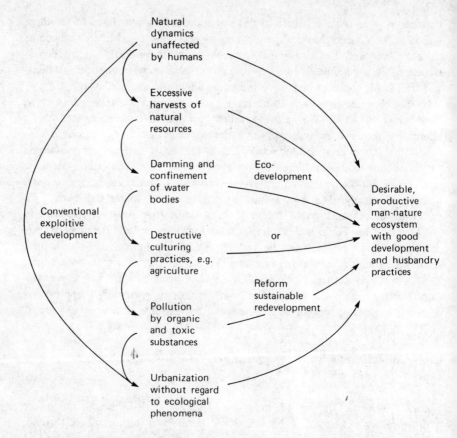

Figure 7.1 Schema illustrating the meaning of conventional exploitive development and ecodevelopment of natural or healthy ecosystems or reform-sustainable redevelopment of degraded ecosystems.

mercantile interests. Its use and rationale have spread to entrepreneurs everywhere, even to the state capitalists of centrally planned economies. To be quite explicit, as currently practised, both state socialism and liberal capitalism are about equally at fault with respect to the practices of CED. We hold a brief for neither ideology.

The CED ideology permeates the science and technique of conventional resourcists and environmentalists (Regier, 1986b), though as technocentrists they may combat the more obnoxious excesses of CED (Pepper, 1984). For example, in fisheries science, the well-known bioeconomic model that relates levels of sustainable harvest (in biomass or financial units) to amounts of effort expended in the harvest (in physical work or financial units) is squarely within the tradition of CED (see Chapter 3). A similar statement applies to conventional forestry (Regier and Baskerville, 1986). More generally CED is central to the conventions that guide international enterprises in the resource-exploitation fields and in their industrial strategies according to which they may locate new polluting industries in foreign pollution havens.

Experts, certified by our schools and professional associations to develop and apply CED policy and techniques, generally do not hold CED to critical account. Programmes intended to protect and enhance valued ecosystem components may be 'assessed', say according to benefit-cost or risk criteria, by techniques firmly in the context of CED (see Chapter 9). Assessment procedures may serve a tempered form of CED. Many professionals serve the vested interests in CED of their employers. The contributions of such professionals may not help to prevent foreclosure of long-term options, or the 'marginalization' of local communities that depended on natural phenomena which were degraded through CED.

The great majority of natural resources that attract the interest of CED entrepreneurs are used in ways that suppress their productivity and then yield harvests below what is considered optimal according to the CED's own hopes. Selective removal of only the most valued ecosystemic component (hygrading), such as the harvest of only certain species in tropical forests, is combined with disruption of ecosystemic productivity due to careless harvesting methods and due to pollution from poorly managed industry and badly planned human communities. Managers may complain that resource and environmental experts do not provide the better information that would prevent such excesses. It is often not a question of inadequate scientific information of the conventional types but rather an approach to development that is fundamentally flawed. When much of the world suffers from conventional exploitive development, one should consider reform-sustainable redevelopment for degraded regions and ecologically sensible development or ecodévelopment for regions still in a healthy state. To put is cautiously, it seems unlikely that mere fine tuning of CED will often lead to progress toward desirable, productive man–nature ecosystems. It might amount to a rather inconsequential fiddling with symptoms rather than corrective of causes (Pepper, 1984). Thoroughgoing reforms are needed.

Figure 7.1 illustrates the role of RSR. Nowadays there exist relatively few ecosystems in a sustainable productive state. Maurice Strong, then of the United Nations Environment Programme, publicized the concept of 'ecodevelopment', implicitly for ecosystems still in a state of general 'health'. The World Conservation Strategy of 1980 has used the similar concept of 'sustainable development'. As yet ecodevelopment or sustainable development has seldom occurred, and large regions have become more degraded. Reform-sustainable redevelopment, RSR, has the task of transforming degraded ecosystems to ones in which enjoyable uses are sustained and allocated equitably.

Many proposals have been made with respect to some goal consistent with what is termed reform-sustainable redevelopment. These include the small community of Arthur Morgan (1942), the land ethic of Aldo Leopold (1949), the intermediate technology of Fritz Schumacher (1973), the communitarianism of Murray Bookchin (1980), the personal naturalistic piety of John Livingston (1981), the ecocentrism of Timothy O'Riordan (Pepper, 1984), the deep ecology of Arne Naess (1985), the ecosystem-as-home doctrine of Jack Vallentyne (1986), and the bioregionalism of Peter Berg (1986). On these questions, the Gandhians may be progressing further than Westeners can imagine (Anarwhal et al., 1982).

Together these ideas provide a collage of thoughts toward RSR and ecodevelopment. Information services and practical policies that follow from these ideas are of a 'post-professional type' in that the actual complexity of an issue is not reduced arbitrarily to the narrow domain of any one professional speciality or discipline (Gamble, 1986). Proposed solutions stress qualities and non-material aspects of evolving relationships: they are not limited to such quantitative, material features as can be reduced into commodities with monetary value. A dominant ethic of respect for the long-term patterns of all nature (including humans) is not suppressed to the here-and-now considerations of the market place.

How do the issues of common property and allocation relate to broad considerations of CED and RSR? We attempt to develop the connections below.

Governance regime

In attempts to understand the reasons for the frequent mismanagement of resources, that issue has often been approached from a consideration of resource ownership and access to the resources by non-owners. In Figures 7.2 to 7.4 we have sketched a broad conceptual framework of how the CPR issue relates to governance regimes. A number of colleagues have contributed over the years to this perspective, and the arguments here continue from Chapter 3.

Figure 7.2 classifies different social practices and political systems with respect to their conventions concerning ownership of property and access to property. 'Property' as used here relates to renewable living resources and the natural environment, and especially to the living but non-human parts of natural ecosystems. No regime uses its favoured approach with every kind of natural resource imaginable, but tends to employ it to manage uses of those phenomena for which there is some competition directly or indirectly.

Concerning the bottom left corner of Figure 7.2, full exercise of private property rights is now virtually impossible in an ecosystemic setting. Air,

	Closed access	Limited access	Open access
Owner-less	Non-legal autarchy, squatters	Protectorate, imperialistic or through U.N. decision	Free anarchy, explorers of uninhabited areas
State owned	Party plutarchy, state capitalism	Democratic socialism and communism	None known
Communally owned	Monastic and idealistic communal movements	Tribal traditions, communitarian groups	None known
Privately owned	Aristocratic autarchy	Liberal capitalistic democracy	Illegal anarchy, poachers

Figure 7.2 Administrative and governance regimes according to dominant norms with respect to ownership and access to natural phenomena. The terms autarchy, plutarchy and anarchy here relate primarily to property rights and not necessarily to all phenomena over which authority may be exercised.

water, inorganic and organic substances, and biota simply cannot be prevented from moving onto, off, or across one's property. Ecological 'neighbours', some as far as thousands of kilometres away, adversely affect these migrant ecosystemic components that in turn affect what is ostensibly private property in some locale. The more intense and/or numerous such adverse systemic interconnections, the less complete will be the package of property rights in practice if not in theory. Thus the 'dimensionality' of the domain of private property/closed access is caused to shrink with ecosystemic degradation.

In the top-left corner may be found those who arrogate to themselves property that was hitherto ownerless. But the class of phenomena that may be construed as entirely ownerless is shrinking rapidly and may soon be non-existent throughout the biosphere.

In the top-right corner of Figure 7.2 may be found historic instances of remote, unsettled islands, mountains and swamps. Few if any of these now remain ownerless. Some 'resources' may as yet seem to be largely ownerless, such as air or offshore oceanic water. But restrictions on the use of these

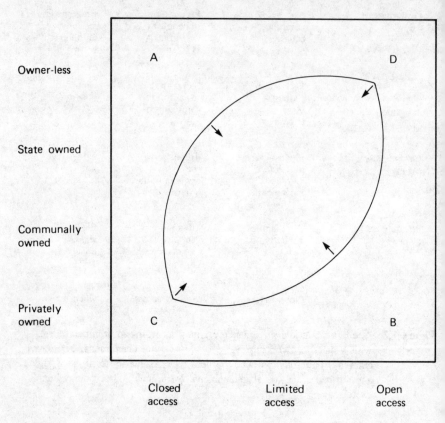

Owner-less

State owned

Communally
owned

Privately
owned

A   D

C   B

Closed   Limited   Open
access   access   access

Figure 7.3   Morally unacceptable, unrealistic and shrinking domains within Figure
7.2:
A – morally unacceptable arrogation of use;
B – morally unacceptable felonious use;
C – naturally unrealistic because of ecological interconnectedness; and
D – a shrinking domain as ownership is established and/or access is
limited or compromised by other uses.

ecosystemic features are increasing and each restriction either imposes some
measure of ownership or some limit to access, or both.

In the bottom-right corner of Figure 7.2 are found felons and poachers who
make illegal use of others' property and are subject to punishment and/or
payment of restitution when apprehended. (To the extent that there is self-
governance here, it is of a pathological type.) Because of the interconnectedness of features within ecosystems it would be an unusual case where
unlawful use left the property unaffected. It might happen by chance that
some extra-legal use would benefit an owner's practical interest in the

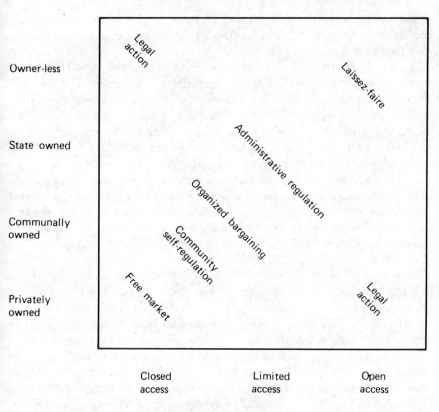

Figure 7.4   Dominant social mechanisms used in allocative decisions as distributed over the full ownership-by-access domain.

property, but the opposite is usually the case.

Also in the first column, the intensity and ubiquity of control by centralized bureaucracies in some socialist countries is waning. Party plutarchy and state capitalism operating under the guise of socialism are gradually being reformed. Similarly closed monastic and idealistic communities now occur less commonly than was once the case.

In summary of the above, the complexity and ecosystemic processes together with the expanding and intensifying impacts by humans on ecosystems are together helping to reduce the incidence of 'regimes' that fall toward the edges of the matrix in Figure 7.2. Of course, social and political forces not closely related to ecosystem phenomena are also at work.

Figure 7.3 illustrates a generalization that regimes that are currently thriving now cluster around the ascending diagonal. The trend may be toward further shrinkage of this domain as degradation of the biosphere by humans comes to be recognized more fully, and institutions are adapted to correct some of the deeper causes of degradation. A generalized form of co-management or joint management (Dorcey, 1986) may emerge with increasing frequency.

Figure 7.4 illustrates the primary focus for some broad types of mechanisms for allocating or apportioning rights to ownership and access to property. Increasingly these are viewed in a systemic and relativistic way, with a primary type being complemented in practice by a secondary and perhaps a tertiary type. For example, where community self-regulation is the dominant mechanism, a free market may exist for allocation of some of the less important resources. With the so-called free market, the legal, administrative and social costs simply for maintaining it may be quite high. The recent resurgence in some Western countries of a rather simple-minded faith in the free market is coming under increasing attack by critical thinkers not themselves bound to other simplistic nostrums. This is not to say that there is no place for free-market institutions in appropriate settings; far from it.

Community self-regulation (Figure 7.4) is attracting more interest, as reflected in the various chapters of this volume. *The Common Property Resource Digest* (see Chapter 1) is 'devoted to community-based resource management'. This wording seems conventional enough, but the thought or implications behind the 'message' is unconventional, at least nowadays.

As the doctrinaire ideological preoccupations with ownership and access questions wane, and with awareness of the complexity and unpredictability of man–nature ecosystems, simple-minded commitments to particular allocation mechanisms lose their charm and innocence. Such a blurring of distinctions might have its disadvantages if some existing regime had demonstrated in practice that it had successfully husbanded the natural environment and renewable resources. But this has apparently not occurred, at least with any of the major regimes of industrialized countries. Each of the latter has practised conventional exploitive development, CED, with severe adverse consequences to valued ecosystem components.

The Heartland–Hinterland Motif

The right or bundle of rights to make decisions, within a jurisdiction, on the use or allocation of use of resources among individuals and groups is not a homogeneous, undifferentiated phenomenon. The schema shown in Figure 7.5 is a version of Figure 3.1 in Chapter 3. It illustrates eight types of allocative conventions arranged as two subsystems. Regier and Grima (1985) noted that examples of all eight types may be found operating in Canada, and in various other countries. One type is usually dominant in a particular setting, with other types serving as support or as illegal disruptions.

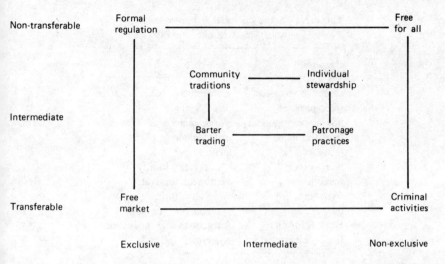

Figure 7.5 A perspective on how rights to use natural phenomena are assumed, arrogated, exercised, confirmed, allocated or assigned.

The four outer corners form an interactive hard shell subsystem centred in a metropolis. This subsystem is characterized by sharply defined power relationships, formality, simplicity, hierarchy and legal accountability. In a sense each corner of the subsystem 'needs' the other corners in order to function in the conventional manner. Free-market entrepreneurs use (or abuse) the commons, administrators find and apprehend miscreants and administrators protect the free market.

The four inner corners comprise a soft-core subsystem which contrasts with the hard-shell sketched above. Dominant features may include negotiation, complex network interactions, a sense of traditional obligations, casualness, equity, social accountability and ecosystem husbandry. The distinction between hard and soft (see Table 7.1) has parallels with the old distinctions of heartland and hinterland, of Gesellschaft and Gemeinschaft by Ferdinand Tönnies (Anon, 1985) and of the state and nation by Randolph Bourne (Resek, 1964). Scholars with a weakness for analogies might add parallel contrasts from religions, psychology, and other disciplines.

Consider further the tensions between the hard-shell and soft-core subsystems in our societies. Groups that practise labour-intensive, diversified, subsistence economies are directly vulnerable to competition from the capital-intensive and technology-intensive processes of other groups, especially if the latter are strongly subsidized by the state through such measures as loans, crop and fuel subsidies. The husbandry skills and related lifestyles thus suppressed may be especially those that could help to heal the ecosystem degradation due largely to excesses of the hard-shell system.

Table 7.1 Some contrasts between the two
subsystems of allocation devices.

Hard-shell	Soft-core
capitalist, socialist	cooperative, communitarian
trade-oriented	use-oriented
urban, metropolitan	rural, hinterland
hard technique	soft technique
technocentric	ecocentric
meritocratic	democratic, locally
maximization	minimax, survival
short-term pay-off	long-term thrift
bureaucratic	voluntaristic, personal
legal arbitration	bargaining and meditation
linear, hierarchic	systemic, egalitarian

Co-option of scientific and scholarly professionals: an example

In Figure 7.6 we have related different social groups of users of 'fisheries resources' to the basis of their interest in them. An examination of this example may invest the discussion above with some practical meaning.

In Canada, fisheries interests have been related to three broad objectives: material well-being, cultural opportunity and environmental harmony (see Loftus et al, 1978). Figure 7.6 shows these three primary values as circles.

An examination of the objectives of different individuals or small groups of users of the fishery resource, say in the North American Laurentian Great Lakes, shows that most of them share two or three of these objectives. This is reflected in their position in those parts of the overall domain of Figure 7.6 in which two or three of the circles overlap.

We have arranged the circles in this figure so that there is a dimensional relationship between Figures 7.5 and 7.6. In Figure 7.6, the hard-shell subsystem operates most strongly for groups at the top of the material well-being circle, and the soft-core subsystem primarily for those at the bottom of the cultural opportunity and environmental harmony circles. But some degree of mix of hard and soft exists with respect to the management of the cases of most interest groups.

Heretofore, fisheries professionals in the Great Lakes have, more or less, explicitly, served primarily one of three interest groups: profit-oriented commercial fishermen, competitive anglers, and commercial services for anglers. Stated in another way, Great Lakes fisheries experts tend to serve the interest of the hard-shell subsystem of users (see Figure 7.5). At a tactical level they compete amongst themselves those serving commercial fishing

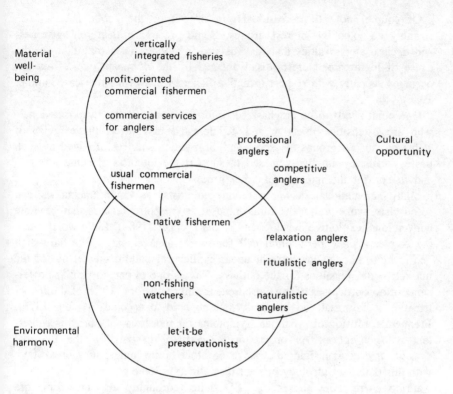

Figure 7.6 A classification schema of types of interest groups in fisheries of the Great Lakes according to the main motivation(s) underlying the interest.

interests engage in adversarial scientific and professional activities toward those co-opted by commercial services for anglers and by competitive anglers. At a more strategic level, those three groups of experts have tended, at least tacitly, to ally themselves against the interests of the soft-core subsystem of society – the groups that fall in the bottom half of Figure 7.6. But new approaches that serve the soft-core subsystem are being developed by unconventional workers in the Great Lakes as elsewhere, as the current volume demonstrates.

The loyalty that binds experts to interest groups, whether it is explicit or implicit, may survive major changes in societal preferences for the fish as valued ecosystem components. If these experts are in fact being paid as civil servants to serve society's purposes, then some primary accountability to society should override the loyalties that relate to an earlier co-option, but professional experts are seldom held to such an accounting. Hence there is a powerful professional inertia that hinders progress with implementation of changed social priorities (see also Chapter 6).

Of course, not all professionals, in or out of the public service, are strongly co-opted by interest groups. Some practise critical self-awareness and declare any loyalties that may bias their advice. They may take up the cause of legitimate interests disadvantaged by the dominant ones. This has occurred recently with respect to native fisheries in North America (Gamble, 1986).

One point needs to be emphasized: informal commitments by professionals who are ostensibly objective and disinterested may affect the exercise of rights by various groups of users. The information services provided by such professionals are implicitly biased to support the interests of some group(s) and to combat the interests of other groups (Regier, 1986a).

Many conventional economists and biologists, as environmentalists and resourcists, work within the same mindset as the entrepreneurs that generate conventional exploitive development, CED (Pepper, 1984). Little wonder that the conventional experts often call for more management of the hard-shell genre: more phenomena brought under explicit regulation; greater use of the market; stiffer penalties for the outlaws. This is due in part to similar professionalization processes of the entrepreneur and regulators. Much of the indoctrination is informal and hence difficult to hold to account (Mason, 1978). Frequent confusion of proximate symptoms for more distant causes is consistent with co-option. As professionals, certified in part for the informal evasion of critical insight, they have no other option unless they break faith with this dominant ideology of their discipline(s). Some reformers who would want to correct the abuses of CED quite thoroughly also call for more stringent regulation and enforcement of the hard-sell type. Can the abusers be beaten at the game that they have, in effect, created?

It has often been said that innovation and reform are difficult to achieve by addressing the entrenched regime (the 'economic system') in its central citadel (The Stock Exchange, Toronto's Bay Street, New York's Wall Street). It may be more effective to mobilize reform forces in the hinterland first, before advancing politically on the metropolis. Throughout the world, many elements compatible with RSR persist in the hinterland where CED has not been entirely successful in sweeping them away. The remnants surviving within tribal, village and rural cultures may be particularly interesting. Reform efforts are now timely: various practical and scholarly initiatives are converging toward this point of view (Regier, 1982, and several other chapters of the present volume).

An ecosystem approach

Gamble (1987) perceives a value shift underlying an 'ecosystem approach' to a form of co-management of the Great Lakes Basin, Figure 7.7. The distinction

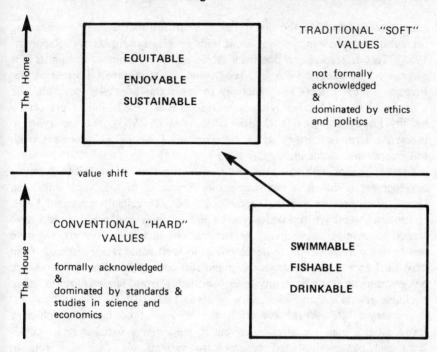

Figure 7.7   An ecosystem approach to water quality in the Great Lakes may serve the purposes of a value shift now underway in our culture (Gamble, 1987).

between practices within a 'house' and those within a 'home' follows Vallentyne (1986). Regier (1988) has discussed some differences between the two sets of values to be served through management of human uses of the ecosystem. Implicitly a value shift was endorsed in the purpose of the 1978 Great Lakes Water Quality Agreement undertaken jointly by the USA and Canada: 'to restore and maintain the chemical, physical and biological integrity of the waters of the Great Lakes Basin Ecosystem.' But RSR and ecosystem rehabilitation are not automatically accomplished with the mere signing of an agreement. There has to be a popular willingness and pressure to implement what has been decided.

With respect to ecosystemic husbandry, Lerner (1986) has described the recent emergence of voluntary stewardship groups and Francis (1986) has shown that some networks now in place resemble what Eric Trist has called referent groups. Both phenomena are consistent with an increasing emphasis on reform-sustainable redevelopment. The initiate critical reform and accountability activities outside the formal institutions of government and the professions. To some extent they reject the central norms of CED progress.

Ecosystem scientists of various disciplines who now cooperate within an ecosystem approach to the Great Lakes Basin are increasingly emphasizing organizational phenomena, consistent with general system theory (Rapoport, 1985). This is becoming a dominant theme especially amongst ecologists (for example, Steedman and Regier, 1987), and social scientists (Lerner, 1986, Francis, 1986). Efforts are underway to apply this approach to rehabilitate a degraded Green Bay in Wisconsin (Harris et al, 1982) and to preserve a healthy Long Point Bay in Ontario (Francis et al, 1985). We are trying to invest the term 'integrity', as in the purpose of the 1978 Agreement, with full operational meaning.

Our experience with the most 'successful' conventional exploitive resource development is that it is not sustainable. Resources of the North American Great Lakes provide striking examples of this. To rehabilitate Great Lakes ecosystems, we have reached beyond CED ideology and practice, and have started to develop alternatives. As summarized in Regier (1986b), we have had to move from exploitive development to sustainable redevelopment; from hard-shell approaches to stewardship and soft-core approaches; from reliance on government to community-based self-help; from laissez-faire to more equitable regulation and husbandry of resources.

In many Third World countries, the equivalent of Lerner's voluntary stewardship groups are already present in the existing social system. Local-level and community-based resource-use systems play a larger role in resource management than do governmental institutions. Examples of these soft-core systems range, in this book, from those in India (Chapter 14) to Pacific Islands (Chapter 16) to Mexico (Chapter 11). These existing communal-property systems, compatible with sustainable development or redevelopment, are 'resources' in themselves; 'folk science' at the service of traditional management systems is in some ways doing a better job than conventional Western science. Regarding Third World resource management and economic development, one important task must be to point out the weaknesses and pitfalls of CED so that Third World governments and managers will not blindly institute CED programs in place of existing community-based systems which may be more compatible with RSR (Berkes, 1987). This is not to say that Third World countries should reject Western science of the appropriate types.

Systemic interconnectedness of resources appears to have been recognized by many societies in the past, as well as by those rediscovering it today in such areas as the Great Lakes, and switching to 'soft' values and approaches. Many of the existing common-property-management systems for the allocation, general governance and sustainable use of these resources make sense in the context of the arguments presented in this chapter. These CPR systems are consistent with the ecosystem view.

Indeed, several chapters in this volume – those by Baines on Pacific island-reef management systems, and Moorehead on integrated wetlands resources-management systems in Mali – are examples of the traditional use of ecosystem approaches. Each of these involves the management of a cluster of interrelated resources as a unity, rather than one by one as in conventional Western science. Planning for sustainable development would do well to recognize the importance of conserving such traditional ecological wisdom and CPR systems in general.

Acknowledgements

Our thanks to Lino Grima, Sally Lerner, George Francis, Milton Freeman and an anonymous reviewer for the help with this chapter. Financial support was provided by the Max Bell Foundation.

References

Anarwhal, Anil, Chopra, Ravi and Sharma, Kalpana, 1982: *The State of India's Environment, 1982: A citizen's report*, Centre for Science and Environment, 95 Nehru Place, New Delhi, India.

Anon, 1985: Ferdinand Tönnies. Chicago, *The New Encyclopedia Britannica*, Micropaedia, 11, p. 843.

Berg, P., 1986: 'Growing a life-place politics', *The Planet Drum Review*, (San Francisco), No. II, pp. 9–12.

Berkes, F., 1987: 'The common property resource problem and the fisheries of Barbados and Jamaica, *Environmental Management*, 11, pp. 225–35.

Bookchin, M., 1980: *Toward an Ecological Society*, Black Rose Books, Montreal, Quebec.

Dorcey, A.H.J., 1986: 'Techniques for joint management of natural resources: Getting to yes', in Saunders, J.O., ed., *Managing Natural Resources in a Federal State*, Carswell, Toronto, Canada.

Francis, G.R., 1986: 'Great Lakes governance and the ecosystem approach: where next?', *Alternatives*, 13(3), pp. 61–70.

Francis, G.R., Grima, A.P., Regier, H.A. and Whillans, T.H., 1985: *A Prospectus for the Management of the Long Point Ecosystem*, Ann Arbour, Michigan, Great Lakes Fishery Commission Tech. Rep. 43, pp. vii and 109.

Gamble, D.J., 1986: 'Crushing of cultures: Western applied science in northern societies', *Arctic*, 39(1), pp. 20–3.

Gamble, D.J., 1987: 'The vital role of citizen's groups in water resource management', *1987 Annual Conf. Assoc. québécois des techniques de l'eau*, 5 March 1987, Montreal.

Harris, H.J., Talhelm, D.R., Magnuson, J.J. and Forbes, A.M., 1982: *Green Bay in the future – a rehabilitative prospectus*, Ann Arbour, Michigan, Great Lakes Fishery Commission Tech. Rep. No. 38, pp. vii and 59.

Lerner, S.C., 1986: 'Environmental constituency-building: local initiatives and volunteer stewardship', *Alternatives*, 13(3), pp. 55–60.

Leopold, A., 1949: *Sand County Almanac*, Oxford University Press, New York.

Livingstone, J., 1981: *The Fallacy of Wildlife Conservation*, McCelland and Stewart, Toronto, Canada.

Loftus, K.H., Johnson, M.G. and Regier, H.A., 1978: 'Federal-provincial strategic planning for Ontario fisheries: management strategy for the 1980s', *Journal of the Fisheries Research Board of Canada*, 35, pp. 916–27.

Mason, R.V., 1978: 'The Critical Potential of Knowledge: environmental studies and the matrix of power', University of Toronto PhD thesis, Toronto, Canada, pp. 319 and Appendices.

Morgan, A.E., 1942: *The Small Community, Foundation of Democratic Life*, Community Services Inc., Yellow Springs, Ohio, p. 313.

Naess, A., 1985: 'Ecosophy T', in Devall, B. and Sessions, G., *Deep Ecology*, Peregrine Smith Books, Salt Lake City, Utah, p. 266.

Pepper, D., 1984: *The Roots of Modern Environmentalism*, Croom Helm, London, UK, p. x and 246.

Rapoport, A., 1985: *General System Theory*, Abacus Press, Cambridge, Mass.

Regier, H.A., 1982: Training course on the management of small-scale fisheries in the inland waters of Africa: conceptual framework and approaches for the acquisition of key resource information. Food and Agriculture Organization of the United Nations, Rome, FAO Fisheries Circular No. 752, pp. v and 25.

Regier, H.A., 1986a: 'Six varieties of ecosystemic science of the natural environment and renewable resources', in Polunin, N., ed., *Ecosystem Theory and Practice*, John Wiley & Sons, New York.

Regier, H.A., 1986b: 'Progress with remediation, rehabilitation and the ecosystem approach', *Alternatives*, 13(3), pp. 445–54.

Regier, H.A., Botts, L. and Gandon, J.E., 1988: 'Remediation and rehabilitation of the Great Lakes', in Caldwell, L.K., ed., *Perspectives on Ecosystem Management for the Great Lakes*, Albany, State University of New York Press, pp. 169–89.

Regier, H.A. and Baskerville, G.L., 1986: 'Sustainable redevelopment of regional ecosystems degraded by exploitive development', in Clark, W.C. and Munn, R.E., eds, *Sustainable Development of the Biosphere*, Cambridge University Press, Cambridge, UK, p. 491.

Regier, H.A. and Grima, A.P., 1985: 'Fishery resource allocation: an exploratory essay', *Canadian Journal of Fisheries and Aquatic Sciences*, 42, pp. 845–59.

Resek, C., ed., 1964: *War and the Intellectuals: Some Collected Writings of Randolph Bourne*, Harper Torchbook.

Schumacher, E.F., 1973: *Small is Beautiful, a Study of Economics as if People Mattered*, Blond and Briggs, London, UK, p. 255.

Steedman, R.J. and Regier, H.A., 1987: 'Ecosystem science for the Great Lakes: perspectives on degradative and rehabilitative transformations', *Canadian Journal of Fisheries and Aquatic Sciences*, 44 (Suppl. 2), pp. 95–103.

Vallentyne, J.R., 1986: 'The necessity of a behavioural code of practice for living in the biosphere, with a special reference to an ecosystem ethic', in Polunin, N., ed., *Ecosystem Theory and Application*, John Wiley, New York, p. 445.

8 Multi-Jurisdictional Resources: Testing a Typology for Problem-Structuring

Susan J. Buck (Cox)

Summary

Marine fisheries are a common-property resource with special biological characteristics: they are both renewable and fugitive, with habitats that range from freshwater rivers to the high seas. Because of these biological characteristics, marine fisheries must be managed in multiple and often antagonistic political jurisdictions. To clarify the management options peculiar to fisheries resources, a typology of common-property resources is developed. The components of the typology are the nature of the resource (fugitive-renewable); the migratory pattern of the fishery (unshared stock, shared stock, highly migratory, anadromous, or high seas); the property right in the fishery (non-transferable or transferable, non-exclusive or exclusive); and the scale of the user pool (traditional, localized, regional, national or multinational). The typology is then applied to Chesapeake Bay fisheries as a demonstration of its usefulness in examining institutional arrangements in fisheries management.

Introduction

What we label as 'common property' is not one but several kinds of property. A fish caught on the high seas, which is no one's property, or *res nullius* (Grotius, 1608, p. 22), becomes its captor's property by virtue of his labour; no nation or individual could lay claim to it prior to the capture. This lack of ownership, however, resides not in the fish but rather in its location. The same fish caught in a Scottish lord's salmon stream is private property before the first line is caste, which is why fishing rights in salmon and trout streams may be leased. Had the fish travelled, instead, into American waters to spawn, it would have belonged to the state (*res publica*) in which it was found and its capture bound by numerous state-imposed restrictions such as season, licences, and gear. However, our peripatetic and biologically unlikely fish may have swum into waters whose fishing is assigned to a tribe of

Native Americans, in which case it would become the property of the entire tribe (*res communes*) rather than of one individual. Thus we cannot casually label a fish as a common property resource: it may be *res nullius*, *res communes*, *res publica*, or simply private property, depending upon where it is found, how it is caught, and by whom.

A new concept of 'common heritage' takes the issue of property further. This idea, first espoused by Arvid Pardo, Maltese ambassador to the United Nations, defines some resources as the common heritage of mankind. They are therefore *everyone's* property (and since they are already owned, cannot legally be appropriated by any one individual or state) and should be subject to joint management (Kent, 1979, p. 242–3). Pardo was calling for the common heritage to apply to the sea resources that are outside national jurisdiction such as deep-seabed mineral deposits and open-ocean or 'high seas' fisheries. 'The common heritage idea should be understood as a wholly new concept of property rights, a modern alternative to the traditional ideas of exclusive ownership or of free and unlimited access' (Kent, 1977, p. 244). Proponents feel this new idea is necessary because changes in environmental pressures and resource availability make old ideas of property obsolete.

How then, are we to define common-property resource? The term 'seems to be a catch-all concept for a variety of essentially different circumstances that require different definitions and formulations' (Dorfman, 1974, p. 9). However, there is general agreement that such a resource is both limited and has a pool of users whose access has not been restricted. The problem of commons management arises when this pool of users is larger than the resource can permanently bear (see also Chapter 1).

To go beyond a general understanding, this chapter presents a heuristic typology of common-property resources. The typology is designed to provide a framework for conceptualizing common-property resources according to their biological, legal, and jurisdictional attributes. I assume that similar resources should have similar institutional arrangements for management; however, it is difficult to determine which characteristics should be 'counted' as contributing to critical similarities and differences. Use of this typology (which is in a preliminary form here but will be elaborated upon in future research) helps managers identify similarities and differences among resources. Future work will refine the typology, apply it to several common-property resources, and correlate resource characteristics with successful management institutions. This chapter describes the basic typological framework, elaborates it to include marine fisheries, and applies the typology to Chesapeake Bay fisheries in the early 1980s.

A typology of common-property resources

Three factors have a major impact in classifying common-property resources: the scale of the endeavour (the size of the user pool); the property right involved (transferable or non-transferable, exclusive or non-exclusive) (Regier and Grima, 1985, p. 853); and the nature of the resource itself (stationary or fugitive, renewable or non-renewable) (Table 8.1).

Table 8.1   A typology of common-property resources

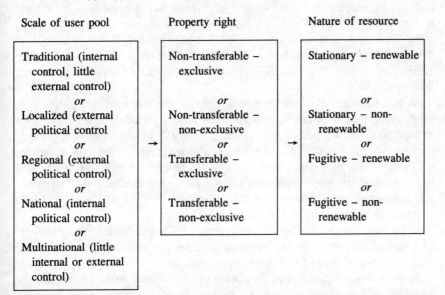

Scale of user pool	Property right	Nature of resource
Traditional (internal control, little external control)	Non-transferable – exclusive	Stationary – renewable
or	*or*	*or*
Localized (external political control	Non-transferable – non-exclusive	Stationary – non-renewable
or	*or*	*or*
Regional (external political control)	Transferable – exclusive	Fugitive – renewable
or	*or*	*or*
National (internal political control)	Transferable – non-exclusive	Fugitive – non-renewable
or		
Multinational (little internal or external control)		

The 'scale of endeavour' was chosen as a factor because much of the discussion of common-property resources revolves about the impossibility of successfully managing extensive resources. Advocates of the inevitability of deterioration in the commons may claim that successful management is possible only in small-scale, relatively unsophisticated resources. Public-choice theorists argue that even with a localized group of users, an individual will not voluntarily contribute to a common goal if the group is large and if the individual cannot be excluded from the collective benefit (Olson, 1965). This theory does not, however, fit consistently with observed facts, and some public-choice theorists (for example, E. Ostrom, 1986) are revising previous concepts to account for the anomalies. Use of 'scale of endeavour' will help test such claims and theories.

Knowledge about the 'property rights' in a resource is essential in setting management options. For example, a manager is able to impose limitations on transferring of property rights only if the biological-physical nature of the resource affects the political jurisdictions over which the resources must be managed, the supply and accuracy of technical data about the resource, and the utilization options for managers.

Scale of user pool

While the scale of the endeavour is not strictly synonomous with political jurisdiction, the two are intertwined. At one end of the scale are small, self-contained communities such as were once found in medieval Europe and are now virtually restricted to developing countries. In these communities the traditional commons system (Cox, 1985b; 1985c; Gonner, 1966; Hoskins and Stamp, 1965) has the most chance of success (Berkes, 1981; Berkes and Pocock, 1983; Berkes and Pocock, 1981, Ruddle and Akimichi, 1984; Ruddle and Johannes, 1985).

At the opposite end of the user-pool scale are the virtually unrestricted user pools comprised of users from many nations and ethnic groups. These user groups have little formalized political control, largely because the resources they use are outside political jurisdiction. High-seas fisheries are, for example, accessible to any user with sufficient capital; restrictions which may be imposed by non-democratic governments on their citizens' participation in the fishery are not limitations on access *per se* but rather are limitations which would be imposed on a particular individual regardless of his activity. In this category, restraints and management restrictions of any kind are difficult to apply because of a lack of agreement among participants, a lack of political jurisdiction, and the extreme difficulty of consistent enforcement.

Between these two extremes lie a wide variety of user pools. Others include localized user pools that are part of a wider political community which impinges upon use of the resource. Access here is rarely restricted because the user pool from any one community is small compared to the resource; the resource becomes endangered by the combination of many such user pools. With such user pools, there are often self-imposed restraints, but a wider political community impinges upon use of the resource and upon local-level management systems (Chapters 12, 14 and 15; Berkes and Pocock, 1981; Pringle, 1985).

A fourth possible category is the regional user pool which is, once again, controlled by an external political community. Examples of this category include river basins, large coastal areas such as the New England region of the American eastern seaboard (Dewar, 1983), or interstate regions such as the Chesapeake Bay area. Political jurisdictions overlap in this category; for example, resources within the Chesapeake Bay area are controlled by three states, the District of Columbia, and the federal government. These overlapping jurisdictions generate complex management problems which require innovative institutional arrangements (Cox, 1985a).

A fifth category is the national user pool; this community of users has an internal political control in that the users are drawn from throughout the political jurisdiction exercising control. Visitors to national parks come from the entire nation and the regulations they face have been devised by a national process, unlike consumers of municipal water who are constrained by state and federal regulations as well as their own municipal ordinances.

These discussions of the scale of the endeavour are not exhaustive; a variety of other categories exist. The possibilities lie on a continuum rather than presenting a finite number of discrete points. The complexity of the management problem is directly influenced by the scale of endeavour and its relationship to the type of resource and the type of property rights involved.

Property rights

Academic discussions of the legal niceties of property law do little to illuminate the practical concerns of common-property-resource management (Johnston, 1965, p. 303). Regardless of how the property rights have been generated, and even if they do not exist in law but rather only in custom, what matters in management is the practical application of those rights.

Rights are either transferable or not (Regier and Grima, 1985). Transferable or individual rights are saleable for goods or money, or are subject to bestowal and removal for services rendered. Non-transferable rights have been removed from individual control and rest with the government or with the community of users. These rights may be assigned to individuals but the individual may not transfer the rights to another. For example, in medieval England, the right of access to a common was attached to the property within the village. A householder could not sell his right to use the common pasture and still retain his house and property. The house could be transferred, thus inevitably transferring the right to common, but the right to common was not severable (Gonner, 1966, p. 3-4).

Similarly, property rights may be exclusive or non-exclusive (Regier and Grima, 1985). Exclusive rights imply a limited access to the resource; grazing permits for public land are exclusive in that only a limited number are issued, and access to public grazing is restricted to those holding permits. A non-exclusive right gives access to the resource to a defined pool of users rather than to individuals; any city resident may use the municipal parks. Access to high-seas fishery is virtually unrestricted; therefore, the right to exploit these fisheries is at present non-exclusive.

The management implications of property rights are considerable. A non-exclusive, non-transferable right is not, by definition, susceptible to political management. For some resources, such as open-seas fishing, there are no legal property rights at all attached to the resource. Therefore, to initiate any management programme, we must first create a property right in the resource. To accomplish this, political jurisdictions of some sort must be imposed upon the resource. In the case of high-seas fisheries, this entails extending political jurisdiction of some nations out into the open seas. The 'common heritage of mankind' proponents would have use give this jurisdiction to all nations; others argue for extending the jurisdiction of only the coastal states. However we decide, the simple recognition of the type of property rights involved begins to direct our managerial options.

Nature of the resource

Resources may be categorized as *stationary*, such as forests, mineral deposits, and oyster beds, or *fugitive* as in wild game and most fish stocks. They may also be considered *renewable*, such as fisheries or forests, or *non-renewable*, as are minerals. Each category generates a set of management issues.

Stationary resources are readily identifiable and rarely is their ownership open to question. For example, oyster beds in Virginia, since they rest on state-owned sea bottom, belong to the state; in other states, oyster beds may be privately controlled as well. National forests are managed by federal agencies; private forest lands are harvested by the corporations which own them. Government may regulate private resources for the good of the political community but the ownership and control are clear.

In contrast, fugitive resources may span several political jurisdictions and are difficult to capture. Ownership of the resource varies with its location. For example, in the United States, the 'state ownership' doctrine applied to fisheries until the 1940s (Bean, 1983, pp. 12–17). Under this doctrine, the right to navigable waters, submerged land, fish, and wildlife was a public trust dating from colonial times. The public character of the rights was passed on to the various sovereign states which therefore owned the fish. However, in 1948, the Supreme Court struck down the state ownership doctrine and declared that federal law was pre-emptive (*Toomer* v. *Witsell*, 1948). This has led to awkward situations in which the American federal government may regulate fisheries inside state waters. Other problems also arise when the fish travel out of one jurisdiction and into another; for example, fishermen in the second territory may feel that the resource is unfairly exploited before they have access.

Given the typology in Table 8.1, resources fit into one of four categories. Forests and public grazing lands are stationary-renewable. Mineral deposits such as coal or copper are stationary non-renewable. Fisheries, wild game, and some water-borne plants are fugitive-renewable. 'Fugitive-non-renewable' remains a null set.

Marine fisheries: an elaboration of the typology

Where do fisheries fit into this typology? All fisheries are renewable resources; beyond that, however, fisheries may be bound to fit virtually any combination of the typology in Table 8.1. Most (excluding the truly sedentary such as oysters) are fugitive. This fugitive character of fisheries may be categorized according to either the political jurisdiction or the type of fish, although clearly these distinctions are closely related.

Christy (1977, p. 237) combines a classification of migratory pattern with political jurisdictions.

1 Unshared stock exists in a single national jurisdiction.
2 Shared stock exists in the jurisdiction of two or more adjacent or opposite coastal nations.
3 Highly migratory stock is within the jurisdiction of two or more nations *and* exists outside any national jurisdiction.
4 Anadromous stock lives in the fresh or estuarine waters of a single nation *and* outside the nation's jurisdiction on the high seas.
5 High seas stock exists outside national jurisdictions (for instance, some whales).

Thus the nature of the resource is closely related to the scale of the user pool because access is frequently determined by political jurisdiction. However, the two are distinct in that the user pool of one jurisdiction may harvest several stocks, or, conversely, one stock may be susceptible to more than one user pool.

Because the fugitive characteristic means the stocks will probably cross several political jurisdictions, the typology in this category will be expanded to include the five migratory patterns discussed above (Table 8.2). This biological characteristic hampers collection of scientific data on fishery stocks, future yields, and any other information usually deemed essential to resource management. Thus social, political, and economic factors may have a proportionately greater influence in a fugitive resource than they might in another resource.

Property rights in fisheries may fall into any category. Some fishery property rights, such as those enjoyed by certain Pacific Northwest Indian tribes, are non-transferable. Others, such as the right to certain salmon runs or trout streams, may be leased and are transferable. Conventional fishing licences convey an exclusive right of access to the fishery, while Asian villages may have non-exclusive rights to the local stocks (Hooper, 1985).

Finally, any one of the almost infinite user pools may describe a group with access to the fishery.

A variety of techniques is available to the fishery manager; the usefulness of each technique depends almost entirely on the type of resource being

Table 8.2 Typology of fugitive fishery resources

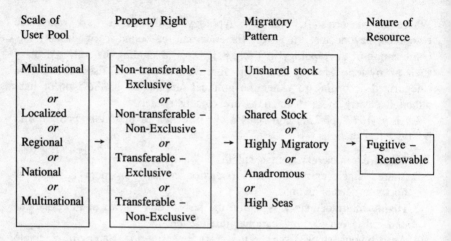

Scale of User Pool		Property Right		Migratory Pattern		Nature of Resource
Multinational		Non-transferable – Exclusive		Unshared stock		
or		*or*		*or*		
Localized		Non-transferable – Non-Exclusive		Shared Stock		
or				*or*		
Regional	→	*or*	→	Highly Migratory	→	Fugitive – Renewable
or		Transferable – Exclusive		*or*		
National				Anadromous		
or		*or*		*or*		
Multinational		Transferable – Non-Exclusive		High Seas		

managed. A small pool of users with exclusive and transferable rights to a fishery will respond to approaches that are inappropriate for a large pool of users drawn from several political jurisdictions. One use of the typology is for managers to organize their perceptions of resources under their jurisdiction. Determining the differences and similarities between resources helps determine the transferability of management techniques. An application of the typology to Chesapeake Bay fisheries follows to serve as a demonstration of the problem-structuring possibilities of the typology.

Chesapeake Bay fisheries

Multiple-management jurisdictions and their effects

The states of Virginia, Maryland and Pennsylvania, and the District of Columbia influence the Bay (Figure 8.1). While Pennsylvania has no bay shoreline, more than 90 per cent of the freshwater discharged to the Chesapeake comes from Pennsylvania (Environmental Policy Institute (EPI), nd, p. 3). The Bay has 8100 miles of shoreline and 4400 square miles of surface, making it the largest estuary in the United States (Cronin, et al, 1977, p. 38). More than 2700 species of plants and animals live in the bay or on its shoreline (Citizen's Program (CP), 1983, p. 3). One-third of the nation's oyster harvest comes from the bay (EPI, nd, p. 3). This harvest provides nearly 70 per cent of the value of Maryland seafood catches, a catch which in 1980 was estimated at US$765,000,000 (CP, 1983, p. 3). Nowhere else is the blue crab found in such quantity, and this highly marketable

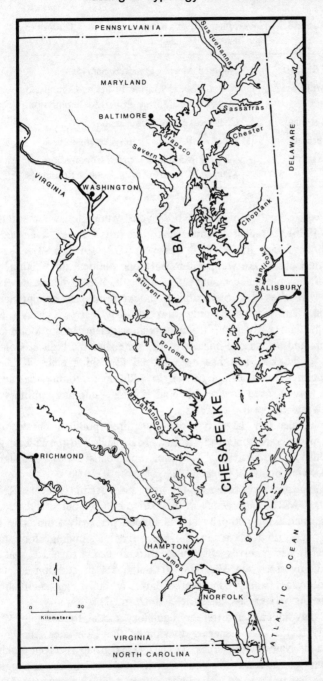

Figure 8.1 Chesapeake Bay and area.

Table 8.3 Government organisations engaged in Chesapeake Bay Fisheries Management

Federal:	National Marine Fisheries Service
Multi-State:	Atlantic States Marine Fisheries Commission
	Mid-Atlantic Marine Fisheries Commission
Tri-State:	Chesapeake Bay Commission
Bi-State:	Potomac River Fisheries Commission
State:	Virginia Marine Resources Commission
	Maryland Department of Natural Resources

crustacean carries out its complete life cycle within the waters of the Bay (Warner, 1976). Recent commercial harvests have averaged over 600,000,000lb of fish and shellfish per year (CP, 1983, p. 3).

Even if the Chesapeake were within only one political jurisdiction, its size and variability would make management difficult. It is a marine environment in its lower reaches that blends to a brackish one as it approaches the Susquehanna. The rivers draining into the bay carry a heavy load of pollutants; the James River in Virginia which originates in the foothills of the Appalachians and drains one-quarter of the state, has the highest Contamination Index in the Bay and has been closed to fishing since 1975 due to Kepone contamination (EPI, nd, 1–4). In addition to commercial and sport fishing, the bay is used for recreational boating, shipping, military operations, and waste disposal.

Fisheries in the bay have not one but three political entities directly controlling management options: Virginia, Maryland, and the federal government. In addition, the District of Columbia and Pennsylvania have significant impacts on water quality (Table 8.3).

Virginia manages bay fisheries through the Virginia Marine Resources Commission (VMRC), an agency in the Office of Commerce and Resources. VMRC has rulemaking authority and is funded primarily from state general funds, although it does received some federal funding for statistical programmes. It also receives some funds through taxes, royalties, and licence fees. VMRC oversees the Virginia Wetlands Act in addition to its other duties of enforcing fishery conservation laws, administering shellfish leases, and replenishing oyster stocks (Jones, 1982, p. 7).

Maryland has adopted a different regulatory model by assigning fisheries responsibility to the tidal fisheries division of the Tidewater Administration (Department of Natural Resources [DNR]). This group receives much of its funding from special funds derived from licences and taxes, although DNR also receives general and federal funds. What rulemaking powers DNR has are much more circumscribed that the powers of VMRC. Unlike VMRC, which has enforcement powers, DNR must rely on the Natural Resources Police and the Licensing and Consumer Services to enforce its rules and decisions (Jones, 1982, p. 7).

The Potomac River Fisheries Commission (PRFC) is the regulatory body formed in 1963 from the Potomac River Compact (1958) between Maryland and Virginia. Under the compact, the river fisheries are managed in accordance with Maryland laws unless the PRFC decides otherwise. Although PRFC regulations may be challenged in court, the commission has never lost a court challenge. Regulations may be changed or revoked by a joint resolution of both Maryland and Virginia legislatures, but this process has never been used. The commission must rely on the states for enforcement, but the licensing power is so well established that effective regulation is easily achieved. The Potomac is managed as a system independent of other bay concerns and will not be considered further in this chapter (Carpenter, 1986).

A second multistate group is the Chesapeake Bay Commission. Originally, the commission was comprised of representatives from Virginia and Maryland; in September of 1985, Pennsylvania became the third participant. Established in 1980, the commission's duties include recommending legislative and administrative action for coordinated and cooperative use of the bay, monitoring resources, representing state concerns to the federal government, and arbitrating interstate conflicts. In 1984, the commission formed a bi-state fisheries advisory group from the scientific and political communities of both Virginia and Maryland. By 1986, the group was no longer functioning. Why the advisory group failed to become a permanent management group, and what it did accomplish, is discussed below.

The federal presence in fisheries management in the bay is felt in two areas: legal constraints, and certain species-specific management plans. The legal constraints arise through court opinions which restrict state managements options such as licensing. For example, in *Bruce* v *Director, Department of Chesapeake Bay Affairs* (1971), the Court of Appeals of Maryland declared unconstitutional the county residency requirement for crabbing licences. In *Douglas* v *Seacoast Products* (1977), the Supreme Court held that fishing vessels operating under federal licences were entitled to fish in states' coastal waters because such vessels are engaged in interstate commerce. Most recently, in *Tangier Sound Waterman's Association* v *Douglas* (1982), Virginia lost her ability to restrict fishing licences to state residents.

The federal impact on certain species arises because these species migrate from the bay into federally controlled waters: striped bass from the bay, for example, are often fished as far north as Massachusetts. The Atlantic States Marine Fisheries Commission (ASMFC), formed by compact in 1940, may adopt fisheries management plans. In general, these plans are only advisory. One notable exception is the plan for striped bass management mandated by the Striped Bass Conservation Act of 1984, although the constitutionality of this plan has been questioned (Bubier and Rieser, 1984). Other federal entities such as the Mid-Atlantic Marine Fisheries Commission and the National Marine Fisheries Service have virtually no jurisdiction within the states' coastal waters, although the council does preempt some coordination efforts of the two major bay states.

It is apparent that although the federal influence in the bay must not be neglected, the major actors in bay fisheries management are the two states of Virginia and Maryland. Unfortunately, their history has not been a cooperative one. Land disputes between Maryland and Virginia go back to colonial times. Critical public opinion sparked by oyster wars which began in the late nineteenth century led to the Potomac River Compact; as late as 1949 a Maryland oysterman was shot to death by a Virginia marine inspector (Warner, 1976, p. 221). The *Tangier Sound* case mentioned above was brought against Virginia by Maryland crabbers eager to leave their own poor fishing grounds to take advantage of Virginia's richer waters. Their success in the suit and their subsequent invasion has led to bitter disputes between crabbers of both states. This multiplicity of political jurisdictions leads to serious management problems in Chesapeake Bay fisheries.

For example, one deceptively simple problem caused by the multiple state jurisdictions is the variation in fishing gear permitted in Virginia and in Maryland. In Virginia a crab pot is defined as a 'structure made of wire or thread net'; hard crab pots may not have mesh smaller than 1 1/2'' but peeler pots have no restrictions at all (Chesapeake Bay Commission (CBC), 1983, p. 5). In Maryland, a crab pot is legally defined as a 'cube shaped device with openings toward inside [with] sides not more than 24'' long [and] constructed of wire.' Hard crab pots in Maryland may not have mesh smaller than one inch, and peeler posts have identical restrictions (Goldsborough, 1984, p. 1). The variation is sufficiently extreme that, prior to 1985, possession of regulation Maryland gear in Virginia waters could lead to an arrest.

A second state-level concern is sociocultural. Virginia and Maryland have been historic rivals for control of the Chesapeake Bay: boundary disputes date back to 1632 (Horton, 1981, p. B6). Although the traditional cultures of fishermen in the two states are very similar to the outside observer, the fishermen themselves view their cultures as dissimilar and cherish those differences in the same spirit as two high schools perpetuate a sports rivalry.

Application of typology

Excluding the sedentary fisheries, Chesapeake Bay fisheries are:

1 fugitive-renewable resources, comprised of
2 shared stock *and* highly migratory stock.
3 Property rights are non-transferable and
4 exclusive.
5 The pool of users consists almost entirely of localized, externally
  controlled users (e.g., Gloucester, Virginia, and Smith Island,
  Maryland).

Setting political considerations aside momentarily, this description raises
several issucs for managers.

Fugitive-renewable resources
The fugitive nature of the resource complicates the calculation of the rate of
renewability of the resource and therefore also complicates calculation of the
allowable harvest. While numerous scientific studies of striped bass, blue
crab, menhaden and other species have been conducted by scientists from
both states, the date from the different states are not compatible for statistical
analysis because of differences in methodology, and the scientists differ
widely on interpretation. Because conflicting reports exist, managers are
hampered in their efforts to legitimate decisions. In addition, opponents of
regulatory proposals have a source of data to counteract management's scientific assumptions.
   The various stocks can be managed for (a) maximum sustainable yield
(MSY) – the level at which the seasonal catch equals the replenishment of
the stock – or (b) the maximum economic yield (MEY) – the level of catch
which maximizes profit by generating the largest possible return per unit of
effort. Since the MEY is usually at a level of catch below MSY, and since
the data which generate the MSY are suspect, partly due to the fugitive
nature of the resource, the fishery should be managed for something less than
the estimated MSY (Eckert, 1979, p. 123; Gulland, 1974, p. 110; Chapter
3, this volume). This may be easier than it first appears because 'among the
public at large there is enough growing awareness of the simpler aspects of
fishery problems for the idea of exceeding the MSY to have achieved the
moral stigma of a specialized form of pollution' (Gulland, 1974, p. 109).

Shared stock and highly migratory stock
Although the stock is both shared and highly migratory, the user pool does
not move outside the shared stock political jurisdictions. Therefore the
manager can discount the need to regulate the user pool in the federal
government's territorial waters. What the manager must do, however, is
insure that the users' behaviour within the shared stock range is consistent
with the demands of the migratory stock management.

Non-transferable property rights

The property rights in the fishery exist already and do not need to be created. Unlike property rights in high-sea fisheries – which to date do not exist in any recognizable or enforceable form – the rights to the bay fisheries have been established by positive law and ratified by custom.

Exclusive property rights

These rights are exclusive in the sense that no one may fish in the bay without a licence. However, as a practical matter, neither Maryland nor Virginia imposes a limit on the number of licences issued. The states would need to justify a licence limit on conservation grounds. At present, bay regulators seem content to manage through catch limits and season and gear restrictions. Bay management therefore has the interesting but unsatisfactory management situation of exclusive rights with unlimited access.

Localized user pool

Finally, the pool of users is comprised of localized, externally controlled users. While in theory regional and multinational pools exist, in practice the users primarily come from Maryland and Virginia. A few Delaware or North Carolina fishermen will venture into the bay but they have no significant impact. The regulatory impact upon the fisheries comes from the two states, but the actual bureaucratic structure in place is very elaborate. Recognition of the size and character of the user-pool suggests that the management focus should be at the regional level. This is generally the case, although management of certain species such as striped bass is so politically sensitive that decisions are made at the state level. Fisheries management in Virginia and Maryland is coordinated through frequent but informal communication between the two states.

Implementation of management options

From this discussion, managers would infer that the following changes in their management institutions and processes might reduce stress on the resource and improve overall resource management.

1 Increase the database and ensure that the information collected by each state is in a form compatible with the data from the other political jurisdictions.
2 Limit licences, and defend the limitation on conservation grounds rather than for territorial reasons.
3 Focus management initiatives at the regional level.

The first suggestion has been implemented: the National Oceanic and

Atmospheric Administration (NOAA) has established a Chesapeake Bay Stock Assessment Committee formed of federal, state, and academic participants to make long-range plans for stock assessments and to implement the plan (Goldsborough, 1986).

The second suggestion is unlikely to be followed in the near future. Such an action would almost certainly be challenged in court, especially as Virginia would be the state most likely to limit access. There is no discontent in Virginia's regulatory agencies about the effectiveness of their current procedures, so no incentive exists to limit licences.

The third suggestion, to focus management initiatives at the regional level, has been tried but without much success. Between 1984 and 1986, a Bi-State Fisheries Advisory Group was initiated and developed under the auspices of the Chesapeake Bay Commission. The commission had ambitious plans for the advisory group: it was to guide the commission in developing comprehensive, cooperative legislation for bay-wide fisheries management policies (CBC, 1984, pp. 13–14). The group first met on July 30, 1984, and consisted of commercial fishermen, representatives from the Mid-Atlantic Fishery Management Council, fishery scientists from both states, management officials, and consultants.

Progress seemed to continue during 1985, culminating in the Work Group Report on Fisheries Management and Living Resources used as the discussion focus for the 1985 Biennial Review of the Action Agenda. The Biennial Review Conference met in Baltimore in September, 1985, and the fisheries participants met throughout one afternoon to prioritize the work group's recommendations. However, these recommendations were already subject to criticism and, unknown to most conference participants, alternative recommendations were circulating among concerned fisheries managers (Rothschild, et al, 1984). By early 1986, the Fisheries Advisory Group was disbanded.

Understanding why the group disbanded provides insights into the difficulties of implementing bay-wide regional management policies. The demise of the advisory group is attributable to any of several causes. Staff at the Chesapeake Bay Commission prefer to say the group has fallen into disuse rather than been abolished. The commission had requested quarterly reports on interstate fisheries issues but the report quality was marginal and the reports themselves were often late. Members of the group tended to represent their administrations or organizational interests rather than their expertise, and thus they never went beyond a discussion of how to proceed. In short, the group lacked clear goals and objectives, and they had no motivation to strive for implementation of issues they discussed. As an advisory group providing input to the Chesapeake Bay Commission, itself an advisory group, the fisheries participants had little expectation of results. However, from the commission staff's perspective, the advisory group did achieve two changes. First, by simply assembling the scientific, administrative, commercial, and sports fisheries users, some degree of familiarity for future cooperation efforts has been established. Second, and perhaps more important, the Chesapeake Bay Commission has established an overview function for bay-wide fishery management. Previously, no single entity had been viewed as empowered to assemble such a group. This reflects a changing perspective on the commission's functions (Jones, 1986).

Various state officials offer slightly different perspectives. One VMRC official sees the advisory group as redundant since the ASMFC is already engaged in drafting cooperative fisheries management plans for the Atlantic coastal states. The only fisheries for which he can justify bi-state plans are crab and oyster, which are generally restricted to the two bay states. He views the efforts of the Chesapeake Bay Commission through the advisory group as regressive because they reintroduced political and legislative factors into an essentially scientific concern (Travelstead, 1986).

However, a fisheries biologist at the Virginia Institute of Marine Science (VIMS) thought the group dissolved because they had accomplished their tasks. They had no authority to force bi-state action and the Virginia representatives were busy with implementation on the state level (Austin, 1986). Officials at Maryland's Department of Natural Resources attribute the group's failure to a lack of communication: no information on the group's decisions, data collections, or recommendations ever trickled down to the DNR managers. However, at DNR this lack of information is not unique to the advisory group. DNR managers heard of the state-wide moratorium on striped bass the same morning the secretary announced the moratorium to the press. Maryland's fisheries management structure may help to explain the lack of information since DNR has little regulatory authority. The legislature in Maryland is apparently willing to trade poorly informed management for political control of the management process, thereby allowing the legislature to blame DNR for both the fisheries problems and the lack of initiatives to resolve them (DNR Staff, 1986).

How can the Fisheries Advisory Group be evaluated? The reaction of those affected is varied. Maryland's DNR saw no impact, while some Virginia managers thought the venture was profitable. There is certainly no consensus on a need for bi-state cooperation for all fishery-management plans. What agreement exists seems to be that blue crabs and oysters are most in need of cooperative efforts, although no manager went so far as to advocate uniform regulations.

It seems unlikely that any state-initiated plan will have much chance for success, primarily because of the deep-seated rivalry and distrust between the two states. The action of the Maryland Secretary in announcing a striped-bass moratorium only three days after publicly assuring the Virginia members of the Chesapeake Bay Commission that such an action was not under consideration is a strong example of the basis for distrust. Maryland DNR staffers question the integrity of research performed by the Virginia Institute of Marine Science (VIMS) because VIMS is a state research laboratory (although it is also the marine science graduate school for the College of William and Mary). Virginians reply that all political pressure from Richmond falls on VMRC rather than VIMS, and they charge in turn that DNR research is done by researchers whose jobs depend on reaching politically acceptable conclusions. Small wonder that fisheries managers cannot agree on management strategies when they cannot accept the validity of their counterparts' research efforts.

In addition to this distrust, there is no uniformly perceived need for bi-state cooperation. Despite federal views that Chesapeake Bay should be managed as one ecosystem (EPI, nd, p. 1), state managers seem to agree that the bay is a composite of several different ecosystems: the highly salt/marine system at the mouth; a middle, relatively stable system from Tangier Sound to Baltimore; and a third system heavily influenced by freshwater incursions from the northern end of the bay. Some managers even assert separate managerial ecosystems for each of the major rivers (Lynch, 1986; Travelstead, 1986). The Potomac River Fisheries Commission certainly manages the Potomac as an autonomous system.

Assessing regional management needs

Thus before we can address in any constructive way the problems of interjurisdictional management of Chesapeake Bay fisheries resources, we must first determine the source of the problems. If there is indeed no need for a unified – or even a cooperative – management strategy in the bay, then strategies for improvement must address existing institutions, improved communications, and standardized data collection and analysis. On the other hand, if a coherent policy is needed for bay-wide application, then strategies must also include institutional development, changing political coalitions, and state-level acceptance of some external control of fisheries resources.

What are the arguments for a coherent policy? First – whether we view the bay as one ecosystem (which justifies a unitary management philosophy) or several ecosystems – we cannot deny that the actions of each state (including Pennsylvania and the District of Columbia) have an interactive effect on the resources of the other states. Issues of water quality, patterns of submerged subaqueous vegetation growth and population expansion affect more than their immediate surroundings. No one is advocating a return to total state autonomy in fishery management, indeed, such total autonomy probably never existed. But such isolationism is driven more by economic fear and greed than by concepts of resource management.

A second rationale for bay-wide management lies in the changing demographics of the bay area. The middle peninsula of Virginia (from Gloucester Point up to the Potomac) and Maryland's Eastern shore are booming areas for tourism, vacation homes, and urban sprawl. Through the 1960s, the predominantly rural character of the bay area allowed localized decision-making. Communities were relatively isolated, and fishing was a low-technology, highly individualized business. However, as population growth continues, the environmental problems generated by concentrated populations become more acute. State-level controls are imposed for pollution abatement and coastal zone planning. Communities change with an influx of new residents who demand more amenities and services, better schools and improved roads. The fishing industry has also changed. Slower, more traditional boats make way for fibreglass boats with sonar and sophisticated technology, and fishermen have become skilled political negotiators (Dewar, 1983; Miller and Von Maanen, 1983).

Finally, the states may well choose to act cooperatively to forestall federal imposition of controls. Despite the publicity surrounding a 'new federalism' in state–national relations, in some areas the federal government has been moving inexorably toward stronger federal control. This trend dates from 1916, when a Canadian–American Treaty for the Protection of Migratory Birds was signed. One practical reason for this treaty was to enable the federal government to by-pass constitutional restrictions on federal control of state-owned wildlife (Caldwell, 1984, p. 29). More recently, the Striped Bass Conservation Act, noted above, provides for federal controls on striped bass within state waters if the states fail to comply with the Act. Although the legality of this Act has been questioned (Bubier and Rieser, 1984), it is still evident that the national government will move to protect important resources if the states fail to act (Cicin-Sain, 1986, pp. 241–3).

Cooperative management is not necessarily regional; another approach is to focus on the local or community-level approach. Such cooperative agreements operate effectively, for example, in Japanese fisheries (Chapter 10).

Community involvement in Chesapeake Bay fisheries is at present confined to fishermen's input in the regulatory process. Both individuals and groups provide comment during rule-making, and information and opinions to elected representatives. Community leaders rightly fear that giving regulatory control to a regional authority would diminish their involvement. In addition, there is no tradition of state-wide cooperation among users. In actuality, reluctance to cooperate across state boundaries is stronger at the local level, where daily contact with competitors and enforcement officials exacerbates rivalry and reinforces parochial solidarity.

Within the states, fishermen have evolved customs of territoriality and norms of behaviour (Carpenter, 1986; Travelstead, 1986). The regulatory process of each state has evolved slowly, and it is therefore accepted by the fishermen. The conflicts arise when fishermen from one state desire access to fish stocks or markets in another state. Because these conflicts involve matters of state law such as gear, seasons, and catch limits, they cannot be resolved at the individual or community level. Thus, any resolution of conflicts caused by the multi-jurisdictional nature of the resource must be resolved at the state level. The management history of the resource, with almost exclusive reliance on complicated government regulation, leaves community-based management as an unlikely option.

In conclusion, of the three changes suggested by using the typology, only one has been implemented without apparent difficulty. The attempt to increase regional cooperation by establishing a fisheries advisory group was not successful. However, one cannot conclude that a different approach to regional management would not succeed.

The primary value of the typology at this point in its development is heuristic. It allows managers to isolate resource characteristics, to identify similarities in management institutions, and to postulate connections between characteristics and successful institutions.

Acknowledgements

The author wishes to thank Northern Arizona University for financial support to conduct research on Chesapeake Bay fisheries in 1985 and 1986.

References

Austin, Herb (Virginia Institute of Marine Science), 1986: Personal interview. 5 August.

Bean, Michael J., 1983: *Evolution of National Wildlife Law*, Praeger, New York.

Berkes, Fikret, 1981: 'Role of self-regulation in living resources management in the north', in Freeman, M.M.R., ed., *Renewable Resources and the Economy of the North*, Ottawa, ACUNS/MAB.

Berkes, Fikret and Pocock, Dorothy, 1981: 'Self-regulation of commercial fisheries of the outer Long Point Bay, Lake Erie', *Journal of Great Lakes Research*, 7(2), pp. 111–16.

Berkes, Fikret and Pocock, Dorothy, 1983: 'Ontario native fishing agreement in perspective, a study in user-group ecology', *Environments*, 15(3), pp. 17–26.

Bruce v. *Director, Department of Chesapeake Bay Affairs*, 1971, 261 Md. 585.

Bubier, Jill and Rieser, Alison, 1984: 'Atlantic striped bass Conservation Act: Unconstitutional amendment of an interstate compact?', *Territorial Sea* IV, No. 4, December, pp. 1–11.

Caldwell, Lynton, 1984: *International Environmental Policy: Emergence and Dimensions*, Duke University Press, Durham NC.

Carpenter, A.C., (Executive Secretary, Potomack River Fisheries Commission), 1986: Personal interview, 4 August.

Chesapeake Bay Commission, 1983: *Summary and Comparison of Laws and Regulations Pertaining to the Commercial Marine Fisheries of Maryland and Virginia: 1983 Update*, Annapolis.

Chesapeake Bay Commission, 1984: *Annual Report to the General Assemblies of Maryland and Virginia, 1984*, Annapolis.

Christy, Francis, 1977: 'Transitions in the management and distribution of international fisheries', *International Organization*, 31(2), Spring, pp. 235–65.

Cicin-Sain, Biliana, 1986: 'Ocean resources and intergovernmental relations: An analysis of the patterns', in Silva, Maynard, ed., *Ocean Resources and the U.S. Intergovernmental Relations in the 1980s*, Westview, Boulder, CO.

Citizens Program for The Chesapeake Bay, 1983: '*Values of the Day*', in *Choices for The Chesapeake: An Action Agenda*, Baltimore.

Cronin, Eugene, Gross, Grant, Lynch, Maurice and Sullivan, Kevin, 1977: 'The Conditions of the Chesapeake Bay – a consensus', in *Proceedings of the Bi-State Conference in the Chesapeake Bay*, EPA, NSF, USFWS, Washington, DC.

Cox, Susan J.B., 1985a: 'Fisheries management and interstate cooperation in the Chesapeake Bay', Paper presented at 1985 Annual Conference, American Society for Public Administration, Indianapolis. March 24–27.

Cox, Susan J.B., 1985b: 'Flawed perceptions in the foundations of public policy: The case of Hardin's tragedy of the commons', Paper presented at the Annual Meeting, Southern Political Science Association, Nashville, TN, 6–9 November.

Cox, Susan J.B., 1985c: 'No tragedy on the commons', *Environmental Ethics*, 7, Spring, pp. 49–61.

Dewar, Margaret, 1983: *Industry in Trouble: The Federal Government and the New England Fisheries*, Temple University Press, Philadelphia.

DNR Staff (Maryland Department of Natural Resources: Tidewater Administration, Annapolis), 1986: Personal interviews, 29 July.

Dorfman, Robert, 1974: 'Technical basis for decision-making', in Haefele, Edwin, ed., *Governance of Common Property Resources*, Baltimore, Johns Hopkins for RFF, pp. 5–25.

Douglas v. *Seacoast Products*, 1977, 431 U.S. 265.

Eckert, Ross, 1979: *The Enclosure of Ocean Resources: Economics and the Law of the Sea*, Hoover Institution Press, Stanford, CA.

Environmental Policy Institute, nd: *Summary of States' Chesapeake Bay Cleanup Efforts*, Washington.

Goldsborough, Bill, 1984: 'Striped bass fishing ban announced', *Chesapeake Bay Foundation News*, 9(3), November, p. 1.

Goldsborough, Bill, 1986: Personal communication, 13 June.

Gonner, E.C.K., 1966: *Common Land and Inclosure*, Cass, 1917 (2nd edn), London.

Grotius, Hugo, 1608: *Freedom of the Seas*, trans. Ralph Magoffin, New York, Oxford University Press, 1916. (rpt. edn, Arno Press, New York, 1972.)

Gulland, J.A., 1974: *Management of Marine Fisheries*, University of Washington Press, Seattle.

Hooper, Antony, 1985: 'Tokelau fishing in traditional and modern contexts', in Ruddle, Kenneth and Johannes, R.E., eds, *Traditional Knowledge and Management* of Coastal Systems, Jakarta Pusat Indonesia, UNESCO (Regional Office for Science and Technology for Southeast Asia), p. 7–38.

Horton, Tom, 1981: 'Border dispute dates back centuries', *Baltimore Sun*, 8 March.

Hoskins, W.G. and Dudley Stamp, L., 1965: *The Common Land of England and Wales*, Collins, London.

Johnston, Douglas, 1965: *International Law of Fisheries*, Yale University Press, New Haven.

Jones, J. Claiborne, 1982: 'Chesapeake Bay fisheries management primer', Chesapeake Bay Commission, Annapolis.

Jones, J. Claiborne (Assistant Director, Chesapeake Bay Commission), 1986: Personal interview, 30 July.

Kent, George, 1979: 'Global fisheries management', in Orr, David and Soroos, Marvin, eds, *The global predicament: Ecological Perspectives on World Order*, UNC Press, Chapel Hill, pp. 232–48.

Lynch, Maurice (Head, Division of Marine Resource Management: Virginia Institute of Marine Science), 1986: Personal interview, 5 August.

Miller, Marc and Van Maanen, John, 1983: 'Emerging and organization of fisheries in the United States', *Coastal Zone in Management Journal*, 10(4), pp. 369–86.

Olson, Mancur, 1965: *Logic of Collective Action*, Harvard University Press, Cambridge, MA.

Ostrom, Elinor, 1986: 'An agenda for the study of institutions', *Public Choice*, 48, pp. 3–25.

Pringle, J.D., 1985: 'The human factor in fishery resource management', *Canadian Journal of Fisheries and Aquatic Sciences*, 42(2), pp. 389–92.

Regier, H.A. and Grima, A.P., 1985: 'Fishery resource allocation: An exploratory essay', *Canadian Journal of Fisheries and Aquatic Sciences*, 42(4), pp. 845–59.

Rothschild, Brian, Lieberman, Warren, Jones, Phillip and Stagg, Cheney, 1984: 'An action program to develop a management system for Chesapeake Bay fisheries', Chesapeake Biological Laboratory (Center for Environmental and Estuarine Studies: University of Maryland), Solomons, MD.

Ruddle, Kenneth and Akimichi, Tomoya, 1984: 'Introduction', in Ruddle and Akimichi, eds, *Maritime Institutions in the Western Pacific*, National Museum of Ethnology, Osaka, Japan, pp. 1–9.

Ruddle, Kenneth and Johannes, R.E., eds, 1985: *Traditional Knowledge and Management of Coastal Systems in Asia and the Pacific*, UNESCO (Regional Office for Science and Technology for Southeast Asia), Jakarta Pusat, Indonesia.

Tangier Sound Waterman's Association v. *Douglas*, 1982, 541 F. Supp. 1287.

Toomer v. *Witsell*, 1948, 334 U.S. 385.

Travelstead, Jack, (Virginia Marine Resources Commission), 1986: Personal interview, 6 August.

Warner, William, 1976: *Beautiful Swimmers*, Little, Brown, Boston.

9 Meeting Environmental Concerns Caused by Common-Property Mismanagement in Economic Development Projects

Robert Goodland, George Ledec and Maryla Webb

Summary

Developing countries face serious environmental degradation problems, often discussed in terms of 'common property' resource mismanagement. Using a broad definition of common property, this paper presents three major categories of environmental mismanagement related to common property resources:

1 the misuse or breakdown of traditional common property management systems;
2 economically unjustified development projects or policies; and,
3 economically justified development projects or policies.

It focuses special attention on aspects of neoclassical economic analysis which need to be modified and supplemented by ecological criteria in order to promote more sustainable forms of development. It also suggests safe minimum standards, or non-market environmental criteria, which development projects or policies must meet in order to correct environmental mismanagement of common-property resources not easily quantified or valued.

Introduction

Many countries worldwide face serious environmental degradation, including deforestation, overgrazing, soil erosion and loss of cropland, misuse of biocides and other agrochemicals, overfishing, and locally severe water and air pollution. These problems result in considerable human suffering and seriously undermine future prospects for sustainable development. As used here, sustainable development is defined as a pattern of social and structural economic transformations which optimizes economic and other societal benefits available in the present, without jeopardizing the likely potential for similar benefits in the future. Many environmental problems are especially serious in the tropical, developing countries on which this paper focuses. Environmental degradation in developing countries also has negative consequences for the international community and for future generations. Of particular concern is deforestation and elimination of wildland habitats which threaten to cause the extinction of a sizeable proportion of the earth's plant and animal species within a single human generation (Ehrlich and Ehrlich, 1981).

The failure of human societies to prevent a wide range of environmental degradation is often discussed in terms of 'common property' resource mismanagement (Hardin and Baden, 1977). Indeed, much environmental degradation has been of resources which are either communal (held in common by a group of people) or freely accessible to anyone. However, severe environmental degradation frequently occurs on privately held lands as well.

Most of the examples used in this chapter are taken from the work of the World Bank; comments, though, are generally applicable to natural-resource-development projects and policies throughout the Third World. The resources that are being 'developed' or impacted by these projects and policies are usually public goods – commodities, services, or other items of value which, if available to one person, can be supplied to other people at no addition cost (Pearce, 1984). These goods can belong to one of the three categories of common property distinguished earlier (Chapter 1): open-access resources (*res nullius*); communally held resources (*res communes*); and nation-state property (*res publica*). We also include as common property 'pure' public goods – goods with infinite, additive benefits such that usage by one person does not reduce the amount available for others. An example would be the scenic value of the sunset. Our definition of common property is therefore intended to encompass the full range of environmental issues associated with development projects in the Third World, including renewable and non-renewable natural resources, environmental services (for example, watershed functions), and 'intangible' environmental benefits (such as those derived from the 'existence value' of rare species).

Using a broad definition of common property, this chapter presents three circumstances which may lead to environmental mismanagement of common property resources in developing countries:

1 the misuse or breakdown of traditional common property management systems;
2 economically unjustified development projects or policies; and
3 economically justified development projects or policies.

The main contribution of this chapter is a critique of central planning-level thinking used by state-level (*res publica*) government planners or economic development advisors. We acknowledge that this paper is possibly too 'macro' and 'Western' and 'formally economic' – but that is the reality of development planning. Therefore, this chapter focuses special attention on aspects of neoclassical economic analysis which need to be modified and supplemented by ecological criteria in order to promote more sustainable forms of development. As used here, 'neoclassical' refers to a spectrum of more or less conventional, market-oriented capitalist economics. Neoclassical, rather than, say, Marxist (cf. Bunker, 1985; Redclift 1984; and Perelman 1974), economic analysis is a principal focus of this paper because of its wide use by international development agencies, government officials, and other development planners. Our chapter also proposes safe minimum standards, or non-market environmental criteria, which development projects or policies must meet in order to correct environmental mismanagement of common-property resources not easily quantified or valued.

Environmental mismanagement involving misuse or breakdown of traditional common-property systems

Environmental degradation occurring in developing countries can be attributed partly to the misuse or breakdown of traditional common-property resource-management practices. Such misuse or breakdown typically occurs as a result of various far-reaching changes in the circumstances involving natural-resource utilization (Table 9.1).

These changes have produced severe degradation of the environment and natural-resource base throughout much of the developing world. The World Bank and other development organizations are continually confronted with these types of common-property management problems. The following examples, taken from World Bank financed projects, illustrate the diversity of forms which such environmental degradation can take.

1 The site of the proposed Lesotho Highlands Water Project is communally grazed by livestock owned by tribal people who are frequently paid with cattle rather than money for their labour in the mines. In the comparatively short period of human settlement, the natural resources of these highlands have suffered. The large native mammals have virtually disappeared; such woodland or forest cover as once existed has been depleted; and the rangeland suffers from accelerated soil erosion and depletion of vegetation palatable to livestock.
2 As industrial and urban development has proceeded in East Java, Indonesia, the use of the Kali Surabaya River as a communal sink for discharging untreated effluents has resulted in severe pollution. Swimming and fishing are dangerous, and water withdrawn for domestic and industrial use requires extensive and costly treatment.

Table 9.1 Changes causing breakdown of traditional common-property systems

---

1 Increased participation in market economies, which encourages the overexploitation for export of natural resources which were previously harvested for local subsistence only.

2 Breakdown of traditional value systems, which often directly or indirectly encouraged resource conservation.

3 Population growth, which often produces pressure for overexploiting fixed natural-resource stocks to meet subsistence needs.

4 Technological change, which often makes it physically easier to overexploit natural resources.

5 Increasing centralization of power and application of inappropriate pricing, subsidies, legislation, or other governmental incentives.

Based on Berkes (1985), Bromley and Chapagain (1984), Kirchner et al. (1985), Norberg-Hodge (1985).

3 Insecure land tenure in Brazil and Thailand is believed to be partially responsible for the rapid and wasteful forest clearing that is widespread in these countries (see also Chapter 4). Several World Bank-financed projects in these countries consist largely of land titling and registration, since more secure land tenure is an important condition for improving land management.

4 Nationalization of forests and wood plantations in Ethiopia has led to an increase in exploitation by commercial charcoal producers, as well as individuals gathering firewood. Moreover, tree planting has ceased because of uncertainty about future access to the resource. As a result, there is a chronic shortage of fuelwood and the country is within a few years of losing virtually its entire tree cover.

Environmental mismanagement involving economically unjustified development policies

Natural-resource policies can be considered economically efficient if resource consumers are charged the full amount of the economic losses borne by society because of the consumption of these resources. Warford (1986) defines these losses as the marginal opportunity cost (MOC). A price less than the MOC would stimulate natural-resource consumption in excess of the economically optimal level.

A wide variety of government policies in developing countries provide explicit or implicit subsidies for natural resource consumption in excess of economically optimal levels, thereby encouraging environmental mismanagement. Some of the most prevalent forms of such subsidies are listed below.

1 Infrastructure is often provided for activities which cannot be justified economically. For example, many governments build expensive roads into forested or other natural areas to encourage settlement, even if such settlement cannot be justified by economic cost-benefit analysis and is ecologically unsustainable. Much settlement and deforestation of the Brazilian Amazon can be explained in terms of explicit government subsidies for infrastructure and various services, not as the result of *laissez-faire* market forces (Goodland and Irwin, 1975; Hecht, 1981; Skillings and Tcheyan, 1980; Bunker, 1985).

2 Individuals or firms involved in natural-resource exploitation often receive generous tax concessions. For example, several Southeast Asian nations have provided substantial tax reductions and waivers to corporations involved in ecologically unsustainable forms of tropical forest logging (NAS, 1980; Ledec, 1985).

3 Agricultural and livestock credit is often heavily subsidized. Such subsidies can occur through below-market interest rates which do not fully cover the opportunity cost of capital, or are not fully adjusted for inflation; they can also occur through lenient collection practices which encourage default (Adams et al, 1984). Subsidized agriculture credit frequently encourages economically excessive use of biocides and fertilizers; numerous ecological problems often result from such overuses (Goodland et al, 1984). Subsidized credit sometimes also supports land clearing for ecologically unsustainable activities. This was the case with the Brazilian government's investment credits for cattle ranching in Amazonia throughout most of the 1970s (Norgaard, 1979).

4 In many countries, land-titling policy requires the clearing of forests or other natural vegetation in order to be eligible for obtaining title or other legal rights to the land. In fact, landowners or land claimants who do not clear the natural vegetation often risk losing their title or other land rights, as noted by Hartshorn et al (1982) for Costa Rica and Chapin (in press) for Panama. Such policies are rooted in the perception that forests or other natural vegetation have no social value unless they are cleared or otherwise directly exploited by people (Ledec and Goodland, 1988b). This perception overlooks the important environmental services which forests or other ecosystems provide, including watershed and soil protection, habitat for threatened species, or climatic stabilization.

Governments can reduce many environmental problems (and save public money) simply by eliminating subsidies such as these. This approach can be justified both by ecological and neoclassical economic criteria.

Environmental mismanagement involving economically justified development policies

Of particular interest and concern are those types of development policies which are unjustified according to ecological criteria but justified by prevailing neoclassical economic criteria. These controversial economic prescriptions are used at both the project and country planning levels.

At the project level, environmentally unsound forms of development are usually justified economically through a variety of cost-benefit analysis (CBA) techniques. Even when CBA is conducted exactly according to the 'rules of the game' (as outlined by Mishan, 1976), it tends to be strongly and systematically biased against basic ecological concerns. The principal reasons for this bias are measurement and valuation difficulties, irreversibility, and the discount rate (Goodland and Ledec, 1986).

Measurement and valuation difficulties

Development projects have many environmental consequences which, while very real, cannot readily be assigned a monetary value. This is due to the difficulties inherent in both physical estimation and monetary valuation of the relevant environmental effects. In terms of physical effects, it may be difficult, as an example, to predict a priori to what extent the building of a rural road through a forested area may affect soil erosion, as well as downstream sedimentation and water quality. Similarly, it may be very difficult to predict to what extent the projected use of agricultural chemicals in an irrigation project may reduce downstream fish catches, particularly in the longer term. In practice, physical estimation of the environmental effects of a proposed project usually amounts to little more than educated guesswork. This uncertainty is due in part to the relative lack of appropriate scientific data and the complexity of environmental processes, as well as the site-specific nature of many environmental effects.

Difficulties in the physical estimation of relevant environmental effects are further compounded by the fact that relatively gradual changes in resource use can sometimes produce discontinuous and catastrophic effects in multispecies ecosystems. These changes may be counter-intuitive and irreversible (Goodland and Ledec, 1986). For example, there have already been a number of unexpected ecological collapses in economically important ocean fisheries.

Even when the physical environmental effects of a proposed project can be predicted with some accuracy, monetary valuation of these effects may still prove impossible or exceedingly difficult (Hufschmidt et al, 1983). For example, soil erosion, loss of fertility, or other (often long-term) reductions in the productive potential of cropland may not be reflected in the market price of the land. This is particularly the case in many developing countries, where land markets are highly distorted and land tenure is often insecure. Even when reasonably accurate monetary valuation of tangible environmental effects is possible, it is usually not done in practice because the required inputs of data and staff time are too great.

To complicate matters further, many environmental benefits, while arguably important, are 'intangible', as noted above. Efforts to measure intangible environmental benefits in monetary terms have been unsatisfactory. For example, some resource economists have attempted to measure people's 'willingness to pay' for the conservation of certain natural areas by measuring the travel costs and other expenditures of visitors to these areas. This approach can account for only a limited proportion of the total value of such natural areas, because it cannot measure the strong, non-market convictions that people (of present or future generations) may have about how these areas should be managed. In this context, it is important to note that individuals' preferences as selfish, market-oriented consumers are often not consistent with their public-policy opinions as socially-minded citizens (Sagoff 1984; Lind et al, 1982). Moreover, a substantial number of people do not share the value judgment implicit in CBA that behaviour towards the natural world should be governed largely by criteria for maximizing economic wealth. Comprehensive valuation of intangible environmental benefits therefore needs to be guided by ethical codes of conduct, not simply economic CBA.

Irreversibility

Many of the environmental consequences of development projects or policies are either completely irreversible or reversible only over a very long time-scale (by human standards). Examples of more or less irreversible environmental effects include species extinctions, groundwater contamination, fossil-fuel depletion, loss of the traditional knowledge of indigenous tribal peoples when they are rapidly acculturated, soil erosion, human-induced climatic changes, and the removal of slowly reproducing ecosystems such as coral reefs and certain types of forests. Species extinctions or other irreversible environmental loses are the ones which future generations are least likely to forgive this generation.

CBA techniques usually treat irreversible costs (if they have even been considered and quantified) no differently from more readily reversible ones. A number of resource economists have attempted to develop appropriate methods for adequately considering irreversible effects in economic analysis (Bishop, 1982; Arrow and Fisher, 1974). However, such methods have yet to be refined and property institutionalized within the CBA procedures of most government agencies and international development organizations (Goodland and Ledec, 1986). The implicit value judgment inherent in CBA is therefore that irreversible consequences are no more important or serious than reversible ones. The inattention of CBA techniques to the special problems posed by irreversibility is unfortunate but not surprising, since CBA is based on the mechanistic concept of a readily reversible 'market equilibrium' (Norgaard, 1983).

The discount rate

Present-day economic CBA invariably involves using a discount rate to obtain the 'present value' of future cost and benefits. Discounting means that the further a benefit or cost occurs in the future, the less value it is given in a CBA. The use of discounting in CBA is often justified as a means of encouraging the economically efficient investment of funds, in order to screen out less profitable projects (Baum and Tolbert, 1985). However, the discount rates used in the CBA of public projects (often 10 per cent or more in real terms, ie after inflation) are strongly biased against environmental concerns, because they favour projects with short-term benefits and long-term costs.

By contrast, ecologically sound management of natural resources often entails the imposition of short-term costs in order to secure substantially long-term benefits. As an example, the logging of timber from a primary forest (which yields immediate economic benefits) will be more favoured by discounting than reforestation (which provides only long-term economic benefits). Similarly, long-term environmental problems which may not occur until 20 years or more into the future (such as the contamination of ground-water by leaking radioactive wastes) are rendered virtually costless by discounting in a typical CBA. Therefore, from an ecological perspective, low (or even zero or negative) discount rates can be desirable, in order to promote projects with long-term benefits, while discouraging those with long-term costs.

Correcting environmental mismanagement

Pricing environmental effects

One approach to correcting the deficiencies of economic CBA in addressing the ecological aspects of development projects and policies is to make CBA more comprehensive in its consideration of important ecological issues by assigning 'shadow prices' to environmental effects. Shadow prices are economic values imputed to goods or services which have no market price (or for which the market price is considered 'distorted', such that it does not accurately reflect actual social costs and benefits).

An example of using shadow pricing to achieve ecological and economic goals is a World Bank-supported irrigated rice project on the island of Sulawesi, Indonesia. A relatively small component of this project provided for the establishment of the 3200 square kilometre Dumoga-Bone National Park. The park's dense tropical forests encompass the entire watershed catchment area for the project's irrigation works. Conserving these forests helps to protect and enhance the productivity of these irrigation works by reducing sedimentation and resulting maintenance costs, and by helping to prevent irregularities in water supply (Ledec and Goodland, 1988a). In this case, the park's other major environmental benefits (including the preservation of threatened endemic forest species) were not even necessary to justify this conservation component. Economic CBA, by considering the watershed protection benefits of forests, was sufficient to justify the establishment of this large forest preserve (Goodland and Ledec, 1986).

Pricing of 'environmental externalities' for the cost-benefit analysis of development projects involves two steps. The first step is the physical estimation of environmental effects. Some of the difficulties in such estimations are noted above. Despite these difficulties, physical estimation is essential for evaluating the environmental effects of proposed projects or policies, whether CBA, 'safe minimum standards' (discussed below), or other decision criteria are used.

The second step is the monetary valuation of the environmental effects. A variety of different CBA techniques can be used in such valuation. These techniques suffer from many deficiencies, and (as noted above) tend systematically to underestimate environmental values. However, they are capable of providing partial, 'lower bound' estimates of many (though not all) environmental benefits and costs. As the Dumoga-Bone National Park example suggests, major environmental improvements in development projects can often be justified through CBA that assigns shadow prices to only a limited range of the total environmental benefits.

Replacement cost
The cost of replacing some environmental benefits through other means can be estimated. For example, the replacement cost of not conserving forests in watershed-catchment areas can include the costs of dredging silt from reservoirs, navigation canals, harbours and irrigation works, or of providing check dams and other engineering works for flood and erosion control. These costs are then added in order to estimate the value of the environmental service.

'Consumer/producer surplus' value of lost production
Certain marketed goods could not be produced in the absence of various

environmental services or other environmental benefits. For example, the benefits of mangroves, coral reefs, or other fish breeding areas can be partially calculated by estimating the decline in output at a fish cannery if these habitats were eliminated. Similarly, some of the economic value of fuelwood (sustainably harvested from a forest or woodland) can be calculated by estimating the loss in agriculture output that would result from substituting animal dung as fuel (so that it is unavailable as fertilizer).

Cost of compensating victims
The cost of compensating victims for certain types of environmental damage (such as increased flooding or air pollution) can sometimes be estimated, to the extent that such victims can be identified. This cost is then taken as an approximate value of the environmental service.

Property values
The maintenance of some environmental benefits (such as flood control from forested watersheds) can enhance the property values of downstream or adjacent lands. An estimate of this rise in value is then used as an estimate of the value of the environmental benefits. Since land markets in developing countries are often disorganized, constrained by sociocultural factors, or otherwise inefficient, an artificially appraised land value is often used (Ledec and Goodland, 1988a).

Willingness to pay or accept
This approach is often used to assign monetary values to intangible environmental benefits. Willingness to pay (WTP) is the maximum amount than an individual or group would voluntarily pay to prevent environmental damage. (The related concept of willingness to accept (WTA) is the minimum payment that the individual or group would accept to allow the environmental damage.) Both the WTP and WTA techniques involve measuring environmental benefits in terms of the estimated satisfaction in monetary terms they provide to people in the present generation. As such, they can be questioned from an ethical perspective (Ehrenfeld, 1981; Sagoff, 1984). Nonetheless, these methodologies are sometimes useful in development policy formulation because they can increase the attention given to intangible environmental concerns by policy-makers and can be of some use as 'lower bound' estimates of intangible environmental benefits. In policy decisions, these incomplete estimates are still preferable to the usual alternatives, which is implicitly assuming that these intangible benefits have zero value.

Safe minimum standards

'Safe minimum standard' (SMS) analysis (Ciriacy-Wantrup, 1972; Bishop, 1978; Bishop and Anderson, 1985) is another approach which can be used to address these ecological concerns which are given little or no attention in economic CBA. An SMS is any non-market criterion which a project must meet to be approved. SMS analysis is a time-tested, standard operating procedure that is widespread throughout engineering design, health planning, industrial-worker safety and other sectors. For example, a bridge is commonly designed with a safety factor of three or more to accommodate the unexpected and the unknown (Goodland and Ledec, 1986).

When used in the appraisal of development projects, SMSs constrain the economic CBA by specifying environmental, social, or other criteria which the project must meet in all cases. If a project is modified to meet SMS criteria, any extra costs of such modification are automatically added to other project costs in the CBA. If a proposed project cannot be modified to meet SMS criteria, it is abandoned in favour of more environmentally or socially prudent investments. CBA which incorporates SMSs is therefore a type of constrained economic optimization.

In recent years, the World Bank has advanced considerably in the use of environmental and social SMSs in the appraisal of proposed development project (Table 9.2). Comprehensive and routine implementation of these relatively new policies would significantly help to rectify many of the above-mentioned conflicts between economics and ecology. The Bank's experience to date has shown that the costs of modifying projects so that they meet the SMSs are usually a very small fraction of total project costs (World Bank, 1984; Ledec and Goodland, 1988a; Baum and Tolbert, 1985). The main exception to this rule is some cases of involuntary human resettlement, when large numbers of people need to be moved to accommodate a hydroelectric or other project. This constraint on conventional economic optimization in project analysis, however, is social, rather than strictly environmental, in nature.

Ecological SMSs can be set at levels that policy-makers can more or less agree upon as 'reasonable', given the particular circumstances of a proposed development project or policy. SMSs are often applied in ways 'tailored' for specific projects, countries, or religions (Baum and Tolbert, 1985). Such tailoring is often appropriate because of the great variation in the natural-resource base, environmental absorptive capacities, population pressure, and economic and social conditions of different areas. For example, applying the appropriate SMSs for forest conservation would differ for Rwanda (which has lost the great majority of its original forest cover) and Guyana (which remains about 90 per cent forested) (Ledec and Goodland, 1988a). By lending their expertise to the development-planning process, ecologists can be

Table 9.2 Safe minimum standard criteria of World Bank projects

---

1 Projects depending on the harvest of renewable natural resources (such as forests, fisheries, and grazing lands) shall adhere to sustained-yield principles, to minimize the risk of overexploitation and degradation (through overcutting, overfishing, or overgrazing) (World Bank, 1984).

2 Projects shall not clear, inundate, or otherwise convert ecologically important wildland ecosystems, including (but not limited to) officially designated protected areas, without adequate compensatory measures (World Bank, 1984; Ledec and Goodland, 1988a).

3 Projects shall avoid knowingly causing the extinction or endangerment of plant or animal species, unless adequate mitigatory measures are provided (World Bank, 1984; Ledec and Goodland, 1988a).

4 Any project based in one country shall not affect the environment or natural resource base of any neighbouring countries without their full consent (World Bank, 1984).

5 Projects shall not contravene any international environmental agreement to which the borrowing country is party (World Bank, 1984).

6 Any groups seriously disadvantaged by Bank-supported projects (such as vulnerable ethnic minorities or communities undergoing involuntary resettlement) shall be appropriately compensated to a degree that makes them at least no worse off (and preferably better off) than without the project. This is to be done even if the compensatory project components do not contribute to the stream of economic benefits (World Bank, 1982; World Bank, 1984).

7 Projects shall not compromise public health and safety to any degree which would be widely regarded as unacceptable by the affected people or by experienced, impartial third parties (World Bank, 1982; World Bank, 1984).

---

indispensable in the formulation and site-specific application of SMSs for different ecosystems.

Limits to throughput

At the national development policy level, an environmentally critical issue concerns the appropriate scale of aggregate resource consumption and waste discharge. Daly (1980) refers to this flow of energy and materials into and out of the economy as 'throughput'. A major operating assumption common in political and socioeconomic circles is that there are no ecological or social limits to the physical scale or rate of throughput, or that these limits are so distant as to be irrelevant. However, substantial evidence is now available to indicate that limits to growth in throughput do exist and in many cases are close to being reached. Recent data indicate that the productivity of basic renewable resource systems, particularly croplands, forests, grazing lands, and fisheries, is now declining in many countries (Brown et al, 1985; WRI and IIED, 1986). The marginal cost of discovering and exploiting many new mineral and fossil-fuel deposits is increasing exponentially. Despite evidence such as this, even the theoretical possibility of limits to growth (not just their imminence) is flatly denied by many economists (Barnet and Morse, 1963; Beckerman, 1974; Simon, 1981).

The 'limits to growth' debate can be clarified by distinguishing between growth in throughput (natural-resource consumption) and in economic output *per se* (as measured by gross national product or a related index). Notwithstanding any conceivable technological advances, growth in throughput (whether due to an increase in population, per capita consumption, or both) is ultimately constrained by the physical laws of thermodynamics, by ecological principles, and by the finite size of the planet. However, growth in economic output might not be similarly constrained, since innovation might conceivably continue to find ways to squeeze ever more economic 'value added' from a natural-resource bundle. Thus, governments concerned with the long-term sustainability of their development programme need not necessarily limit growth in economic output, so long as they limit the extraction and harvesting of natural resources to sustainable levels.

'Steady-state economics' (Daly, 1977), one major attempt to define a theory of economics that admits limits to growth in throughput, has not been well received by mainstream neoclassical economists. Nonetheless, steady-state economics and similar alternative theories deserve more careful consideration and study from the economics profession, as well as from ecologists and other natural scientists. Current development strategies, which follow conventional economic prescriptions, often result in environmental degradation and reduced ecosystem stability. If policy-makers wish to ensure that their chosen development strategies are sustainable, they need to ensure that natural-resource throughput is limited to sustainable levels.

Conclusion

Widespread environmental degradation characteristic of economic development in Third World countries indicates ongoing mismanagement of common-property resources and environment in general. While environmental mismanagement occurs for a variety of reasons, much of it can unfortunately be justified by present-day techniques of neoclassical economic analysis. Application of neoclassical economics to development policy has profound and pervasive effects upon human societies and the natural environment worldwide. Ecologists and other scientists who have important insights about the functioning of the natural world can help ensure that these insights are adequately reflected in the formulation of development policy.

It is recognized that resources look different to the local community of users than to state planners; locals worry about access and are likely to have different discount rates and economic planning horizons. The formal economics discussed in this chapter often does not accurately reflect daily resource decisions in many societies. The practical survival strategies of many traditional communities toward common-property resources cannot be explained in Western economic terms, but in any case it is not particularly relevant to do so (Emmerson, 1980; Collier, 1977).

On the other hand, national decisions can determine the nature and economic optimality of property rights governing a resource. For example, state (*res publica*) or communally (*res communes*) owned land can be privatized through land-titling programs or, conversely, privately or communally owned land can be nationalized. Less stringent policies such as granting tax or licensing concessions to communes while charging higher fees or taxes to individuals or private firms, can also favour one form of resource management over another. Chapters in Part 3 address the strengths and weaknesses of the *res communes* type of common-property management and whether there is an environmentally optimal form of property rights.

Acknowledgements

The World Bank does not accept responsibility for the views expressed herein, which are those of the authors and should not be attributed to the World Bank or to its affiliated organizations. We gratefully acknowledge the advice and improvements generously received from Fawzi Rihane, Jeremy Warford, Richard Ackermann, and Hans-Eberhard Köpp.

References

Adams, D.W. et al., eds, 1984: *Undermining Rural Development with Cheap Credit*, Westview Press, Boulder, Colo.

Arrow, K.J. and Fisher, A.C., 1974: 'Environmental preservation and irreversibility', *Quarterly Journal of Economics*, 88(2), pp. 312–19.

Barnet, H. and Morse, C., 1963: *Scarcity and Growth*, Johns Hopkins University Press, Baltimore.

Baum, W.C. and Tolbert, S.M., 1985: *Investing in Development: Lessons from World Bank Experience*, Oxford University Press, Oxford, UK.

Beckerman, W., 1974: *In Defense of Economic Growth*, Jonathan Cape, London.

Berkes, F., 1985: 'Fishermen and "The Tragedy of the Commons"', *Environmental Conservation*, 12(3), pp. 199–206.

Bishop, R.C., 1978: 'Endangered species and uncertainty: The economics of a safe minimum standard', *American Journal of Agricultural Economics*, 60(1), pp. 10–18.

Bishop, R.C., 1982: 'Option value: An exposition and extension', *Land Economics*, 58(1), pp. 1–15.

Bishop, R.C. and Anderson, S.O., 1985: *Economics, Institutions and Natural Resources: Collected Works of S.V. Ciriacy-Wantrup*, Westview Press, Boulder, Colo.

Bromley, D.W. and Chapagain, D.P., 1984: 'The village against the center: Resource depletion in south Asia', *American Journal of Agricultural Economics*, 66, pp. 868–73.

Brown, L.R. et al, 1985: *State of the World 1985: A Worldwatch Institute Report on Progress Toward a Sustainable Society*, W.W. Norton & Co., New York.

Bunker, S.G., 1985: *Underdeveloping the Amazon: Extraction, Unequal Exchange and the Failure of the Modern State*, University of Illinois Press.

Chapin, M., (in press): 'Nusagandi: An indigenous project in environmental conservation', in Schumann, D.A. and Partridge, W.L., eds, *The Human Ecology of Tropical Land Settlement in Latin America*, Westview Press, Boulder, Colo.

Ciriacy-Wantrup, S.V., 1972: *Resource Conservation: Economics and Policies*, University of California Press, Berkeley.

Collier, W.L., 1977: *Agricultural Evolution in Java: The Decline of Shared Poverty and Involution*, Land Tenure Center, University of Wisconsin, Madison, Wis.

Daly, H.E., 1977: *Steady-state Economics: The Economics of Biophysical Equilibrium and Moral Growth*, W.H. Freeman, San Francisco.

Daly, H.E., ed., 1980: *Economics, Ecology, Ethics: Essays Toward a Steady-state Economy*, W.H. Freeman, San Francisco.

Ehrenfeld, D., 1981: *The Arrogance of Humanism*, Oxford University Press, Oxford, UK.

Ehrlich, P.R. and Ehrlich, A.H., 1981: *Extinction: The Causes and Consequences of the Disappearance of Species*, Random House, New York.

Emmerson, D.K., 1980: *Rethinking Artisanal Fisheries Development: Western Concepts, Asian Experiences*, World Bank, Washington, DC.

Goodland, R.J. and Irwin, H.S., 1975: *Amazon Jungle*, Elsevier Scientific, New York.

Goodland, R.J. et al, 1984: *Environmental Management in Tropical Agriculture*, Westview Press, Boulder, Colo.

Goodland, R.J. and Ledec, G., 1986: *Neoclassical Economics and Principles of Sustainable Development*, World Bank, Washington.

Hardin, G. and Baden, J., eds, 1977: *Managing the Commons*, W.H. Freeman, San Francisco.

Hartshorn, G. et al, 1982: *Costa Rica Country Environmental Profile: A Field Study*, Centro Cientifico Tropical, San Jose, Costa Rica.

Hecht, S., 1981: 'Deforestation in the Amazon Basin: Magnitude, dynamics, and social resource effects', *Studies in Third World Societies*, 13, pp. 61–108.

Hufschmidt, M. et al, 1983: *Environment, Natural Systems and Development: An Economic Valuation Guide*, Johns Hopkins University Press, Baltimore.

Kirchner, J.W. et al, 1985: 'Carrying capacity, population growth, and sustainable development', in Mahar, D.J., ed., *Rapid Population Growth and Human Carrying Capacity: Two Perspectives*, World Bank, Staff Working Paper No. 690, Washington, pp. 41–89.

Ledec, G., 1985: 'The political economy of tropical deforestation', in Leonard, H.J., ed., *Divesting Nature's Capital: The Political Economy of Environmental Abuse in the Third World*, Holmes and Meier, New York, pp. 179–226.

Ledec, G. and Goodland, R., 1988a: *Wildlands: Their Protection and Management in Economic Development*, World Bank, Washington.

Ledec, G. and Goodland, R., 1988b: 'Epilogue: An environmental perspective on tropical land settlement', in Schumann, D.A. and Partridge, W.L., eds, *The Human Ecology of Tropical Land Settlement in Latin America*, Westview Press, Boulder, Colo., pp. 372–383.

Lind, R.C. et al, 1982: *Discounting for Time and Risk in Energy Policy*, Johns Hopkins University Press, Baltimore.

Mishan, E.J., 1976: *Cost-benefit Analysis*, Praeger, New York.

Myers, N., 1980: *Conversion of Tropical Moist Forests*, US National Academy of Sciences, Washington.

Norberg-Hodge, H., 1985: *The Ladakh Project* (Transcript of an oral presentation), World Bank, Washington, DC.

Norgaard, R.B., 1979: *Agricultural Development and Environmental Transformation in Terra Firme Amazonia*, University of California, Agricultural Experiment Station Working Paper No. 112, Berkeley.

Norgaard, R.B., 1983: *Equilibria, Environmental Externalities and Property Rights: A Coevolutionary View*, University of California, Department of Agricultural and Resource Economics, Berkeley.

Pearce, D.W., ed., 1984: *Dictionary of Modern Economics*, MIT Press, Cambridge, Mass.

Perelman, M., 1974: 'An application of Marxian economics to environmental economics', *Review of Radical Political Economy*, 6, pp. 75–7.

Redclift, M., 1984: *Development and the Environmental Crisis: Red or Green Alternatives*, Methuen, London.

Sagoff, M., 1984: 'Ethics and economics in environmental law', in Regan, T., ed., *Earthbound: New Introductory Essays in Environmental Ethics*, Random House, New York, pp. 147–178.

Simon, J.L., 1981: *The Ultimate*, Princeton University Press, Princeton, NJ.

Skillings, R.F. and Tcheyan, N.O., 1980: *Economic Development Prospects of the Amazon Region of Brazil*, Johns Hopkins University, School of Advanced International Studies, Washington.

Warford, J.J., 1986: *Natural Resource Management and Economic Development*, World Bank, Projects Policy Department, Washington.

World Bank, 1982: *Tribal Peoples and Economic Development: Human Ecologic Considerations*, World Bank, Washington.

World Bank, 1984: *Environmental Policies and Procedures of the World Bank*, World Bank, Office of Environmental and Scientific Affairs, Washington.

WRI and IIED, 1986: *World Resources 1986: An Assessment of the Resource Base That Supports the Global Economy*, Basic Books, New York.

Part 3 Single Resource Case Studies

'Almost every basic fisheries conservation measure devised in the West was in use in the tropical Pacific centuries ago,' observed Robert Johannes in a 1978 paper in the Annual Review of Ecology and Systematics. But traditional conservation worked only as long as communities had control over access to the resource, and were able to enforce rules to regulate joint use.

There have been detailed accounts of the traditional ecological knowledge of Indonesian medicine men, Brazilian Amerindian forest managers, and African hunters of the rainforest. Traditional ecological knowledge of dazzling complexity can be cited from many geographic areas and for many kinds of resources, as done for example in Gary Klee's World System of Traditional Resource Management (see Chapter 1 for references).

Yet, throughout the world, resources are abused and people dependent on them are left impoverished. Thus, the mere possession of traditional ecological knowledge does not appear to be sufficient for sustainable resource management. What is missing?

It seems that successful systems of management require the ability to institute and maintain appropriate social and political organization (or 'common property institutions'). Traditional resource management systems such as those listed in Chapter 1, Table 1.1, require well-functioning common-property institutions. These institutions are susceptible to external (and presumably internal) disturbances but also have a capacity to recover from past abuses, as illustrated by the case study of the Cree Amerindian hunting territory system in Chapter 5. One of the keys to success involves adaption of appropriate science and technology without destroying well-functioning common-property institutions.

How do common-property institutions work? What makes them tick? How does success come? The chapters in Part 3 provide detailed case studies of a variety of common-property institutions in practice. The section deals with single-resource cases and consists of four chapters on aquatic resources – the first three on fisheries and the last one on water.

Chapter 10 by Ruddle is a success story in common-property-resource management, and explains how the community-based management system of Japanese coastal fisheries works. Japanese coastal fishermen enjoy legally guaranteed equitable access to and 'ownership' of aquatic living resources. In contrast to many Western nations, in Japan no conceptual distinction exists between land tenure and sea tenure. Communal fishing rights have a legal status equal to that of communal land ownership. The system, in which ownership is vested in local cooperative associations, has a great many variations in implementation, no doubt related to the deep historical roots of the system and the elaboration of locally adapted practices over time.

Chapter 11 by Miller describes a lobster fishery on the Caribbean coast of Mexico which developed as a commercial enterprise only after the mid-1950s. The case provides insights as to how a 'mature' communal management system such as that in the previous chapter may have evolved. Two of the cooperatives in the study area have been able to develop a system of limiting access and recognizing use rights, thus giving individuals and the cooperatives as a whole incentives to work harder, invest more and, at the same time, reduce the problem of free ridership or cheating.

Chapter 12 by Acheson deals with the evolution of a joint, community-level and state-level management system (co-management). The lobster fishery in Maine, Northeastern United States, which Acheson describes, is historically older than the fishery in Chapter 11 but probably more recent that the one in Chapter 10. In contrast to Japan and Mexico, a major difference in Maine is that there are no legal communal (or cooperative) use rights to the resource. Despite official state property and open-access policies in United States fisheries, Maine lobster fishermen have nevertheless maintained a sustainable fishery, with community-held territories, for at least a century. In more recent years, with increasing costs of fishing and a locally perceived need for tighter controls, the fishermen have started asking for more stringent regulations than those advocated by government managers. The author points out the irony of this, and calls into question the Hardinian axiom that users of common-property resources have no interest in long-term conservation.

Chapter 13 by Cruz provides a case study of water as common property in the Philippines where traditional water-management systems are well known. The chapter is an evaluation of the 1976 Water Code of the Philippines which was developed with the aim of using irrigation water resources efficiently and equitably. Water coming from a natural source is under state ownership in the Philippines. As Cruz explains, however, the very nature of water as a flow resource and the difficulty of controlling its distribution to many users, argue strongly for the establishment of collective rules on water allocation. The Water Code protects the rights of legitimate users – members of irrigation associations – by specifying the collective management of such waters. This case thus reflects the role and limitations of state-level controls in promoting equity among users, and provides an insight as to how state-level management may complement traditional systems.

The four aquatic-resource case studies in Part 3 provide a range of examples from the most complicated and elaborate (Japanese coastal fisheries and Philippines irrigation systems) to the relatively rudimentary and simple (Mexican lobster fisheries). They are useful in demonstrating the importance of historical factors (Chapter 10), the evolving nature of common-property systems (all four), and specifically the emergence of the integration of communal-level and state-level controls or co-management (Chapters 10, 12 and 13).

Co-management is an increasingly significant development in the contemporary world in which local-level traditional controls alone are in many cases insufficient. Because of ecological interconnectedness (see Chapter 7), relevant scientific information and sound technical knowledge have a role to play alongside traditional ecological knowledge and resource-management systems. State-level management becomes important in dealing with shared resources, such as irrigation water and migratory fish. The state is crucially important also in providing legal recognition for common-property institutions, one of the major findings of the Conference on Common Property Resource Management. The integration of science and technology with traditional practice, and the integration of government-level and local-level management are two major themes that run through this section. The success of resource management in Japanese coastal fisheries and other cases may be explained in part through such integration.

10 Solving the Common-Property Dilemma: Village Fisheries Rights in Japanese Coastal Waters

Kenneth Ruddle

Summary

Through a rights system and membership in local cooperative associations, Japanese coastal fishermen have legally guaranteed equitable access to and 'ownership' of the living aquatic resources in their tenured waters. Contemporary Japanese coastal sea tenure involves time-honoured village customary procedures that have been incorporated into modern legislation. Among other things, these complex and locally varied systems consist of the intimate interplay of community rules of conduct, local social sanctions and the interpersonal behaviour of fishermen with the formal institutions. This chapter examines the main features of fisheries rights, cooperative associations, and the use of sea territory in Japanese coastal waters.

Introduction

Understanding of non-Western traditional systems of coastal sea tenure has long been hampered by the dominant Western theories of the fishery as the epitome of an open-access natural resource, from which it was postulated fishermen's competitive social behaviour, overcapitalization of the industry, and overexploitation and the eventual crash of the resources arise. More recent research, however, has demonstrated this to be patently untrue for a wide range of societies (Ruddle and Akimichi, 1984; Ruddle and Johannes, 1985). Indeed, many Oceanian societies, for example, had centuries ago implemented fisheries management schemes that Western-trained administrators are now striving to design (Johannes, 1978).

Another example, not well documented until recent years in Western languages, is the case of Japan. Unlike the prevalent maritime tradition in the Western world, that in Japan never included the idea that the sea is a resource owned at once by everybody and nobody. On the contrary, there developed gradually over many centuries a complex system of locally varied customary village tenure and rights to fisheries in coastal marine waters.

These were incorporated into national legislation through the fisheries laws of 1901 and 1949. As a result, the local Fisheries Cooperative Association (FCA) has emerged as the principal corporate fisheries-rights-holding group in Japanese coastal waters.

During feudal times (1603–1868) there was a notable lack of nationwide uniformity in the importance, definition and regulatory procedures governing coastal fisheries. This characteristic has persisted at the village level, where customary laws and traditional patterns of behaviour continue to be of primary importance. Thus the contemporary management of Japanese coastal waters can be properly understood only if both the formal and informal bodies of law are examined, and the continuity of tradition appreciated (Ruddle, 1985).

This chapter describes the Japanese alternative in the management of coastal fisheries. There is no pretence at completeness since, perforce, only several main topics can be examined, and only at a general level.

The chapter demonstrates that, based on deep historical roots, communities of Japanese fishermen enjoy legally-guaranteed equitable access to and 'ownership' of the living aquatic resources in coastal waters. Further, no conceptual distinction exists in Japan between communal land holdings (*iriaichi*) and land tenure, and sea holdings (*iriai*) and sea tenure. Fisheries rights have a legal status equal to that of such communal land ownership. This is in contrast with many Western countries in which fisheries are considered 'common property' only in the legal sense of state property (*res publica*) to which access is free. The importance of the Japanese coastal fishery case is that it demonstrates that a communal-property arrangement (*res communes*) is both possible and feasible.

Japanese marine fisheries and their administration

Japanese marine fisheries are divisible into coastal, offshore and distant water types. Although never legally defined, an operational distinction can be made among them.

1 Distant water fisheries operate beyond the Japanese Exclusive Economic Zone (EEZ) and in those of other nations;
2 offshore fisheries, usually employing boats larger than ten gross tons, operate seawards of coastal fisheries but within the Japanese EEZ; and
3 coastal fisheries, mostly using boats of less than ten gross tons, operate landwards of the offshore fishery.

The fisheries are administered through a system of licences and fishing rights.

Fishing licences govern those types of fishery that move gear over considerable distances in search of highly mobile fish. They are issued for coastal, offshore and distant-water fisheries. In the coastal fishery they therefore occupy the same seaspace as the fishing rights areas. However, in principle, licences are issued for fishers not covered by fishing rights and in particular for migratory species taken from trawlers larger than 15 gross tons and purse seiners over 40 gross tons. Unlike fishing rights, fishing licences are not regarded as a legally protected use right. On the contrary, licensed fisheries operate under free competition.

Fishery rights in the marine environment apply to coastal waters, and cover those types of fishery that employ fixed gear or exploit a relatively immobile fauna, fish and invertebrates of the benthos. All coastal waters except port areas and reclaimed industrial zones are divided up among FCAs or federations of FCAs.

Three principal categories of rights are recognized under Japanese law: joint rights, demarcated rights and set net rights. All can – and not uncommonly do – exist within the same seaspace, to which, in coastal waters, licences are also granted.

Demarcated fishery rights are issued for small-scale aquaculture. Two classes exist. 'Special demarcated fishery rights' to coordinate and manage equitably different types of aquaculture operated in the same general area, and 'demarcated fishery rights' for more isolated sites where little coordination with others activities is necessary.

Rights for large-scale set-net fisheries are applied mainly to herring, migratory trout and salmon fisheries, as well as in Hokkaido, using gear set at depths greater than 27 metres. Since the high capital investment and large operating budget demanded by this technique effectively limit the number of nets, the area and sites of operation can be restricted easily by the prefecture. (Small- and medium-size nets, on the other hand, can be operated by many small-scale fishermen within a given area and so they are managed by the FCAs as a part of the joint fishery rights.)

In every instance joint rights embrace the entire sea territory of an FCA, whereas demarcated rights and those for set nets are granted only for specific areas within the joint-rights area. Further, whereas all fishermen belonging to a specific FCA are entitled to fish in that associations's joint-rights areas only, a limited number are granted set-net and demarcated rights. Whereas all FCAs have a joint-rights area the same is not true of the other two types of rights. These are granted only if an FCA has areas within its sea territory suitable for them.

Joint rights are granted exclusively to an FCA or a federation of FCAs for the coordinated use of its entire fishing area and aquatic resources by its membership. The FCA distributes them among the members, all of whom are entitled to fish in that associations's joint-rights area(s).

All FCAs have a joint-rights area but the other rights are granted by the prefectural fisheries office only if an FCA has areas within its sea territory suitable for them. Joint-rights areas always embrace the entire sea territory of an FCA. Three categories of joint rights are recognized: for the benthos catch; for small stationary gear set at a depth of less than 27 metres; and for beach seines.

The 1949 Fisheries Law and fisheries rights

The 1949 Fisheries Law gave fishery rights and licences to working fishermen only, and placed routine local fishery management in their hands through the local FCA (Zengyoren, 1979). FCA membership was restricted by the *Fisheries Cooperative Association Law* (1948) to fishermen resident in the jurisdictional area of the association who worked 90 to 120 days a year (the period being determined by each FCA). This law also ensured that the membership controlled an FCA. Professional fishermen cannot work without being a member of an FCA. As a consequence the FCA emerged as the vital organization linking the central and prefectural government with the individual fisherman. An FCA belongs entirely to a local community of fishermen. It constitutes the social and economic hub of modern Japanese fishing communities.

The fishing-rights system basically continues historical practices and protects coastal fishermen against other fisheries and economic sectors by granting them fully protected use rights. However, these rights cannot be loaned, rented or transferred to others; nor can they be mortgaged. These use rights are regarded as belonging exclusively to the fishermen to whom they are granted. Further, any infringement or loss of rights must, as has traditionally been the case, be compensated by monetary payment (Ruddle, 1987).

Although the details vary somewhat according to the specific fishery, those eligible to apply for fisheries rights must possess prior fishing experience, must not have been found guilty of flagrant violations of the Fisheries Law or pertinent labour regulations, and must not hold other fishery rights.

Thus under the Japanese system of coastal fisheries administration the FCA represents a community of local fishermen. Rights to exploit the bottom fauna, fish and invertebrates of the benthos in the adjacent coastal waters are granted jointly to the FCA by the prefectural fisheries office, acting on behalf of the ministry of agriculture, forestry and fisheries. In turn, the FCA then allocates these use rights to eligible individual fishermen that comprise its membership. Japanese coastal fishermen therefore possess the right to use a communal resource.

The role of the FCA

Any Japanese FCA has three principal management roles. The first, and principal role, is planning and managing the sustained development of its sea
territory according to the Fisheries Law (1949). This it does mainly by
implementing and enforcing national and prefectural legislation and regulations, supplemented or complemented by those made locally. The latter
generally cover closed seasons, conservation measures, and the membership
of individual fishing types. These rules are formalized in an FCA's
'executive rules for licensed fisheries' and approved by the prefecture.

A second main role is to represent its membership at the higher levels of
fisheries administration: the prefectural fisheries office, and the ministry of
agriculture, forestry and fisheries. Regular meetings are held with prefectural
officials to negotiate licensing and fisheries rights issues, as well as to obtain
higher-level approval of rules locally made by the FCA.

A third role, less frequently performed by most FCAs, is to defend the
rights of its membership against other sectors of government or private
parties whose actual or potential activities might have a deleterious impact on
fishery rights. When necessary, an FCA negotiates compensation rates for
losses or damage to those rights, or for relinquishing them outright.

In routine operational terms, Japanese coastal fisheries are essentially self-
managed by the individual FCAs or federations of FCAs. This enables
fishermen, through their role of committees and at general meetings, to determine the division of access rights among individual members and to ensure
that all interests are accounted for. It also permits higher-level fishery regulations to be adapted to regional differences in ecology, target species, fishing
effort and level of industrialization, among other factors. Further, it
guarantees that management strategies, processes of conflict resolution, and
interpersonal and intergroup relationships will be, to a large extent, based on
local customary law and codes of conduct.

Continual interaction among the levels of the fishery administration to
verify the various interpretations and understandings of laws and regulations
permits the incorporation of customary law within the regulations made at the
higher levels, and serves to foresee, prevent and resolve conflicts that might
otherwise arise between the two bodies of law. The control of resources from
within a fishing community as well as from above are two complementary
and mutually reinforcing channels that constitute a viable administrative and
management system for coastal fisheries.

The functioning of FCA administration

The ultimate control of an FCA is the general assembly of its entire

membership. The routine functioning and external relations of an FCA are
handled by an executive committee elected by and responsible to the general
assembly. This is usually comprised of a president, vice-president, advisors,
and regular members. The president and vice-president are professional
administrators, paid by the FCA, whose re-election is virtually a certainty.
But regular members are all fishermen who must win votes from within their
community to ensure re-election.

Conflicts tend to occur fairly frequently within an FCA but their impact is
mitigated by the full participatory consensus approach to decision-making that
is characteristic of Japanese organizations (Vogel, 1975). Squad or group
leaders and the directors of an FCA have no authority to make decisions on
behalf of the membership. Policy and other major decisions are always made
at meetings where everybody involved is in attendance and which are
governed by the normative objective of attaining a consensus that embraces
the interests of all concerned, rather than a simple majority approval. Decisions made otherwise are unacceptable. Such meetings are essentially negotiations involving concessions and counter-concessions, compromises and the
accommodation of various interests. They may be protracted and extend over
several weeks until a consensus has been achieved.

In most FCAs, fishermen are organized into fishery-type squads and
residential location groups. Through these, individual fishermen retain control
of their affairs, especially those pertaining to access to a fishery, since the
board of directors is obliged to follow closely the decisions of these small
groups. Thus, the fishery squads and residential groups are the main entities
in resource allocation. At the annual meetings of the various squads, the main
issues usually discussed are use rights, the equitable use of territory, and the
resolution of intersquad conflicts. The resolutions adopted are regarded as
formal within the squad and a secretary records them in a 'rule book', with
which potential conflicts are anticipated and managed, or resolved.
Commonly, the individual types of fishery covered by joint fisheries rights
are strictly controlled by the fishery squads, and the overall FCA is little
concerned with operational details within a specific fishery.

Equal access to an entire exclusive-rights area is not necessarily enjoyed by
all fishermen in all types of fishing within an FCA. In some FCAs, particular
waters are reserved for the exclusive use of individuals or squads, and operational strategies can vary greatly among the different types of fishery
conducted within an FCA. For example, whereas gill-netters in an FCA in
Hokkaido may fish anywhere in the FCA's territory, fishermen operating
small-scale fixed nets are regularly assigned the same fishing spots, since nets
must be individually tailored to the bottom topography in each spot fished
(Short, in press). In Tobishima, in northern Honshu, octopus holes within a
joint-rights area are held and inherited as personal use rights (Nagai, 1951).
In other fisheries, as in the live-bait fishery of Yaeyama in southern

Okinawa, for example, a lottery is used to allocate valuable fishing spots among squad members, whereas free competition and first-comers' rights prevail in less-productive locations (Ruddle, 1987; Ruddle and Akimichi, in press).

FCA membership and the acquisition of joint fisheries rights

Birthright – together with the requisite training, residence and full-time fishing – function additively in the acquisition of FCA membership and fishing rights. Some communities formalized this through rigorous apprenticeships, although this was uncommon. Most entry was and is informal, based on years of on-the-job training within a family or kin group, supervised by and in partnership with older kinsmen and family members. A man then applies to the FCA for fishing right, after which he works either independently or, more commonly, with his instructor – to whose fishery rights he will eventually succeed. Most coastal fishing units involving more than one person are crewed by a father–son team or by brothers. In many FCAs the senior person holds the fisheries rights as a full, voting member of the association, whereas the others are associate members (non-voting).

The requisite experience to qualify for FCA membership can also be gained by crewing on a boat. Marrying into a community and then working with the in-laws is also another traditional means of effecting entry.

The methods by which joint fisheries rights are acquired in present-day Japan vary greatly in detail among FCAs and are strongly influenced by local historical, economic and sociopolitical factors, as well as by everyday face-to-face interpersonal relationships within a village (Kada, 1984; Kalland, 1981; Ruddle, 1987). This precludes easy generalization, since local practice, even though upholding the spirit of the national law, may differ considerably from its letter. In many fishing villages the 'subjective legitimation logic' regarding the allocation of joint fisheries rights also either consciously or unconsciously reflects an FCA's membership's perception regarding equity and social justice. This refers not just to present-day circumstances but just as strongly – if not more so in some cases – to social justice for the ancestors and its implication for long-term reciprocity in paying off the debts incurred by descendants of former upper-class families, who for centuries had discriminated against other social strata (Kada, 1984).

For example, in one cooperative along Lake Biwa (which is administered for fisheries as a 'small sea', *koumi*) the use of fish weirs was allocated about a century ago solely to the village paupers. With passage of the Fisheries Law (1949), which democratized control of coastal fisheries by placing them in the hands of working fishermen, the paupers became the dominant class in local fisheries, since local landowners lost their absentee rights. For reasons of historical precedent, and by assent of the membership, weir fishing remains allocated exclusively to the descendants of the pre-war pauper class. This practice is regarded as fair by that group since it represents social justice for the descendants of the paupers who had been long discriminated against (Kada, 1984).

Another rural FCA that is highly dependent on joint fisheries rights for trap and weir fishing, received its rights in 1098 AD. Its territory has remained unchanged since that time. Membership is not open to all residents. New residents must wait one generation (or 30 years) before they become eligible to apply for membership and fishing rights. Further, a branch family established by a son of a stem family of this village must wait ten years before it can apply. On the other hand, succession of stem family members to fisheries rights has been automatic through the generations.

The above exemplifies conditions where traditional values and behavioural norms remain dominant. Conditions differ enormously in areas like the Inland Sea that have undergone massive cultural and economic structural change during the last 40 years. In a rapidly changing society, with easier access to education and wider range of employment opportunities than hitherto, the role of kinship in ensuring succession in coastal fishing has diminished. Indeed, finding a successor has become a serious problem nationwide for many ageing fishermen, in areas where young people are going into other professions. But this has increased the opportunities for persons of non-fishing backgrounds to enter the sector.

Sea territory

Definition

Owing to such factors as sociopolitical history, geographical circumstances, level of market development and the general economy, which varied by region, the formation of village inshore sea territories did not occur either at the same time or at the same rate throughout Japan (Arai, 1970). Although village sea territories were formed largely during the feudal era (1603–1867) their historical roots penetrated much deeper (Ruddle, 1987). Usually, as the early-feudal codification established or reconfirmed, a particular local fishing ground belonged to a single village. But some were the shared property of several settlements. Generally, those old village territories correspond to present-day common-rights fishing grounds.

Virtually without exception, the coastwise extent of such village sea territories was defined by the projection seawards of the terrestrial boundaries of the village. But the seaward limit was not defined precisely nor was it defined by the same criteria nationwide. This might have reflected the special importance of defining rights to sandy beaches for beach seine operations, whereas offshore areas were less important. In Okinawa, waters in which an adult could walk were reserved exclusively by the adjacent village. In Japan proper the criteria varied, and location of the offshore boundary ranged from 12 to 18 kilometres offshore along sparsely populated Sea of Japan coasts to about four kilometres from the high-tide mark in the Inland Sea, where demand for access was heavy.

With the implementation of the 1901 Fisheries Law, village sea territories established during the feudal era were mapped, codified and registered at the prefectural fisheries office. Typically, these modern boundaries coincided with those established through prior customary usage.

Around smaller islands and more isolated coasts on the main islands, the seaward boundaries of fisheries tenurial rights were characteristically set at a uniform distance offshore along the entire coastline. Thus the seaward boundary of such rights ran parallel to the shoreline all along the coast.

Nor was the distance uniform throughout the nation or within prefectures. In Okinawa, boundaries varied to ensure that all the resource-rich waters within a fringing coral reef plus the seaward-reef slope were included within a village's sea territory. In that way an FCA was ensured of the exclusive right to a particular tract of reef fishing, unless separate access agreements were made with other associations. Some sea territories were defined by using clearly visible onshore bases to fix imaginary points that were then linked up to create a seaward boundary. Following the 1949 law, most FCAs used the latter system.

Shared usage of seaspace

In feudal Japan, the concept of shared land (*iriaichi*) used jointly by villages for the collection of fuelwood, thatching materials and the like, was also extended to sea territories. This was done particularly in bays, which would have been difficult to divide among villages, and for fishing rights within fishing villages (Hara, 1977). Within the shared fishing territory (*iriai*) the use of a given technology or the harvest of a particular species was reserved for one village, whereas other species could be taken by a fisherman from another village, using different gear.

Fundamental to the *iriai* concept was that a particular seaspace was to be held jointly and equally by two or more villages. In some areas, reciprocal access rights or access in return for payment was more widespread. Under other circumstances the *iriai* concept was applied among the fishermen of a single village where a portion of the village sea territory would be licensed to a particular individual for a beach seine operation. The remainder of the area would be regarded as *iriai* for the free use of non-netting techniques.

The open sea beyond a village sea territory was also known as *iriai*. These waters could be worked by boats from any village. However, access was controlled since owners of these larger boats formed guilds, which were taxed and licensed or required to perform various duties.

Village sea tenure appears to have developed gradually according to a general pattern and was widely established by the middle and late years of the feudal era. In the first stage, the privileged or 'real' fishermen – the full-time specialists of village A, which was exclusively a fishing village – could fish freely in the waters off neighbouring farming villages, B and C, whose inhabitants were prohibited by law from fishing. With the passage of time the second stage emerged. The need arose to regulate access to coastal waters as the strict segregation of villages by economic role diminished: villages B and C claimed their own sea territories. However, since at that stage the inhabitants of A were still regarded, according to the implicit caste system, as 'true fishermen' they retained limited exclusive rights within the territories of the adjacent villages, such as those to use netting techniques, for example. But the inhabitants of B and C henceforth held all other marine-resource rights. The third stage was reached when each village decided to enforce exclusive rights to its own sea territory.

Just prior to the Meiji restoration in 1868, it appears that the second stage of the model was the dominant tenurial mode, that stage one was still common, and that the final stage was just beginning to emerge in the most highly developed and productive fisheries. It was that final stage which was institutionalized by the Fisheries Law of 1901.

Following passage of the 1901 law, the merging of FCAs and integration of their sea territories occurred. This process intensified after the 1949 law, particularly in rural areas experiencing depopulation. In heavily fished and more productive waters, territorial integration represented a simplification of a multitude of bewildering, mutual inter-FCA access agreements.

The integration process has continued until the present. Some formerly separate FCAs have merged into a single unit. Others retained their own individual administrative identity but henceforth had to share their tenured waters with other separate associations. Whereas in many instances this is a simple arrangement whereby just two FCAs share a seaspace, other administrative arrangements are far more complex (Akimichi and Ruddle, 1984). The sharing of seaspace has occurred only in the most productive and heavily claimed areas and in those where conflict has been most frequent and intense. On the other hand, where historically there has been little inter-FCA rivalry for resources, individual village FCAs have retained sole rights to a particular tract of inshore water.

The sharing of seaspace is one administrative mechanism employed by prefectures to resolve the many tenurial and customary law conflicts that arose between and among FCAs over the most productive and conveniently located fishing grounds. The prefectural fisheries office designated the territory to be shared and then left it to the FCAs concerned to formulate, implement and monitor the detailed executory rules concerning access, gear and representational authority to the higher administrative levels.

Other access rights

Together with the provisions of the *iriai* system, the granting of other access rights functioned to make the bureaucratically rigid sea-tenure system of the feudal era more flexible. In that way it became better adapted to the heterogenous nature of different yet proximate fishing grounds by enabling fishermen to exploit a range of locations, to work year round and to specialize in particular fisheries.

It is often asserted that a common reason for granting access rights to outsiders within an exclusive sea territory of a village was to afford fishermen from villages with small or resource-poor territories access to better fishing grounds. Yet almost invariably restrictions were imposed on such entrants by the resident fishermen's association (or 'guild', as it was known in feudal times). Most commonly this took the form of limitations on technology; boat and gear numbers; target species and seasonality; and timing of operations. Further, fishermen granted access were required to pay a fee equivalent to 10–33 per cent of the value of their catch taken in the waters to which they were given access. Since the higher figure represents a hefty 'tax', it may well have been that the real motivation was to extract further rents rather than to provide more equitable access.

Access to sandy beaches located in exclusive-rights territories was also commonly granted during the feudal era, since these were critical sites for hauling and drying nets and for sun-drying fish in beach-seine operations. A fee was levied on those grated such access for net- and fish-drying (Fukuoka Prefecture 1963, cited in Kalland, 1984).

Those practises were continued into the modern era. With the implementation of the 1901 Fisheries Law, any fisheries association (or individual) that wished to obtain rights within the tenured waters of another association had to reach an agreement on the terms and conditions of the entry contract with that association, and then officially register the access rights. These were generally based on customary precedent (Akimichi and Ruddle, 1984). In some cases entry was permitted only for closely specified techniques and/or target species. Invariably a rent was extracted for such rights. In other cases, old-established genealogical links among highly specialized fishing communities were utilized to gain entry to the waters of other associations (Ruddle, 1987; Ruddle and Akimichi, in press). Neighbouring fisheries associations made more frequent entry claims than did specialists from more distant locations. In many instances these became highly complex and overlapping.

Territorial behaviour and *de facto* ownership of the sea

Although legally all fisheries-rights waters belong to all members of an FCA, in practice small spots within such a sea area are conceived of as temporarily belonging to an individual fishing unit. This private 'ownership' within the common domain arises in several ways, both formal and informal. The fundamental function is to promote equitable access to resources and to minimize and manage interpersonal conflict among fishing units.

Among the principal formal ways in which such temporary private tenure arises is the licensing by an FCA for several years of a given tract of the joint-rights area to a particular fishing unit and for a particular purpose, such as aquaculture. Another is through the annual exclusive award by the FCA lottery of specified spots to a particular unit of capture fishermen for a specific target species, as in the live-bait fishery in the Yaeyama archipelago (Ruddle and Akimichi, in press).

The commonest way in which temporary private tenure arises is through the exclusive use of fishing spots as a result of closely guarded personal knowledge. In the Yaeyama archipelago, for example, fishermen observe that territorial behaviour and *de facto* 'ownership' of particular fishing spots emerges naturally through individually acquired knowledge and experience (Ruddle and Akimichi, in press). The use of fishing spots is largely determined by experience, physical abilities and capital availability for investment in fishing. Also important is where a man received his early training in fisheries, his place of residence and accessibility.

Fishermen in the complex, coralline lagoonal environment of Yaeyama reef fisheries traditionally maintain four informal tenurial levels: fishing spots that are well known to everybody ('the known sea'); sites regarded as personal ('the place where I usually fish'); a favourite fishing spot ('my sea'); and secret fishing spots ('concealed little sea') (Ruddle and Akimichi, in press). Knowing many 'good' spots guarantees a regular income, and, more importantly, demonstrates a man's knowledge, skill and experience. This enhances his prestige, ensures him respect, and guarantees him an influential role in the FCA, where his views will be carefully considered during the resolution of intra- and inter-community disputes.

Fishermen are faced with the fundamental problem of arranging the spatial and temporal allocation of their effort among the different categories of fishing spot, a technique known in Yaeyama as 'allocating the sea' or 'taking a small piece of the sea' (Ruddle and Akimichi, in press). This requires the balancing of a large number of fixed, cyclic and unpredictable environmental, human and social variables which are rendered more complex by the efforts of competing fishermen who might know and also exploit a man's supposedly 'secret' spots. This contest of skills and wits is governed by interlocking sets of formal regulations as well as community-sanctioned rules of behaviour. Fishermen skilled at allocating the sea invariably attain a high rate of success for effort expended. This, too, serves to enhance their prestige within the community.

By not revealing information verbally and by avoidance behaviour, Yaeyama fishermen preserve their 'secret' fishing territories. Only sons who work regularly with their fathers inherit this detailed information throughout the many years of on-the-job training. These issues are intimately bound up with pride and notions of self-esteem among fishermen, and therefore again with a man's status within the fishing community, and all that arises from it.

Among Yaeyama fishermen several customary techniques are employed to ensure that the likelihood of interpersonal conflict is avoided or at least minimized. Among these the most important are avoidance behaviour on the sea and the acknowledgement of a first-comer's rights.

At sea, avoidance behaviour is practised assiduously whenever there is the slightest chance of inadvertently revealing the location of a 'good' secret spot. All activities are stopped, and a man leaves a spot rapidly when another boat is seen approaching the general area. Other locations are chosen if another fisherman has already reached the general vicinity of a man's pre-selected spot. Since the tenured waters of an FCA are open to all members there is nothing legally sacrosanct about an individual's secret or favourite fishing spot. Apart from those places specifically allocated to individual fishing units for particular purposes, any spot can be used freely.

In Yaeyama (Ruddle and Akimichi, in press) and off the main island of Okinawa (Akimichi, 1984), and most likely in many other places too, the priority right to a fishing spot by a first-comer is absolutely sacrosanct. Again, there is nothing in the formal law to uphold this right, but it is ironclad in customary law. The first man to reach and work a particular spot temporarily 'owns' that location until he stops working it. This rule applies within and among all types of fishing. In some places on Okinawa Island, spots for temporary fixed nets are selected by individual fishermen on the previous day. These are marked by sticking a bamboo pole in the bottom and attaching the fisherman's personal sign to the bamboo. Once so marked, they cannot be used by another fisherman employing the same technique (Akimichi, 1984).

Sometimes, more aggressive fishermen attempt to intimidate first-comers into leaving a 'good' fishing spot. If this occurs repeatedly, an influential and respected third party helps resolve the conflict. Community opinion and peer pressure will be brought to bear on the offender, since the first-comer is always supported. Only rarely and in extreme cases of repeated intimidation will the assistance of the coastguard be sought. In Yaeyama, intermediaries and peer pressures are used to resolve informally a variety of other relatively minor conflicts.

When time-honoured, informal community mechanisms prove inadequate to resolve a particular conflict, more formal – yet still informal – channels are resorted to. Such procedures were used by Yaeyama fishermen to resolve the conflict over sites for lift-netting for live bait. Until just over a decade ago, no formal regulations were applied to this fishery, and as a consequence there was considerable discord over the use of fishing spots. A basic problem is that the fishing spots are small and close to others with which they are intimately linked by daily migratory behaviour of the target species. Fishing at one therefore interferes with operations at the other. Lift-netting groups with first-comer rights to a particular spot claimed those rights were being infringed upon by other groups that had decided to work the adjacent spots at the same time and therefore were, in effect, stealing the first-comer's fish.

This intergroup problem occurred frequently and without satisfactory resolution. Eventually it was taken up by the 'lift-netting squad'. Since the squad was unable to resolve the problem it was eventually taken before the FCA executive board. Its solution was finally accepted by the annual general meeting of the FCA, which included all the lift-netters. The outcome was the acceptance of a 'formal agreement on bait fisheries for bonito' and the institution of an annual lottery for the reallocation of registered lift-netting spots among all the lift-netting groups.

The defence of fisheries rights

The history of Japanese fisheries is replete with incidents of conflict over fisheries rights. Some were relatively easily and amicably solved; solutions to others were found only after outbreaks of violence and bloodshed. Some have been only local-level, intra-village disputes between different factions in a fishing community or between different villages within a prefecture over access to shared or adjacent seaspaces. Others, the more important ones, have involved fishermen from two or more prefectures and have had to be resolved at the national level. Some such major incidents have had a long and continual history, going back to feudal times; others have been relatively short, sharp and quickly settled. The causes of these major disputes have been varied, having stemmed from entry-rights disputes, gear conflicts, illegal fishing, island ownership, boundary jurisdiction and institutional reform problems. As would be anticipated, the differential rates at which different communities adopted new technologies was one of the major sources of fisheries conflict.

Potential conflicts among the membership of an FCA are, as discussed above, generally foreseen and managed by traditional methods. Those which do emerge are also generally contained within a small group and resolved informally and interpersonally. More intractable cases are discussed and resolved by a formal mechanism, such as the annual lottery described above. Persistent theft or violation of either prefectural or FCA regulations is referred to the coastguard for action, although this is usually a last resort, taken when traditional methods have failed.

If they cannot be resolved by the direct negotiations of the FCAs concerned, larger-scale conflicts, such as those between or among FCAs belonging to the same prefecture, are taken before the prefectural sea-area adjustment commission. The decision of that body is binding. Similarly, those between FCAs of different prefectures are resolved by a joint or regional sea-area adjustment commission. Major disputes at the prefectural level are often resolved by the ministry, or in more difficult cases by a special law enacted by the diet.

Another major source of fisheries conflict in postwar Japan has been that between fisheries and other sectors of the national economy, most notably industry, transportation and public services. The traditional methods of mediation, conciliation and, to a lesser extent, arbitration, which have a long legacy in Japan, are also those preferred to settle this category of formal dispute. Further the Dispute Law (1970) essentially represents a modernized version of these traditional methods (Ruddle, 1987).

Intersectoral conflicts are in essence a symptom of a much larger rural–urban dichotomy in Japanese society, with the generally parochial worldview of the former conflicting with the relatively cosmopolitan and global perspective of the latter. Although traditional means of conflict management remain the favoured methods in rural and urban society alike, the former cleaves to them more closely. In a rapidly changing society like present-day Japan many traditional values and behaviour patterns may be cast aside. Management of conflicts between entities such as industry that represent the urban (modern), and fisheries that represent the rural (traditional) sector, becomes complex. Traditional processes are sometimes neglected, and atypical conditions become imposed on the process of finding a solution.

Thus in the late 1960s the traditional vehicles of conflict management were supplemented by resort to the judiciary, when, as a consequence of industry's neglect of basic traditional behavioural norms of the rural sector, some particularly intractable cases were brought before the courts for settlement. Although still not a widely accepted method of resolving conflicts, owing in large part to the legacy of intra-community strife that it uncommonly heralds, judicial solutions are occasionally sought to fishery problems. Such cases remain relatively rare, and most conflicts are managed at the local level, by traditional methods (Ruddle, 1987).

Conclusion

According to the Fisheries Law (1949) fisheries rights in the sea area under the jurisdiction of a fisheries cooperative association (FCA) are the bona fide personal use rights of the individual members of that association to its communal property: bottom fauna, fish and invertebrates of the benthos in the adjacent coastal waters. These use rights are distributed by the association to its membership. Each FCA also establishes regulations for the control and operation of various types of fishery in its joint-rights area in an equitable, efficient and sustained manner, as local conditions dictate. This situation has its origins in both customary law and in the formal legislation of the Japanese feudal era.

Thus, sea tenure in Japanese coastal waters is a complex subject. It represents a continuity of tradition and involves time-honoured customary procedures that have, after suitable modification, been gradually incorporated into modern legislation. It operates at various levels, ranging from the national government, through the prefecture and the local FCA, to the fishing squad and finally to the individual fisherman.

In contemporary Japan, the FCA is a vitally important intermediate organization that links the central and prefectural governments with the individual fisherman. Although comprising the fundamental unit of governmental fisheries administration and being the key organization for the implementation of official fisheries projects, an FCA belongs entirely to the local community of fishermen. But, as throughout modern history, its principal function remains the planning, management and continuing sustained development of the local sea territory to which a community has tenure.

In many ways the modern Japanese FCA is really only an elaborate variant of the traditional fishing-village organization that has persisted since at least feudal times. The beneficial aspects of traditional village institutions were not abandoned during the modernization of Japan. Instead, they were transferred to fishery associations and later to fishery cooperative associations. Therein, on the one hand, lies an abiding strength. Yet, on the other hand, by giving such strong control to local fishermen the system does complicate and often precludes comprehensive coastal-zone planning. This is a major drawback. Nevertheless, regardless of perspective, there is no doubting that Japan provides one of the few workable examples of how the common-property-resource dilemma can be avoided.

References

Akimichi, T., 1984: 'Territorial regulation in the small-scale fisheries of Okinawa', in Ruddle, K. and Akimichi, T., eds, *Maritime Institutions in the Western Pacific*,

National Museum of Ethnology, Osaka, pp. 89–120.

Akimichi, T. and Ruddle, K., 1984: 'The historical development of territorial rights and fishery regulations in Okinawan inshore waters', in Ruddle, K. and Akimichi, T., eds, *Maritime Institutions in the Western Pacific*, National Museum of Ethnology, Oska, pp. 37–88.

Arai, E., 1970: *Fishing Villages in the Early Modern Period*, Yoshikawa Kobunkan, Tokyo (in Japanese).

Fukuoka Prefecture, 1963: *The History of Fukuoka Prefecture*, Fukuoka Prefecture, Fukuoka, vol. 2, pt.1 (in Japanese).

Hara, T., 1977: *On the History of Institutions in Japanese Fishery Rights*, Kokushokankokai, Tokyo (in Japanese).

Johannes, R.E., 1978: 'Traditional conservation methods in Oceania and their demise', *Annual Review of Ecology and Systematics*, 9, pp. 349–64.

Kada, Y., 1984: 'The evolution of joint fisheries rights and village community structure on Lake Biwa, Japan', in Ruddle, K. and Akimichi, T., eds, *Maritime Institutions in the Western Pacific*, National Museum of Ethnology, Osaka, pp. 137–58.

Kalland, A., 1981: *Shingu – A Study of a Japanese Fishing Community*, Curzon Press Ltd, London.

Kalland, A., 1984: 'Sea tenure in Tokugawa Japan: the case of Fukuoka Domain', in Ruddle, K. and Akimichi, T., eds, *Maritime Institutions in the Western Pacific*, National Museum of Ethnology, Osaka, pp. 11–36.

Nagai, S., 1951: *Ethnography of Tobishima*, Kobundo, Tokyo (in Japanese).

Ruddle, K., 1985: 'The continuity of traditional management practices: the case of Japanese coastal fisheries', in Ruddle, K. and Johannes, R.E., eds, *Traditional Knowledge and Management of Coastal Systems in Asia and the Pacific*, UNESCO, Jakarta, pp. 157–79.

Ruddle, K., 1987: *Administration and Conflict Management in Japanese Coastal Fisheries*, FAO Fisheries Technical Paper No. 273, Rome.

Ruddle, K. and Akimichi, T., eds, 1984: *Maritime Institutions in the Western Pacific*, National Museum of Ethnology, Osaka.

Ruddle, K. and Akimichi, T., (in press): 'Sea tenure in Japan and the southwestern Ryukyus', in Cordell, J.C., ed., *A Sea of Small Boats: Customary Law and Territoriality in the World of Inshore Fishing*, Cultural Survival, Cambridge, Mass.

Ruddle, K. and Johannes, R.E., eds, 1985: *The Traditional Knowledge and Management of Coastal Systems in Asia and the Pacific*, UNESCO, Jakarta.

Short, K., (in press): 'Self-management of fishing rights by Japanese cooperative associations', in Cordell, J.C., ed., *A Sea of Small Boats: Customary Law and Territoriality in the World of Inshore Fishing*, Cultural Survival, Cambridge, Mass.

Vogel, E.F., ed., 1975: *Modern Japanese Organization and Decision Making*, Tuttle, Tokyo.

Zengyoren, 1979: The Fisheries Law: Law No. 267 of 1949. Zengyoren, Tokyo.

11 The Evolution of Mexico's Caribbean Spiny Lobster Fishery

David L. Miller

Summary

During the past decade Mexico's Caribbean-spiny-lobster fishery has matured into a well-developed industry. The lobster resource is now heavily exploited. In the state of Quintana Roo, fishermen of the cooperatives 'Cozumel' and 'Vigia Chico', have developed a common-property resource-management system which limits access and grants individual property rights, yet still recognizes that the fishery belongs to the community. Elsewhere in this rapidly developing region, pressures have resulted in the establishment of open-access situations which appear to favour short-term exploitation rather than sustainable management of the resource.

Fishermen of the cooperatives Cozumel and Vigia Chico co-ops construct small artificial habitats ('casitas', 1.5m square) and place them on the sea floor to attract and concentrate lobsters. They have divided most of the zone originally granted to their co-ops into individually held parcels or 'campos' (0.3 to 2km square). One fisherman may have 50 to 300 casitas in each of two or three campos. Campos can be sold or bartered, inherited by a spouse or divided among children. Formal titles do not exist, although where disputes have been resolved by officers of the co-op, written agreements stipulate boundaries.

Casitas were originally introduced in the north of the state where the fishery was best developed and most heavily exploited. Fishermen enjoyed the benefits associated with casitas, but the open-access situation led to the eventual abandonment of the enhancement technology. No provision for individual use rights could be easily admitted. The casita/campo system developed where the resource was initially only periodically exploited. The advantages of casita use became apparent and, as the fishery developed, the campo system evolved in response to competition for fishing space.

The casita/campo system seems to provide fishermen with incentives to maintain a sustained harvest. Individuals have an incentive to work harder, invest more and actively participate in the regulation of their fishery. The system's use rights, and their access-limiting nature, reduce the problem of free ridership.

Introduction

This paper focuses on the evolution of limited property rights associated with a spiny lobster (*Panulirus argus*) fishery located at Ascension Bay and Espiritu Santo Bay, in Quintana Roo, Mexico (Fig. 11.1). It provides a case study of a newly developed fishery changing rapidly from an open-access to a closed-access condition. Elsewhere in this rapidly developing part of Mexico, development pressures have resulted in the establishment of open-access situations which appear to favour short-term exploitation rather than sustainable management of the resource. Some other studies of coastal fisheries throughout the world subjected to similar development pressures document the disruption and demise of local common-property-resource institutions (for example see Johannes, 1978; Ruddle and Johannes, 1985; for additional context see Berkes, 1985a, 1985b; Acheson, 1975). Thus, the origin and persistence of what may be a more ecologically sensible resource-exploitation pattern bears examination.

The purpose of this study is to explore, in the context of this fishery,

1 the reasons underlying the creation of limited property rights;
2 changes in the system of organization and their rationale;
3 the relationship between informal rights and legally defined rights; and
4 the 'robustness' of this particular system of organization for harvesting of the resource in light of current biological and cultural landscapes.

The area and its historical background

Quintana Roo's nearly 900km of coastline includes all of Mexico's Caribbean shore, and a short stretch in the north that technically belongs to Gulf of Mexico shores. Fishing activity at the northern end of the state is focused on the Yucatan Bank of the Campeche Shelf, an area richly endowed with marine resources. Shelf area along the Caribbean shore is relatively limited. Within a few kilometres of the shore the seafloor quickly drops away in a series of terraces to depths of 900 metres. Here, fishing activity seldom occurs out of sight of land, most of it taking place near or at the reef which fringes the shore.

In terms of earnings, the state's fishing industry is second only to tourism. The bulk of the lobster and shrimp harvest is exported to the USA and is an important source of export earnings. In 1980, there were less than 800 registered fishermen in the state. By 1986, I estimate there were more than 1500 fishermen. Fewer than 20 per cent of them were born in Quintana Roo, and a minority of the native sons were of Mayan ancestry. Most of the immigrant fishermen were from either Campeche, Tabasco or Veracruz.

Extensive harvesting or Quintana Roo's marine resources did not begin

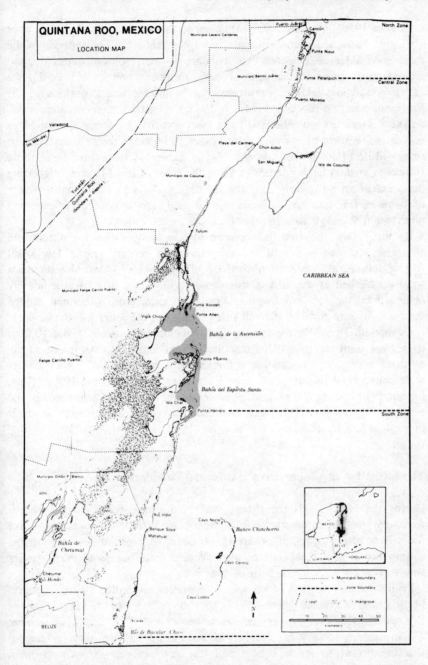

Figure 11.1   Map of the Mexican state Quintana Roo. Shaded areas show locations of lobster 'campos' held by fishermen of the Cooperatives 'Vigia Chico' and 'Cozumel' within Ascension and Espiritu Santo Bays.

until after 1950. For some 400 years prior to that time the state's coasts were virtually abandoned and its marine resources relatively undisturbed. While there is considerable evidence that abundant marine resources were harvested quite actively prior to the time of early European contact (1511–91), the native population declined drastically due to disease and disruption as the European conquest proceeded (Miller, 1982a). Coastal settlements were abandoned as survivors moved inland for greater security. Evidence that the Maya utilized some form of marine tenure system to organize their fishery remains scant. Miller (1982b) records the Mayan names of three traditional turtle (*Chelonia mydas*) fishing locations along the coast of Isla Mujeres, suggesting the presence of an orderly resource-use regime. It is probable that a wealth of fisheries tradition and technique based on generations of experience and observation was lost as a result of European disruptions.

By the 1700s, the area had become a base of operation for pirates and smugglers; it was not until the mid-nineteenth century that a few small fishing settlements were established on offshore island. Coastal settlements were established at the turn of this century, the focus of economic activity being Chicle-tapping and logging. With few exceptions, fishermen limited their activities to turtling and salt-fish production, the latter mostly for local consumption. By 1930, the territory's population had reached about 10,000; it was not until the mid-1970s that the current inhabitants outnumbered the estimate of the Maya population at the time of first European contact. Large-scale commercial fishery production did not begin until the mid-1950s. Thus, for about 400 years, the marine resources of the Mexican Caribbean enjoyed respite, and new equilibria were established based on greatly reduced levels of exploitation by man.

The formation of cooperatives and formal boundaries

During the early 1960s the fishery was in the process of shifting from a relatively small-scale enterprise to a larger-scale commercial industry. Effort focused on the production of luxury products such as lobster, conch, and shrimp for export. Cooperatives were formed since access to these species was reserved by federal law to co-ops.

Prior to the formation of co-ops, independent fishermen ('permissionario libres') were granted permits to harvest lobster in certain locations ('campos'). However, older fishermen report that this was a convenient fiction made necessary to comply with federal law. In actuality, a 'campo' was interpreted to mean a boat and its crew. In exchange for permits, fishermen were required to report their captures and pay a modest tax on their captures. (L. Manzanilla, personal communication). A campo permit was interpreted to grant rights to a site only with respect to the location of beach weirs ('trampa de corazon y cola') and turtle nets. Stations were held by individual fishermen, and their right to maintain gear in these locations was supported by local convention. Frequently, fishermen notified the local port captain or fishery officer prior to positioning gear at the beginning of each session. This was considered prudent in the case of turtle nets, and was apparently necessary for weirs as late as 1978.

The first co-ops were established at the northern end of the state. The newly formed co-ops immediately obtained permits to exploit lobster, and each group was assigned a site ('campo') where they could fish. Boundaries were established in conformity with the traditional range of fishermen. Since petitions by independent fishermen for lobster permits were denied, most fishermen saw that it was necessary to join cooperatives.

The division of fishing grounds into exclusive zones for exploitation of reserved species reflects a policy established in the early days (1930s) of Mexico's fishing cooperatives. They were structured like land-based agrarian collectives ('ejidos') and given title to fixed areas for exploitation (McGoodwin, 1980). By 1980, six co-ops had been formed, and campo boundaries readjusted several times (Miller, 1982b). At that time, efforts underway to establish additional co-ops were being actively resisted by members of existing groups who realized the campos would have to be further subdivided. By 1985, however, additional co-ops had been formed. These groups managed to overcome resistance by initially applying only for permits to take finfish. After receiving charter, they successfully solicited lobster and conch harvesting permits which they could not be legally denied.

As of 1986, there were more than a dozen co-ops in Quintana Roo and, with the exception of campos held by two of the co-ops boundaries were generally ignored. Only the cooperatives 'Cozumel' (in Espiritu Santo Bay) and its spinoff 'Vigia Chico' (in Ascension Bay) have been generally successful in maintaining their territorial boundaries. Despite some difficulty in resolving boundaries within their zone, fishermen of the 'Cozumel' and 'Vigia Chico' co-ops have so far managed to forestall incursions or invasions by others seeking to exploit the zone's lobster resource. Their success seems largely related to the unique organization of their fishery, and to the harvest technology that they employ. These will be discussed, following some background on the two cooperatives and the area.

Background to the Ascension Bay and Espiritu Santo Bay Fisheries

Fishermen of Vigia Chico and Cozumel co-ops limit their efforts to the near shore and concentrate on harvesting lobster. Each cooperative has about 100 members. Cooperative Vigia Chico fishes Ascension Bay. During the open season (July 16–16 March), most Vigia Chico members live at Punta Allen (see Fig. 11.1). In 1986, the village's population was estimated to average 500. In contrast, members of cooperative 'Cozumel' commute to Espiritu Santo Bay in a mother ship from Cozumel Island. Their voyages typically last one or two weeks. When they are not fishing, many co-op members are employed in some aspect of Cozumel's tourist industry.

Members of both cooperatives harvest from large fibreglass skiffs (8–9m) powered by 40hp outboard motors. In 1986, there were 48 skiffs in Punta Allen. Members of 'Cozumel' had perhaps 30 skiffs. Lobsters are harvested with a short gaff, and occasionally by using tangle nets. Capture of other species such as finfish or shark is, for the most part, incidental. The bulk of both cooperatives' production is exported to the USA.

The 'Casita' or Artificial Habitat Fishery

Members of the Cozumel and Vigia Chico co-ops have divided their fishing zones into individually held capture areas ('parcelas' or 'campos') ranging from 0.5 to more than $3km^2$ (Fig. 11.1). These divisions were typically arrived at informally, with boundaries being established as fishermen were stopped from expanding in a given direction by the presence of another fisherman's gear or boundary marker. Conspicuous bottom features such as rocks, reefs or the edge of a clear, sandy bottom area were frequently agreed upon as boundary points. Shallow water boundaries are marked by long poles driven into soft substrate, or by buoys. In deeper water, triangulation assists the placement and replacement of buoys serving to delimit campos. As of the mid-1980s, virtually all areas within Ascension and Espiritu Santo Bay were occupied and areas further offshore were being claimed.

Fishermen position artificial habitats – shelters ('casitas') that simulate niches and crevices in rocks and reefs (Fig. 11.2) – on the sea floor within their campos. Most casitas are placed in shallow (2–7 metre depth) water and are spaced some 20 to 30 metres apart. Fishermen make harvests by free-diving to the shelter and removing lobsters with a gaff or herding them into a net. Typically, from seven to ten lobsters are harvested from each casita, but it is not uncommon for some casitas to add several dozen lobsters to the catch. Some 30 to 50 casitas are checked in a day, and then not revisited for a week to ten days.

The shelters attract lobsters because juveniles and adults are gregarious; because they remain in dens during the day; and because they do not modify existing habitat or build new habitat. The enhancement of natural habitat may also increase productivity, since casitas provide additional and perhaps optimal refuge sites from predators (sharks, grouper, triggerfish, turtles). In addition, casitas located near feeding grounds have the potential to reduce predation risk (Miller and De la Torre, 1985).

Figure 11.2   A 'casita' constructed with a frame of thatch palm logs (*Thrinax* sp.) and roof of reinforced concrete. Approximate dimensions are 1.5 metres square.

Currently, the 107 members of the Vigia Chico co-op utilize more than 10,000 shelters positioned throughout some 160km^2 of Ascension Bay. Their lobster fishing grounds are divided into approximately 150 individual held campos. By common accord, fishermen do not position their casitas with 25 metres of their boundary. This arrangement minimizes the chance for conflict in the ambiguous near-border area. Occasionally, a buoy will be tied to a casita for use as a reference point, but most fishermen do not mark their shelters in order to make poaching more difficult. The situation of the Cozumel co-op, fishing in the twin bay to the south, is similar.

Individually held campos and limited property rights

Campo owners have exclusive right to harvest lobsters within their boundaries. Ownership also transfers considerable control over access to most other marine creatures within the campo. Line fishing by anyone is allowed, but spearing of fish is permitted only during the first three months of the closed season for lobster. No spearfishing is permitted during the last quarter of the closed season (June 15 to July 15). In practice, few fishermen exercise the option to dive in another's campo. The majority of fishermen want to avoid any possible suggestion of impropriety. Friends and relatives, on the other hand, will typically be granted permission to make reasonable harvests.

Rules regarding diving in or around another's 'parcel' have changed. Generally, regulations have become more restrictive. Initially, areas of barrier reef were treated as 'commons'. In 1974, placement of casitas within 150 metres of the reef was forbidden (Gutierrez Memorandum, 1974). This arrangement proved problematic; divers had trouble determining where the reef ended; campo owners had trouble determining where it began; both complained of violations of the distance rule. Also, some divers were tempted to harvest from shelters located closest to the reef. By 1980, placement of shelters within 100 metres of the reef was forbidden (Miller, 1982a); four years later the control of adjacent areas of reef passed to parcel owners (H. Leon, 1986 personal communication).

As of the mid-1980s, permission will sometimes be granted to others wishing to set gill nets within a campo. In this instance, the campo owner will get some share of the catch or simply credit for some reciprocal assistance in the future. However, nets which are set along the bottom can snare large numbers of lobsters and therefore a campo owner could justifiably refuse such a request.

Campos are sold, bartered and traded among co-op members. Valuation is based on a fisherman's judgement regarding the potential for profit. To some degree, an individual contemplating a purchase will consider prior production at the level of effort applied by the owner, the capacity of an area for casitas based on a rough estimate of usable bottom, and how the location might enhance his harvesting options. With respect to the latter, relative travel time is factored into the decision-making process. The presence of areas of shallows and reefs necessitates circuitous routes to many campos. Also, access to some areas is difficult during certain months. Changes in prevailing winds alter wave and current patterns in some areas, making travel arduous and diminishing water clarity.

Several campos are sold or bartered each season and such transactions are common knowledge. On occasion, sales are registered with the co-op. Campos can also be inherited by a spouse or divided among children, male or female. Formal titles do not exist, although where disputes have been resolved by officers of the co-op or with the assistance of fishery officers, written agreements stipulate boundaries. In at least one instance, the result of mediation was registered in a court of law. On that occasion, one campo's location was described as follows: 'from Punta Hualastock, to the east where the third clear sandy bottom area ('blanquizar') ends, and from north to south [on the shore] to the house of [the campo owner's name] . . .' This document also stipulated that gear was not to be placed within 25 metres of boundary lines, and that campos ended 150 metres from the reef (Gutierrez Memorandum, 1974). Such property descriptions, based largely on landforms or water features are characteristic of the 'metes-and-bounds' survey system. With time, more temporary landscape elements are altered, resulting in boundary uncertainty and dispute.

Fishery origin and the evolution of regional variation

Casitas were introduced to Quintana Roo fishermen by Cuban refugees in 1968. The shelters were first tried at the north end of the state, where their advantages became immediately apparent. They were introduced into Ascension Bay the following year. By 1980, two distinct patterns of casita-based fishery organization had evolved (Miller, 1982a). In the northern part of the state, there have never been individually held campos. Any fisherman could place a shelter anywhere within his cooperative's territory, but harvests could be made from it by any member discovering the location of any casita. To the south, around Ascension and Espiritu Santo bays, co-op members individually held campos. Here, only the 'owners' could make harvests. Only areas of reef remained common property of the group or 'mencomunados'; any co-op member could harvest lobsters from them. In 1981, some 4000 casitas were being used by fishermen in the north, and these were estimated to have been responsible for 12 per cent of the area's harvest. Members of the Vigia Chico and Cozumel co-ops used from 15,000 to 22,000 shelters, which produced perhaps 95 per cent of their harvest (Miller, 1982a).

Currently, the systematic use of habitats by fishermen in the north has been suspended. Apparently, their 'campo libre' system (where anyone has the right to harvest from any casita) has proved untenable. Co-op members state that the few who were constructing shelters could no longer justify the cost and effort. Everyone was exploiting (legally) the results of their investment, an example of the 'free-rider' phenomenon and the classical commons dilemma.

Evolution of harvesting strategies

Reasons for the regional evolution of the distinctive styles of organization are complicated, but are in part related to the regional imbalance of fishing effort at the time of introduction of the casita technology. By the late 1960s, the northern zone's fishery was already well developed and heavily exploited. A 'campo-libre' system had been established, and no provision for individual use rights could be easily admitted. By contrast, the situation around Ascension and Espiritu Santo bays was different. This area was sparsely populated, and initially, the lobster resource was only periodically exploited by fishermen visiting the area from Cozumel Island. The advantages of casita use became apparent and, as the fishery developed, the individual campo system evolved in response to competition for fishing space.

The explosive growth of the tourist industry in the north has also contributed to evolution of distinct strategies. Increasing pressures have been visited upon marine resources as coastal areas have become developed and the demand for seafood has increased. The original northern cooperatives have pressured the government to limit the access of others to species reserved for co-op members, but the results have been minimal. The fishery department does not have the resources to enforce regulations adequately. The situation has also been complicated by the fact that new cooperatives have been formed in the region, thereby qualifying even more fishermen to make lobster harvests.

Also complicating efforts to restrict individuals or cooperatives to certain areas or certain species has been the widespread adoption of outboard motors. This has dramatically increased the mobility and range of fishermen. The construction of numerous roads to the coast has also complicated the efforts to police the harvest. Development to the south has lagged behind that in the north, and population growth has been relatively modest. For the most part, access to more southern coastal areas remains limited. This circumstance favours the efforts of the Cozumel and Vigia Chico cooperatives to retain their patrimony.

Aspects of the organization to exploit the lobster stocks of the two bays remain dynamic. Fishermen are becoming more sophisticated about use of the technology. For example, notions about spacing of casitas have changed. Fishermen are placing shelters an average of 20 metres apart, rather than the 30 metres which I reported earlier this decade (Miller, 1982a). In some instances, fishermen appear to have encountered diminishing returns, and have adopted a strategy of maintaining, rather than increasing, the shelter density in a particular parcel. Fishermen still attempt to position their habitats over vegetated or rocky bottom, but they are becoming more selective about the style of casita they position on certain types of bottom. As a rule, lighter materials such as wood and sheet metal are selected for areas of softer sediment, while heavier materials are used for firmer substrates where wave action or current complicate matters. Recent field surveys tend to confirm that lobster preference for habitats constructed of certain materials is associated with substrate type (De la Torre and Miller, 1987).

The distribution of fishing effort has changed. Members of the Vigia Chico group have abandoned parcels in some interior bay areas, reflecting empirical estimations of a gradient of productivity which exists in the bay. As is the case elsewhere (for a review see Kanciruk, 1980), lobster habitat preference and overall distribution in Ascension Bay appear to be associated with life-history stage of the species. Young juveniles (approximately 8–50mm in carapace length [CL]) are solitary and seem to reside in habitats different to older juveniles (approximately 40–80mm CL) which aggregate conspicuously under shelters in shallow areas. As lobsters mature, they move from shallow nursery areas to deeper water. Thus, legal (harvest) size lobsters (13cm tail length or larger – about 72mm CL) are in the minority in most shallow areas. Some fishermen have also quit shallow-water campos because of highly variable rates of production. During a typical year, the salinity of near-shore areas is reduced during the rainy season. This apparently forces lobsters out of the area, in effect rendering gear idle. Annual rates of precipitation have varied considerably in recent years, complicating the informal calculus of risk assessment which underlies a fisherman's decision to reduce, maintain or expand effort in a locale.

Recent fieldwork at Ascension Bay suggests that some Vigia Chico co-op members are attempting to diversify the base of the their production. Based on a preliminary survey, it appears that the more successful fishermen hold campos which are geographically dispersed. In this manner, they hedge their bets, and maintain access to stocks when changes in water quality (salinity, temperature, turbidity, current) or life-stage related migrations contribute to spatial variations in productivity. Weather also limits harvesting activity. The option to harvest in a protected area during heavy weather is valuable. Thus, while some campos are located along 'corridors' of lobster migration and are consistently productive, other campos which are periodically productive are also valued. For example, campos along the south-east shore of Ascension Bay are quite productive during December, when large numbers of lobster exit the bay, and migrate towards the south.

Thoughts on the 'robustness' of the casita/campo system

Successful management of Quintana Roo's lobster stocks will require a thorough understanding of how the area's biological and cultural landscapes interact, and an appreciation of the distinct patterns which have evolved. Each fishermen of the cooperatives using casitas may have from 50 to 300 casitas in each of two or three campos. This represents a considerable investment of capital. Thus, the casita/campo system appears to provide co-op fishermen with an incentive to maintain sustained yields, thus reducing chances of fishery collapse.

Although habitat enhancement appears to represent a possibility for increasing spiny-lobster captures, the long-term impacts of the strategy are uncertain. Casitas attract and concentrate lobsters from surrounding areas and thus facilitate harvest. Casitas may also increase the biological productivity of fishing grounds. The preliminary results of a recent series of field experiments suggest that casitas significantly reduce the rate of natural mortality due to predation. However, if increases in captures associated with concentration of stocks are not offset by gains in biological productivity, then the strategy may facilitate overexploitation.

At the state level, spiny-lobster production has declined somewhat in recent years; yet it is not clear that overharvesting has occurred. Efforts to determine the reasons for declines are complicated by aspects of the species' early life cycle. Once hatched, early larva stages are transported offshore by surface currents; after some six to 12 months, the last larval stage migrates inshore, seeking a protected habitat (Phillips, 1981). Thus, the origin of recruits in one area may be a considerable distance away. At the present time, no method has been devised which reliably distinguishes origin of post-larvae. If recruitment of postlarvae is predominantly local, then decreasing captures may signal that casitas may be concentrating stocks and facilitating capture to such a degree that overharvesting is underway. If recruitment is basically non-local, then declining harvests may be due to increases in fishing effort 'upstream' (at the source of recruits). Also, at the present time it is not possible to determine whether the failure to maintain shelters in areas primarily inhabited by juveniles has had an impact on harvests.

From the standpoint of resource management, the casita/campo system seems superior to the open-access situation in the north. Fishermen holding campos are very conscious of their investment and will not hesitate to inspect the boat of any fisherman found in their campo. Fishermen are quite aware of who should be where, and will investigate or report suspicious activity in a neighbour's campo. Penalties for poaching are stiff. For example, if an inquiry by the Vigia Chico co-op's officers determines guilt, the offender loses his cooperative membership and his right to hold a campo. Outsiders caught poaching have their equipment confiscated, and must pay substantial fines for its return (Acta Levantada, 1975).

During the closed season (lobster reproduction season) the co-op fishermen frequently visit their campos to repair casitas and position new ones. Thus, a considerable amount of vigilance is maintained and illegal harvests are minimized. In contrast, efforts to enforce the closed season in the northern zone meet with minimal success. A black market flourishes. Although fishery officers occasionally do make arrests, their resources are inadequate to police the fishery effectively.

The 'robustness' of Bahia Ascension and Espiritu Santo fisheries may have been enhanced by the recent designation of their area as part of the Sian Ka'an Biosphere Reserve. This could lend added weight to arguments regarding the efficiency of the campo system. Currently, the area is effectively closed to fishermen of other co-ops; this is a source of some considerable tension. If the casita/campo system fishermen can manage to sustain yields, or at least manage better relative yields than groups in other areas, then fishermen and fishery managers will have an easier time defending the common-property resource-management system which has evolved.

Conclusions

Quintana Roo's casita/campo system seems to provide fishermen of the Vigia Chico and Cozumel cooperatives with incentives to maintain a sustained harvest. The system limits access and grants individual property rights yet still recognizes that the fishery belongs to the community. Individuals have an incentive to work harder, invest more and actively participate in the regulation of their fishery.

To the north, where the fishery was well developed before casitas were introduced, the campo system could not be accommodated. Casitas were initially used, and fishermen enjoyed their benefits, but the open-access situation led to the eventual abandonment of the enhanced technology. To the south, a tradition of recognized and enforceable property rights evolved during the infancy of the fishery. These use rights, and their access-limiting nature, reduce the problem of free ridership. In this instance, use rights make the common-property resource more manageable.

Acknowledgements

This work was supported by a World Wildlife Fund grant to the Centro de Investigaciones de Quintana Roo (CIQRO) and by the Office of Sponsored Research of the State University of New York at Cortland. Field assistance was provided by members of the Vigia Chico Fishing Cooperative, numerous members of the CIQRO staff, and by volunteers from Earthwatch of Watertown, Massachusetts. I thank R. De la Torre, F. Berkes, J. Acheson and A. Grima for insightful critiques of the manuscript.

References

Acheson, J., 1975: 'The lobster fiefs: Economic and ecological effects on territoriality in the Maine lobster industry', *Human Ecology*, 3, pp. 183–205.

Acta Levantada, 1975: Document titled 'Acta Levantada en Dicha Colonia, Punta Allen Q. Roo', dated October 28, 1975, summarizing complaint of poaching made against two fishermen of the Cozumel co-op. Document filed in Expediente 'Actas' [1975], at the Vigia Chico Cooperative office in Punta Allen, Quintana Roo.

Berkes, F., 1985a: 'The common-property resource problem and the creation of limited property rights', *Human Ecology*, 13(2), p. 187–208.

Berkes, F., 1985b: 'Fishermen and the "tragedy of the commons"', *Environmental Conservation*, 12(3), pp. 199–206.

De la Torre, R. and Miller, D., 1987: 'Update on the Mexican Caribbean's habitat-based spiny lobster (Panulirus argus) fishery: The evaluation of design, material and placement optimums', *Proceedings of the Gulf and Caribbean Fisheries Institute*, 38, pp. 582–589.

Gutierrez Memorandum, 1974: (Untitled) document dated June 12, 1974, summarizing agreement certified by Lic. Oscar Jose Gutierrez Flores, Juez Mixto de Primera Instancia en el Territorio. Filed in Public Records office at Chetumal in Escritura Publica Numero 825, Volumen LIX.

Humberto, J., 1985: Personal communication, Presidente de Administracion, SCPP, Pescadores de Vigia Chico, SCL, Vigia Chico, Quintana Roo.

Johannes, R.E., 1978: 'Traditional marine conservation methods in Oceania and their demise', *Annual Review of Ecology and Systematics*, 9, pp. 349–64.

Kanciruk, P., 1980: 'Ecology of juvenile and adult Palinuridae (spiny lobsters)', in Cobb, J. and Phillips, B., eds, *The Biology and Management of Lobsters, vol. 2, Ecology and Management*, Academic Press, New York.

Lipcius, R., 1985: Personal communication, Postdoctoral Research Associate, Environmental Research Laboratory, Hatfield Marine Science Center, Newport, Oregon 97365.

Manzanilla, L., 1979: Personal communication, Head Fisheries Inspector, Isla Mujeres Office of Dept. of Pesca, Isla Mujeres, Quintana Roo.

McGoodwin, J., 1980: 'Mexico's marginal inshore Pacific fishing cooperatives', *Anthropological Quarterly*, 53(1), pp. 39–47.

Miller, D., 1982a: 'Construction of shallow water habitats to increase lobster production in Mexico', *Proceedings of the Gulf and Caribbean Fisheries Institute*, 34, pp. 168–79.

Miller, D., 1982b: 'Mexico's Caribbean fishery: Recent change and current issues', PhD thesis, University of Wisconsin, Milwaukee.

Miller, D. and De la Torre, R., 1985: 'Spiny lobster (Panulirus argus) fisheries and artificial habitats: Increasing the yields by merely concentrating stocks?' Paper presented at Lobster Recruitment Workshop, St. John's, NB.

Pallares Memorandum, 1972: (Untitled) document dated June 29, 1972, summarizing meeting held at office of Lic. Lauro Pallares R., Director de Planeacion y Promocion Economica del Gobierno del territorio de Quintana Roo. Document filed in Expediente 'Convenios' at the Vigia Chico Cooperative office in Punta Allen, Quintana Roo.

Phillips, B., 1981: 'The circulation of the southeastern Indian Ocean and the planktonic life of the western rock lobster', *Oceanography and Marine Biology Annual Review*, 19, pp. 11-39.

Ruddle, K. and Johannes, R., eds, 1985: *The Traditional Knowledge and Management of Coastal Systems in Asia and the Pacific*, UNESCO, Jakarta.

12 Where Have All the Exploiters Gone? Co-Management of the Maine Lobster Industry

James M. Acheson

Summary

The case of the Main lobster industry reinforces some parts of the theory of common-property resources and calls into question others. The data on the biological and economic effects of territoriality certainly reinforce the idea that property rights do help conserve resources. However, these need not be individual property rights; communal property rights may serve just as well. Further, the case study calls into question one of the central axioms underlying the common-property model, namely the proposition that the users of common-property resources have no interest in the long-term well-being of those resources, and that they cannot generate institutions to conserve them. Under certain conditions, users of common-property resources can effectively generate such institutions: the existence of the territorial system, the hatcheries, and recent legislative initiatives all underscore this point. The case of the Maine lobster industry should also speak volumes to those who assert, with Hardin, that 'Tragedies of the Commons' can only be averted by draconian action by an authoritarian state.

Introduction

For the past two decades, one of the most important concepts behind fisheries management in the United States and many other nations has been the theory of common-property resources. According to this body of theory, resources which are owned in common such as oceans, rivers, common grazing grounds, parks, and public lands are doomed to overexploitation. Such resources are owned by no one and thus protected by no one. In the absence of ownership rights the users of such resources have no incentive to protect them. Why should one fisherman reduce his own harvest to conserve the fish when they will be taken by someone else in the near future?

It is not just that such resources are abused by a callous public; they are subjected to escalating overexploitation as people compete with each other to plunder them. According to Garrett Hardin, perhaps the most famous proponent of this theory, it is only rational for the users of common-property resources to increase their exploitive efforts until the resource is depleted beyond recovery. Hardin has called this remorseless process the 'Tragedy of the Commons' (1968). Several economists have pointed out that the tragedy is not only a waste of natural resources, but inefficient use of those resources because of the externalities involved (Cheung 1970; see also Chapter 9). Since many fish stocks are a classic type of common-property resource, overexploitation of stocks, low catches, overcapitalization, economic inefficiency and low income are inevitable consequences (Crutchfield, 1964).

If common property causes nothing but problems, the theory suggests private ownership conveys only benefits. Ownership of property will give the owner strong incentive to conserve the resource and use it most efficiently (Gordon, 1954: Scott, 1955).

Underlying the theory of common-property resources is a set of axioms about the institutions surrounding common property and human motivation. First, the theory assumes that oceans and fish are 'open access' resources. Second, it assumes that the users of common property are interested only in short-term material gain and that they cannot or will not erect institutions to preserve the resources on which their livelihood depends. However, in the Maine lobster fishery, neither of these assumptions holds true. Although the fishery takes place in the open sea, a public domain, it is not an open-access fishery. Lobster fishermen have property rights in that they maintain lobster-fishing territories and limit access to them. In addition, fishermen have long been concerned about the resource, and are increasingly entering the political arena to lobby for protective legislation. Both the territorial system and the legislative effort help to conserve the resource; such action by the users runs counter to the predictions of the current commons theory.

The Maine lobster industry

The Maine lobster fishery is an inshore trap fishery. In the 1980s there were an estimated 2200 full-time fishermen, although 9000 licenses are issued a year. Full-time fishermen typically have inboard-powered boats between 28 and 36 feet long, and fish between 300 and 450 traps in the mid coast region, where most of this research has taken place. Most of the fishermen own their own boats, which they work alone, or with one helper called a 'sternman'. The study area is shown in Figure 12.1.

Lobstering is a highly seasonal activity. In the midwinter months catches are low because water temperatures cause lobsters to go into a state of near hibernation and the stormy weather makes it difficult to fish. At this time of year, lobsters (*Homarus americanus*) are best caught in deep water so that

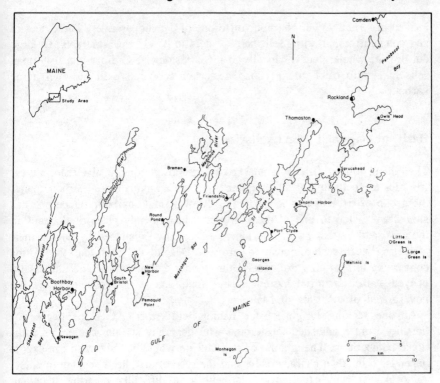

Figure 12.1 The study area.

fishermen who do go 'winter fishing' are placing their traps offshore, perhaps three to ten miles from the coast. Many fishermen do no fishing at this time of year, but rather devote all their time to repairing their gear.

As waters warm in the spring, lobsters begin to migrate inshore and can be caught in larger numbers. Thus there is a spurt of activity in April and May during the 'spring fishing' season. From mid-June to August, a large percentage of the lobsters are moulting. During this 'shedding season' they are hiding in the rocks close to shore and not inclined to be caught; many fishermen again reduce their fishing activity, and traps are placed very close to shore.

The height of the lobster season is late summer and early autumn. The number of lobsters that can be taken has been augmented by a new-year class which has moulted into legal size; and lobsters are again inclined to climb into traps. Over 65 per cent of the total catch occurs between mid-August and the first of November. As summer turns to autumn, lobsters begin to migrate offshore again. By January, fishermen are again placing traps in deep water.

Lobster fishermen sell their catches to one of the many local dealers located in virtually every harbour or to one of the cooperatives. These dealers and cooperatives, in turn, sell their lobsters to hotels or restaurants, to large out-of-state wholesalers, or locally to retail customers. Ordinarily a fisherman sells his entire catch to only one dealer or cooperative in his own home harbour.

Harbour gangs and their territories

The Maine lobster fishery is marked by group or communal territorialities. In order to go fishing at all, one must become a member of a harbour gang, the group of fishermen who go fishing from a single harbour. Once one has gained admission to one of these groups, one can only place one's traps in the area held by that gang. Interlopers are usually sanctioned by having their lobstering gear surreptitiously destroyed. Despite the fact that the norms concerning territoriality are general throughout the industry – and universally obeyed – the territorial system is informal, and is not recognized by the government of the state of Maine.

Anyone seeking to go lobster fishing will experience some degree of hostility from established lobstermen who generally see newcomers as additional competition. The amount of resistance a would-be fisherman can expect depends on his own characteristics and the type of area he is seeking to enter. A local boy will experience relatively little difficulty entering mainland harbour gangs – particularly if he comes from a family with a long fishing history and has kinsmen who are members of the harbour gang. His entry into the gang will ordinarily be especially easy if he begins fishing as a teenager and then goes fishing on a full-time basis after he is finished with school. People 'from away' will have more difficulty in establishing themselves in a harbour gang; they can expect to be harassed for a period of months, and some are never accepted. Resistance will be especially stiff if a newcomer begins fishing in middle age and has another source of income. Such people are violating an important principle of equity. By going fishing, they are taking 'more than their share' – a sort of 'double dipping'. The feeling against 'part-time' fishermen is particularly strong. Not only do they have another source of income, but they are apt to be poor fishermen and thus commonly follow good fishermen around, putting traps on top of theirs and even taking lobsters on occasion.

The most important factor influencing acceptance into a particular gang is the willingness to abide by local fishing norms. A man who gets the reputation of meddling with other men's traps or stealing lobsters will not last long in the business, regardless of family history and local ties.

Usually a person can enter only one harbour gang. However, under unusual circumstances, a man may be able to enter two. This may occur, for example, when a person moves from one harbour to another and gains admission to the harbour gang in his present home without losing membership in the gang in his former location.

Gaining admission to island harbour gangs is a more difficult task. Some islands are privately owned, in which case fishing rights are granted only to members of the owning family. On permanently occupied islands such as Frenchboro, Matinicus, and Isle au Haut, fishing rights are reserved for residents and it is difficult to buy land (Acheson, 1979, p. 264ff.).

Lobstering territories are typically small, no more than 225 square kilometres. Since lobster fishermen are confined to a single territory, they come to know their own area in great detail but have little knowledge of other areas. They know the details of the boundaries of their own areas but have little knowledge of other's boundaries. Territorial boundaries are typically relatively small features: a cove, a big rock, perhaps a tree. Boundaries further offshore are delineated by reference to prominent features on the mainland or islands.

One cannot predict with any certainty what will occur when territorial boundaries are violated. A high-status fisherman with many potential allies might get away with his incursion for weeks or months, while another man might be sanctioned almost immediately. If the incursion lasts long enough, however, someone – usually a single person acting alone – will seek to defend the boundary. Usually the interloper is first warned by tying two half-hitches around the spindle of his buoys, or conspicuously leaving the doors on his traps open. If he persists in fishing in the area of another gang, his traps will then be destroyed – usually by cutting the buoy line so that the trap is irretrievably lost. Usually the man or men defending the boundary will not 'cut off' any more traps than is necessary to force the interloper to move. Touching another man's traps is considered somewhat shameful, and is certainly illegal. In many cases, the interloper will retreat without a fight, in the knowledge that he has violated a boundary. Sometimes the victim will retaliate and a small 'cut war' will occur, in which men destroy the traps of guilty and innocent alike. Large-scale 'lobster wars', involving dozens of fishermen and the destruction of hundreds of traps, do occur – but they are very rare, occurring perhaps only once in a decade.

Information about trap-cutting incidents rarely escapes from the harbour gangs involved. The police or wardens are rarely called. Efforts to enforce the law are apt to be ineffective since it is very difficult to get evidence that will stand up in court. After all, traps are not cut off when witnesses are around. Moreover, there is a strong feeling that fishermen should handle their own problems and not involve external enforcement agencies.

There are two different types of territory in the Maine lobster industry. At present, the mainland harbours exhibit 'nucleated' territoriality. That is, the sense of ownership is very marked near the mouth of the harbour and grows progressively weaker as one goes further away. At a distance of perhaps ten miles from the harbour mouth, there is no strong sense of ownership at all. Any interloper placing traps close to the harbour mouth is certain to have trouble; but in the middle of bays and offshore, fishermen from as many as five different harbours may place their traps together. Some fishermen call this 'mixed fishing'.

Perimeter-defended areas are the rule on the offshore islands where boundaries are known to a yard and strongly defended; the sense of ownership remains strong up to the perimeter of the island's territory. As is to be expected, it would be more difficult to join harbour gangs on these islands where perimeter defence is found. The object of maintaining strict boundaries is to reserve an area for the exclusive use of harbour-gang members. Clearly, there is little sense maintaining strict boundaries if anyone could join.

At the turn of the century apparently, virtually all lobstering areas were perimeter-defended. On the mainland, these areas have virtually disappeared; nucleated areas have taken their place through a slow process of boundary movement and the easing of requirements for joining some harbour gangs (Acheson, 1979, pp. 253–76). However, a combination of factors has allowed the small perimeter-defended territories to be maintained around some of the outer islands. Men from mainland harbours have not been aggressive in pushing offshore to form areas where mixed fishing is allowed. They have been unable to organize the kinds of effective political alliances that will allow men from one harbour to push into the territory of another with any degree of success. Moreover, they do not need to make such incursions since they control sufficient territory. The islanders are able to form effective teams due to their small numbers, closely knit kinship system, and the ideology reinforcing their ownership claims. The forcefulness of their defence results partly from the fact that their lobstering territory provides their sole means of gaining a livelihood; there are few alternative opportunities on islands.

Regulating the fishing effort

The fishing effort in perimeter-defended areas is far less intensive than in nucleated areas. First, fishermen in perimeter-defended areas have more severely restricted entry into their harbour gangs than those from nucleated areas. (This is not to suggest that nucleated areas are 'open access' areas.) In three nucleated areas there were a total of 170 boats in 225 square kilometres of fishing area – or 1.32 square kilometres per boat. By way of contrast, in three adjacent perimeter-defended areas there was three times as much fishing area per boat. In these three areas, there were only 27 boats, with 94 square kilometres of equally good fishing area – or 3.48 square kilometres per boat (Acheson, 1975a p. 196).

Second, there is less fishing pressure in perimeter-defended areas because of certain local-level conservation practices. On Matinicus and Green Islands, fishermen have agreed to limit the number of traps they use. In 1984 Swan's Island fishermen successfully lobbied for a trap limit to permit each fisherman to fish only 400 traps. The advantages of such conservation measures are not immediately apparent. Trap limits do not cut down on total catch. Using fewer traps merely means that the same catch will be landed but may take a longer time. The advantage is that they increase profits for fishermen by lowering production costs. Fewer traps means smaller expenditures for bait, gas, maintenance, and so on. More important, a person using a smaller number of traps keeps track of them more effectively, loses fewer, and pulls them more frequently. All this reduces mortality by handling and cannibalism. There are fewer lost or 'ghost' traps which may incarcerate lobsters permanently. When traps are pulled frequently, soft-shelled, moulting lobsters, which would have been eaten by other lobsters, are released.

In addition, Monhegan Island, another perimeter-defended area, has persuaded the legislature to pass a law prohibiting fishing from January to June. This aids in conserving the lobster resource by prohibiting fishing during the midsummer moulting season when mortality is high on lobsters caught in traps.

There is strong evidence that the reduced fishing pressure in perimeter-defended areas due to fewer boats and conservation measures is having favourable economic and biological effects. This evidence was provided by a study done on the catches of 14 lobster fishermen from both nucleated and perimeter-defended areas in the same region of the coast. During this study, the carapace length of 9089 lobsters was recorded along with additional information on all the egged and notch-tailed lobsters (proven breeding stock) in the sample (Acheson, 1975a, pp. 199–200). It was found that lobsters caught in perimeter-defended areas are larger than those caught in nucleated areas. The mean carapace length of lobsters caught in perimeter-defended areas was 89.9mm, compared to only 87.9mm in nucleated areas. (This difference in means was significant at the 0.005 level by a t-test.)

The difference in mean size undoubtedly has an influence on the numbers of lobsters that survive to become breeding stock, and thus on the well-being of the fishery itself. Only 6 per cent of female lobsters become sexually mature under 90mm, but a very large percentage become mature between 90mm and 100mm; virtually all females are sexually mature by 105mm (Krouse, 1973, pp. 170–1). The percentage of lobsters in the critical size range (90mm to 100mm) is much higher in the perimeter-defended areas than in the nucleated areas. In the sample, 1.9 per cent of the lobsters caught in perimeter-defended areas were over 98mm but only 0.8 per cent of the lobsters caught in perimeter-defended areas were females with eggs as opposed to only 1.2 per cent in the nucleated areas.

Some of the most experienced lobster biologists conclude there are not enough eggs in the water and that the fishery will benefit if a larger number of females are allowed to survive to the sizes where they can spawn (Thomas, 1973, pp. 43–56). If this is true, then it can be argued that fishermen in perimeter-defended areas are doing more to conserve the lobster breeding stock than those in nucleated areas.

In addition, our study supports the idea that stock density of lobsters (number of lobsters on a given unit area of sea bottom) is much higher in perimeter-defended areas than in nucleated areas (Acheson, 1975a, p. 201). In the lobster fishery, the best indicator of stock density is expressed as catch-per-unit-of-effort. This is calculated as the catch per number of traps hauled, divided by the number of days the trap has been in the water (catch/trap/day). This takes into account the working time of the bait. At all seasons of the year, the catch per unit of effort was found to be substantially higher in perimeter-defended areas than nucleated areas. Late in the autumn, for example, perimeter-defended areas produced 0.11kg of lobster per trap per day, compared to 0.02kg per trap per day from nucleated areas – only 1/5 as much. In the summer, the differences between perimeter-defended and nucleated areas, although not as great as in the autumn, were still substantial. Fishermen in perimeter-defended areas were catching more – and larger sized – lobsters, and catching them with less effort (Table 12.1).

Table 12.1 Catch characteristics: Nucleated v. perimeter-defended areas

	Nucleated	Perimeter-Defended
Number of lobsters caught	3169	6180
Number of lobsters caught/trap hauled	0.31	0.51
Mean kilograms of lobsters caught/trap hauled	0.36	0.55
Mean weight of lobsters (in kilograms)	0.53	0.54

A man fishing a perimeter-defended area will earn more money with the same fishing effort than one fishing a nucleated area. Not only is he catching more lobsters per trap hauled, but the larger size of the lobsters caught translates into more premium 'dinner lobsters' in the catch – selling for a higher price per pound. The difference in earnings of fishermen from these two different areas can be quite substantial. In 1973, eight lobstermen from perimeter-defended areas earned an average gross income of $22,929 from lobster fishing. The same year fishermen from nearby nucleated areas earned only $16,499. (Although the sample was small, the difference of $6,430 is highly significant statistically; see Acheson, 1975a, p. 203.)

This is not to suggest that all fishermen from perimeter-defended areas inevitably earn more than those from nucleated areas. Men from nucleated areas can earn higher incomes than fishermen in perimeter-defended areas, but they need to work many more traps to do so.

In summary, it is easier to enter nucleated areas than perimeter-defended areas, resulting in a higher number of boats per unit of fishing area and hence relatively more fishing effort per unit of area. In such nucleated areas, lobsters are smaller, and catches, stock density and the average incomes of fishermen are lower than they are in perimeter-defended areas where fishing effort has been lowered by local-level conservation measures.

Despite the fact that the perimeter-defended areas operate to conserve the lobster stock better than nucleated areas, perimeter-defended areas are decreasing in numbers. At the turn of the century, all of the lobstering areas on the coast were perimeter-defended. Over the course of decades, the boundaries of most of these perimeter-defended areas have broken down due to political pressure from men from harbour gangs up in the estuaries, resulting in nucleated areas (Acheson, 1975a, pp. 192–3). At present, perimeter-defended areas persist only around some of the offshore islands. It remains to be seen how long they will remain there, since some of the boundaries of some of these areas are becoming increasingly costly to defend against incursions of fishermen from mainland harbours.

This is not to argue that the coast of Maine is in the process of becoming an open-access fishery. Entry into nucleated areas is controlled, if not as stringently as entry into perimeter-defended areas. Nowhere along the coast can 'just anyone' get a lobster licence and go fishing without opposition.

Politics of lobster management

In the 1980s, efforts to manage the lobster fishery are in a state of flux, and the fishermen and their organizations are playing an increasingly important role in lobbying to change the regulatory environment with conservation in mind.

Lobster fishermen have long presented themselves as independent beings who want nothing so much as to have the government off their backs. In reality, they have never been as apolitical as they would like to pretend. In the past, however, their efforts have been devoted largely to opposing attempts to regulate the fishery. Currently, they are seriously worried about the state of their industry and are interested in promulgating far more regulations than are the federal and state agencies charged with lobster management. In order to understand this turn of events, it is necessary to know something about both the regulatory environment and the circumstances that have produced this change of attitude with respect to regulations.

Until 1976, at the time of the passage of the Fisheries Conservation and Management Act, regulation of coastal fisheries was the responsibility of state governments; since that date, the federal government has had the authority to regulate all fisheries. However, to date, no federal regulations of the lobster fishery have been passed. This means that since the 1870s, when the first regulations went into effect, all regulations have been promulgated by the state of Maine.

There are very few laws pertaining to the lobster industry. To go lobster fishing, a person must have a licence, which can be obtained by all for a nominal fee. There is also a law that all traps and equipment must be marked with the fisherman's licence number and that his buoys must be marked with a distinctive combination of colours registered with the state. These regulations are for administrative purposes, and are designed to ease problems of enforcing laws prohibiting molestation of traps. In addition, there are a number of laws designed to conserve the resource, the most important of which are size regulations. Currently, it is illegal to take lobsters smaller than 3 3/16 inches (81mm) or larger than five inches (127mm) measured on the carapace. In addition, it is illegal to take 'berried' lobsters (female lobsters with eggs attached). Fishermen may also mark such berried lobsters by cutting a v-shaped notch in one of their tail flippers. Once such lobsters are 'notched', they may not be legally taken again. Both the so called 'oversized' lobsters and 'v-notched' lobsters are considered proven breeding stock. In addition, a 1984 law mandates that all traps be equipped with vent, which will allow small, illegal-sized lobsters to escape.

Regulation in the lobster industry is scarcely new. The strong propensity to regulate the industry is clearly the result of a long series of predictions of disaster, which have almost as long a history as the industry itself.

The commercial lobster fishery began in the 1840s when the advent of the lobster smack, with circulating seawater tanks, made it possible to ship lobsters to cities along the eastern seaboard. Shortly thereafter, very large numbers of lobsters began to be canned. By the 1870s there was fear that the lobster fishery might crash, and a consensus was reached to do something about the situation. In 1872 a law was passed prohibiting the taking of berried females, and in 1874 fishing was prohibited during the summer shedding season and it was made illegal to take lobsters under 10.5 inches (267mm) carapace length. In 1932, a legal maximum size was also established, largely at the urging of biologist Francis Herrick, who argued that large lobsters were prolific breeders. These laws were later revised, but from the 1870s to the present, the basis of lobster management has remained size limitation and protection of the breeding stock.

This long-standing tradition of regulation is a response to an equally long tradition of emphasizing the 'problems' facing the industry. Even in the 1880s, one of the largest canners was worried about the industry's future; and in 1901 one Holman Day was prompted to write a humorous poem called 'Good-bye Lobster'. Francis Herrick was at the forefront of those proclaiming the demise of the industry from the early years of the century to the Depression. Such concerns continue to be expressed to the present, and every year a number of articles are published with titles such as 'Where Have All the Lobsters Gone?' (Keiffer, 1973), and 'A Fishery Under Fire' (Kreis, 1986).

In large part this crisis atmosphere is engendered by the fishermen, who themselves advertise the difficulties of their business while minimizing any successes. It is exacerbated by the press with their penchant for disaster stories.

The crisis atmosphere cannot be explained by a history of disasters or by evidence that a disaster is imminent. In reality, the lobster catch has proven remarkably stable over time. Since 1947, when the modern record-keeping system was introduced, the total Maine lobster catch has fluctuated from a low of 7227 metric tons (15.9 million pounds) in 1948 to a high of 11,091 metric tons (24.4 million pounds) in 1957. In most years, the catch hovers around the 9000 metric ton (20 million pound) mark. Moreover, catch per unit of effort has also been stable for the past 20 years (Thomas et al, 1983). From 1968 to the present, about 0.2 lobsters have been caught per trap per layover day (Thomas et al, 1983, p. 164).

Nevertheless, the past 15 years have witnessed virtually all lobster biologists advocating a change in the regulations to save the industry. In general, they feel that the industry may be poised on the brink of disaster because the breeding stock is at such a dangerously low level and because there are not enough eggs in the water. These biologists point out that at least 90 per cent of all lobsters are caught in the first year after they reach legal size. Only 6 per cent of females are mature at 81mm (3 3/16 of an inch) at which size they can be legally caught. This suggests that the vast majority of lobsters do not survive to the size at which they could possibly extrude spawn even once. The solution, from the biologist's point of view, is to increase the legal minimum size to 3.5 inches (89mm) carapace length, thereby allowing a much larger number of females to survive to breeding size. In the early 1970s increasing the legal minimum size to 3.5 inches became a key feature of the Comprehensive Management Plan for American Lobsters produced by the Northeast Marine fisheries Board (Anon., 1978), and more recently of the lobster-management plan proposed by the New England Regional Council. In addition, lobster biologists recommend an end to the five-inch (127mm) maximum legal size on the grounds that there are very few such lobsters and that they show a marked tendency to migrate south west out of the local area (Anon., 1978, p. 3–4). Last, biologists and bureaucrats would like to abolish the 'notched tail' law because cutting notches in the tail of a lobster presumably leaves the lobster prone to infection.

Lobster fishermen are generally not in favour of these proposed regulations but their attitudes towards management have undergone considerable change in the past few years. If they are not in favour of exactly the same regulations that the federal and state officials would like to see passed, they are in favour of regulations which they feel would be more effective.

In the early 1970s, fishermen were against management in general and certainly against the kinds of regulations being proposed for their industry at that time. Fishermen were questioned about a scheme that would place a moratorium on fishing and subsidize fishermen to replace lost income while the stock recovered. Fishermen were vociferous in condemning this plan. They were also solidly against any tax on traps, even though many admitted that there were too many traps in the water; they argued that such a tax would not only be unfair, it would be ineffective. At that time, fishermen were also overwhelmingly against raising the legal minimum size to 3.5 inches, reasoning that a very large percentage of all lobsters caught were just over the existing legal minimum size. Raising the size limit would thus make illegal a very large part of the catch, which in turn would lower their incomes. They were not convinced that any of these proposals would result in long-term benefits to the industry (Acheson, 1975b, pp. 654–6).

Fishermen were divided on the question of whether the five-inch (127mm) rule should be repealed: 78 per cent favoured abolishing the oversize rule because it would open another fishery and make it possible to land the large lobsters caught in numbers offshore in Maine. However, 24 per cent were sufficiently worried about the state of the breeding stock to want to retain this 'oversize' or five-inch-maximum rule (Acheson, 1975b, p. 655ff.).

In the early 1970s there was general support for a limit on the number of lobster traps. Eighty-eight per cent of the fishermen stated that there were too many traps in the water and that a trap limit would not only help to conserve the lobster, but would lower their business costs. (Fishermen felt that a trap limit would not reduce the total catch; it would simply take a little longer to catch the same number.) It would also be 'fairer' in that it would prevent overly competitive fishermen from taking a disproportionate share of the catch.

There was also mixed support for a limit on the number of licences issued. The idea of limited entry came as no shock. After all, fishermen have been limiting entry into harbour gangs for decades. However, fishermen's interest focused on who would be allowed to go fishing and who would be excluded. Basically, they wanted the law to exclude those who had traditionally been excluded and allow those who had always been permitted.

In the mid-1970s, there was no attempt to introduce legislation to change the legal size limits since there was no support in the industry for such legislation. One serious attempt was made to limit traps and licences, but it did not pass through the state legislature. Despite the fact that there was general support in the industry for such legislation, groups of fishermen were violently opposed and mounted a very effective and successful lobbying campaign against the bill in the legislature.

Political initiatives: 1986–87

In the 1980s, incomes of lobster fishermen have gone down in general; they have been caught in a cost-and-price squeeze. The cost of things they have to buy (boats, traps, bait, insurance, etc) have increased far faster than the selling price of lobster. In addition, catches have remained stable while the number of fishermen has increased, particularly in the mid-1980s.

This economic decline has made lobster fishermen more inclined towards government management. In 1986 and 1987, 61 full-time fishermen were interviewed in regard to proposed legislation for the industry. There was marked unanimity expressed on many issues. The strong ambivalence towards government action and the range of opinion on most issues concerning management that was so marked in the mid-1970s no longer existed. Fishermen still favoured limited entry and a limit on the number of traps, for virtually all agreed that there were too many traps in the water and too many fishermen. Many spontaneously pointed out that a trap limit and licence limit had to be combined, for they recognized that it would do no good to limit the number of licences if the remaining fishermen could increase the number of traps they fished. Conversely, they observed that fishing effort would not be reduced by limiting the number of traps if additional fishermen entered the industry. In addition, *all* the fishermen interviewed unanimously approved of the passage of the 1984 law requiring escape vents on traps to allow undersized lobsters to escape.

There had been a reversal of attitudes regarding the five-inch (127mm) maximum-size law; of the 61 lobster fishermen interviewed, 59 now said they would like to see the measure retained. Fishermen reasoned that abolishing the oversize measure would increase their catches by only a few dozen lobsters a year since there are so few oversized lobsters in inshore waters; yet retaining the measure probably helped to conserve the resource. Lobster dealers, however, would like to see the oversize measure abolished as this would allow large lobsters, caught offshore, to be handled by Maine dealers rather than landed in other states.

Fishermen were also adamant about retaining the 'punched tail' law. None of the men interviewed wanted to see this law abolished. In their view, this law does more to maintain the breeding stock than any other factor since it ensures that millions of females carrying eggs are not only returned to the water, but are protected so they can breed again. As one fisherman expressed it, 'If you do away with that law, you do away with the industry. It is that important.'

Opinion was divided on the question of raising the legal size to 3.5 inches (89mm). Thirty-eight men interviewed wanted to see the legal size raised, while 23 disagreed, arguing that this measure would cut their catches and incomes. These men also wondered about its effectiveness as a conservation measure. Several suggested that increasing the legal size would only mean that lobsters would live another year before they could be caught. During that year, they would not only be subjected to additional natural mortality, but would also be caught in traps. This would entail a certain proportion of lobsters damaged from increased handling, and an increased proportion of females 'notched' and thus illegal. Others wondered if the industry was really so close to collapse that such drastic measures were needed to increase egg production. Many wondered if additional eggs would enhance recruitment because so many factors play upon lobster-stock growth rates besides the number of eggs in the water.

Many of the men who favoured raising the measure to 3.5 inches were only moderately supportive. These men, by and large, felt that an increase in the legal measure would help the industry in the long run by ensuring that there would be more eggs in the water and larger lobsters which could be sold at a higher price per pound. They knew that such a law would cut their catches in the short run, but they were willing to make the sacrifice in the best long-term interests of the industry.

It needs to be stressed that the attitudes of fishermen towards these various management proposals cannot be dismissed as 'unscientific' and that the position of the federal and state bureaucracies is not as rational as one might suppose (for a parallel case, see Chapter 6). Recent studies by Bayer et al (1985) of the University of Maine demonstrate that the v-notch law is doing a good deal to maintain the breeding stock by ensuring that a large proportion of the females that have borne eggs survive to do it again. A study by Waddy and Aiken (1985) suggests that the five-inch maximum measure ('oversize' law) is probably doing the same. At the same time, my own research indicates that the 3.5-inch measure – which many federal and state officials see as the cornerstone of lobster management – would not result in the kinds of economic benefits its proponents have assumed. It would certainly substantially reduce catches and income for the lobster industry during the years the measure was being increased incrementally to 3.5 inches (Acheson and Reidman, 1982, p. 10).

The current lobster-management plan, under discussion at the state and federal levels, calls for increasing the legal minimum size from 3 3/16 inches (81mm) to 3.5 inches (89mm) in 1/16in increments. If this were done, our model indicates that in each of the years when the measure was being increased there would be 4 per cent to 7 per cent loss of revenue to fishermen; once the legal limit had reached 3.5 inches, there would be a permanent gain of 5.5 per cent in total revenue to the industry. There would most likely be long-term benefits to the industry, but fishermen are quite correct in assuming that implementing such a law would result in economic hardships (Acheson and Reidman, 1982, p. 10).

Recently, fishermen have had a substantial effect on efforts to manage their industry. In the spring of 1986, bills were presented in the Maine legislature to increase the legal minimum size measure, abolish the 5-inch (127mm) maximum-size measure, and introduce trap limits for various classes of licences. There was also a bill that would establish lobster hatcheries. However, no change was proposed for the v-notch law. Intense lobbying activity by fishermen and industry leaders persuaded the legislature to postpone action until the next legislative session when the results of a study, mandated by the legislature, would be available.

Throughout the early 1980s, federal and state bureaucracies continued their efforts to have enacted into law the federal fisheries management plan which features increasing the minimum size limit to 3.5 inches (89mm), abolishing the v-notch law and the five-inch (127mm) (oversize) measure. The fishermen were against this proposal because it would make the 3.5-inch measure the cornerstone of conservation, a measure which fishermen suspect will be costly and ineffective, and abolishes the two laws they feel are conserving the resource – the v-notch law and the law protecting lobsters of over five-inch carapace length. Eddie Blackmore, president of the Maine Lobsterman's Association, who generally has strong backing from the industry, has proposed an unusual compromise. The fishermen will support the 3.5-inch measure, which he and many fishermen see as ineffective, if the federal government will agree to maintain the five-inch-maximum measure and the 'notched tail' law. This would permit both sides to have the laws they feel are most essential for conservation of the resource. At this writing, the fate of this compromise is uncertain but progress has clearly been made. In June 1987 the New England Regional Council voted to begin raising the legal minimum size and to maintain the v-notch. If the Maine Lobsterman's Association succeeds in this endeavour, the result will be the ironic situation in which a group of fishermen have entered into an agreement to have one conservation law imposed as a means of retaining others.

A speedy resolution of the issue cannot be expected given that the New England Regional Council, the Federal Government, and the coastal New England states would all have to adopt such regulations. (The coastal states exert control out to the three-mile line; the federal government exerts control from the three-mile line to the 200-mile line.)

The concern for the welfare of the lobster stock has been demonstrated in a more tangible way: groups of lobstermen in cooperation with the University of Maine have begun to establish small hatcheries at various points along the coast. These hatcheries release small lobsters after they have passed through the first four moults, during which time mortality is highest (Plants, 1986, p. 1).

Although these small hatcheries cost only a few thousand dollars to build, groups of fishermen are paying much of the cost. More important, there is wide enthusiasm in the industry for the hatcheries. Fishermen are not certain how effective they will be, but none of the 61 fishermen interviewed during 1986 and 1987 thought they were a waste of time and money: many were certain they would help to maintain the stock.

In January 1987 a bill was being prepared which would limit entry into the lobster industry and provide for a trap limit. This bill is being drafted by the commissioner of the Department of Marine Resources in coordination with the Lobster Advisory Council, which is composed of fishermen. The exact form this bill will take and its ultimate fate at the hands of the Maine Legislature and New England Regional Fisheries Management Council remain uncertain at this time. However, the bill appears to embody the most far-reaching management proposal for the lobster industry in many decades. It will clearly get substantial industry support.

Even if the legislation proposed by the Lobsterman's Association and the hatcheries fail completely, the strong support such measures have received from the industry should not go unnoticed, for an interest in conservation is not supposed to be a characteristic of those exploiting common-property resources. Where have all the overexploiters of common-property resources gone?

The Maine lobster industry and the theory of common-property resources

The case of the Maine lobster industry calls into question one of the central axioms underlying the common-property model – namely the proposition that the users of common-property resources have no interest in the long-term well-being of those resources and that they cannot generate institutions to conserve them. This case study shows that under certain conditions, users of common-property resources can effectively generate such institutions. The existence of the territorial system, the hatcheries, and recent legislative initiatives all underscore this point.

At present, there are two different kinds of management systems in operation in the lobster industry. The first is the older territorial system, which continues to operate in its traditional fashion. The second is co-management of the industry with the state of Maine and the federal government. That is, fishermen and their representatives are seeking to shape legislation through a long process of lobbying and negotiation with legislative and bureaucratic officials. Each of these managerial institutions helps to modify the common-property model in different ways.

There is strong evidence that the territorial system does help conserve the resource. Certainly, we have evidence that the perimeter-defended areas produce more favourable biological and economic results than the nucleated areas where access is easier. It is reasonable to assume that nucleated areas do more to preserve the stock and result in higher incomes for fishermen than would be the case in true 'open access' areas. The latter hypothesis is untestable since there are no areas 'unowned' by harbour gangs where anyone can set traps.

These data on the territorial system in the Maine lobster industry reinforce one of the most important axioms of the common-property-resource theorists – namely that property rights help conserve natural resources. However, it is crucial to note that the theory of common-property resources asserts that it is *private property* that results in efficiency and conservation. Yet in this particular case, lobster territories are owned jointly or communally by a group of fishermen. This underlines the fact that communal ownership – not just private ownership – can result in conservation. The potential of such communal ownership was noted by Ciriacy-Wantrup and Bishop (1975), and by others working in other parts of the world (for example Switzerland; Netting, 1972).

Lobbying activity is a very common strategy in the USA, where industry leaders preserve legislative bodies to provide them with a protected niche, all the while extolling the virtues of free enterprise and freedom from government interference. Fishermen have been less hypocritical than most. Most have said they did not want any government interference and they have meant it. However, in the past few years, as fishing has become a more difficult occupation in which to earn a living, there have been increasing efforts to generate legislation which will conserve the stock of lobsters. These efforts have not gone unopposed because federal and state officials charged with the management of the fisheries have strong ideas about how management should be effected. Thus, fishermen cannot properly be said to direct legislation for their industry. Rather, they influence its direction by bringing the weight of membership to bear on the legislature and representatives to the regional fisheries council. Fishermen are not managers of the lobster stock; they are what Pinkerton (1987) calls co-managers.

This particular situation is not consistent with the current theory of common-property resources: Hardin holds that resources such as fish can only be preserved through draconian and not very democratic government action. Recent events in the Maine lobster industry argue strongly against those who assert, with Hardin, that 'Tragedies of the Commons' can only be averted by an authoritarian state. Moreover, the economists interested in the management of such resources see salvation only in the institution of 'sole ownership' or private property. The lobster industry points out that at least two other means of effective management can exist:

1 local-level management of jointly owned assets (the territorial system); and
2 joint management with the state and federal governments.

Neither depends on sole ownership, and neither is unusual in worldwide perspective (Acheson, in press; McCay and Acheson, 1987).

Conclusion

In conclusion, it would appear that the political environment surrounding lobster management is undergoing substantial change at present. In the past, fishermen sought to conserve the lobster mainly by informally and illegally limiting entry into the industry through the territorial system. Recently, they have added another strategy, namely, legislation – a means they have been most reluctant to use in the past. In short, fishermen are moving into a situation in which they will exercise both local-level management, and co-management with the state of Maine.

References

Acheson, James M., 1975a: 'The lobster fiefs: Economic and ecological effects on territoriality in the Maine lobster industry', *Human Ecology*, 3(3), pp. 183–207.

Acheson, James M., 1975b: 'Fisheries management and social context: The case of the Maine lobster industry', *Transactions of the American Fisheries Society*, 104(4), pp. 653–68.

Acheson, James M., 1979: 'Traditional inshore fishing rights in Maine lobstering communities', in Raoul Anderson, ed., *North Atlantic Maritime Cultures*, Mouton, The Hague, pp. 253–76.

Acheson, James M. and Reidman, Robert, 1982: 'Biological and economic effects of increasing the minimum legal size of American lobster in Maine', *Transactions of the American Fisheries Society*, 111(1), pp. 1–12.

Acheson, James M. in press: 'Economic anthropology and the management of common property resources', to be published in Plattner, Stuart, ed., *Economic Anthropology*, Stanford University Press, Palo Alto.

Anonymous, 1978: *American Lobster Fishery Management Plan*, Northeast Marine Fishery Board, Gloucester, Massachusetts.

Bailey, Frederick, 1969: *Strategies and Spoils: A Social Anthropology of Politics*, Schocken, New York, p. 240.

Bayer, Robert, Daniel, Peter C. and Vaitones, Scott, 1985: 'Preliminary estimate of contribution of v-notched American lobsters to egg production along coastal Maine based on Maine Lobsterman's Association v-notch survey: 1981–1984', *Bulletin of the Department of Animal and Veterinary Sciences*, University of Maine, Orono, Maine.

Cheung, Steven N.S., 1970: 'The structure of a contract and the theory of a non-exclusive resource', *Journal of Law and Economics*, 13(1), pp. 45–70.

Ciriacy-Wantrup and Bishop, Richard C., 1975: 'Common property as a concept in natural resources policy', *Natural Resources Journal*, 15, pp. 713–27.

Crutchfield, James, 1964: 'The maritime fisheries: A problem in international cooperation', *American Economic Review Proceedings*, 54, pp. 207–18.

Gordon, H.S., 1954: 'The economic theory of a common property resource', *Journal of Political Economy*, 62, pp. 124–42.

Hardin, Garrett, 1968: 'The tragedy of the commons', *Science*, 162, pp. 1243–8.

Keiffer, Elizabeth, 1973: 'Where have all the lobsters gone?', *New York Times Magazine*, November 18, pp. 36–7.

Kreis, Donald, 1986: 'A fishery under fire', *Maine Times*, September 26, p. 1.

Krouse, Jay S., 1973: 'Maturity, sex ratio, and size composition of the natural population of American lobster, *Homarus americanus*, along the Maine coast', *Fisheries Bulletin*, 71(1), pp. 165–73.

McCay, Bonnie and Acheson, James, 1987: 'Human ecology of the commons', introduction to *The Question of the Commons*, University of Arizona Press, Tucson.

Netting, Robert McC., 1972: 'Of mice and meadows: Strategies of Alpine land use', *Anthropological Quarterly*, 45(3), pp. 132–44.

Plante, Janice M., 1986: 'Inside lobster hatcheries', *Commercial Fisheries News*, August, p. 1.

Pinkerton, Evelyn, 1987: 'Intercepting the state: Dramatic processes in the assertion of local co-management rights', in McCay, Bonnie and Acheson, James, eds, *The Question of the Commons*, University of Arizona Press, Tucson.

Scott, Anthony, 1955: 'The objectives of sole ownership', *Journal of Political Economy*, 63, pp. 118–24.

Thomas, James, 1973: *An Analysis of the Commercial Lobster (Homarus americanus) Fishery along the Coast of Maine, August 1966 through December 1970*. National Oceanic and Atmospheric Administration, Technical Report, National Marine Fisheries Service, Washington, DC.

Thomas, James, Burke, C.C., Robinson, G.A. and Parkhurst, J.R., 1983: *Catch and Effort Information on the Maine Commercial Lobster (Homarus americanus) Fishery, 1967–1981*, Lobster Informational Leaflet No. 12, Maine Department of Marine Resources Lobster Research Program, Boothbay Harbor, Maine.

Waddy, Susan and Aiken, D., 1985: *Proceedings of the Lobster Recruitment Workshop*, St. Andrews, New Brunswick.

13 Water as Common Property: The Case of Irrigation Water Rights in the Philippines

Ma. Concepcion J. Cruz

Summary

Two factors motivated the institution of a framework for water-resources utilization and development in the Philippines. The first was the need to evolve efficient and rational use of scarce water supplies. This is especially true in the case of irrigation, where water supply is unevenly distributed across geographical regions and throughout different growing seasons.

The second factor has to do with protection of use rights of all legitimate users of a water resource in a manner that guarantees equitable distribution of water. The advantages of upstream farms over their downstream counterparts makes a strong case for the enforcement of rules for water sharing. The Water Code of the Philippines attempts to address these two concerns of efficiency and equity in the use of water resources by explicitly defining in both substantive and juridical terms rules for water allocation.

To differentiate water-distribution rules which are covered by the Water Code and rules which are governed by informal norms and practices, the view of water right as the legal or formal concession granted by the state is adopted. Water in this instance comes from a natural source and is treated as an 'object' that is subject to state control.

On the other hand, water below the source becomes a 'commodity' that acquires a cost so that allocation rules and the institutional setting differ. This distinction of water as object and water as commodity permits the separation of rules for water distribution along the source (for example, a river) and below the source.

The case study of water-rights conflict in Ilocos Norte province is between a federation of 13 irrigation associations (called *zanjeras*) with a legal water right and three unfederated associations without water rights. A technical solution has been proposed to resolve the conflict but it is the enforcement of rules for water sharing that recognize the prior claims of holders of the water right, that has more significance in establishing common-property management of the resource.

Five factors are identified as significant in promoting collective control of water.

1 environmental conditions that affect seasonal fluctuations in water supply;
2 technology requirements;
3 size of the irrigation system and population serviced;
4 social and political relationships of users; and
5 presence of water rights.

Introduction

Awareness of and concern for the problems associated with the use of water resources have been increasing worldwide. Two major aspects of these problems involve the alarming rates at which water supplies are being depleted and the conflicts arising from competition in allocating the scarce water supply. In addition, a common problem among developing countries is the lack of guidelines for the development of water resources and for the distribution of water among competing users. These problems have become especially critical for the Philippines, resulting in considerable administrative encumbrances in water-resources projects and growing conflicts among rival claimants to the use of a common water source.

This chapter offers an analysis of the effectiveness of the Water Code of the Philippines in addressing problems related to water distribution and control for irrigation purposes. A brief description of traditional irrigation water use is presented in the next section. Section II discusses basic principles governing water use. Section III reviews the Water Code in terms of its effects on common-property-resource management through an evaluation of enforcement and allocation procedures. A case study of water-rights dispute in Ilocos Norte province is examined in Section IV, and a conclusion is provided in Section V.

Section I: Traditional water use in the Philippines

There are numerous documented cases of water sharing in the Philippines that have existed as early as the eighteenth century (Christy, 1914). The most popular, the *zanjeras* (a term from the Spanish word *zanja*, meaning canal), are found mostly in the northern Ilocos provinces. *Zanjeras* are generally small-sized irrigation societies, though some are as large as 1000 hectares. All *zanjeras* are community-built and managed (Siy, 1982).

Many of the existing *zanjeras* were formed through the initiative of groups of individuals who offered to construct irrigation structures in exchange for the right to cultivate a portion of the land. In building the irrigation system, individual *zanjera* members often contributed 20 to 30 days of labour per year, although in the early periods of construction as much as 80 days per year were contributed (Christy, 1914).

Mobilizing local resources for managing the *zanjera* irrigation system depended on two sets of 'rules'. These rules pertain to the manner in which land is distributed among *zanjera* members and the principles by which individual services and rights are valued in proportion to the land. Individual landholdings are allocated in several equal-sized parcels. Each parcel is located in both upstream and downstream segments of the system to minimize problems associated with unequal water allocation. The land parcel is defined collectively with respect to *atars* or shares in the water coming from the system. Each *atar* is directly proportional to area cultivated and defines the member's obligation to contribute labour and materials for operating and maintaining the system.

The *atar* shares are inherited and transferable whenever the land is sold. Work obligations, because they are based on landholding size, are roughly equal for all members of the *zanjera*. Such equitable sharing of benefits and costs, which is embedded in the local culture, has contributed to the success of the *zanjera* organization in dealing with conflicts and mobilizing local resources (Siy, 1982).

The *zanjeras* have existed for many years with minimal government interference. However, in 1976, the Water Code was enforced and all *zanjera* ancestral claims to the use of water from rivers and streams now had to be registered with the government's National Water Resources Council (NWRC). The case study presented in Section IV of this chapter shows an example of how the new Water Code has eroded some of the traditional values of water sharing among *zanjeras*.

Section II: Approaches to irrigation water use

Irrigation in the Philippines has traditionally been characterized either by open-access exploitation or common-property management. Open-access conditions obtain when there is an absence of rules on resource use and thus advantages based on socioeconomic status or community influence govern access to and control of resources. For example, certain families located near the water source appropriate sole use of the water.

Common property has been defined as the 'distribution of property rights in resources in which a number of owners are co-equal in their rights to use the resource' (Ciriacy-Wantrup and Bishop, 1975, p. 914). A water resource governed by the common-property concept is collectively managed or used under specific conditions of access. Easter and Palanisami (1986) define common-property-access rules to irrigation in terms of the double nature of irrigation water as public good and as private property. Water ceases to be subject to exclusive individual ownership (private property) since the nature of the water resource lends itself to greater cooperative control. Thus, the very nature of water as a flow resource, and the difficulty of controlling its distribution across many users, argue strongly for the establishment of collective rules on water allocation.

The operational rule that explicitly distinguishes the appropriation of irrigation water from open-access conditions is the institution of rules governing users of the resource. Such rules cover the acquisition, allocation and distribution, and operation and maintenance of the irrigation system. The collective performance of these activities necessitates the enforcement of formal or informal rules which define the individual water user's rights to receive a reliable water supply.

In the Philippines, the right to divert water from a river or stream is defined through a water permit. The conditions of use are well defined in the water permit (or grant) and the physical arrangements and technology for diversion and storage of water are identified. The water right establishes a legal basis for use of the resource that is enforced and protected by the state.

The water permit embodies the 'privilege granted by the government to appropriate and use water' and is based on the underlying principle that 'all waters belong to the state' and that the water 'cannot be the subject of acquisitive prescription' (Water Code, Sec. 1). Thus the water permit guarantees the right of 'administrative concession' to specific users of the resource. The right of 'use and concession', which is subject to the rules embodied in the Water Code, restricts open-access exploitation and defines the conditions of actual use and allocation of the water supply.

Framework for classifying irrigation water rights

Table 13.1 shows a framework for classifying water rights, as either *formal* or *informal*, in terms of interactions among water users. The formal rules are set by the state (through the Water Code) while other (informal) rules of access operate through existing social, cultural and political rules for cooperative sharing of water. In some instances, however, holders of a formal right may in fact be ineffective in actually controlling the water supply as long as such informal factors as social status and prestige (for example, of an influential landowner) are the dominant forces in the community.

To differentiate between formal water distribution rules (which are covered by the Water Code) and rules which are governed by informal norms and practices, the view of the water right as a legal or formal right granted by the state was introduced in the promulgation of the Water Code in 1976. All existing claims to water prior to the code are considered non-binding unless a new water permit is secured from the government (through the NWRC).

Table 13.1 A framework for classifying use-rights for irrigation water in the Philippines

	Rules pertaining to water from a natural source	Rules pertaining to water from a man-made source (canal)
FORMAL RULES		
'Ownership' of the water source	State as owner of all natural water bodies issues water permits	Water fees or services in exchange for water delivery
	Rules based on the 1976 Water Code of the Philippines	Rules based on community practices; in case of water fees, based on the 'market price' of the water
Boundary for defining ownership/use rights	Always defined *above* the point of diversion of water *along* a natural water body (river, stream, etc)	Sometimes use rights defined at the point of diversion (eg among two competing irrigation associations) but oftentimes rules defined *below* the source (eg rules on water distribution along the canals)
INFORMAL RULES		
Agreements regarding use of water	State grants water permits for a single water body on a 'first come, first served' basis	Social, cultural, and political norms are used in determining priority rights to water
Settlement of conflicts	Normally done through the courts; sometimes through intervillage agreements	Generally settled within informal kin-based systems (elders, local officials, etc)

Such claims include ancestral rights to water sources and rights which have been previously granted by local government and Bureau of Public Works officials.

The water permit specifies the location, volume and scope of the right to divert water from an identified water source. Thus water comes from a natural source and is treated as an *object* that is subject to state control (through the issuance of water permits).

On the other hand, the informal rules of access that govern water distribution ('below the source') operate in a context of sociocultural and political obligations which permit users of the water resource to act with considerable flexibility in enforcing their rights. The informal rules governing the allocation of water are made among various competing users. However, such rules may in fact be operational with or without the legal water right. Another important distinction is to consider the legal right as the state's claim to ownership of 'all natural water bodies', while the informal use rights to water pertain to individual or collective rights to receive a portion of the supply in return for services rendered (for example, in the form of water fees or labour services to the irrigation society).

Water distribution below the source can thus be treated as a *commodity* which acquires a cost so that allocation rules and the institutional setting differ. This distinction between water as object and water as commodity underlies the separation of rules for water distribution along the source (through the water permit) and below the source (through informal rules of access). The existence of the water right itself serves the efficiency criterion by producing a 'rent' or value for the resource that, under conditions of open-access, will generally be dissipated.

Section III: Implementation of the Water Code

Legitimate claims to a water resource are formally recognized through the issuance of a water permit. The permits are granted by the National Water Resources Council (NWRC) which is also authorised to impose and collect fees and to settle disputes concerning rival claims to water supply usage.

Granting water permits

As of December 1984, a total of 7601 water permits have been granted by NWRC for various types of water uses. Of this, 71 per cent, or 5407, permits were used for irrigation purposes and 27 per cent, or 1685, permits were for domestic water supply. Industrial and hydropower uses accounted for 5 per cent (or 377 permits), the rest being used for livestock, recreation, fisheries, and multiple uses.

Table 13.2 provides a summary of the distribution of water permits by year the permit was awarded. The table illustrates that a majority of the permits were issued during the period of the Water Code, accounting for almost 86 per cent of total permits granted. The years immediately before the Water Code (1970–1975) accounted for another 6 per cent.

Table 13.3 contains the distribution of water permits issued for irrigation purposes by geographic area and type of user. For all regions, the major users are individuals or groups of individuals, comprising more than half (55 per cent) of the permits granted. This is followed by irrigation associations with 22 per cent (1208 permits), 39 per cent of which were issued to *zanjeras*

Table 13.2 Distribution of water permits by type of water use and year permit granted

Type of water use	Colonial period pre-1990s–1946	Pre-Water Code 1947–1975	Water Code period 1976–1984	TOTAL
1. Irrigation	222	549	4583	5354
2. Power	–	6	95	101
3. Domestic water supply	8	158	1479	1645
4. Industrial use	1	29	242	272
5. Fishery	–	2	28	30
6. Livestock, recreation, and other types of uses	2	18	71	91
TOTAL	233 (3.1%)	762 (10.2%)	6498 (86.7%)	7493* (100%)

* an additional 108 grantees have no dates written on their water permits, bringing total to 7601.

Source: National Water Resources Council compilation of water permits granted as of December 1984.

in the Ilocos region. (The water permit represented the *zanjeras'* attempt to legalize what they have recognized as their legitimate, ancestral rights to the water.)

Collection of fees

An application fee of 100 pesos is collected from every applicant for a water permit, except for government agencies, water districts, and irrigation or water-supply organizations. On water permits issued for irrigation purposes, the NWRC is authorized to collect an annual water charge at the rate of 0.5 pesos for each litre per second (lps) withdrawal of water up to 30 lps; 0.75 pesos for water use exceeding 30 lps but not more than 50 lps; and 1.00 peso for water discharge exceeding 50 lps. In 1982, the NWRC generated over 0.31 million pesos from water fees and charges.

Settlement of water rights conflicts

A total of 173 cases of water-rights conflicts were filed with the NWRC in

Table 13.3 Distribution of irrigation water permits by type of user and region

Region	Irrigation Association	Government agency: NIA	Government agency: local government	Individual or group of individuals	Private[a]	Total
I. Ilocos	471	96	4	349	17	937
II. Cagayan Valley	117	83	2	481	9	692
III. Central Luzon	61	122	7	436	20	646
IV. Southern Tagalog	120	119	14	514	30	797
V. Bicol	52	104	2	269	3	430[b]
VI. Western Visayas	58	157	23	297	68	603[c]
VII. Central Visayas	61	8	2	202	9	282
VIII. Eastern Visayas	37	107	20	128		292[d]
IX. Western Mindanao	17	36		1		54
X. Northern Mindanao	73	53	15	59	9	209
XI. Southern Mindanao	94	36		158	21	308
XII. Central Mindanao	47	32	11	41	1	132[e]
All regions	1208 (22%)	953 (18%)	100 (2%)	2935 (54%)	187 (4%)	5382 (100%)

Notes: a. *Private users include plantations, corporate farms, and haciendas.*
     b. Total unclassified users = 2.
     c. Total unclassified users = 32.
     d. Total unclassified users = 11.
     e. There is one unclassified user.
     f. Including unclassified users, the total should be 5429 grantees.
NIA = National Irrigation Administration

Source: National Water Resources council compilation of water permits granted as of December 1984 (see Cruz, et al. 1987).

1982, of which only 17 per cent (30 cases) have been resolved. The rate at which disputes are settled in court has since improved; however, this may be due to a substantial reduction in the number of cases filed with the NWRC. In 1984, a total of 21 cases were filed, but 15 of these were settled amicably.

For the period 1974 to 1978, over 45 per cent of water-rights claims filed with the NWRC dealt with groups of individuals, 35 per cent with landowners, and 17 per cent with irrigation associations. Cases involving individuals generally pertain to removal of flow obstructions, while cases concerning associations relate more to the settling of rival claims to a water source. In general, over 70 per cent of water disputes sought an interpretation of the legality of previously granted water permits.

The NWRC has ruled in favour of associations over landowners in 54 per cent of the cases filed regarding removal of obstructions in the waterway. In terms of prior-use interpretations, or those concerning legality of previously granted water permits, the NWRC has supported associations in only 20 per cent of cases during the period 1974 to 1978.

Enforcement problems in the granting of irrigation water rights

Table 13.4 shows the procedure for processing of water permit applications for irrigation. Steps 1 through 5 are often completed in the field; the process can take anything from a month to one or more years depending on the extent of the field survey. The water application is processed in the NWRC office starting with step 7.

A major problem related to the allocation of water as common property is the unusual advantage of individual landowners over associations in the appropriation of water rights. While the Water Code is explicit in its support for collective versus individual control of irrigation water, processing procedures for water permits have tended to discourage cooperative use of the resource. Since the water permit is given on a first-come, first-served basis, influential landowners will have the advantage in getting their water permits processed ahead of the irrigation associations. It normally takes much longer for an association to assemble all the materials pertinent to a water permit application – documentation for which in some cases is needed for each member of the association. There is also a lack of clear guidelines in the Water Code specifying the conditions under which applications by irrigation associations may be given precedence over individual applications.

A second problem related to the granting of water permits concerns overappropriation of the water supply. Overappropriation occurs when the total volume of discharge rates given to grantees exceeds the actual available supply. This happens when other users, not know to the NWRC, draw water from the source by virtue of a prior claim, without having been included in

Table 13.4 Schematic diagram of procedures in processing of water permit applicants for irrigation purposes

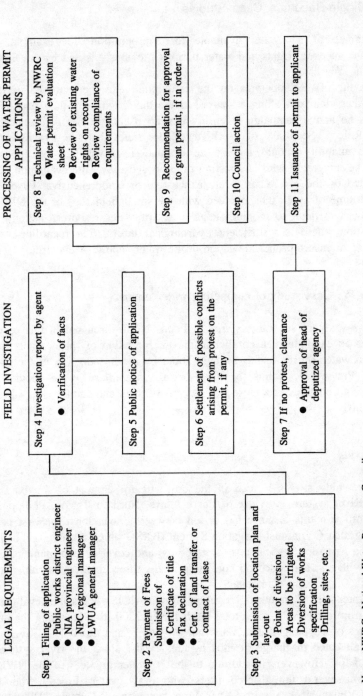

Notes: NWRC National Water Resources Council
         NIA   National Irrigation Administration
         NPC   National Power Corporation
         LWUA   Local Water Utilities Administration

Source: Implementing Rules and Regulations of Water Applications (Water Code) and Interview of NWRC Staff as of December, 1984.

the estimate of net water available for appropriation (for example, the numerous ancestral rights and water permits previously issued by the Bureau of Public Works).

Since the NWRC operates on the assumption that there are no existing legal water claimants along a source, unless their rights are duly registered, there is no active campaign to ensure that all users are taken into account. While Rule 1, Section 9 of the Water Codes states that 'the assessment of water availability should include an evaluation of whether the applicant should be integrated with an existing or proposed user', the evaluation often conducted by the NWRC is rarely exhaustive or comprehensive. Given the large volume of applicants, coupled with the small field staff of the NWRC, it has been difficult to monitor actual users of water resources nationwide. In addition, there is insufficient hydrological information regarding water resources to ensure proper allocation of the water supply (Alejandrino, 1982).

Section IV: Case study of competing water claims

The case study of several *zanjeras* in Ilocos Norte discussed in this section provides an example of a conflict in the interpretation of 'prior rights' to a common water source that is brought about by the introduction of the water permit. Previously, claims to water among the *zanjeras* were decided by inter-village councils, composed of *zanjera* officers and family elders in the community.

Background

The case-study site is located in the downstream segment of the Bacarra-Vintar River system, province of Ilocos Norte, Northern Luzon, Philippines. The conflict in this instance has arisen between associations, the first being the Integrated Communal Irrigation System (ICIS), which is composed of two federated irrigation associations (or *zanjeras*) and covering two municipalities and 13 villages, and a second consisting of the three unfederated *zanjeras* of Curarig, Dibua, and Camongao.

The Integrated Communal Irrigation System (ICIS) holds the legal water permit from the NWRC for a total discharge of 2800 lps. Excluding the three tributaries of Teppang Creek, Cabayaoasan Creek, and Cabatulaan River, the overall allocated discharge granted by the NWRC along the river system is 14,082.5 lps. However, in addition to the 26 water grantees of the NWRC, there are several unregistered users who draw water directly from the Bacarra-Vintar river system. The three *zanjeras* of Curarig, Dibua and Camongao have been users of this category. While they have no legal claim to the water, their rights as water users were established by a long-standing 'prior right' (some of their irrigation structures date back as far as 1762).

Institutional set-up for water sharing

Three levels of collective control over the management of the irrigation system govern water use among *zanjeras*. The first is the *panlakayen* or board of directors, which determines the enforcement procedures across municipal or administrative boundaries. *Panlakayen* officers apply for water permits from the NWRC on behalf of the association and supervise follow-up of the application. They also coordinate administration of the water permit with other users along the river. This involves creating a suitable rotation schedule for the different associations of the federation and settling water-rights conflicts among minor member associations.

The second level is that of the *maestro* or supervisor, who controls the activities of working groups which are defined at the canal level. Each working group is composed of four to ten farmers sharing a common canal, where membership is based either on kinship ties or on the labour-exchange grouping called the *ammuyo*. In many of the affiliated *zanjeras*, ammuyo members engage in an equal exchange of labour hours for cultivation work. In addition, the *maestro* assigns canal-cleaning and repair work to different *ammuyo* clusters. The *maestro*, however, does not engage in activities directly related to the enforcement of the water permit.

The third level of water control is at the canal segment or cluster of farm parcels. Among the clusters conflicts are resolved through *lakays* or farm elders. The *lakays* provide the critical function of mediator for problems related to water use below the canal turn-out.

Description of the irrigation system

In the Integrated Communal Irrigation System (ICIS), water is diverted through a brush dam and conveyed to member villages on continuous basis along a main canal. Distribution to individual farmlands then takes place through smaller channels (such as the connecting laterals and sub-laterals) on a rotation basis. The rotation schedule occurs on alternate days. In the case of the unfederated *zanjeras*, however, water flows continuously along the main and lateral canals. Each *zanjera* has its own temporary brush dam, which is repaired and replaced annually. While both systems make use of a brush dam with connecting canals to deliver water to farm parcels, the federated system (such as the ICIS) – using only one brush dam for 13 villages, instead of three dams for three villages (such as the unfederated *zanjeras*) – has been found to be more efficient.

When a water body changes course or has numerous flow obstructions, water control becomes more difficult. Coupled with low precipitations, the need for coordinated work in maintaining a river becomes important. No established rules existed regarding the cleaning of debris along the Bacarra-Vintar river, and thus there was less incentive for upstream users periodically to remove flow obstructions. Following a decline in the water supply for irrigation in the dry season, water-allocation rules had to be strictly enforced.

Water-rights competition

Competition for water rights began with the proposed construction by the ICIS of a 400-metre canal from the point of diversion at the source to the farthest affiliated *zanjera* at Barrio Pasayacan (see Fig. 13.1). The canal would permit the planting of a dry season crop. The nearby *zanjeras* of Curarig, Dibua, and Camongao contended that the proposed 400-metre canal would result in a reduction of the water supply to their fields. The reduction in rainfall had already diminished the net water available in the canal and, in addition, the NWRC had overallocated water to present users. The leaders of the three *zanjeras* therefore approached the National Irrigation Administration (NIA) to study the layout for a new, shorter canal. Subsequently an 80-metre canal was proposed by the NIA to cut across the Paratong main canal. Fig. 13.1 shows the location of the two planned canals with respect to the Bacarra-Vintar River.

ICIS officials opposed the 80-metre canal alternative, arguing that construction of the 400-metre canal was still within their legal water allotment of 2800 lps from the NWRC. Since the three competing *zanjeras* had no water permits from the NWRC, from the legal (or formal) standpoint, leaders of the ICIS argued that building the 400-metre canal was justified as long as it remained within the discharge rate prescribed by the NWRC, regardless of whether the rate was now considered to be inflated.

The case is still pending with the NWRC despite several meetings among officers of both the ICIS and the three contending *zanjeras*, in addition to NIA engineers and lawyers from the NWRC. The NIA and the NWRC are inclined to rule for a reallocation of the water permit to the federation (ICIS). A reduction in the allocation from the 2800 lps to 980 lps is under review. However, NWRC lawyers will require the three *zanjeras* to federate and apply for a common water permit and to construct only one brush dam having a connecting channel link to the 80-metre canal.

The help of local village officials was solicited to make representations with concerned government agencies such as the NWRC, NIA, and the trial courts. Leadership roles, as in this case the settling of water disputes,

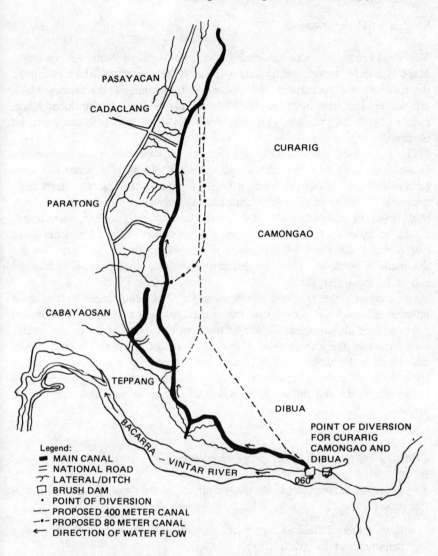

Figure 13.1 Layout of the integrated communal irrigation system in the Bacarra-Vintar river

legitimize the formal decision-making functions of the association and village officials.

Section V: Conclusions

The emergence of rules governing the allocation of water as common property can be understood by describing first the conditions which prompted the necessity for such rules, then secondly, by examining the factors which affected enforcement of the rules. While the discussion uses the Ilocos Norte case study as an example, similarities with other irrigation systems can be observed.

The case study shows that of the different possible water uses, irrigation presents a unique case in which inequities in the allocation of water are more pronounced than in others. Along a single water source, upstream users have greater advantages in receiving adequate water than downstream lands. Also, it is easier to enforce one's 'rights', and consequently, affect other users' rights by merely blocking water flows downstream. Without a water code that protects the rights of legitimate users, especially those located at the downstream portions, it will be difficult to enforce rules preventing unequal access to the water supply.

For example, the resulting competition for water anticipated by the three unfederated *zanjeras* shows that the context of water scarcity provides an important condition upon which stricter enforcement of rules for water distribution is likely to emerge. However, it is also the breakdown of informal social and political ties that made the presence of a legal water permit from the NWRC more significant. Having the legal recognition of prior right to the water, the federation (ICIS) now had a stronger case for justifying its actions.

Critical elements for common-property management

Five elements contribute to effective common-property management of irrigation water.

1 Environmental factors, such as the natural conditions of the water resource and its availability;
2 nature of technology for water distribution;
3 size of the system and population serviced;
4 relationship of users (social and political ties); and
5 presence of formal or legal water rights.

1 Environmental factors
Situations of perceived water scarcity occur as users experience seasonal fluctuations in water supply. These fluctuations are conditioned by changes in the natural environment and climate, particularly rainfall.

2 Technology

While it has been found that a water system having one dam supplying water to numerous farm parcels is more efficient than a system of multiple dams, it is important to recognize that the decreasing marginal costs of expanding area irrigated are often offset by increased marginal costs for conveyance. Operation and maintenance costs also increase as the command area expands. Lastly, as the technology for water delivery improves, a stronger institutional set-up is required for more efficient collective management of the water supply.

3 Size

Rules for water allocation are more difficult to implement as the number of users increases and as more administrative units are involved. On the other hand, the federation set-up is shown to be more conducive to intervillage coordination. For example, it was easier for the federation (ICIS) to institute rotation schedules based on hydrological units (such as canals) rather than using village boundaries such as the one adopted by the unfederated *zanjeras*. This is so since the composition of the ICIS *panlakayen* leadership also enabled greater cooperation among member-village associations where the officers of the federation were also the village elders and local village officials.

4 Users' relationships

The close social and political ties among Ilocano *zanjeras* are well known to be effective for collective management of water (Bagadion, 1986). Previously, open access to water was respected under the riparian (river shore) rights of land owners near the river. Non-riparian lands were allowed access based on social ties, the only form of payment for water passage being participation in the maintenance of the canal (cleaning and repair work and so on).

By setting up the federation, access to water is now based on intervillage relationships. The participation of local village officials, therefore, is crucial if strong linkages among villages are to be established.

5 Presence of water rights

The ICIS federation had the formal or legal water right to draw water from the Bacarra-Vintar river at a rate of 2800 lps as specified in the permit. To obtain this right, officials underwent the intricate application process, paid fees, and incurred other costs incidental to enforcement of their right. By thereafter sharing their right with the unfederated *zanjeras*, a situation of 'free riding' obtained – where non-holders of a water permit benefit from the water allocation but it is only the federation that carried the burden of acquiring the right (Olson, 1965).

Acknowledgements

The author wishes to thank the Ford Foundation for its financial support, in particular Dr. Frances Korten. This chapter is based on research findings presented in the book *Legal and Institutional Issues of Irrigation Water Rights in the Philippines* (Los Banos: University of the Philippines at Los Banos, 1987).

References

Alejandrino, Angel A., 1980: *Philippine Water Resource Policies: An Appraisal*, paper presented at the International Centennial Symposium of the US Geological Society, Reston, Virginia.

Alejandrino, Angel A., 1982: *Coordinated Water Resource Activities: The Philippine Experience*, paper presented at the UN-ESCAP seminar on water resources development planning, Kiev, USSR.

Bagadion, Benjamin U., 1986: *Water User Organizational Needs and Alternatives*, (mimeographed).

Bromley, Daniel W., 1982: 'Land and water problems: An institutional perspective', *American Journal of Agricultural Economics*, 64, (December), pp. 834–44.

Bromley, Daniel W., 1982: 'The rights of society versus the rights of landowners and operations', in Halcrow, Harold G., Healy, Earl O. and Cotner, Melvin L., eds, *Soil Conservation Policies, Institutions and Incentives*, Soil Conservation Society of America, Iowa.

Christie, Emerson R., 1914: 'Notes on irrigation and cooperative irrigation societies in Ilocos Norte', *The Philippine Journal of Science*, 9(2), pp. 99–113.

Ciriacy-Wantrup, S.V. and Bishop, R.C., 1975: 'Common property as a concept in natural resources policy', *Natural Resources Journal*, 15(4), pp. 713–27.

Cruz, Ma. Concepcion J., 1984: *A Review of Irrigation Water Rights in the Philippines: Conceptual Framework and Selected Case Studies*, University of the Philippines, Los Banos.

Cruz, Ma. Concepcion J., Cornista, Luzviminda R. and Dayan, Diogenes C., 1987: *Legal and Institutional Issues of Irrigation Water Rights in the Philippines*, University of the Philippines, Los Banos.

Easter, K. William and Palanisami, K., 1986: 'Tank irrigation in India and Thailand: An example of common property resource management', *Proceedings of the Conference on Common Property Resource Management*, National Academy Press, Washington, DC.

Fox, Irving, 1971: *Water Resources Management in the Soviet Union and the United States: Some Similarities, Differences and Policy Issues*, The Water Resources Center, Madison.

Oakerson, Ronald J., 1986: 'A model for the analysis of common property problems', *Proceedings of the Conference on Common Property Resource Management*, National Academy Press, Washington, DC.

Olson, Mancur, 1965: *The Logic of Collective Action*, Harvard University Press, Cambridge.

Siy, Robert Y., 1982: *Community Resource Management: Lessons from the Zanjera*, University of the Philippines Press, Quezon City.

Part 4 Multiple-Resource Cases and Integrated Development

Commercial forest contractors operating in the Himalayan foothills in the early 1970s started running into a well-organized, non-violent Gandhian resistance movement. Groups of local people were embracing trees to prevent loggers from cutting them down. The Chipko ('to embrace' in Hindi) movement was born.

The Chipko movement in India is perhaps the best known case of opposition to outside interests trying to appropriate local common-property resources. The movement has been successful in forcing a slowdown of commercial felling in the Himalayas and generating pressure towards a national forest policy in India, a policy which would be sensitive to both local peoples' needs and environmental concerns.

Initially, some observers thought that the protesters were simply after a bigger share of the immediate commercial benefit of logging. But the Chipko movement evolved into a lobby group demanding ecological rehabilitation as well as social justice. A Chipko slogan says that 'soil, water and oxygen' are the main products of forests, emphasizing the importance of restoring the forest cover of the Himalayas. The Chipko movement has come to symbolize a new brand of grass-roots Third World environmentalism, and the integration of ecological concerns with social concerns.

Saving trees by embracing them is an ancient idea that goes back many centuries in Indian culture, and so does the stewardship of the forest. Prior to the colonial era, large tracts of natural forests, as well as village forests, used to be husbanded by local communities. During the British rule, village commons were transformed into private property, and natural forests were logged on a large scale for commercial purposes. Thus, from a common-property point of view, the Chipko movement is an example of the re-assertion of traditional communal resource-use rights. Is there a continued role for communal-property regimes in the complex contemporary world?

The three chapters in Part 4 provide examples in the use of multiple, interconnected resources. They deal with historical aspects of traditional management systems, transformation of societies and of common-property institutions, and grapple with policy issues in a world of many pressures against the sustainable use of resources.

Chapter 14 by Gadgil and Iyer is concerned with a variety of resource types: cultivated lands, grazing lands, fish and wildlife, and wild plant resources. Gadgil and Iyer use caste groups in India as an ecological analogue of 'species' specializing in different resources. Before colonization, such ecological-niche diversification ensured monopoly for a local group in the use of specific common-property resources, and was instrumental in the long-term sustainable use of these resources. The historical trend of a deteriorating resource base throughout India is traceable to the forced conversion of communal property into state and private property, increased commercialization, and the generally increased demand for resources. Gadgil and Iyer conclude with an exploration of the means and policies by which some of the positive attributes of communal-property systems can be conserved and rejuvenated.

Chapter 15 by Moorehead analyses a case study from a different geographical setting (Mali) but with a parallel set of problems. Dealing with grazing land, agricultural land, wildlife and fishery resources in the inland delta of the Niger River, an extensive wetland area, Moorehead explains how the traditional integrated resource-management system (*dina*) has disintegrated due to a variety of factors, including the stress of low water levels as a result of prolonged drought in this part of Africa. Some resources have been degraded, others converted from communal property to state property and private property. Rather than trying to recreate the original traditional system, Moorehead suggests instead that new policies be adopted to strengthen local management of resources, reinforce traditional reciprocal access rights of existing groups, and generally facilitate controlled-access common-property management.

Chapter 16 by Baines deals with a resource system which is no less complicated than those in the preceding chapters but with an important difference: traditional common-property management systems of the South Pacific are generally alive and well. It has been said that island peoples perceive their limits more readily than do continental peoples; most appropriately, some of the best-documented and most sophisticated traditional management systems come from the Pacific area. Baines deals with a range of resource types, marine and terrestrial, consistent with the notion of many Pacific island peoples that land and water components of an island resource assemblage is one and indivisible. The chapter provides an overview of commons management from the South Pacific, addresses the issue of balancing development and traditional conservation, and provides clear policy directions for strengthening and securing communal-property management.

The case studies in Part 4 show that, as common-property institutions come under stress, they receive increasing competition from state-property regimes and private-property regimes. Privatization may be economically more efficient for certain resource types but tends to concentrate wealth in the hands of few, at the expense of equity – as shown for example in the Mali case. State management, while undermining traditional communal controls, is often unable to replace these controls with an effective alternative system. This argument was made earlier in Chapter 2 by Gibbs and Bromley; it is illustrated in all three chapters of Part 4. It may not be possible in many cases to 'turn back the clock', but the knowledge base that would enable sustainable resource use nevertheless remains with local users. Hence, it makes management sense to leave as much control and responsibility as possible at the communal level while coordinating activities of users at the government level.

All three cases demonstrate the ecological wisdom of traditional management systems; clearly some traditional management systems perceived the essential unity and interconnectedness of man–nature systems. Like the Chipko view of the function of Himalayan forests, these traditional systems are consistent with the ecosystem view. This raises the intriguing possibility that some traditional management systems come close to implementing an ecosystem approach akin to that detailed in Chapters 3 and 7.

Going back to one of the perennial debates first introduced in this volume in Part 1, the case studies here provide insights regarding the role of population pressures. All three cases provide evidence that population growth is an undeniably important factor in the degradation of the environment and resources. But population is not the only, or even the overriding factor. It is simply one of the major variables in a tangle of socioeconomic problems which lead to increased pressures on natural resources.

The case studies in Part 4, supplemented by those in Part 3, provide insights on the impact of foreign political regimes, economies and technologies on communal-property systems. Massive change seems to result in the disintegration of common-property systems, especially if accompanied by environmental change as well, as in the case of Sahelian drought. However, change that is rather more gradual, at a pace that could be accommodated by the society in question, seems to allow the successful survival and evolution of common-property systems – for example, in Japan and to some extent in the Philippines and Pacific island nations as well. In this sense, the health of social systems seems to go hand in hand with the health of resources, through the interface of common-property systems.

14 On the Diversification of Common-Property Resource Use by Indian Society

Madhav Gadgil and Prema Iyer

Summary

The different endogamous groups of Indian caste society have so diversified their patterns of resource use that many specialized resources – such as palm leaves for mat weaving – were, and often still are, the monopoly of one particular group in any given locality. Other more commonly used resources, such as fuelwood, were controlled by small multi-caste village communities in which the different caste groups were linked to each other in a web of reciprocity. This organization had favoured sustainable use of common-property resources under communal management by the Indian society until the colonial conquest. British rule led to disruption of communal organization and converted communally managed resources into open-access resources. These have subsequently been used in an exhaustive fashion. However, pockets of good resource management under communal control have persisted and are now serving as models for the reassertion of such communal control. It is hoped that this would contribute significantly towards bringing about a sustainable use of the country's natural resource base.

Introduction

The well-being of all human populations significantly depends on the availability of a variety of renewable resources. Such resources – be they ground water, soil nutrients, pastures or fish stocks – may either be utilized sustainably, at rates which permit harvests at a given level over long time intervals, or exhaustively, at rates that in the long run lead to a decline in the total stocks and possible harvests therefrom. Since humans are believed to be primarily motivated by self-interest, it is widely held that sustainable patterns of resource use would be restricted to individually controlled territories, and that any resource to which several individuals have common access is apt to be overused and exhausted (Hardin, 1968). There are many examples of such 'tragedies of the commons', from the presumed Pleistocene overkill and the exhaustion of whale populations in recent years to the deforestation of the Himalayas.

The most remarkable feature of human behaviour is, however, its flexibility, and there is a great deal of empirical evidence that the tragedy of the commons is by no means inevitable. Pre-colonial New England supported abundant populations of fur-bearing mammals which apparently yielded a sustainable harvest to the American Indians (Cronon, 1983); the village commons of pre-enclosure England were sustainably used by the village communities (Cox, 1985); and woodlots in some of the Himalayan villages are even today being harvested in a sustainable fashion (Gadgil, 1985a). While some of these instances may relate to levels of demands too low to cause resource depletion, others are likely to have resulted from culturally determined patterns of resource use that served to prevent resource exhaustion and thereby conferred a positive advantage on the group practising it (Gadgil, 1987). Yet others may relate to pursuit of self-interest by small numbers of individuals interacting repeatedly over long time intervals (Axelrod, 1984; Joshi, 1987; Berkes and Kence, in press).

These considerations suggest that sustainable use of common-property resources is indeed possible, but requires certain special conditions. In general it is favoured when:

1 the number of parties sharing access to the resource is small;
2 the parties sharing access repeatedly interact with each other over a long period;
3 such parties share the harvests in an equitable fashion; and
4 such parties are linked to each other by bonds of kinship or reciprocation in contexts additional to the resource use.

Human populations have evolved a diversity of mechanisms to regulate utilization of the resources they required. Where such mechanisms restrict the access to a particular set of resources to a small group of individuals who interact over long time intervals and may be tied together by bonds of kinship or reciprocity, we thus expect the resources to be used in a sustainable fashion. The most widespread method of achieving this is the establishment of some form of property right over land being cultivated by a small kin group – a nuclear or an extended family. However, family proprietary rights are less prevalent when the resource involved is not being produced but foraged. Foraging for resources such as fish or fuelwood entails the use of relatively large tracts of land or water which are often controlled by somewhat larger groups of people – either a clan or a village community or the state. A combination of these two, involving family control of a plot of cultivated land and clan or village control of a territory from which resources are foraged for has been a characteristic pattern of regulation of resource use in most hunter-gatherer, shifting cultivator and traditional agricultural societies. This pattern by and large seems to have permitted the sustainable utilization of many renewable resources (McNeely and Pitt, 1985; Ruddle and Johannes, 1985).

Indian caste society

The Indian caste society that crystallized around the fifth century AD developed one other way of restricting access to a particular resource in a particular habitat to a small group of people tied together by bonds of kinship or reciprocity. This was the diversification of ecological niches of the different coexisting endogamous groups. There are, of course, parallels to this in other cultures and from other times. Two groups of Neanderthals living near the Dordogne in France are believed to have specialized in hunting horses and reindeer respectively (Leakey, 1981). Such diversification in terms of resource use as well as other economic activities became far more sophisticated in Indian society which was an agglomeration of some 40,000 endogamous caste groups (Gadgil and Malhotra, 1983). This promoted sustainable resource use in two ways: by restricting access to many specialized resources of any given locality to members of just one endogamous group, and by linking together members of different endogamous groups in a network of reciprocal exchanges and mutual obligations.

We would like to illustrate this organization on the basis of a case study of a cluster of villages from the west coast of India. These villages are situated near the mouth of the river Aghanashini close to the town of Kumta in the district of Uttara Kannada of Karnataka State (Fig. 14.1). Spurs of the hill range of the Western Ghats run all the way to the sea in this region, creating a rich mosaic of terrestrial, riparian and coastal habitats supporting a great diversity of natural resources. Populations of as many as 19 different endogamous groups – 18 professing Hinduism and one Islam – inhabit this region. There are essentially no marriages outside of the endogamous groups, and members of the groups to a large extent continue to follow their traditional, hereditary occupations. Some of the hereditary occupations are, of course, no longer viable. Tapping of coconut trees for alcoholic beverages and temple dancing are now defunct, while a number of newer occupations have been introduced in the modern economic sector and bureaucracy. All of this has, however, changed the subsistence patterns of the communities remarkably little. A quite complete reconstruction of the traditional subsistence patterns of the groups is possible on the basis of information in sources such as the first gazetteer of the region (Campbell, 1883), as well as the folk tradition we collected in the field over the period 1984 to 1987. These 19 endogamous groups may for our purpose be grouped in seven categories:

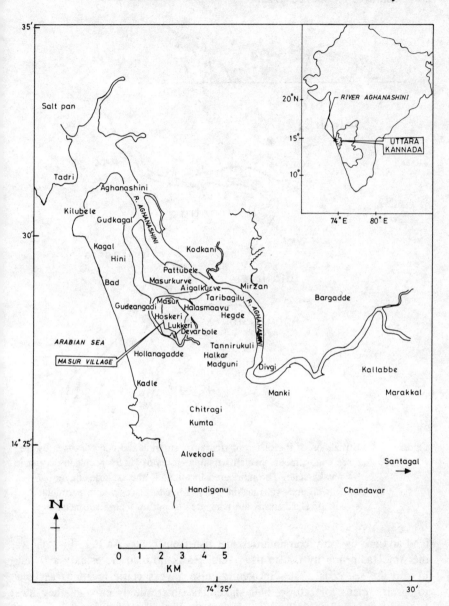

Figure 14.1 A map showing the location of the human settlements and the course of the river Aghanashini in Uttara Kannada district of Karnataka state.

1 Fishing communities

Three of the endogamous groups, the Hindu Ambigas and Harikantras, and the Islamic Jalajirs, subsist almost entirely on fishing. They own little or no

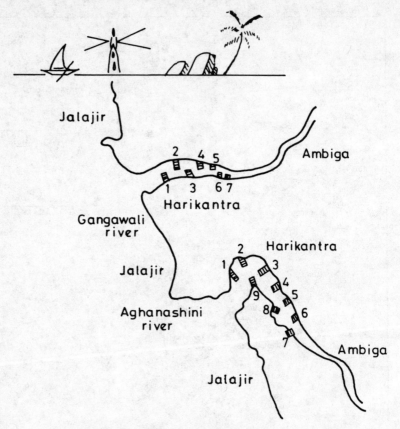

Figure 14.2 Utilization of the different riparian, estuarine and coastal zones by the three endogamous specialist fishing castes of Uttara Kannada district in Karnataka state. The numbered locations in the estuaries of the Gangawali and Aghanashini rivers refer to places where particular groups of Harikantras are permitted to put up their stake nets.

land and are the only communities that fish from boats. As Fig. 14.2 shows, the Ambigas primarily fish in the rivers, Harikantras in the estuary and Jalajirs on the sea coast. The Harikantras also have specific locations assigned to specific clans for setting their stake-nets. Interestingly enough, they meet a good part of their fuel needs through collection of driftwood during the floods.

2 Agriculturists

The traditional agricultural communities include Halakki Vakkals or Gowdas, Gam Vakkals or Patgars and Namdhari Naiks. Their primary occupation is paddy cultivation, but they also indulge extensively in collection of shellfish and fishing from the shore, as well as hunting birds and mammals. The Namdhari Naiks were traditionally soldiers and petty chieftains as well. Notably enough, Halakki and Gam Vakkals undertake weaving mats; for this purpose Halakkis use *pandanus* and Gams *cyperus*. Members of no other endogamous groups of this locality use either.

3 Horticulturists
Havik Brahmins are the only endogamous group in this region to specialize in horticulture. In particular they raise multistorey orchards of banana, arecanut coconut and pepper in moist valleys protected from the evening sun. They also serve as priests for all other endogamous groups of the region.

4 Entertainers
Two endogamous groups, the Bhandaris and Deshbhandaris traditionally served as musicians and dancers, especially attached to the temples. This occupation still continues but now only contributes marginally to their subsistence. The Bhandaris also used to tap toddy from coconut palms, but this was banned by the British in order to raise excise from liquor contractors. Both Bhandaris and Deshbhandaris now depend on agriculture.

5 Service castes
There are two service castes: Kodeyas, the barbers, and Madivals, the washermen. Kodeyas still follow the traditional occupation; Madivals have largely taken to agriculture. However, unlike the traditional agriculturists, Halakki and Gam Vakkals, these other groups - Bhandari, Deshbhandari and Madival - rarely fish and never hunt.

6 Artisans
The artisans include Shet (goldsmith), Achari (carpenter and blacksmith), Gunaga (potter), Uppar (lime makers from molluscan shells), Uppanad (salt makers), Mukhri (stone workers), and Holeyas (tanners of hide and weavers of basket and mats). Notably enough, the Holeyas use only bamboo, cane and *corypha* palm for their mat and basket weaving, thus having no overlap in the raw material requirements with Halakki and Gam Vakkals.

7 Traders
Gowd Saraswats, a Brahmin caste, are the chief trading group of this region. During the British regime they became landlords as cultivator castes such as Halakki and Gam Vakkals were dispossessed of their lands. However, they did not themselves take to agriculture or horticulture. The fishing caste of Jalajirs have also traditionally engaged in some coastal maritime trade.

This picture is quite representative of the non-tribal areas of India. The different endogamous caste groups even to this day largely adhere to their traditional modes of subsistence. Since each one tends to have its own special way of obtaining this subsistence, competition between different endogamous caste groups is very limited. Rather, they are linked together in a network of reciprocal exchanges. This is not at all to claim that there are no inequities; indeed the terms of exchanges are often asymmetrical, with the lower castes giving much more than they receive and having access to an unfairly low proportion of resources. Nevertheless, in this system, each endogamous caste group tended to have assured access to certain resources. Thus the Holeyas, who were earlier treated as untouchables, were the only ones to claim the meat of dead buffaloes and cattle, and the only ones using bamboo, cane or *corypha* for basket and mat weaving. Similarly, Halakki Vakkals were the only ones to hunt deer, and Ambigas the only ones to fish the deeper waters of the rivers. This was based entirely on the force of social custom, although also related to some specialized knowledge and skills. The traditional subsistence pattern of one's own endogamous caste group was adhered to by all members as the only socially acceptable pattern of life, both within the caste and within the multi-caste village society. These social conventions, albeit very much weakened, still persist and control patterns of resource use in the Indian countryside.

Prudent resource use

The basic elements of Indian society were the closely knit multi-caste village and the endogamous caste groups. Both were made up of a relatively small number of individuals, interacting repeatedly with each other and with bonds of reciprocity (in case of members belonging to different endogamous groups) and of kinship as well as reciprocity (in case of members of an endogamous group). The village community as a whole foraged on land or water with common access to several people for resources such as fuelwood needed by all; members of any given endogamous group foraged on land or water with common access for more specialized resources such as *cyperus* reeds for mat-weaving. In the pre-colonial times, the local communities were quite strong and autonomous and while the king in theory owned all land and waters, its actual control was vested in local communities. These local communities apparently not only regulated the harvesting practices of their own members, but also excluded others from access to resources controlled by them (Dharampal, 1983).

This was a situation clearly favouring sustainable resource use, and indeed there is evidence of many traditions promoting restraint in the Indian society, a number of which persist to this day albeit in a much attenuated form (Gadgil 1985a,b).

1 Quantitative quotas
In the communally managed village-council forest of Kallabbe in the focal locality described above, people still accept limitations on the quantity of wood extracted by each household in a season, while in the village-council forest of Halakar they only remove dead and fallen wood. Nevertheless, people from both these villages tend to overexploit the open-access minor forests in other localities such as Chandavar.

2 Closed seasons
In many South Indian villages people do not hunt birds such as storks, herons and pelicans during the breeding season at the heronaries, although they may be hunted at other times of the year. The farmers are conscious of the value of guano as manure. Similarly, collection of green leaves from the village-council forest of Halakar is restricted to certain months of the year only.

3 Protected life history stages
Phasepardhis, a group of nomadic hunter-gatherers of semi-arid tracts of Western Maharashtra earlier had a monopoly on the antelopes and deer of their locality. They traditionally set free any fawn or pregnant doe caught in their snares (Malhotra, Khomne and Gadgil, 1983).

4 Protection to individual species
Banyan, peepal and other fig species of the genus *Ficus* continue to be widely protected and even today are rarely cut down in Uttara Kannada district, as over most of India. Figs are now recognised by ecologists as 'keystone resources' – dry-season staples for many species of birds and mammals (especially monkeys) which play a preeminent role in the ecosystem (Terborgh, 1986). *Prosopis cinerarea*, a key fodder and fencing species of the Indian desert, is strictly protected in the villages of the Bishnoi community.

5 Protection to entire communities in specific localities
Complete protection was accorded to patches of forests, stretches of rivers or ponds where no disturbance was permitted. Sacred groves are even now important reservoirs of genetic resources in the Uttara Kannada district as well as in many other parts of India (Gadgil and Vartak, 1976).

Takeover by the state

Pre-colonial India was a land of strong local communities and endogamous caste groups with relatively weak central authorities. Extensive areas of land and water were therefore controlled by local communities and were presumably used in a sustainable fashion (Dharampal, 1983). This picture changed dramatically when the British established strong state control. The imperial interests lay in establishing control over as much of the country's resources as possible. This was attempted by two means: raising the taxation level on cultivated land as far as possible, and establishing state control over as much non-agricultural land as possible.

These interests are well reflected in the report submitted by Francis Buchanan, who travelled through Uttara Kannada including the localities described above, in February and March 1801, two years after the British had established their rule (Buchanan, 1870). To the east of Mirzan (Fig. 14.1) he describes hills devoted to the cultivation of pepper. Buchanan remarks that 'The landlords pretend that all the timber trees are their property, but that none of them are saleable.' He goes on to describe a sacred grove, further north in the same district and remarks that

> The forests are property of the gods of the villages in which they are situated, and the trees ought not to be cut without having obtained leave from the . . . headman of the village, whose office is hereditary, and who here also is priest to . . . the village god. The idol receives nothing for granting this permission; but the neglect of this ceremony of asking his leave brings his vengeance on the guilty person. This seems, therefore, merely a contrivance to prevent the government from claiming the property.

The British Government certainly did not accept any such 'contrivances' and claimed rights over all lands not under cultivation, as well as all waters. Unlike the indigenous population, the British were interested in a much narrower diversity of resources, primarily teak for ship-building. Furthermore, in the initial period they were unsure of retaining their control over these newly acquired territories and therefore had little motivation to utilize the resources sustainably. What happened in the early period of British takeover is best narrated in words of Cleghorn (1861), the first conservator of forests of the Uttara Kannada district.

> In 1805, the . . . Government, for the first time laid claim to the indigenous forests of the western coast . . . from this period up to 1822 a partial and somewhat ill-advised attempt at conservancy was made, but it thoroughly failed in its object; and all the restrictions which had been imposed during its existence were removed. This relaxation, or rather abandonment of law, however, in course of time led to results of a still more disastrous nature, which threatened the speedy and complete destruction of the forests themselves. The attention of the Government was again seriously directed to the question; but it was a matter of . . . difficulty to establish a system of conservancy which would not infringe upon private rights.

Evidently the government takeover of the resources earlier controlled either by individuals or communities led to a rapid exhaustive use. This pattern of usage prevailed from 1805 to 1850. The demand for all resources rose greatly with the construction of the Railways in the 1850s; and this led the British government to systematize the management of forests under the direction of Brandis, a German forester (Stebbing, 1922). The system of management thus introduced classified the forests in two categories: 'reserved' – being the forests in which the local people enjoyed no rights or privileges – and 'protected' – being those in which they enjoyed certain privileges. The operative term was 'privileges', implying that the state permitted local people access to these forests to harvest fuelwood or to graze their cattle and so on, but without any formal rights. The local communities were deprived of the power either to keep others out of protected forests, or to regulate the harvests by their own members.

Thus common-property resources earlier under communal control now became open-access resources and were consequently liable to exhaustive usage. The overuse of the protected forests was then cited as a justification for their conversion into reserved forests. The area of protected forests in Uttara Kannada was 780,288ha in 1880, 718,592ha in 1890, 256,000ha in 1900 and only 35,328ha in 1910 (Masur, 1918). This progressive contraction of protected forest (called 'minor' forest in Uttara Kannada district) meant its accelerated degradation. The resulting protests led to a modification of the forest settlement by Collins (1921). The condition of these forests at that time is best described in his words:

Except in a very few cases each village has its own quotum of forest. But in the case of many villages, it is forest only in name and . . . it is only the outlying villages on the east which have forests with good tree growth. These are preyed upon by other villages which lie between them and the sea, all along the line. They too are not sufficient to meet the wants of the large population . . .

Collins's proposals for coastal Uttara Kannada reverted 10,800ha of reserve forest to minor forest category to create 13,324.4ha of minor forest. However, the assignment of minor forests was made not for each village, but by groups. As Collins himself remarked, 'in the interests of future generations it is essential that there shall be a system of strict preservation, which however is rendered somewhat difficult by the group system, under which the privileges will be exercised.'

Local forest councils

Through all these vicissitudes of British rule some villages had still managed to retain hold on the village forests and maintain them properly. Collins (1921) commends these, for instant 'the Forest of Chitragi which had long been preserved' and notes that the villages on their own had been appointing watchmen to keep out non-residents and to enforce regulated harvest by the residents. He went on to recommend that it would be desirable to form group or village committees to look after the minor forest. However, he recognized that there were serious difficulties in accomplishing this as often the forests were too far away for the members of the committee to exercise supervision, and in most cases there were so many villages in the group that the possibility of fixing the responsibility for offences on the right persons was remote.

These recommendations led to a 'section 27' in the Indian Forest Act 1924, providing for the establishment of village forest councils. Thus in our focal locality forest councils were established at three of the villages: Chitragi, Halakar and Kallabbe, in 1929. These councils had elected members who supervised the management of the minor forest under their control. The council collected contributions from the villagers for the privilege exercised. They used part of these funds for paying a watchman to look after the forest and ensure that non-residents were kept out and that the residents observed a number of regulations that led to sustainable harvest. In fact, two of these council forests – Halakar and Kallabbe – are still in very good condition. The Kallabbe minor forest even retains a number of evergreen species that have been exterminated from other forest localities, including reserved forests.

These, however, remained exceptions. Most of the minor forest areas were not supervised by a forest council and thus remained open access. As expected, they were indeed utilized exhaustively and gradually depleted further. Some of the council forests were also used exhaustively, especially when they embraced too many different villages or could not exclude outsiders effectively. Throughout the period that has followed the constitution of the village councils half-a-century ago, the state machinery has been consolidating its hold and attempting to dedicate the common-property resources of the country totally to the requirements of the urban-industrial section (Singh, 1986). The forest administration has therefore continued the approach of doing away as far as possible with the 'burden of privileges enjoyed by the local population'. It was in this spirit that the new Karnataka Forest Act, 1963 made no provision for village forest councils. The wheels of bureaucracy, however, move slowly and it was in 1979 that the Karnataka Government advised the village forest councils that:

> The village forest panchayat (council) was constituted under the provisions contained in Bombay Forest Manual. These provisions no longer exist in the Karnataka Forest Act; 1963 and the Karnataka Forest Manual 1976. Hence the forest panchayat stands dissolved as of 1st June 1969 on which day the Karnataka Forest Act came into force.

The three forest councils of Kallabbe, Halakar and Chitragi which has been functioning very well since 1929 in their present form (and were presumably based on centuries of tradition before that), were thus disbanded by the state without second thought in 1979. The Chitragi council accepted the dissolution because they felt that management had become difficult because of the pressures of the town of Kumta that had grown up next to Chitragi. Following the acceptance of dissolution of the forest council the residents of Chitragi themselves liquidated the well-preserved forest in a matter of a few months.

The forest councils of Halakar and Kallabbe, on the other hand, refused to accept the dissolution and moved the courts to stay the order. The orders were stayed by the court and the legal issues arc still unresolved. Both these forest councils continue to this date to exercise their authority over the council forests. The Halakar council, for instance, employs a watchman to apprehend outsiders and to enforce its regulations. The residents are permitted on a fee to collect only dead and fallen wood and to lop twigs and leaves for green manure in certain months. The council auctions the rights to collect flowers and fruits and levies fines for any infringement of the regulations. It also charges residents for the privilege of quarrying stones. This money serves to pay the watchman's salaries.

New initiatives

India attained independence in 1947 under the leadership of Mahatma Gandhi and Jawaharlal Nehru. Gandhi wished India to become a country of self-reliant villages; his attitude towards industry was ambivalent. Nehru wanted India to become a modern industrial nation. The state policies after Independence were largely moulded by Nehru's vision backed by the interests of the urban middle and trading classes. The state policy therefore continued to serve the urban-industrial interests with an ongoing effort to do away with the involvement of local rural population in the utilization and management of common-property resources, be they forests or fisheries (Gadgil, Prasad and Ali, 1983). These policies have led to a further erosion of the country's resource base, and the consequent pressures have begun to tilt the balance of power between the rural masses and the urban-industrial sector a little in favour of the former.

There have been two consequences of this shift. Firstly, voluntary agencies involved in rural development efforts have become increasingly concerned with issues of resource management and participation of the local people in this context (Fernandes and Kulkarni, 1983). Simultaneously, the state policies have shifted towards welcoming people's involvement in resource management (National Wasteland Development Board, 1985). The governments have also begun to experiment with decentralizing development decisions. In 1986 the government of Karnataka launched an experiment in establishing stronger elected authorities at the village level. We ourselves have been involved in an effort to work with the local people in an ecodevelopment effort in four localities in the Uttara Kannada district (Prasad et al, 1985). One of these is the focal locality described above.

At the local level, the headmaster of the high school at Masur has assumed a leadership role. This gentleman, Mr H.H. Patagar has been able to initiate and coordinate a number of programmes in the Masur-Lukkeri cluster of villages on an island in the estuary of river Aghanashini. At the centre of the island is a hillock with a minor forest of 127ha. This minor forest has lost all tree growth, except for a solitary tree spared because of the taboo against cutting any *Ficus* trees. Around 1977, when there was some tree growth still left, the local villagers, numbering about 400 households, got together and appointed a watchman to ensure that only deadwood and dry leaves were removed. This move, however, failed, and the remaining tree growth was destroyed. The people now cross the river to the minor forest of Mirjan to bring fuelwood and leaf manure.

We became involved in working with the headmaster and the villagers in 1983. This was also the time that the forest department was beginning to shift its policies and recognize the need of producing biomass to fulfil rural requirements. We were successful in organizing the villagers to agree to protect minor forest areas newly afforested by the state forest department. Consequently, an area of 1ha was afforested in 1984, 2ha in 1985 and 25ha in 1987. At the same time we have been attempting to revive the traditional protection given to sacred groves, and this too is beginning to yield some positive results. One consequence has been the decision by the state forest department to establish new 'sacred' groves, primarily with indigenous species of religious significance. Eight such groves have been established in the district of Uttara Kannada beginning in 1985 (Gadgil, Hegde and Shetty, 1987). The attempt to establish a sacred grove at Lukkeri in 1987 was, however, unsuccessful as no modalities could be worked out for providing adequate grazing lands.

Prospects

There are thus a number of trends, not only in Uttara Kannada but all over the country, giving hope that the tide of degradation of common-property resources can after all be turned around (Agarwal and Narain, 1986). The new initiatives would have to be grounded in the realities of the Indian situation and must take full advantage of what is desirable in our traditions of resource management. The hard reality is that Indian society is fragmented amongst thousands of endogamous caste groups which are increasingly coming into conflict because of the destruction of traditional occupations and the erosion of the resource base. We have to work with the caste groups and rebuild the resource base so that it benefits all in an equitable fashion. The diversification of resource use by the different endogamous groups is of considerable relevance in this context. This is because many of the specialized resource needs of such groups, for instance *pandanus* for mat-weaving by Halakki Vakkals, have been totally ignored by the government machinery which continues to think in terms of a very small number of resources of commercial significance (such as teak).

Identification of these needs and attempts at fulfilling them can play an important role in involving a whole range of caste groups in the effort to take good care of the resource base. It is also vital to create new social institutions at the local level to control and manage local resources. These institutions should obviously attempt to ensure that a small number of individuals inter-acting with each other on a long-term basis and with their interests genuinely tied to the health of the resource base should have control over access to the resources of a given locality.

This is still very much a neglected issue, although there is increasing talk of involving local village councils and voluntary agencies in resource management. Precisely how this is to be done has not yet been spelt out, and the powerful state machinery is still reluctant to confer any real powers on the local institutions. There are, however, clear signs that the local communities would increasingly come to reassert their key role in the management of common-property resources and every hope that this would eventually lead to a major nationwide effort at ecorestoration.

Acknowledgements

We are grateful to the many people of Uttara Kannada who have worked with us and taught us much of what is narrated here. We wish to thank our colleagues at the Indian Institute of Science for their help in field work and for many helpful discussions. Finally we appreciate the stimulating inputs provided by Fikret Berkes.

References

Agarwal, A. and Narain, S., 1986: *The State of India's Environment 1984–85. The Second Citizen's Report*, Centre for Science and Environment, New Delhi.
Axelrod, R., 1984: *The Evolution of Cooperation*, Basic Books, New York.
Berkes, F. and Kence, A., in press: 'Fisheries and the Prisoner's Dilemma game: Conditions for the evolution of cooperation among users of common property resources', *Middle Eastern Technical University Journal of Pure and Applied Sciences*, Ankara.

Buchanan, F.D., 1870: *A Journey from Madras Through the Countries of Mysore, Canara and Malabar*, vol. 2, Higginbothams and Co., Madras.

Campbell, J.M., 1883: *Gazetteer of the Bombay Presidency*, vol. XV – Part 1 Kanara, Government Central Press, Bombay.

Cleghorn, H., 1861: *Forests and Gardens of South India*, W.H. Allen and Co., London.

Collins, G.F.S., 1921: *Modifications in the Forest Settlements Kanara Coastal Tract*, Part 1 No. F.O.R., S.R.VI. 7/1920, 'Extension of minor forests for the purposes of forest privileges in Ankola, Kumta and Honavar Talukas and Bhatkal Petha', Mahomedan Press, Karwar.

Cronon, W., 1983: *Changes in the Land: Indians, Colonists and the Ecology of New England*, Hill and Wang, New York.

Cox, S.J.B., 1985: 'No tragedy on the commons', *Environmental Ethics*, 7, pp. 49–61.

Dharampal, 1983: 'A note on the disruption and disorganization of Indian society in the last two centuries', *PPST Bulletin*, 3(2), pp. 18–47.

Fernandes, W. and Kulkarni, S., 1983: *Towards a New Forest Policy – People's Rights and Environmental Needs*, Indian Social Institute, New Delhi.

Gadgil, M., 1985a: 'Cultural evolution of ecological prudence', *Landscape Planning*, 12, pp. 285–99.

Gadgil, M., 1985b: 'Social restraints on resource utilization: The Indian experience', in McNeely, J.A. and Pitt, D., eds, *Culture and Conservation: The Human Dimension in Environmental Planning*, Croom Helm, Dublin, pp. 135–54.

Gadgil, M., 1987: 'Diversity: Cultural and biological', *Trends in Ecology and Evolution*, 2(12), pp. 369–73.

Gadgil, M., Hegde, K.M. and Shetty, K.A.B., 1987: 'Uttara Kannada: A case study in hill area development', in Saldanha, C.J., ed., *Karnataka State of Environment Report, 1985–86*, Centre for Taxonomic Studies, Bangalore, pp. 155–72.

Gadgil, M. and Malhotra, K.C., 1983: 'Adaptive significance of the Indian caste system: An ecological perspective', *Annals of Human Biology*, 10, pp. 465–78.

Gadgil, M., Prasad, S.N. and Ali, R., 1983: 'Forest management in India: A critical review', *Social Action*, 33, pp. 127–55.

Gadgil, M. and Vartak, V.D., 1976: 'Sacred groves of Western Ghats of India', *Economic Botany*, 30, pp. 152–60.

Hardin, G., 1968: 'The tragedy of the commons', *Science*, 162, pp. 1243–8.

Joshi, N.V., 1987: 'Evolution of cooperation by reciprocation within structured demes', *Journal of Genetics*, 66(1), pp. 69–84.

Leakey, R.E., 1981: *The Making of Mankind*, Abacus, London.

Malhotra, K.C., Khomne, S.B. and Gadgil, M., 1983: 'Hunting strategies among three non-pastoral nomadic groups of Maharashtra', *Man in India*, 63, pp. 21–39.

Masur, G.R., 1918: *A Representation to the Collector, Treating at Length Some of the Grievances Embodied in the Preceding Statement*, Agricultural Association, Kumta.

McNeely, J.A. and Pitt, D., eds, 1985: *Culture and Conservation: The Human Dimension in Environmental Planning*, Croom Helm, Dublin.

National Wastelands Development Board, 1985: *Wastelands Development Programme: Guidelines for Action*, Government of India, New Delhi.

Prasad, S.N., Hegde, M.S., Gadgil, M. and Hegde, K.M., 1985: 'An experiment in ecodevelopment in the Uttara Kannada district of Karnataka', *South Asian Anthropologist*, 69(1), pp. 73–83.

Ruddle, K. and Johannes, R.E., eds, 1985: *The Traditional Knowledge and Management of Coastal Systems in Asia and the Pacific*, UNESCO.

Singh, C., 1986: *Common Property and Common Poverty, India's Forests, Forest Dwellers and the Law*, Oxford University Press, Delhi.

Stebbing, E.P., 1922: *Forest of India*, vol. I, John Lane The Bodley Head Limited, London.

Terborgh, J., 1986: 'Keystone plant resources in the tropical forest', in Soulé, M.E., ed., *Conservation Biology*, Sinauer Associates, Inc. Sunderland, Massachusetts, pp. 330–44.

15 Changes Taking Place in Common-Property Resource Management in the Inland Niger Delta of Mali

Richard Moorehead

Summary

Common-property management systems have developed over hundreds of years in the inland Niger delta, and served to control access to resources between several ethnic groups using different production systems within the same area. They were particularly adapted to the bioclimatic diversity of the region, and underlay the coping strategies of rural inhabitants who moved each year to gain access to different resources in different ecological areas in the delta, between different seasons.

Over the last 15 years these management systems have been increasingly undermined, and with them the coping strategies customarily pursued by rural inhabitants. Twelve years of low flood levels and rainfall, leading to a dramatic fall in production, has diminished the resource base of the area, and made rural inhabitants more dependent on the market for the provision of basic necessities.

In these circumstances the more productive and reliable resources of the delta have fallen under the increasing control of powerful interests in rural communities and influential outside groups. On more marginal lands, the Malian state increasingly exercises an ambiguous authority proclaiming conservation goals as justification for fining rural inhabitants for breaking forestry laws and issuing permits for the exploitation of natural resources. At the same time, the government pursues a fiscal policy raising rural producers' cash needs, and hence diminishing the amount of choice they have in how they exploit the environment from which all their income is derived. Formal ownership of natural resources by the Malian state, which has neither the manpower nor the knowledge necessary effectively to manage access to these resources, is undermining customary common-property management systems, and providing access to and control of resources to those who never had these rights before.

Introduction

The inland delta of the river Niger is a flood plain situated in central Mali, covering an area of approximately 40,000 square kilometres. Running on an axis from south-west to north-east, the delta bridges the Soudano-Sahelian climatic zone to the south and the Sahelian climatic zone to the north. About 550mm of rain falls in the southern, upstream regions, and 250mm in the northern, downstream parts of the delta.

As shown in Figure 15.1 the inland Niger delta is one of the most important wetland areas of West Africa. Technical details of the Niger river system may be found in the chapter by Welcomme in Davies and Walker (1986). Data on floodplain land use and productivity (herding, meat and milk production, fisheries and agriculture) are summarized by Marchand (1987). For other background information and details of current conservation efforts, various IUCN reports may be consulted.

The major characteristic of this area is the extreme variation in natural conditions between seasons, between years, and between the delta and adjacent territories. Throughout the year, water levels in the delta change. Between June/July and September/October they rise in the main watercourses, fed by rainfall in the Futa Jallon and the mountains of the Mali–Ivory Coast border many hundreds of kilometres away to the south-west and west. Between October and December the flood reaches its full height, with floodplains underwater. Between January and March flood levels shrink into the main watercourses and between April and June water only flows in the deepest river beds, and the area becomes a vast dry plain. The inland delta has one short rainy season, stretching from June/July to September/October.

In this area not only are total amounts of rainfall and flood level of primary importance for the productivity of resources, but the timing of each in relation to the other often makes the difference between a good and a bad year. Such is the variability in the amount and timing of rainfall and flood levels both within years and between them, across topographically heterogeneous parts of the delta, that within local areas there may be considerable differences in productivity.

Five major production systems are found in the inland Niger delta and its surrounding drylands: semi-sedentary farmers (both rice and millet producers); agro-pastoralists; agro-fishermen; and transhumant fishermen and herders. A basic principle of their exploitation of the area is movement. Optimal use is made of differences in productivity in different ecological zones of the area according to highly variable local flood and rainfall characteristics between seasons and years.

Clearly, a critical factor underpinning the ability of rural producers to move between different ecological zones is the system of access rules governing resource use in various parts of the delta. Generally speaking, in the

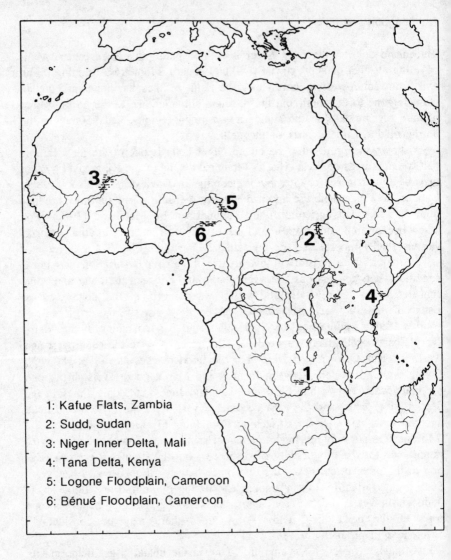

1: Kafue Flats, Zambia
2: Sudd, Sudan
3: Niger Inner Delta, Mali
4: Tana Delta, Kenya
5: Logone Floodplain, Cameroon
6: Bénué Floodplain, Cameroon

Figure 15.1 Major river systems, floodplains and wetlands of Africa. Inland Niger delta is shown as number 3. *Source:* Marchand (1987).

inland Niger delta and on its adjacent lands, these rules were in the past part of common-property management systems. These rules were codified in the nineteenth century when the area was under the control of a theocracy imposed by the dominant tribe of the region, the Fulani.

This system, which was relatively well adapted to specific circumstances of ethnic and production-system diversity and ecological variability, has been disintegrating. Twelve years of low rainfall and flood levels have diminished the resources available in the area, leading to falling production despite more intensive use and decreasing incomes for rural producers at a time when households are becoming more reliant on the market for the provision of essential foodstuffs. This is exacerbated by a movement of the terms of trade against delta products, and by rising population levels – both within the delta and through people moving into the area from the dry lands. Also, there is a proportional increase in the level of export of resources from the area, without any matching reinvestment in primary production.

Though elements of the nineteenth century organisation are still important today, the overarching power of Fulani hegemony in the area is no longer operational. The Malian state – which considers the rights of producers to exploit their resources as part of their status as citizens rather than as members of diverse ethnic groups practising different livelihoods – has neither the manpower nor the knowledge needed to manage the resources effectively. On a more general level the customary social and economic ties that bound communities together are becoming weaker. There are increasing levels of conflict both within and between rural communities, and a general decline in the quality of environmental management.

Very broadly, there would appear to be three processes at work changing common-property relations in the delta. On the more residual, marginal commons the central government administration is attempting to set up parallel management systems to replace customary ones. However, these new state management systems are unable on the one hand to manage access to commons effectively, and on the other hand are undermining the customary institutions that persist. On the more reliable, productive commons, fewer people are gaining access. This takes the form either of efforts by communities or groups within them to lay claim to resources ungoverned by access rules before. Or, where access rules did apply in the past at the level of the community, it takes the form of powerful groups within these communities (often now tied to non-rural interests) capturing customary common-property management systems. These groups either exploit the resources directly, or endeavour to increase their revenue by raising the fees they charge for access, these fees being used to meet their own needs rather than being distributed through the community.

Lastly, former open-access (*res nullius*) resources have become state property (*res publica*), subjecting exploiters of these commons to fines and taxes, and requiring permits for certain activities, such as cutting wood for sale or fishing. Recently, communities have also begun to lay claim to former open-access property as symbiotic relationships between production systems have broken down. An example of *res nullius* becoming *res communes* is where cultivators formerly gave animals to pastoralists to herd, but now, through investing in small stock which they pasture themselves, lay claim to forage resources close to their settlements.

This chapter will firstly describe in greater detail the production systems that exploit the inland Niger delta, and the manner in which rural inhabitants pursue their livelihoods. Secondly, it will explain how the management and use of common-property resources in the delta are changing, with reference to the nineteenth century system that controlled the area. In the concluding section, some likely long-term trends will be outlined and some policy options for the management of common-property resources tentatively advanced.

The production system

The inland Niger delta is characterized by the diversity of ethnic groups that inhabit or exploit the zone, reflecting on the one hand an ancient division of labour between the original inhabitants of the area, and on the other the progressive colonization of the region by neighbouring peoples. In the majority of cases, ethnic allegiance implies dependence on one main line of production, while the original presence or later arrival of particular ethnic groups can be linked to period in the delta's history.

The fishing peoples of the delta consist of the Bozo and Somono peoples in the central and southern reaches of the delta, and the Sorko in the north. The Bozo are widely accepted to be the original inhabitants of the region and are specialized in shallow-water fishing techniques (harpoons and trap fishing), while the Somono are more specialized in net fishing and river transport. The Somono were created by the Malian Empire in the thirteenth century out of an heterogeneous group of peoples. They were to be boatmen on the main river, assuring the transport in gold and slaves crossing the Sahara from Timboctou, upon which the economy of the empire rested. The Sorko are of less importance, occupying primarily the sector of the delta north of Lake Debo. They arrived in the area in the fifteenth century, when the region was under the control of the Sonrai empire, whose capital was at Gao in the east of present-day Mali (for historical background, Gallais, 1967).

The farmers of the region are made up of four ethnic groups: the Marka, Bambarra, Sonrai and Rimaibe peoples. Of these the most important are the Marka and Rimaibe, the Bambarra and Sonrai being largely confined to the north of the delta and its surrounding dry lands.

The Marka owe their name to the Mali empire, the translation of 'Mali-ka' being literally 'the people of Mali'. Again, as with the Somono, their ethnic origins are diverse: elements of their society include some of the oldest inhabitants of the delta, being the Noninke people – said to be the original rice cultivators of the region. These original inhabitants have been joined by others from a varied background linked by a common involvement in trade. The term 'Marka' denotes not only a commercial specialization and practice of agriculture, but also a strong Muslim religious belief. Thus, trading and farming communities in the delta became Marka as the empire disseminated the Islamic religion down the main waterways of the delta between the thirteenth and fifteenth centuries.

The Rimaibe are the former cultivating slaves of the Fulani, who were established for the most part on the floodplains in the seventeenth and eighteenth centuries. Captured from varied ethnic groups inhabiting both the delta and its borders, they were implanted into the area by their herding masters to grow floating rice, and, in some places, millet. Bambarra communities, specializing in millet production, migrated into the zone in the sixteenth and seventeenth centuries, when the power of the Bambarra kingdom at Segou to the south-west was at its height. The Sonrai arrived in the fifteenth century when their empire based at Gao was at its most influential; while also farming millet, they have a more diverse set of cultivating activities, including counter-season crop production in flood and rainfed pools.

The dominant ethnic group in the delta are the Fulani herders, who migrated into the area in successive waves between the eleventh and nineteenth centuries. As mentioned above, they ruled the area from the early nineteenth century until the arrival of the French (1893). Other herders seasonally using the area include the Tamasheq and their former slaves, the Bella (these latter having now largely settled down and taken up cultivation), who come down into the delta in the dry season from the north and north-east to graze their animals on the flood pastures.

Calculations from the national census of 1987 reveal about 500,000 people living in the delta. Of these, approximately 38 per cent are Fulani herders or Rimaibe, 30 per cent other farmers (Marka, Bambarra, Sonrai) and 32 per cent fishermen.

The description of the inhabitants of the delta as a set of ethnic groups, each specializing in one main productive activity, conceals the importance of secondary activities in how rural producers make their livelihoods in the area. It is rare to find households pursuing one occupation alone: in the majority of cases a primary activity is supplemented by a secondary occupation of strategic importance to the overall economy. Rural producers' flexibility in coping with highly variable climatic conditions through movement to different ecological zones is complemented in this way by diversification of activities.

The clearest examples of this flexibility are the two major dual-production systems of the delta: agro-pastoralism and agro-fishing. Both agro-pastoralists and agro-fishermen cultivate one cereal crop a year, aimed at meeting their subsistence needs: for the former, who live on the drylands, a millet crop between July and October, and for the latter a floodland rice crop between

July and December. To meet their cash needs, agro-pastoralists also keep livestock, primarily goats, which they graze or browse in the forests of the zone. Agro-fishermen fish the floodplains at high water, the secondary streams and deep pools in the transition seasons, and the main watercourses in the dry season.

Transhumant pastoralists also cultivate, but on a lesser scale, and the revenue from their cattle herds is used both to supplement their subsistence needs and to meet their cash requirements. Their households are generally divided into two productive units, one cultivating and the other moving with the herds. The latter leave the delta after the onset of the rains and, depending on where their village is situated within the delta, migrate either to the Sahelian pastures to the north and west, or to the dry lands to the east and north. In October they return to the delta and graze their animals on the rich pastures left by the receding flood – until June, when the transhumant cycle begins once again.

Transhumant fishermen come primarily from the upstream regions of the delta. Again, households are frequently split, with one part of the productive unit remaining in the village to bring in the rice crop while the other follows the retreating flood. Between November and February there is a mass movement of transhumant fishermen downstream towards the lakes in the northern part of the delta, where they remain until the first rains. At that moment, with the arrival of the flood, they turn for home to help with farming the rice fields.

The farmers of the area in average-rainfall years are perhaps the least dependent on a secondary occupation. They grow primary millet between July and October, supplemented by rice in rainfed pools, when water levels begin to fall, they plant a variety of flood-retreat crops – sorghum, maize, peanuts, cotton – which occupy them right through to the rains.

All the production systems in the delta rely to a greater or lesser extent (given the climatic conditions each year) on wild food found in the area, and some producers (agro-pastoralists, farmers and agro-fishermen) have important reciprocal access to different harvests. Between August and October, wild dry land crops (fonio, forest fruits and so on) are of cardinal importance to production systems waiting for the millet to ripen, and there are important population movements out of the delta on to its borders by rural inhabitants seeking wild food. Many of these people – depending on the success of the crop – then remain in the dry lands to participate in the millet harvest.

In December, a reverse movement takes place, with inhabitants on the delta's borders moving into the floodplains for wild food (such as grains from the floating pastures, water-lily seeds and tubers). These same people then move into the most productive rice cultivating areas to take part in the harvest in December and January. The harvest of young wild birds is equally important at this time, primarily for fishing communities on the floodplains.

Another important activity (particularly for the poor) is wood cutting during the season when water levels are sufficiently high for its transport (October to February in the downstream areas of the delta) either for sale for smoking fish, or for domestic use.

Finally, migration out of the area is a key strategy adopted by rural communities to cope with climatic risk. Farmers in particular move to the towns during the dry season to look for seasonal wage labour, and fishermen frequently migrate as far as the Ivory Coast looking for work, remaining absent from their communities for periods of two to three years. Herders in particularly bad years generally move to the south-west and south with their herds, returning when conditions ameliorate.

Changing patterns of resource use

What has been said above demonstrates that the various production systems and ethnic groups exploiting the inland Niger delta, using flexible strategies to mitigate the effects of a high-risk environment, require sets of access rules allowing inhabitants of different ecological areas of the region to use different resources at different seasons of the year. In the delta, these rules concern common-property systems, evolved over hundreds of years, which allocate resources between groups within the same production system and between the production systems themselves.

The discussion which follows will describe common-property institutions in the northern sector of the delta, around Lake Debo, where two-and-a-half years of research into the use and management of natural resources has recently been carried out by an IUCN project (IUCN, 1986). The area covers three ecological zones: drylands to the north-west; an area of alternating sand dunes and watercourses to the east, known as the Erg of Niafunke; and the lakes and floodplains to the south. The most important resources in the drylands are browse and forest, millet fields, pasture during the wet season and wild food. In the Erg of Niafunke, the main resources are much the same, together with flood pools where counter-season crops are grown as well as rainfed rice and fisheries. On the floodplains fisheries, pastures, rice fields and wild food are the main resources.

The most ancient resource-management system found in the delta rests upon the primacy accorded to the founding lineage. Throughout the area, and across production systems, it is possible to differentiate between rural communities according to whether they are indigenous to the area or outsiders, and within communities between founding lineages, lineages that arrived later and married into the former, and more recently arrived strangers. In general, founding lineages were the inalienable owners of resources; heads of these lineages were called the 'sacrificers', with clearly delimited territories. These lineages also provided resource managers, who might or might not be the same person as the sacrificer.

These managers, called 'masters of the water' and 'masters of the land' were responsible for the allocation of resources, for bringing new resources into production, the adjudication of disputes, and setting dates for important economic activities at different times of the year (sowing, harvesting, collective fishing, and so on). These traditional resource managers almost invariably came from the founding lineage of a community and derived their power from supernatural ties with the water and land spirits. Their powers were dual: those of appeasing the spirit when angry through sacrifices guaranteeing a good harvest or fishing season, and the feared ability to summon up the wrath of the spirit to do harm to transgressors. Stranger fishermen paid the sacrificer to sacrifice for them when they arrived in his area. They paid in kind (for fishermen the traditional amount being a third of the catch) for permission to fish or farm. The master of the water, master of the land or sacrificer was responsible for distributing the proceeds among the community.

The positions of master of the water and master of the land were hereditary. These traditional managers carried out their functions in consultation with the council of elders comprised of the heads of other lineages making up the community. The principal rule governing access to resources was that members of the community (that is, founders, consanguine lineages and later settlers) had a right of access which was essentially free or for a small tithe, while outsiders had to pay. Revenue from these sources was used by the head of the community to pay for visitors, grain stores, marriages and other ceremonies – and was also shared out between the founding and consanguine lineages of the community.

In the nineteenth century a Fulani theocratic state extended its control over the entire delta and imposed a system of resource management, call the *Dina*, on all major production systems. The *Dina* divided the area into a number of grazing territories allocated to loose Fulani clan groupings within which were to be found groups of wholly subordinate farmers (the Rimaibe) and more independent farmers, farmer fishermen, and hunting and gathering fishermen, who paid tribute. Two of the most important effects of the *Dina* system were to sedentarize groups of nomadic herders and fishermen, and to formalize grazing, fishing and farming territories in the area. In doing this, resource-management systems that already existed in the delta were formally established (and recorded in texts), and adapted to the interests of the Fulani.

Forest, browse and wild food resources were *res nullius* during the *Dina* period. A communal-property regime concerned agricultural land, pasture rights and fisheries in both the Erg and on the floodplains, while on the drylands only fields were allocated by community resource managers as *res communes*.

Particularly detailed rules of access surrounded pasture and fishing resources on the floodplains. There were three types of pasture: that which belonged to the political heads of the Fulani clans; that which belonged to the founding lineage groups within clans; and that which belonged to Fulani settlements. Each Fulani clan set dates at which animals could enter their territory as the floodwaters retreated each year, arranged herds in the order of priority of entry, and controlled the number of animals in line with pasture availability in any given year. The Fulani also distributed land for cultivation on the floodplains to their dependent farming and to other subordinate communities in the area. The principal Fulani manager was the *Dioro*, the head of the founding lineage of the clan.

Access to fishing grounds was managed by masters of the water. In the dry season, when fishing was concentrated in the main river courses, highly organized collective-fishing techniques were managed by these same authorities. Particular types of fishing (for example, using seine nets, or certain kinds of hand-held nets) were banned by fishing communities owning adjacent parts of the river at certain seasons of the year. When the time came around for fishing these areas (the date being set by the master of the water in consultation with the council of elders) the traditional authorities would claim a tithe from identified 'stranger' fishermen who came each year to take part. (See also the description of the indigenous fishing management system by Malvestuto and Meredith, 1986.)

In the drylands to the west and north of the delta, masters of the land managed access to fields, as was also the case in areas of higher population density to the north-east and east (the Erg of Niafunke). In addition, in the latter zone, fisheries were managed by masters of the water and grazing by masters of pasture.

Institutions within production systems that formerly controlled access to resources are no longer able to work effectively. Within cultivating communities, links between individual households and managers of resources (masters of the land) are weakening, with customary payments to managers, requests to put new land into use, and payments of rents all falling into disuse. In fishing and farming communities on the floodplains, masters of the water no longer have powers to deny rights of access to outsiders, or to prevent them from using more intensive techniques. Herding and agro-pastoral communities similarly lack the ability to keep outsiders away.

This is linked to weakened relations between traditional herding managers, other herders belonging to the same clan, and formerly dependent cultivators. Work in fishing communities has shown how different households within the same production system with varying amounts of capital equipment, different status, and different access to labour, pursue very different production strategies. Smaller, poorer households specialize in only one major activity, while larger, richer households are able to diversify their production.

Access rules in recent years show a marked movement towards the 'privatization' of resources in comparison with the epoch of the *Dina*. Open-access rules are being replaced by communal property relations, and former community-controlled resources are falling into the hands of individuals or individual households. This is especially so in the Erg of Niafunke, where fields are private property not because they can be sold (though there have been reports of this) but because all production belongs to the household head. These fields can be inherited, and efforts by traditional authorities to reclaim land or charge rents meet with resistance. In recent years, cultivators in the area have put individual plots into production to grow pasture for sale on prime flooded sites. The same breakdown in links between customary authorities, members of the community and strangers is also evident on the drylands and the floodplains.

The more reliable resources in the Erg of Niafunke and on the floodplains have fallen under the control of more powerful groups within rural communities, where founding lineages, merchants and other advantaged groups (for example, retired soldiers who fought in the French colonial army) are able, through their access to credit, capital equipment and labour, to monopolize the more productive resources. In both areas, this narrowing of control over resources formerly shared by the community as a whole involved pasture and fisheries. Both direct production and revenue in fees from strangers is used by these privileged groups to meet their own cash and subsistence ends rather than being redistributed to other members of their society.

Resources that had no formal rules of entry before are now becoming subject to restraints. In all three ecological zones, access to browse is becoming more difficult or subject to payments of fees where there were none before. This coincides with a general movement of agro-pastoralists into goat-herding rather than cattle ownership, as 12 years of low rainfall and flood levels have made it easier to raise goats. On the floodplains, access to some wild food (grains from wild pasture, for example) may well be becoming more controlled, as such resources become particularly valuable during the drought.

At the same time, a new resource manager – the Malian state, differentiated into its component parts of administration, technical services (livestock and forestry agencies, the political party and so on – is transforming the former communal-property regime into a state-property regime. This new regime takes the form of a system of fines and permits for the exploitation or deemed abuse of natural resources: for cutting green wood, for fishing, and for trading in forest products, for example.

On the floodplains and in the Erg of Niafunke, intervention by the state is operating in a reverse way, converting resources that formerly had a more rigorous community-controlled management system into public property. This is taking place at strategic moments of the year when resources are particularly valuable. The state, through its agencies, now manages the majority of collective fisheries that take place in the early dry season (February to May) by setting dates and overseeing the allocation of fishing places. Throughout the delta, the crossing dates of herds into the flood retreat pastures are fixed through a regional administrative conference, following which at each crossing, state officials attend to keep order and collect a fee for each herd that traverses.

The state's formal ownership of all natural resources, and the central role it plays in the adjudication of disputes, offers the opportunity of access to resources to exploiters who may never have had a right of entry. At the same time the proliferation of authorities with the ostensible power to grant access (administration, foresters, livestock service, political party, and so on) undermines the authority of traditional managers. Further, the imposition of administrative frontiers unrelated to customary fishing and herding territories has led to the transfer of control over resources from one production system to another (where farmers have been able to lay claim to fisheries near their villages, for example). That control formerly belonged to masters of the water now in neighbouring administrative areas or to the reallocation of resources between communities practising the same way of life.

The major consequences of this situation are twofold. Firstly, the quality of management of the commons is declining. Rising cash needs within communities are obliging influential groups to monopolize the more productive resources, while using revenue from their management for their individual interests. At the same time the state, while undermining customary common-property management institutions (which were based upon an inherited and practised knowledge of the area) is unable to replace them with an effective and knowledgeable alternative management system. In these conditions, the increasing numbers of rural poor are being obliged to exploit more marginal commons. They are disproportionately taxed by the state, and have increasing cash needs. As a result, they have less and less choice in how they manage their environment and almost no opportunity to develop institutions conducive to better resource management in the future.

Secondly, either common-property resources are being directly controlled, or the revenue from their management is being organized in such a way that the export of resources from the rural sector is taking place without any comparable reinvestment being made in traditional rural economies. This production and revenue from the exploitation of the commons is flowing out of the region. At another level, revenue from state management of resources on the residual commons goes to the national exchequer, whose principal concern is with liquidity to pay for national current-account costs, consisting mostly in payment of civil-service salaries and educational grants.

Long-term trends and policy options

For many of the natural resources in the inland Niger delta, the longer-term future looks bleak. Especially if the drought continues, it is plausible that the more productive resources will fall under the control either of powerful traditional groups within communities living in the delta, or outside interests with strong links to the administration and the political party. At the same, more and more rural inhabitants will be obliged to exploit marginal common land where rules of entry will be conditioned solely by their policing by the state. For these rural inhabitants, the way in which they exploit their environment will have less and less of an element of choice because of the conditions in which they are obliged to pursue their livelihood in rural areas, and the almost complete lack of long- or medium-term employment opportunities outside the rural sector.

It is unlikely that these groups will consider environmental conservation as a priority, either because of their increasing cash needs or because investment in production by non-rural groups will be dictated by concerns lying outside the delta economy. For instance, many merchants and functionaries wish to invest in livestock using the delta; these animals are destined eventually for the Bamako meat market. The technical services of the state in policing the marginal commons are equally unlikely to manage the environment with a view to conservation, for the reasons set out above.

Even if climatic conditions were to improve in the delta – and there would have to be a prolonged improvement over a period of several years to regenerate resources and the economies dependent upon them – the effect of the drought will have been to accelerate longer-term trends of differentiation within rural communities. This is linked to increased dependence on the market and increased numbers of people using the resources of the area. The state's requirement for cash revenue (accentuated dramatically in the last two years following the fall in cotton prices on the international market, which accounted for well over half of Mali's foreign earnings) makes it unlikely, without the help of foreign aid, that their policy of disinvestment in the delta will cease.

In these conditions it is plausible to imagine the delta composed of a set of pockets of richer resources owned and managed by wealthier households within communities or powerful outside interests, surrounded by much larger areas of common land that is progressively more degraded by poorer households pursuing short-term production strategies. Customary coping strategies of moving between ecological areas of the delta are being undermined by the degeneration of the diversity of natural resources in the area. At the same time, the closing-off of the better resources, accompanied by an increase in sedentary activities, means that the majority of people in the delta will become more and more vulnerable to climatic risk.

Development initiatives undertaken over the last 15 years in the delta, involving an expenditure of something over US$70m, and concentrating on the provision of fixed technical inputs (irrigation works, well and borehole digging, vaccination campaigns and the like) have, broadly speaking, met with failure. Fish production is down 50 per cent from the early 1970s; over 60 per cent of the area's livestock was lost between 1983 and 1985; and cereal production has fallen by 70 per cent since the last reasonable year in 1977. (Unpublished data from Operation Pêche Mopti; Opération pour le Développement de l'Elévage dans la Région de Mopti; Opération mils Mopti.)

Yet the rural sector has been able to support increasing levels of revenue for the government over this same period, and the resilience of rural producers to increasingly adverse climatic conditions has been remarkable. This resilience is based on the common-property relations described above that allow delta inhabitants access to resources in different parts of the area in different seasons, and by their ability to diversify into new activities. After 12 years of low rainfall and flood levels, however, many of these coping strategies are now at risk.

Given the almost complete lack of employment opportunities outside the rural sector, future priority in addressing the needs of the rural poor must be given to finding ways of regenerating rural economies to provide an improved livelihood for the inhabitants of the delta. This involves implementing policies to reinforce the adaptive strategies that have allowed rural producers to survive so far. At the same time, steps must be taken to alleviate the structural conditions instrumental in obliging rural producers to abuse their environment – in particular those relating to the export of revenue from rural communities either through taxation, fines, or through dependence on markets where they suffer negative terms of trade.

Policy options for the future thus require that measures be taken to reinforce the ability of rural producers to move between different ecological areas, and that they have access to the more productive resources once they arrive. Coordinated action has also to be taken to regenerate the natural resources of the zones that are already degraded and conserve those that remain. Inevitably, such a process requires limits to be placed on the numbers of exploiters allowed to use a particular area in any season.

While the re-imposition of the traditional *Dina* system is unrealistic, elements of the nineteenth century organization remain of sufficient importance to this day to make them useful. Grazing territories on the floodplain included within them fishing and farming domains that are still recognized by local inhabitants. In areas of higher population density inhabited by mixed farming, fishing, and herding peoples, village territories exist, again recognized by local inhabitants. Within these communities the structure of traditional authority is still present. Even though many of the powers of customary leaders are being undermined as described, the majority of community members still look to them to represent their interests in their dealings with the administration. Reciprocal access agreements are still important for communities living in different ecological zones.

However, one of the principal results of research carried out by the IUCN (1986) project in the northern sector of the delta since 1984, has been the discovery of the extent of differentiation that now exists within communities living in the area. Within production groups that formerly practised a similar livelihood, there now exist important differences between, for example, animal-rich and land-rich households; between large households that can diversify their activities and smaller ones that are obliged to specialize; and between seasonal visitors and sedentary inhabitants.

Thus, future management systems would have to represent the varied interests that are more entrenched in the economic self-interest of individual households than in the kinship links that bound communities together in the past. They would also have to take into account the latter-day importance of the Malian state in the management of natural resources. Mali is not unique in this regard. Some studies in other parts of Africa – for example, in Botswana (Peters, 1987) – indicate many parallels with the case study described here.

Research by IUCN project has shown that it is possible to identify particular interest groups within communities dependent on a specific resource. It is hoped that by working with groups of households sharing a particular interest in these specific resources within customary territories, the basis for a management system might be created. Reciprocal access agreements between interest groups inhabiting different ecological areas might then be negotiated, based on customary agreements that existed in the past. Management committees, on which traditional managers would be represented, would be set up in a framework allowing government and technical services to contribute, though the accent would be on the *local* management of resources. The main work of these management committees would be to control access and to undertake actions to regenerate and to conserve resources, and to manage credit and other schemes.

If unchecked, present trends indicate that the better resources of the delta – those which continue to be productive even in drought years – will become increasingly privatized, and that increasing numbers of poorer rural inhabitants will move on to marginal lands. Resources on such lands will be progressively degraded because the people using them will have little choice in how they are managed as they search for a basic livelihood. The progressive sedentarization of some communities around the better resources, accompanied by the degradation of the more marginal lands, will make the delta as a whole, and the people who inhabit it, more vulnerable to climatic risk.

This doom-laden prognosis for the future need not necessarily be fulfilled. But action needs to be taken in the near future to reinforce the traditional coping strategies of rural inhabitants who made good use of a wide variety of resources in different parts of the delta in different seasons of the year. For these strategies to be encouraged, communal-property management systems need to be created, incorporating various existing interest-groups found within rural communities. The development of regional and community-level fishery and other resource-management authorities 'is not a vague possibility but a current reality that must be carefully nurtured because these . . . [offer] the only real possibility of implementing management programs with enforcement potential' (Malvestuto and Meredith, 1986). For rural producers faced with different climatic conditions each year, reinforcing traditional common-property systems would help promote a flexible and viable subsistence strategy based upon their own tried-and-tested knowledge of the area.

The need for decentralized management systems is being increasingly recognized in government policy, and several efforts are being made to implement local management agreements. The Malian 'Programme Nationale de Lutte contre le Désertification', published in 1985, promotes the devolution of responsibility to local communities for the management of their own natural resources as part of a national development plan based on different 'agro-ecological' areas of the country. The development debate in Mali is increasingly concerned with how changes may be made in legislation offering rural communities legal title to their resources, and how local ideas and initiatives can be promoted through the single political party, the Union Démocratique du Peuple Malien.

In this context, workable management systems based on the traditional knowledge or rural inhabitants of their environment, have a greater opportunity of being supported now than at any time since Mali became independent in 1960.

References

Davies, B.R. and Walker, K.F., eds, 1986: *The Ecology of River Systems*, Junk, Boston.

Gallais, J., 1967: *Le Delta Intérieur du Niger. Mémoires de l'Institut Fondamental d'Afrique Noire*, 2 vols, IFAN, Dakar.

IUCN, 1986: *Rapport de Synthèse, IUCN Project pour le Conservation de l'Environnement dans de Delta Intèrieur du Niger*, IUCN, Gland.

Malvestuto, S.P. and Meredith, E.K., 1986: *Assessment of the Niger River Fishery in Niger (1983–1985) with Implications for Management*, International Large Rivers Symposium, Toronto.

Marchand, M., 1987: 'The productivity of African floodplains', *International Journal of Environmental Studies*, 29, pp. 201–11.

Peters, P.E., 1987: 'Embedded systems and rooted models: The grazing lands of Botswana and the commons debate', in McCay, B.J. and Acheson, J.M., eds, *The Question of the Commons*, University of Arizona Press, Tuscon, pp. 171–194.

16 Traditional Resource Management in the Melanesian South Pacific: A Development Dilemma

G.B.K. Baines

Summary

Traditional natural-resource management systems of the indigenous communities of the Pacific islands, based on communal-property concepts, continue to function in the face of many changes in the circumstances in which they operate. All have been weakened by changes accompanying economic development – yet they have adapted, and persist.

Independent Pacific island governments accept that these systems, being expressions of social structure itself, are basic to the continued welfare of their societies. At the same time these governments are proceeding to implement forms of economic development which are in conflict with these traditional systems. This poses a development dilemma which is crucial for the future of the people of the South Pacific islands. To what extent can the traditional systems accommodate further change? Will serious efforts be made to adjust approaches to economic development so as to ease those disruptions to traditional resource-management systems which are eroding Pacific island societies themselves?

With an emphasis on the resource-rich Melanesian islands of the Pacific island region, practical examples of the development dilemma in the areas of forestry and fisheries are presented. Suggestions are made as to how with more patience and better understanding, agents of development might yet give practical meaning to official policies of support for traditional systems of resource management. Melanesia still has a chance, if excessive population growth rates can be curbed.

Introduction

Indigenous systems for the administration and allocation of land and sea resources have long prevailed in the Pacific islands region (Figure 16.1). These are not strictly systems of property, in the Western sense, or of territory, though involving elements of both. They are integral components

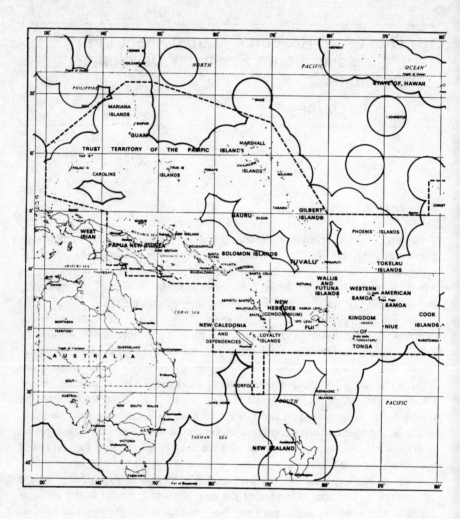

Figure 16.1 The new Pacific is largely made up of sea territories. Circles
surrounding islands indicate Exclusive Economic Zones; dashed
outlines indicate membership in the South Pacific Forum. *Source:*
Nietchmann (1987).

of Pacific Island societies, and are very complex.

For these societies, land above water and land which is covered by freshwater or seawater conceptually is one and undivided, though with some form of seaward limit – often the outer edge of the outermost coral reef. Further, there is a strong sense of close interdependence between an individual, his or her descent group, and the land with which that group is traditionally associated.

It is difficult for persons of Western cultures to understand this close identification of Pacific islanders with their resources. Land and reefs are not viewed as commodities to be sold, or exchanged – although certain use rights might be granted by resource 'custodians', 'guardians', or 'owners'. The word 'owner', though widely used, is misleading since it indicates a possessive and dominating relationship, rather than the sense of an individual having an intimate association with land, reef, and all that grows upon them. (See Chapter 5 for an analogous case.)

In Fiji this concept is embraced by the term *vanua* (Ravuvu, 1983). *Vanua* has interrelated physical, social and cultural dimensions. It means the land–water area and its plants, animals, soils and other natural resources; and it refers also to the human occupants of the area, with their traditions, customs, beliefs, values and institutions. As a whole, *vanua* refers to a social unit that is identified with physical territory, in which its roots have been established for many generations – from the time of a founding ancestor.

In Vanuatu

> custom land is not only the site of production but it is the mainstay of a vision of the world. Land is at the heart of the operation of the cultural system . . . Each man must have some place, some land which belongs to him, which is his territory. If he does not control any land, he has no roots, status or power. In the most extreme cases this means he is denied social existence (Bonnemaison, 1984).

The relationship of a Pacific islander to the area with which his or her hereditary social group is associated is more custodial – though economic development stresses are now effecting changes. Formal recognition of traditional land-tenure systems in the administration of land above water is widespread in Pacific Islands countries. In some, such as Cook Islands, Fiji, Niue, it is firmly based on legislation – as, for instance, in Fiji's Native Lands Act, 1905: 'Native lands shall be held by native Fijians according to native custom as evidenced by usage and tradition . . .'

Elsewhere, including Solomon Islands, Vanuatu and Papua New Guinea, it is a matter of policy, with some supportive references in legislation. The provision of formal status for traditional arrangements relating to the submerged land of coastal waters, however, has received relatively little attention.

The colonial experience

The Melanesian nations of Fiji, Papua New Guinea, Solomon Islands and Vanuatu experienced periods of colonial rule by administrators from alien cultures prior to regaining their political independence. Two Melanesian areas still lack that right – West Irian, administered by Indonesia, and New Caledonia, ruled by France.

British colonial administrations tolerated, and sometimes even made special provision for, the continuance of traditional resource-management systems. There was probably little altruism in this; it was largely a device to facilitate indirect rule, a cheaper form of colonialism. Colonial administrators did not always properly understand the true nature of these systems. France (1969), for instance, explains how an inaccurate model of Fijian traditional land administration was imposed in the early part of this century in the course of efforts to rationalize the land-administration system along traditional lines. And the early twentieth century 'wasteland' policy of the British administration of the Solomon Islands – whereby all land deemed to be unoccupied or unused was interpreted as being outside traditional jurisdiction and therefore forfeit to the administration – was a gross misunderstanding of the prevailing traditional system.

On the other hand, Akin (personal communication) has reason to believe that, being aware of the extent to which the British colonial administration was prepared to leave certain matters to traditional jurisdiction, in some cases Solomon Islanders labelled certain non-traditional matters 'custom' so as to restrict colonial influence in their affairs.

Traditional systems under French rule apparently have been afforded little recognition. Even so, the traditional association of New Caledonian Melanesians with their land remains very strong, long after that land had been taken from their jurisdiction and allocated to French settlers. Land loss, and not least the spiritual implications of this deprivation, is at the core of determined efforts by these Melanesians to wrest their land back from French control.

With political independence has come a heightened respect for tradition. This, coupled with the political reality that the electorate of Melanesian nations is made up largely of rural groups closely concerned with the maintenance of traditional resource-use rights, has focused attention on traditional resource-management systems. These rights are seen by agents of economic development as frustrating resource exploitation – as where Murphy (1973), in reference to them called for 'a thorough look at the real extent of the problem'.

This chapter addresses the issue of traditional resource management in the problematical context of economic development. 'Tradition' in this sense is not, of course, unchanging. While many features of ancient tradition have changed, however, certain other characteristics of traditional resource-management systems remain strong – not least being the intensely felt man–land association. The subject of traditional land and marine tenure in Melanesia and elsewhere in the Pacific islands is so complex and varied as to make it impractical to attempt a detailed discourse here. Crocombe (1987) offers the most comprehensive coverage of land tenure in the region. Since marine tenure systems have only recently become a subject of interest outside those groups involved with them there is, as yet, no published report which gives an accurate overall view.

The objective of this chapter is to address, in general terms, a development dilemma relating to resources held under traditional arrangements which is crucial not only for the future of the Melanesian countries which are the focus but for all countries in the South Pacific island region.

A development dilemma

Recognition of Melanesians' traditional means of administering and allocating natural resources may be found in the texts of policy statements by independent governments, or in special provisions in legislation. In some cases specific constitutional provisions are made.

One of Papua New Guinea's 'national goals and directive principles', incorporated in the nation's constitution is: 'Development should take place primarily through the use of Papua New Guinean forms of social, political and economic organisation.'

Vanuatu's Constitution is even more explicit: 'Article 71 – All land in the Republic belongs to the indigenous custom owners and their descendants.' 'Article 72 – The rules of custom shall form the basis of ownership and use of land in the Republic.'

While the constitution of the Solomon Islands provides only a weak reference to traditional rights, some national legislation is written so as to make special provision for tradition, or to exclude communal-property resources from an Act's coverage. The Provincial Government Act, 1981, for instance, quite specifically restricts Provincial powers: 'Nothing in this section shall be construed as affecting traditional rights, privileges and usages in respect of land and fisheries in any parts of the Solomon Islands.'

Fiji, the only Pacific island nation where traditional land and fisheries rights have been systematically investigated and officially recorded, provides for the former through a Native Land Trust Act, 1940, while the latter are dealt with in the Fisheries Act, 1942. Among other things, this Act provides for a native fisheries commission and a register of native customary fishing rights. Under the guise of policy, specific administrative arrangements are also used – as in a procedure agreed by cabinet in 1974 for recompense for loss of traditional fishing rights as a consequence of foreshore development.

Irrespective of the legal and administrative devices of which the above are examples, there is a consistent tendency by agents of resource development to characterize traditional forms of resource administration as 'problems' impeding development. And, for all the rhetoric of official statements, governments are vulnerable to strong economic pressures to exploit natural resources quickly. These pressures are intensified by the efforts of international economic-assistance agencies arguing for increased natural-resource exploitation so that debtor nations can sustain loan repayments.

Shared resource 'ownership' means that a relatively large number of people is likely to be involved in decisions concerning proposals for commercial development. Consensus, in some form, is usually required before a decision on the use of these resources can be reached. Older people generally have more authority and tend to be conservative, even suspicious, in respect of development proposals. This frustrates some younger members of a communal property group – as it does the officials promoting development. Lending institutions seek the security provided by private-property rights and, so as to facilitate the necessary flow of development funds, seek conversion of customary group tenure into some form of freehold.

Traditional resource-management systems, reflecting the societies of their origin, are built on principles of allocation and cooperation within hereditary groups. Originally, they were geared to produce a surplus beyond subsistence needs only to the extent that allowed for a local exchange of goods or for the maintenance of food reserves. The essence of economic development, of course, is the production of a surplus for monetary gain. This new mode of resource use strains the traditional management system and tests its adaptability. It has adapted to encompass the limited development of cash crops such as copra and cocoa. Yet these, grown on a smallholder basis, produce little more than the cash needed for the basic necessities which constitute today's subsistence needs.

Over the years since Pacific island societies made their first tentative moves towards involvement in the cash economies of the world, there have been many changes in indigenous resource-management systems. Their potential for adaptation has been demonstrated, and essential principles in the systems have remained relatively intact. The changed nature and greater scale of economic development now facing the Pacific islands region does, however, place much greater strain on them. Should traditional systems be accommodated? Political decisions to do so have been taken. So, in the face of intense economic pressures and the impact of burgeoning populations, can they adapt and survive? To what extent might government intervention in their evolution be appropriate? The essence of the development dilemma addressed here is the hope of building on tradition, while at the same time subscribing to forms of development which in so many ways appear opposed to that tradition and are, in fact, contributing to its demise.

Change and adaptation

It was during the early part of the nineteenth century that fairly regular trading contacts were established with many of the island communities of the Pacific. Sandalwood, beche-de-mer, and turtleshell became commodities traded for a variety of European articles, not least weapons. Natural resources were managed to produce the necessary surplus, though not without important political and social consequences. A particularly vivid explanation of the consequences of turtleshell trading in the western Solomons is provided by McKinnon (1975) who showed that those islanders with best access to turtling grounds were able to use the axes and rifles taken in the turtleshell trade to strengthen their control and – of social importance at that time – to enhance their spiritual power through the acquisition of greater numbers of human heads, which caused an upsurge in headhunting raids.

Once traders began to consider establishing land bases for their Pacific island operations, a new threat to traditional resource-management systems arose. Traders presumed to 'buy' land which, by definition, could not be 'owned'. Their presentations of goods, accompanied by impressive displays of superior technology, were not infrequently accepted and land was made available for their *use*. It was later, and to some extent continues to be, a surprise to the traditional custodians of the land that these transactions had been interpreted as outright sales, rather than as grants of use rights, a form of lease.

Yet there was sometimes a sinister secondary element to these transactions. Relatively few Melanesian islanders at the time were able to communicate with the foreigners wishing to use their land. Those with some limited ability with the English language or, more commonly, with one of the Pidgin dialects, were able to monopolize communications with the outsiders. McKinnon (1972) explained how this effected important shifts in power and influence in the western Solomons in the late nineteenth century. The effect on traditional resource rights was profound, and its repercussions are still felt. 'Communicators' conducted land transactions with the traders, sometimes on behalf of those who had authority to allocate the land in question, sometimes in spite of them. The traders were often unaware of the social complexities of traditional resource jurisdiction but, in any case, are unlikely to have cared. Europeans assumed that the islanders who carried out the transaction had the traditional right to do so, and his name was written into the associated documentation! In this way he attained a status in respect of that land to which he may not have been entitled, and the land was subsequently identified with his hereditary group. Once aware of this deviation from proper traditional practice those who did have the right to 'speak' for that land would attempt to correct the situation. Yet the powerful, intimidating authority of the European purchaser implicitly provided the man named in the document with protection. In many cases the mistake was not rectified, even where land so alienated was subsequently returned to traditional jurisdiction. Some of today's disputes in Melanesia over rights to the use of land under customary tenure originated in this way. Descendants of the duped land custodian are still trying to regain their traditional rights.

Following the traders came the planters. They were interested in acquiring tracts of coastal land to plant coconuts so as to produce copra. Much larger areas of land were involved yet, on being asked to allocate land for the purpose of growing this crop – in traditional terms, an application for secondary (usufruct) rights – those representing landholding groups often agreed. The introduction of the plantation mode of land use, however, was to bring far-reaching changes to communal-property resource systems. The coconut is such a long-lived crop, of the order of 100 years, that land planted to it was effectively removed from the pool of land available to a landholding group. In any case, plantation land was regarded by colonial administration as alienated – no longer part of the traditional system.

Today, it is islanders who plant coconuts. Recognizing that this long-term crop effectively ties up the land on which it grows, some individuals have succeeded in gaining control of land under customary tenure through applying for secondary use rights to establish a food garden, and then planting coconuts!

A resource-management system implies the existence of a body of resource knowledge, and the presence of individuals skilled in applying that knowledge. Pacific island societies provided for such roles. From the Lau islands of Fiji, for instance, Thompson (1940) reported on the roles of a 'chief of crops' who, among other things, determined harvest times. A 'master fisherman' had overall control of fishing grounds and organized and supervised fishing activities. The British colonial administration of Fiji, either unaware of the significance of these roles or underestimating their relevance, did not provide for them the official support which it provided for other traditional roles when establishing a Fijian administration. Through neglect, the roles now appear to be extinct, and the effectiveness of Fijian traditional resource-management systems, accordingly, weakened.

These few examples of the varied stresses to which the traditional systems have been subjected since first contact with European influences serve to illustrate two important points. First, that the resource-management systems in operation today have changed since first contact with Western technology; but that, secondly, these systems have demonstrated a capacity to adapt and persist.

Traditional tenure and forest development

A quick and relatively easy source of foreign exchange for the Pacific island countries of Melanesia is provided by logging of their tropical rainforests. The trees involved are large, and felling and extraction involve the use of heavy machinery, some of it tracked. Soil disturbance by this machinery is a serious environmental problem. Forest canopy destruction worsens the overall damage to the soil resource, allowing solar radiation to penetrate and causing soil temperature to rise. Rainfall, no longer intercepted by the forest canopy, falls heavily to the ground, impacting and scouring the flimsy rainforest surface soil.

Those remaining forests which are attractive to loggers are all communal-property resources under traditional jurisdiction. Logging, a crude form of forest development, is a continuing source of controversy. The controversy arises from the environmental disturbance, because of logging's sudden and drastic alteration of the community's resource base, and because of the socially damaging disputes which it generates in areas where the boundaries of group lands have not been clearly determined and marked.

Attempts have been made to establish legislation and procedures which might to some extent recognize reality and accommodate traditional concepts of group resource ownership. Fiji's Native Land Trust Act, 1940, provides a legal basis for forestry activities on customary land. While not ideal, it can be said to have met with reasonable success. This arrangement is still in operation after almost 50 years. Experience with the Solomon Islands' North New Georgia Timber Corporation Act, 1979, indicates that it is unlikely to be used as a model for other areas of the country. This legislation is an attempt to overcome customary landowner-group fears of alienation of their land through logging. The Act makes a distinction between land and trees, vesting timber rights in the corporation while leaving traditional land rights unaffected. This idea is borrowed from Papua New Guinea, where government purchases timber rights from forest-'owning' lineages and then arranged logging – leaving rights to the deforested land with the traditional 'owners'. Legally it may be an attractive concept, but it is inconsistent with the holistic man–land–resources concept of Melanesian societies. It has, however, met with some grudging acceptance, despite its quite serious erosion of tradition.

In a situation where the limits of a particular group's forests are known (perhaps only to a few individuals of the group, and known in terms of a distinctive ridge crest, certain hill-tops, conspicuous boulders, prominent trees and ancient burial sites) but not surveyed, nor even roughly marked on a map – how can the boundaries be established quickly, and without disagreement? There will inevitably be individuals from outside the group who will claim some right, possibly spurious, to determine the allocation of that forest area, and the location of its boundaries. Within the group recognized as having ownership rights there are likely to be differences of opinion with respect to subdivisions of the group area. Some group members will be ready to approve of logging; others will not. The land of the latter may well be downstream of that of those willing to permit logging. The rights of downstream groups may, then, be at risk from sediment pollution of streams from upstream soil disturbance.

Further, the primary rights (usually by birth) of a landholding group are likely to be restricted, in tradition, by the secondary rights of people entitled to harvest the products of individual trees or of groves of trees on that land. In the matter of logging legislation and procedures, no specific provision is made for secondary rights. Since secondary rights are affected – perhaps even extinguished – by logging, should secondary-rights holders be party to decisions on logging, and should they be entitled to a share of the monetary benefits which arise from it?

A decision to log is momentous. Unwisely, it usually involves all of a landowning group's forest. If only a portion were so allocated, options on the future use of the remaining forest could be kept open for decisions by a different generation facing different circumstances. Logging liquidates a resource which may have served a lineage for many centuries, which harbours all of that line's historical links with its past, and which has traditionally been viewed as a resource borrowed from future generations. For all the official rhetoric about reforestation ('we can replace your forest'), the ecological and sociological truth is that tropical rainforest cannot be replaced. The logging of a landholding group's forests may be the most dramatic development impact they will experience. Its environmental and social consequences can be very debilitating.

Instances are known where landholders have gone to a logged area to resolve some boundary uncertainty. There, they have encountered extensive landscape disturbance by logging machinery: the forest canopy reduced to a fraction of its original cover; the ground surface, once relatively open and of easy access, now blocked by fallen tree debris and presenting an altogether unfamiliar topography; and sacred ancestral sites obscured, where not damaged. Individuals accustomed to positioning themselves, and their land boundaries, by reference to natural tree and boulder landmarks, and sometimes by subtle changes of surface topography, become disoriented. The ensuing uncertainties about boundary location are the direct cause of fresh land disputes. This is but one of the manifestations of the resulting social trauma.

Often, because they lack the required basic mechanical skills, relatively few of the members of a landowning group whose forest is being logged might be employed in the logging. Heavy machinery is usually operated by what are regarded as 'outsiders', even though Solomon Islanders and perhaps of the same language group. While these workers will harbour the usual intense, protective feeling towards the forests of their own lineages, experience has shown that they are unlikely to be sensitive to the feelings of those on whose land they are operating. As a consequence, bulldozer operators pay little attention to measures which would minimize soil damage and erosion, nor are they concerned that in the course of their work they damage, and sometimes destroy, the archaeological sites which are so important as identifiers of land 'ownership'.

Ideally, large-scale forest utilization should be preceded by measures to identify properly those individuals who have landholding and use rights; to locate, survey and mark their boundaries; to help them fully to understand the implications of decisions to develop their resources – and the implications of not commercially utilizing these resources. Some policy statements and legislation are written with this in mind. The reality is that economic development pressures are acute, and that documenting and formally recognizing traditional rights is a very complex, costly and lengthy matter. Meanwhile, logging continues erratically, the establishment of a proper forestry sector based on sustainable use of a renewable resource is stalled, and the courts which arbitrate on disputes over customary land are over- whelmed by a growing backlog of land-dispute cases.

In the midst of this uncertainty, efforts to establish a 'national forest estate' through pure stand reforestation continue. Yet it is proving extremely difficult for Solomon Islands' forestry division, for instance, to plant trees on land under customary tenure. It seems that the reasons are both traditional and historical. Tradition allows that whoever is permitted to plant is entitled to harvest the resulting produce, no matter on whose land the plant grows. If, therefore, the forestry division is granted permission to plant trees on customary land then that agency is seen to own those trees – irrespective of whether this government intervention is intended merely as a stimulus to landowner involvement, with no intention by the division to claim any right to the crop. History also hinders. There is a history of land having been isolated from customary control in practice, even if not in law, through the planting of long-term tree crops such as coconut. Irrespective of the fact that Solomon Islands have been politically independent since 1978 there remains the continuing fear of a repetition of early twentieth-century colonial- government moves to remove land from customary tenure for copra planta- tions, and of 1970s efforts to alienate customary land with the specific purpose of gaining access to its timber resources.

It is not, however, necessary to end this observation in pessimism. In Fiji, after similar suspicions frustrated early efforts, it has proved possible for a statutory organization, the Fiji Pine Commission, to establish softwood plan- tations on land under customary tenure, on the basis of a partnership with communal-property groups. It is noteworthy that the initiative which led to this arrangement came from the landowners themselves.

From the Solomon Islands itself comes an example which, involving natural forest rather than planted, should prove to be an even more useful model. On the basis of traditional jurisdiction over the land and forests of portion of the western Solomons island of Parara, a Rarumana Association of involved lineages was established for the purposes of community development of those resources – under traditional leadership and respecting traditional resource rights, while utilizing new technology and ideas. The first step was to have a portion of the forest logged. Cash from this activity was fed into the initial agricultural development – in areas selected *before logging* on the basis of topography and soil type for specific crops. Special care was taken while logging areas destined for the cocoa crop. A 'carpet' of logs of the smaller, commercially unusable trees was first felled so that tracked log extraction machinery did not churn and compact the fragile soil. The logging was undertaken by a large industrial logging company operating at what was, for it, an unusually small scale of some 20,000 cubic metres per annum. The company, Levers Pacific Timbers Ltd, aware of the antagonism towards industrial logging, was prepared to sacrifice some economies of scale and experiment with an approach to logging on land under traditional tenure along lines determined by the 'landowners' themselves. That company no longer operates in the Solomon Islands and no other logging company has shown any interest in following its lead. Meanwhile the Rarumana Association is kept busy with agricultural operations, a small sawmill fed by timber from the forest areas which were kept outside the logging agreement with Levers, and development of new village infrastructure.

Commercial fisheries and traditional marine tenure

Increasing attention is being paid to traditional South Pacific island marine resource-management systems (Johannes, 1978; Klee, 1980, among others). There is a growing realization of the utility of building modern fisheries administration systems on a base of tradition, and an interest in pursuing this possibility. This is despite the difficulties being experienced with customary land. The task should be easier in marine areas since in most places a lineage group's area is not subdivided for allocation among individuals, as is done for food gardens and plantations.

Traditional marine management systems have become modified over the years in response to changing circumstances and their adaptability is now being further tested by individualistic, commercial forms of inshore-fisheries development. Another consideration is the introduction of industrial fisheries into adjacent coastal waters, beyond the reef, which in most cases are probably not under traditional jurisdiction. Such areas are, however, ecologically linked with the traditionally administered waters. There are high hopes for the establishment of such industrial operations, but particular care is needed to avoid risks to the primarily subsistence fishery inshore. Bailey's (1986) examination of the widespread trawler/artisanal fisherman conflict of South-East Asia has brought him to reflect on what form of communal-property resource system may once have existed in that region. By placing the prevailing 'endemic conflict in the fisheries sector' of South-East Asia in the context of the probable existence of such systems, he provides a scenario for what could happen throughout the South Pacific island region if there is no government intervention to support and protect effective traditional systems.

Despite the resilience they have displayed there is reason to be concerned about the prospect of traditional marine resource-management systems surviving the various economic development pressures. In many areas, too, the ecological knowledge which is an integral part of such systems is not being transferred to younger generations. Traditional authority is being weakened by a number of factors, significant among these being the exploitative element of the 'development elite'. This elite is produced by formal education which, for all its importance, does, nevertheless, have the consequence of educating Melanesians away from their tradition. There is a tendency for some of the development elite to be more concerned with persuading their rural cousins to open up their resources to large-scale, quick-cash-flow exploitation than with persisting with the often frustrating business of assisting with the development of true community enterprises. On the other hand the development elite also includes individuals of the type which brought success for the Rarumana Association, discussed above.

Fishing is popularly believed to be a mainstay of Pacific island societies. For small island communities it certainly is. Yet for those of the many 'high' islands, having much better soils, terrestrial resources tend to greater importance than those of the sea – even though these communities, too, are likely to have extensive knowledge of the marine environment. It should be pointed out that Polunin (1984) believes that in Papua New Guinea, which mostly comprises land-resource-rich islands, traditional marine tenure systems are poorly developed. This finding, presented somewhat cynically, should be treated with caution.

Planning for much of the inshore-fisheries development undertaken in the island region often does not reflect this part-time interest in marine resources. A project model widely tried is that of artisanal reef fisheries based on modest improvements in fishing craft, new gear, and iced fish storage in insulated boxes – the catch transported by larger vessels to a commercial market. Difficulties are inevitably encountered with supply and technical support for such projects. By default, through inconstant supplies of ice and irregular sailings of transporting vessels, projects conceived as continuing become occasional. For most participating fishermen – at least for that majority which has traditional rights and access to terrestrial resources – this pattern would not be unacceptable (indeed, perhaps preferred) except for its unpredictability. They need time for other activities, not all of them income-earning. In any case, the harvesting of other resources at times is more attractive than fishing. When the widely fluctuating copra price is high, commercial fishing may hold little attraction. On the other hand, where the copra price remains low for long periods, loan-agency repossession of outboard motors bought during a copra price 'flush' reduces the capacity for commercial fishing.

The phenomenon of 'landlessness' among those technically holding traditional use rights to communal-property systems is spreading, mostly as a consequence of rapid population growth. Virtually all countries of the island region are experiencing, somewhere, sufficient depletion of inshore resources to have made the fear of localized malnutrition very real. Those short of land resources have sometimes been responsible for overfishing their inshore areas and some of these have proceeded to encroach on the traditional fisheries areas of others. The indications are of more trouble ahead.

Some efforts have been made to provide financial returns, or 'resource rents' to those groups which have jurisdiction over marine resources surplus to their present needs and which are of use to outsiders. Tuna baitfish for an industrial pole-and-line tuna fishery in the Solomon Islands, for instance, are harvested by outsiders in areas subject to traditional marine tenure. Resource rents are paid for this harvest, to individuals who represent the groups concerned. There is no fixed formula for the allocation of these rent monies within the group. That is regarded as a matter to be settled 'according to custom'. Custom, in this respect, is very uncertain, subject often to the personal interpretation of the representative, or trustee, for the group. Some follow what are known to be customary procedures of consultation to seek consensus on allocation. In such cases, much of the money is invested in community projects such as schools, piped water supplies and churches. Others regard the rent money as primarily a perequisite of their relatively high status within the group. They personally decide how the money is to be allocated. Under these circumstances, little money is likely to find its way to community projects.

This latter example is, of course, symptomatic of an erosion of the otherwise egalitarian values of Melanesian Solomon Islands societies. In Polynesia, where hereditary chieftanships are the norm (Sahlins, 1958), this behaviour might be regarded as less inconsistent. Indeed in Fiji, which sustains a traditionally chiefly system, rents paid on land leased from customary landowning groups to outsiders through a native land trust board are allocated in such a way that traditional leaders at three levels of administration down to the Fijian equivalent of sub-clan receive a percentage of these rents, while the major portion is distributed among all other members of the group.

Understanding indigenous resource-management systems

There remains a widespread feeling among agents of economic development that traditional systems of land and sea tenure are a hindrance to economic development and that their associated resource-management systems have little contemporary relevance. Nevertheless, there is a growing realization by some that it is better to work towards accommodating these systems rather than displacing them. A smaller, but growing, group recognizes the intrinsic merit of the systems themselves – their social importance, the pragmatic management principles which often underlie them, and the often rich store of ecological knowledge on which management is based. This point of view is reflected in the basic document of the South Pacific Regional Environment Programme (1982) – agreed by all governments of the island region: 'Traditional conservation practices and technology and traditional systems of land and reef tenure adaptable for modern resource management shall be encouraged. Traditional environmental knowledge will be sought and considered when assessing the expected effects of development projects.'

The point has also been expressed at technical meetings; as in these Unesco (1980) recommendations: 'that the possibilities of retaining and reinforcing traditional marine conservation methods or of incorporating their essential elements and philosophies into new management practices to be studied . . . that attempts be made to record traditional knowledge of environmental and fisheries biology and of marine resources . . .'

Yet, though there is now a greater willingness to know, to understand and to document these systems, few appreciate their complexity or the significance of variations between culture groups. There is confusion and misunderstanding among planners, administrators and legislators – even some of those who exercise traditional rights themselves are not altogether clear about the origin and nature of those rights. In such circumstances, there is considerable risk that new policy, administrative arrangements and legislation designed to resolve the development dilemma embracing traditional institutions may be based on half truths and distortions. A superficial, generalized version of the communal-property systems of a Pacific island nation, if written into law, is more likely to provide a new base for socially disruptive disputes rather than the desired accommodation with contemporary development.

Much has been written on traditional land-tenure systems of Pacific island societies and some of these writings have addressed the practical implications which customary land tenure has for contemporary development. For a practical guide, Crocombe (1960) excels. The most comprehensive coverage of the subject is to be found in Crocombe (1987). Legislative and administrative arrangements have been made to accommodate these land-management systems in most of the island regions' countries – with varying success.

Marine tenure systems, however, have received relatively little attention until lately (see, for example, Johannes, 1978; Baines, 1985; Wright, 1985). Some published attempts to explain them reflect the author's inability to comprehend their complexities and nuances. An understanding of Fijian traditional marine tenure, for instance, is not helped by the erroneous basic assumption of Iwakiri (1983) that marine area rights follow land rights in being based on the *mataqali* social unit. Unlike land, contemporary fishing rights in Fiji are based on the higher order social unit of *yavusa*; even, at times, the *vanua* – a grouping of *yavusa*.

The proper identification and definition of the social unit on which primary rights are based is, of course, crucially important. Particular care is needed, also, to clarify various secondary rights and their origins. There is a tendency to talk loosely of rights to fish in a particular area being 'village rights', the implication being that all residents of a particular village have rights to use adjacent communal-property resources. This is too simplistic. A common pattern in coastal Melanesia, for instance, is that, through marriage and adoption, a village is made up of a number of different lineages – as many as ten or more. Primary use rights are inevitably held by only one of those lineages and that lineage alone has the power to allocate use rights in the marine area adjacent to the village. This lineage, then, allocates secondary use rights to others who have been accepted as residents of the village or, sometimes, temporarily, to visitors.

For purposes of harvesting for subsistence needs, there is probably no practical difference between primary and secondary rights. However, only those with primary rights have a say in the allocation of secondary rights. This right to accept or reject is keenly felt. The distinction between the primary and secondary rights of a village community may not be noticed by an outside observer until, say, a commercial fishing venture is proposed. Primary rights holders are likely to assert their status and refuse to accept a project intended to be based on the village community as a whole. Yet they may not make this clear, and fisheries development agents may proceed, unknowingly, to operate through a group with secondary rights. Inevitably, the distinction will be expressed, but probably too late to ensure success for what technically may have been a good development project.

There has been a tendency to underestimate, or even ignore, the role of women in traditional fisheries. Traditionally, men assume the more adventurous fishing roles. Some of these, involving prestige animals such as shark, dugong, porpoise or dolphin and bonito are, or were, associated with 'magic' and mystique. Women largely 'glean' on the reef, in shallow lagoons and on foreshores. The nutritional contribution of these gleanings to community welfare is very considerable. Gleaning success depends on considerable knowledge of the environmental requirements and behaviour of a very wide range of marine foods – fish, algae, seagrasses, crustaceans, molluscs, cephalopods, annelids and echinoderms. Some of the valuable fisheries knowledge of Pacific island fishermen has been documented (notably by Johannes, 1980, 1981). The rich source of ecological knowledge about the nearshore environment which is held by women remains unrecognized by marine scientists and fisheries managers.

The tradition of marine communal-property systems is dynamic and changing. The extent to which it has changed and, in particular, the extent to which it now includes what were once foreign concepts and practices, varies between and within the island countries. If these marine systems are to be given the recognition and support necessary to sustain them in the new environment of economic development then prompt action is required. It will not be possible to await detailed documentation and analysis of these systems. While such detail should still be pursued, a compromise level of information must meanwhile be accepted.

In the case of the Solomon Islands, Baines (1985) recommends an approach geared to the reporting, not of every nuance of a system, but to what he terms a 'basic fisheries tradition' made up of key elements such as principles of inheritance, nature of and allocation of use rights, boundary concepts, and rules for the distribution of harvest and of other benefits from the use of resources. This concept has since been developed into a manual (Baines, et al, in preparation) to provide practical guidance for those investigators of traditional marine resource-management systems whose task it is to facilitate economic development through them.

Commercialization of the resources of areas subject to traditional fisheries rights need not be socially disruptive if carefully approached. In striving to develop new approaches, based on traditional systems, it is useful to examine experience elsewhere. In this respect, through culturally quite different, the Japanese experience is worth studying. There, traditional fisheries rights are legally vested in fisheries cooperative associations. The origins and practice of this arrangement are explained by Ruddle in Chapter 10.

Guiding the evolution of traditional resource-management systems

Traditional resource-management systems of the South Pacific island region are unlikely to survive in a meaningful form without government support – institutional and legislative. Without such government intervention it appears inevitable that the forces of economic development will overwhelm them. Regarding the marine element of such systems, from an international perspective Christy (1982), while pointing to the need for 'strong legal and institutional protection' of traditional fisheries rights, stated bluntly that 'these have not generally been able to withstand the pressures resulting from a large increase in the value of access' to the resources concerned.

There is a vast conceptual gulf between traditional institutions and those which presently serve economic development. Pacific island governments are firmly committed to the latter, in 'free-market' forms only mildly tempered by other considerations. Yet these governments continue to proclaim a determination to recognize and support appropriate traditional institutions. In particular, they seek to preserve communal resource rights. Here, then, is the development dilemma, illustrated in this paper by examples from the forestry and fisheries development sector. Can it be resolved?

Most attempts to resolve the differences between the two systems for natural resource use have emphasized alterations to traditional communal-property systems so as to make them more amenable to economic development. The traditional systems have shown a capacity for adaptation and, despite many contraindictions, it could yet be possible to effect a relatively untroubled transition to a form of economic development in which communal rights can be maintained. Little attention, however, has been paid to the idea of modifying approaches to economic development so that some bridging of the gap might be effected from this 'other side'.

It might appear to be a contradiction in terms to speak of 'guiding' the evolution of a system. Nevertheless, this approximates the role which governments would best adopt, rather than attempting to force change and, in particular, the conversion of communal to individual forms of land and marine tenure – the objective of many agents of development.

There needs to be more effort by the various agents of development – agriculture and fisheries extension staff, development planners and, not least, officials of international economic-assistance institutions – to understand better the nature of traditional resource-management systems. They also need to display greater patience with the slow pace which characterizes traditional community decision-making on the allocation of resources for economic development. So long as traditional systems themselves are viewed as 'the problem' there can be little progress towards such understanding. In this respect credit is due to one notable effort, in the name of the World Bank (Goodland, 1982), to address this issue in a more positive manner.

A distinctive new approach to the development of resources under traditional jurisdiction has manifested itself recently in the Solomon Islands. It is particularly threatening to rural communities. The threat arises externally but is given expression through individuals who are members of groups with traditional resource-use rights. These are individuals with greater knowledge than others of their lineage about commercial possibilities for the group's resources. They have access, often through foreign intermediaries, to capital and technology, and they are adept at influencing administrative decisions. They are the manipulative component of the development elite. Indeed, they are the contemporary equivalent of the nineteenth-century opportunists who, through monopolizing communication with European traders, greatly enhanced their power and wealth at the expense of their own people. Legislative support for traditional resource-management systems could do much to curb this form of exploitation, and, in consequence, give encouragement to the other arm of the development elite – that which seeks to apply its knowledge and understanding to working *with* its kin towards socially and environmentally sustainable forms of development.

Better understanding of these complex systems requires that much more attention be paid to their documentation, interpretation and analysis. This is best done as cooperative research ventures – with scientifically trained investigators and those whose societies are being examined working together – rather than the usual externally inspired research interventions.

Traditional landowning groups, too, have a special educational need. To help them make good decisions on natural-resource allocation and to give them the confidence needed for effective involvement in economic development they must be helped towards a better understanding of development options and consequences. Much of traditional community resistance to development activities arises from fears – a fear of what appears to be the unknown consequences of economic development, and a fear of the history of land alienation through government involvement. Though it is mainly with Melanesian societies in mind that this discussion proceeds, much is relevant for the Pacific island region as a whole.

The adage that 'a little learning is a dangerous thing' is particularly apt in the circumstances discussed here. Any attempt to introduce legislation to formalize customary law, if this is based on only a superficial understanding of the custom in question, could inadvertently produce new opportunities for dispute among those holding traditional rights. Secondary rights, for example, might be overlooked. In consequence, not having the support of formal law, they weaken, and a crucial element of social interrelationships is lost. On the other hand, it could happen that legislation is written so loosely that it becomes possible for manipulative secondary-rights holders to assert primary rights – and sometimes succeed. Though such a ruse would be evident, and disapproved of, in terms of current customary law it might well succeed were legislation to provide an opportunity.

Certain basic principles of traditional resource-management systems need careful examination before decisions are taken to accept them as bases for legislation. Among these is the crucial matter of whether customary rights are to be regarded as rights of use or as rights of ownership. And what is to be done about secondary rights? Fijian legislation for the protection of land and sea areas under customary control does not provide for these. The legislation has been so long in effect (almost 50 years) that secondary rights, not having been given legislative support, appear to have atrophied. Rural Solomon Islanders still have high regard for secondary rights – placing great importance on the notion that a group with the opportunity to grant these has an obligation to help others and that, in return, that group derives support and security in other ways. On the other hand, there are factors which tend to undermine the concept of secondary rights. First, there is the tendency for the primary group to lose control of portions of its land as those allocated secondary rights move to make permanent their right by planting very long-term crops such as coconut. Then there is the matter of population growth. Already there are areas where primary-right holders are short of land, so cannot fulfil their obligations to others. The current annual population growth rate of 3.5 per cent ensures that this problem will worsen very quickly.

The inheritance principle for primary rights must be clearly decided, with the agreement of each culture group. Where it is strictly patrilineal or matrilineal it may not be particularly difficult to determine which individuals are entitled to primary rights through inheritance. Groups whose custom provides for ambilineal inheritance – through both parents, so offering more potential landholdings – are particularly vulnerable to manipulation and spurious claims.

It will be a lengthy, difficult, and expensive task to conduct the detailed examination which is a necessary prerequisite to legislation. In Fiji, the process of determining land ownership and registering rights was spread over almost 70 years. Few resources were applied to that task, however, and there was not the same urgency as is now faced by the other Melanesian countries – New Caledonia, Papua New Guinea, Solomon Islands and Vanuatu. Unless traditional resource-management systems are given special attention and protection they are likely to succumb to development pressures.

Where the legislation is intended to proceed beyond the provision of general support for a communal-property system and on to codification of the traditional law itself, additional difficulties arise. Not the least of these, as pointed out by Crocombe (1960) is that codification freezes what is essentially a flexible system, able to adjust to population changes and other new circumstances. One approach to this difficulty might be to provide for a review of secondary aspects after perhaps ten years, where circumstances warrant. Legally and administratively this is untidy, but it would be a relatively small cost to pay for the benefit of an opportunity for some 'fine tuning' to ease the difficult transition from tradition to formal law.

Yet much progress can be made towards resolution of the development dilemma through extra-legal devices. Suggestions have been made above regarding the importance of education – both for customary groups and for the 'development agent' group – in ways which will serve also to build trust between these groups. Consultation by government officers with traditional communities is often little more than an exercise in persuasion. Consultative procedures could be reorganized on a partnership basis in which traditional jurisdiction over resources is not just grudgingly recognized but is acknowledged with respect. In return, with more information provided about resource-development options and their consequences, together with training designed to improve their ability to make decisions and to manage their resources in today's changed circumstances, communal-property-resource holders will be better prepared to join with governments in attaining national development objectives.

Finally, there is the delicate matter of the distribution of resource benefits within a communal-property group. In most countries that has been left to the groups themselves to determine. This might be expected to have been the proper approach, and certainly has the advantage of avoiding paternalism. However, the erosion of traditional leadership and of the relatively egalitarian Melanesian values on which it was based, has caused a shift towards self-interest. Governments could intervene with legislative prescriptions for allocation of financial benefits from the use of communal resources. A reasonably fair distribution of wealth, in the form of a share of communal-property resources, is a fundamental principle of traditional tenure systems.

Should governments fail to reinforce this traditional principle then a characteristic of tomorrow's Melanesian society will be a growing class of dispossessed poor. The traditional systems will have adapted further, but in ways which suit the self-interested manipulators as they exploit the flexibility of these systems to rationalize their position. Only prompt and sensible interventions by governments to guide the evolution of communal-property systems can avert this social catastrophe.

Those island nations which, despite acute development pressures, choose to face the development dilemma and apply the necessary time and resources to working out a development which embraces traditional resource-management systems, still have some chance of achieving sustainable resource development with their cherished communal-property systems intact – if they can overcome current excessive population growth rates.

Acknowledgements

Thanks to the anonymous reviewers whose comments stimulated me to further effort on this chapter; to David Roe and Chris Radford for their comments on a draft; and to my friends in the western Solomons who shared their knowledge, experience and frustrations and so helped me towards some measure of understanding of their traditional resource-management systems.

References

Akimichi, T., 1981: 'Perception and function: traditional resource management in three Pacific islands', *Resource Management and Optimization*, 1(4), pp. 361–78.

Bailey, C., 1986: 'Conflict in the commons: the case of Indonesian fisheries', paper presented at the annual meeting of the Association for Asian Studies, Chicago, March.

Baines, G.B.K., 1985: 'A traditional base for inshore fisheries development in the Solomon Islands', in Ruddle, K. and Johannes, R.E., eds, *The Traditional Knowledge and Management of Coastal Systems in Asia and the Pacific*, Unesco Regional Office for Science and Technology for Southeast Asia, Jakarta, Indonesia.

Baines, G.B.K., Johannes, R.E., Pulea, M. and Ruddle, K. (in preparation): *Traditional Fisheries Rights in the South Pacific: A Guide to Their Investigation and Application*.

Bonnemaison, J., 1984: 'Social and cultural aspects of land tenure', in Larmour, P., ed., *Land Tenure in Vanuatu*, Institute of Pacific Studies, University of the South Pacific.

Christy, F., 1982: 'Territorial use rights in marine fisheries: definitions and conditions', FAO Fisheries Technical Paper No. 227.

Crocombe, R.G., 1960: 'Improving land tenure', South Pacific Commission Technical Paper No. 159.

Crocombe, R.G., 1987: *Land Tenure in the Pacific*, 3rd edn, University of the South Pacific, Suva, Fiji.

France, P., 1969: *The Charter of the Land: Custom and Colonization in Fiji*, Oxford University Press.

Goodland, R., 1982: *Tribal Peoples and Economic Development: Human Ecologic Considerations*, The World Bank, Washington.

Iwakiri, S., 1983: 'Mataqali of the sea: A study of the customary right on reef and lagoon in Fiji, the South Pacific' (sic), *Memoirs of the Kagoshima University Research Center for the South Pacific*, 4(2), pp. 133–43.

Johannes, R.E., 1978: 'Reef and lagoon tenure systems in the Pacific', *South Pacific Bulletin*, 4th quarter, pp. 31–4.

Johannes, R.E., 1980: 'Using knowledge of the reproductive behaviour of reef and lagoon fishes to improve fishing yields', in Bardach, J., et al, eds, *Fish Behaviour and Fisheries Management (Capture and Culture)*, ICLARM, Manila.

Klee, G.A., 1980: 'Oceania', in Klee, G.A., ed., *World Systems of Traditional Resource Management*, V.H. Winston and Sons, New York.

McKinnon, J.M., 1972: 'Bilua changes: culture contact and its consequences, a study of the Bilua of Vella Lavella in the British Solomon Islands', PhD thesis, Victoria University of Wellington, New Zealand.

McKinnon, J.M., 1975: 'Tomahawks, turtles and traders', *Oceania*, 45, pp. 90–307.

Murphy, G.I., 1973: Fishery development problems in Southeast Asia and the Pacific Island Area (Oceania). East-West Center, Honolulu, Hawaii.

Nietchmann, B., 1987: 'The new Pacific. Geopolitics of Pacific island fisheries', *Cultural Survival Quarterly*, 11(2), pp. 7–9.

Polunin, N.V.C., 1984: 'Do traditional marine "reserves" conserve? A view of Indonesian and New Guinea evidence', *Senri Ethnological Studies*, 17, pp. 267–83.

Ravuvu, A., 1983: *Vaki i Taukei: The Fijian Way of Life*, Institute of Pacific Studies, University of the South Pacific.

Sahlins, Marshall, 1958: *Social Stratification in Polynesia*, American Ethnological

Society Monographs, University of Washington Press, Seattle.

South Pacific Regional Environment Programme, 1982: *Report of the Conference on the Human Environment in the South Pacific*, Rarotonga, Cook Islands, 8–11 March.

Thompson, L., 1940: 'Southern Lau, Fiji: An ethnography', *B.P. Bishop Museum Bulletin*, 162, Honolulu, Hawaii.

Unesco, 1980: *Marine and Coastal Processes in the Pacific: Ecological Aspects of Coastal Zone Management*, Unesco Regional Office for Science and Technology for Southeast Asia, Jakarta, Indonesia.

Wright, A., 1985: 'Marine resource use in Papua New Guinea: can traditional concepts and contemporary development be integrated?', in Ruddle, K. and Johannes, R.E., eds, *The Traditional Knowledge and Management of Coastal Systems in Asia and the Pacific*, Unesco Regional Office for Science and Technology for Southeast Asia, Jakarta, Indonesia.

Notes on Contributors

James Acheson is professor of Anthropology and Marine Studies at the University of Maine. He has worked for the National Marine Fisheries Service and has written extensively on maritime anthropology and modernization in Latin America. He has co-edited *The Questions of the Commons* (1987) and has authored the *Lobster Gangs of Maine* (1988). His current research concerns fisheries management policies in northeastern United States; the herring fishery of the north Atlantic; and economic development in Mexico.

Graham Baines was trained in agricultural science and ecology and has made his home in the South Pacific where he has worked since 1970 – most of that time in natural resource development advisory roles with island governments. Dr Baines has a keen practical interest in indigenous systems for resource management and chairs the Traditional Ecological Knowledge Working Group of IUCN's Commission on Ecology.

Fikret Berkes teaches environmental studies at Brock University. Trained in marine ecology, Dr Berkes has studied human ecology since 1974, mainly in the Canadian subarctic. He has developed case studies also in other parts of Canada, his native Turkey, and the Caribbean to study the relationships of societies and living resources – in particular, how sustainable resource-use practices evolve and persist in small-scale, community-based fisheries.

Daniel W. Bromley is Professor of Agricultural Economics at the University of Wisconsin, Madison, editor of *Land Economics* and author of *Economic Interests and Institutions* (1989). Dr Bromley was a major contributor to the Conference on Common Property Resource Management. He has written extensively on institutional economics, property rights and the management of renewable resources in both developed and developing countries.

Susan J. Buck (formerly Susan J.B. Cox) is Assistant Professor of political science at the University of North Carolina-Greensboro. She writes primarily on environmental policy with a focus on coastal and marine management issues. Recent publications include commons management in medieval English villages, interjurisdictional problems in Chesapeake Bay fisheries, and British environmental policy. Dr Buck is currently applying cultural theory to environmental management.

Ma. Concepcion J. Cruz is Assistant Professor, College of Economics and Management, and the Chairperson of the Graduate Program on Environmental Studies at the Institute of Environmental Science and Management, University of the Philippines at Los Baños. Dr Cruz has worked extensively on irrigation management issues and has recently published a book on water rights in the Philippines.

M. Taghi Farvar, presently with the United Nations Environment Programme, Pilot Ecodevelopment Project for Africa, has served as Senior Advisor to IUCN on Sustainable Development. Iranian-born and US-educated, Dr Farvar has been active in global environmental issues since the 1972 Stockholm Conference and has recently drafted the section on common property resources for the revised *World Conservation Strategy*.

Milton Freeman (PhD, marine sciences, McGill University) is Professor of Anthropology and Senior Research Scholar at the Boreal Institute for Northern Studies, University of Alberta in Edmonton, Canada. Dr Freeman's current research focuses upon local-level and traditional management of renewable resources in northern regions of the world.

Madhav Gadgil (b. 1942) is currently a Professor of ecological sciences at the Indian Institute of Science, Bangalore, India. He holds a PhD (1969) in biology from Harvard University. His research interests include plant, animal and human ecology and ecodevelopment.

Christopher J.N. Gibbs is a natural-resource economist who has worked on the local management of renewable resources in Asia, West Africa and the Caribbean. He is with the Environment Department of the World Bank. This chapter was prepared while Dr Gibbs was a Research Associate at the East-West Environment and Policy Institute, Honolulu, Hawaii.

Robert Goodland is a tropical ecologist and Chief of the newly created Environment Division in the Latin American Office of the World Bank in Washington, DC. Dr Goodland has published extensively in environmental aspects of the Trans-Amazon highway, the cerrado ecosystem in Brazil, tropical hydroelectric projects and agriculture, tribal peoples, wildland management, and cultural property.

A.P. Lino Grima teaches geography and environmental studies at the University of Toronto. Born in Malta and educated in England and Canada, Dr Grima applies his training in economic geography widely: water resource management, fishery allocation, the role of natural resources in economic development, environmental and social impact analysis, and ecosystem rehabilitation.

Prema Iyer (b. 1960) assists Professor Gadgil in research in the area of human ecology. She holds a Master's degree (1985) in Marine Biology from Karnataka University.

George Ledec, a PhD candidate at the Department of Forestry and Resource Management, University of California, Berkeley, has conducted environmental assessments of World Bank-supported projects in Columbia and Kenya. This chapter was prepared while Mr Ledec was conducting his dissertation research in Panama on the linkages between livestock credit and deforestation.

Richard Mason holds a PhD in education and sociology, and teaches at Hobart and William Smith Colleges, Geneva, New York. He has been interested in the sociology of science, and has studied the distribution of power in society and how the allocation of resources of any sort relates to power relationships.

David L. Miller teaches in the Department of Geography at the State University of New York, College at Cortland. A biogeographer, his current research focuses on spatial and temporal variation in the lobster harvest in Mexico's Biosphere Reserve Sian Ka'an. Dr Miller is a member of the Board of Directors of the Gulf and Caribbean Fisheries Institute.

Richard Moorehead is a London-based economist and the Director of the IUCN Project for the Conservation of Nature in the inner Niger delta in the Sahel region. Dr Moorehead wrote this chapter while working out of the Bureau des Eaux et Forêts, Mopti, Mali.

Henry Regier is Professor of zoology and environmental studies at the University of Toronto. Dr Regier has served as research scientist and policy advisor on fisheries for a number of governmental and intergovernmental agencies at all levels, from local to global, including the Great Lakes Fisheries Commission, FAO, UNESCO and INTECOL. He is perhaps best known for his pioneering work on ecosystem rehabilitation, initially applied to the Great Lakes and now extended to other degraded ecosystems.

Kenneth Ruddle is with the National Museum of Ethnology, Osaka, and holds a PhD in geography with minor in anthropology. He has held positions with the United Nations University in Tokyo, East-West Centre in Honolulu, Syracuse University, New York; and has chaired the UNESCO-IABO Steering Committee on traditional management of coastal zones. He has published extensively also on integrated agriculture-aquaculture systems and tropical agriculture and ecology.

Dwight Watson is the manager and a former field advisor for the Sulawesi Regional Development Project in the School of Rural Planning and Development at the University of Guelph. He is also a PhD candidate in the university's Department of Zoology. This chapter is based on earlier development planning work conducted in Sarawak, Malaysia while acting as advisor to the Baram and Samarahan River Basin Development Projects. He has published several articles on fish production, ecology, and development in Sarawak.

Maryla Webb is an applied ecologist employed at the time of writing as a researcher/consultant in the Environment Department of the World Bank. She has worked with Robert Goodland on wildlands and cultural property in development projects. She holds a Masters from the Yale School of Forestry and Environmental Studies.

Index